Sachin Tendulkar

Vaibhav Purandare grew up playing cricket at Shivaji Park, Mumbai, at the same time as the school-going Sachin Tendulkar was amassing loads of runs on the field. He watched helplessly as Tendulkar and Vinod Kambli walked away with a world-record partnership against his school. Purandare was taught in college by Tendulkar's father, Professor Ramesh Tendulkar, and was coached as a right-hand batsman and off-spin bowler by Tendulkar's coach, Ramakant Acharekar.

He began his journalistic career in 1993 with the political newsmagazine *Blitz* and has since worked with India's leading newspapers like *The Indian Express, The Asian Age, Mid Day, Mumbai Mirror* and *DNA*, apart from writing for a host of other publications. His first book, *The Sena Story*, a history of the Hindu militant political party Shiv Sena, was published in 1999, when he was only twenty-three. He is currently Senior Associate Editor with the *Hindustan Times*, Mumbai.

a definitive biography

vaibhav purandare

Sachin Tendulkar

foreword by
Ramachandra Guha

LOTUS COLLECTION
ROLI BOOKS

Lotus Collection

© Text: Vaibhav Purandare, 2005
© Photographs: Pradeep Mandhani, 2005

First published in 2005
Fifth revised edition 2011
The Lotus Collection
An imprint of
Roli Books Pvt. Ltd
M-75, Greater Kailash II Market, New Delhi 110 048
Phone: ++91 (011) 4068 2000
Fax: ++91 (011) 2921 7185
E-mail: info@rolibooks.com
Website: www.rolibooks.com
Also at Bangalore, Chennai, Jaipur, Mumbai & Varanasi

Cover Design: Bonita Vaz-Shimray
Production: Naresh Nigam, Shaji Sahadevan

ISBN: 978-81-7436-360-2

Typeset in Fairfield LH Light by Roli Books Pvt. Ltd and
printed at Rajkamal Electric Press, Haryana

~

In memory of my
grandparents Suryakant Chemburkar
and Lilawati Chemburkar

~

contents

acknowledgements

'See how he bats, and see how *you* bat' my father once told me when I was in Class IX. He was talking about Sachin Tendulkar, then a student of Shardashram High School in Mumbai.

Tendulkar was scoring tons of runs in schools cricket; I, playing the same Harris Shield Tournament in the same city, was struggling to find form. Yet my dad mentioned my name in the same breath as Sachin's. I must first thank him for that.

He didn't stop at that. He went on to analyse Tendulkar's game for me. My father, Jagdish Purandare, knows his cricket. He's technically a flawless batsman and played for the top division in Mumbai in the Seventies and Eighties, the glorious days of the city's cricket. His analyses, to this day, have enriched my own study of the game and of Tendulkar in particular.

My brother Kunal, the greatest admirer of Sachin's partner-in-runs Vinod Kambli on this and other planets, read some of the chapters carefully and made many corrections. I can't thank him and my mother, Jyotsna, enough for their solid support.

My debt to Kiran Nagarkar, one of the world's finest fiction writers in English, is really incalculable. He went out of his way to ensure the successful completion of this project, contacting people, offering suggestions and despite being a confirmed recluse, taking my persistent calls which were actually fervent appeals for help. Without his encouragement, this book would not have seen the light of day.

Eminent historian Ramachandra Guha, whose book on the social history of Indian cricket has been acknowledged the world over as a seminal work comparable to C.L.R. James' *Beyond a Boundary,* not only agreed to write the foreword but did it days ahead of the deadline, a practice relatively unknown amongst accomplished authors.

Tulsi Vatsal made the all-important call to Sachin; Clayton Murzello, the unassuming sports editor of *Mid Day*, set up a meeting with him; and Ramakant Acharekar, Tendulkar's coach and also my own during my college days, recollected for me his fondest memories of his most illustrious disciple.

Former India Test cricketer and now a successful television commentator, Sanjay Manjrekar gave me fascinating insights into Sachin's game. Former India captain Ajit Wadekar, former India wicket-keeper and Sunil Gavaskar's uncle Madhav Mantri and former Test cricketer Praveen Amre granted extensive interviews as well.

A rich fund of anecdotes was provided by Sachin's closest friend Atul Ranade, his Shardashram mate and Mumbai Ranji player Amol Muzumdar and former first-class cricketer Ashok Gadkari a brilliant left-hand batsman who in the Seventies used to open the innings in club cricket with Sunil Gavaskar.

Sudha Sadanand, the editor of this book, cast a sharp eye on the manuscript and disciplined my prose; Ashwati Maya-Franklin, with her fine attention to detail, read the final draft before I sent it to the publishers; Pradeep Mandhani, who has shot Tendulkar more extensively during his international career than any other photographer in the world, granted his pictures; and Jayapriya Vasudevan of Jacaranda Press always offered support.

Special thanks to my publisher Roli Books and Roli's managing editor Renuka Chatterjee, and to my close friends Pankaj Upadhyaya, K. Balachandra, Suyash Padate and Jhilik Sen, all of whom I badgered for suggestions and who always conveyed a certain confidence in the ultimate outcome of this project. That kept me going during some of the lean periods of research and writing in the two-and-a-half years that this project has taken for completion.

All these people are responsible for the good things in this book. For any error, I alone am accountable.

MUMBAI   VAIBHAV PURANDARE
12 JANUARY 2005

foreword

In cricketing terms, Sachin Tendulkar defines the Age; indeed, he *is* the Age. In the history of the game, there have been only three other cricketers who, in terms of skill and impact, can be compared with him.

First, there was the bearded Dr William Gilbert Grace, mammoth in size and personality, a vigorous, extroverted and often domineering character who was the best-known Englishman of his time. Then there was Donald George Bradman, who brought to the art of batsmanship a clinical and almost frightening efficiency. After him came Garfield Sobers, who was, without doubt, the most accomplished and variously gifted man ever to grace this most graceful of games.

And now there is Tendulkar. No batsman since Bradman has had quite such a range of strokes, quite such an ability to dominate attacks, quick and subtle, on wickets dusty or green. And, coming of age with the one-day game, he has mastered challenges the Don never faced; such as flaying away at the top of the innings, or nurturing a shaky middle order to reach what looks like an impossible target. Moreover, in social terms Tendulkar has had to bear a burden no other sportsman could even remotely contemplate. Grace was loved by fifteen million Englishmen. Bradman was idolized by ten million Australians, Sobers worshipped by a like number of West Indians. But Sachin is answerable to a billion hyper-expectant and too-easily dissatisfied Indians.

Tendulkar, like Grace and Bradman and Sobers before him, will be remembered principally as a batsman. Yet like those other geniuses he has other strings to his bow. Grace was a handy slow medium bowler. Bradman was a brilliant cover point. And Sobers was a world-class seam bowler and a world-class spinner; and a superb short-leg besides. Tendulkar lacks Sobers' skill in these departments, but he certainly has a comparable versatility. He has been a successful medium-pace bowler in the one-day game. He has taken key wickets in Test cricket with sharply spun leg breaks. In his youth, he fielded capably at slip; now, he fields capably in the outfield. Who ever saw it, will not easily forget the remarkable, match-and-series winning catch he took, high over his head at long-on, to dismiss Inzamam-ul-Haq under the lights of the Gaddafi Stadium in Lahore.

Future cricket historians will speak of the Age of Tendulkar, as we speak of the Age of Grace and the Age of Bradman and the Age of Sobers. What is particularly nice is that these men happen to represent four different countries, indeed four separate continents. Yet, and this is what marks them out from everybody else, one never had to share the colour of their passport to revel in their greatness. For, as the writer Suresh Menon has pointed out, when India plays its old enemy at cricket 'the ideal solution for many Pakistani spectators is for Tendulkar to score a hundred and Pakistan to win.'

Vaibhav Purandare recognizes, appreciates and lovingly documents the impact of Sachin Tendulkar on the world of cricket. Yet it is the singular merit of his book that it also returns him to the city in which he was reared. Here, for the first time, we have a rich and sensitive account of his early years, of his family and social background, of his confident steps to cricketing greatness. Purandare is uniquely qualified for this task. He is a child of the city himself, who in his adulthood, has acquired a deserved reputation as one of Mumbai's most knowledgeable journalists. And he has played some cricket too. In fact he even had an extended early acquaintanceship with the great man's greatness, when Tendulkar and Vinod Kambli, playing for Shardashram High School, kept poor Purandare's St Xavier's School in the field for days upon end.

That battering from Tendulkar is feelingly described in this book, but so is much else. We have here a vivid portrait of the Maharashtrian middle class in which he was reared, and of the relentless dedication and ambition of his coach Ramakant Acharekar. We learn of how and where Tendulkar fits into the Mumbai School of Batsmanship, a school exemplified, before him, by the likes of Vijay Merhant and Vijay Manjrekar, Sunil Gavaskar and Dilip Vengsarkar. And we read crisp analyses of the great innings he has played for India. At the same time, Purandare does not shirk from detailing the errors of judgement made by Tendulkar on and off the field.

In the end, though, this is a celebration, a deeply informed celebration, of a great cricketing life. That is how it should be. Reading Vaibhav Purandare's book, I was reminded of what the original Little Master, Pakistan's Hanif Mahammed, once said of Garfield Sobers namely, that 'God has sent him down to earth to play cricket.' The Almighty appears to have had the same thought with regard to this little Mumbaikar as well.

NOVEMBER 2004   RAMACHANDRA GUHA

(Ramachandra Guha is the author of several books, including, 'A Corner of a Foreign Field' and 'Environmentalism: A Global History'.)

the bandra boy

Someone's a witness, Someone a bearer,
Someone's a narrator, Someone a listener..., What
then, is life?

A tale told by someone to someone, about
someone else:

That is its only meaning

— Ramesh Tendulkar, *Prajakta*
(A collection of his Marathi poems)

Twenty-sixth November 1983. A sizeable crowd had gathered at
Mumbai's Wankhede Stadium for the third day of the fourth Test
between India and West Indies. It wasn't the prospect of India
batting that had drawn the crowd. It was one name that had: Isaac
Vivian Alexander Richards. Part of this eager mass of cricket-crazed
humanity that trundled up the stands of the Wankhede that morning
was a ten-year-old boy from Bandra, Sachin Ramesh Tendulkar. He
had come along with his elder brother, Ajit Ramesh Tendulkar.

India had scored 463 in their first innings, and on a slow,
turning and rather scuffed wicket, the West Indians were expected to
stay subdued against the home team's spinners. All of them did,
except Richards.

The West Indies were forty-seven for two when Richards
arrived and began only as he could have, with a "hell-I-care" attitude.
Casual but exuberant, he cut and drove savagely, crunching good-
length balls from middle and off-stump away through mid-wicket.

Throughout this assault, it wasn't as if he didn't give a chance to the Indians. He did. Two, in fact: the first when he was at forty and then at fifty-eight. But as was the opponent team's wont, both catches were missed.

In the post-lunch session, Richards launched a particularly brutal assault on Shivlal Yadav's off-spin. In less than half an hour, Yadav was hit for five fours, four of them between long-on and mid-wicket. It was a combination of sheer physical prowess and fine art. There was power, a fine eye for detail, timing and placement, all rolled into one. The crowd applauded deliriously as Richards reached his hundred off just 130 balls, with thirteen fours and a six.

Childhood impressions are forever. Ten-year-old Sachin saw in Richards an entertainer, a master stroke-player, a skilful improviser who didn't have a pile-on-the-runs approach, but batted as if he didn't bother either about the sniff of a hundred or a double hundred. He just wanted to enjoy his cricket. Above all, Viv Richards was the embodiment of the modern game. A killer of the cricket ball.

A day earlier, Sachin had seen Dilip Balwant Vengsarkar (the two later played together in several matches) in full flow being suddenly snapped up at gully by Richards. The catching too was imperious, and the fielding bossy.

If little Tendulkar desired an endorsement of his own natural attitude toward cricket, this was it. If he wanted a bolstering of the belief that this attitude was right, again, this was it.

It is therefore my contention that this match marked the psychological birth of a great cricketer.

*

The imperious are, in a strange way, impervious to tradition. Even when they have one foot firmly rooted in it, the other is a long way forward or behind – in either case, distant. Sachin Tendulkar has had this distance since early childhood. The very fact that he became a cricketer from a locality called Sahitya Sahwas is proof of that.

A more "uncricketing" place than Sahitya Sahwas for the birth of a great cricketer is hard to imagine. This colony of litterateurs (as the literal translation of Sahitya Sahwas goes) in suburban Bandra in Mumbai boasts of an academic culture where traditions of scholarship, collections of books and ways of writing are handed down from one generation to another. Cricket, its culture and cricketing equipment would struggle to find a place on the last rung of Sahitya Sahwas legacy ladder.

The government of the western Indian state of Maharashtra set up the Sahwas as a co-operative housing society for writers and poets in the 1960s. The plan was twofold: one, to bestow State honour on well-known litterateurs by offering them houses at concessional rates, and two, to create an atmosphere for intellectual activity. The plan succeeded as leading members of the literary community came to settle here.

One such family that moved into Sahwas from its small home in Dadar was that of Marathi poet and professor, Ramesh Tendulkar. Tendulkar bought a flat in a building called Ushakkal, meaning, "The Dawn". It is unlikely this choice of building had anything to do with his poetry, but it is interesting because Professor Tendulkar had often tended toward darkness in his verse. In one of his poems he wrote:

Surya vishwala prakashit karto
Hey ek ardhasatyach...
Ardhe vishwa tya kshani
Purna andhaarat budalele aste

(It is a half-truth that the sun lights up the universe... for in that moment, half the universe is plunged into total darkness.)

In the same poem, he expressed concern over the discovery of dark spots on the sun, saying this finding had fuelled a new fear in his heart. However, all that was to change soon after as the professor's youngest son, Sachin, who was to prove the brightest spot in his life, was born on 24 April 1973. And it was in Ushakkal that he grew up.

*

The year 1973 was a curious one in the history of post-independent India. The rate of inflation had registered an all-time high of twenty per cent as international oil prices went through the roof; the monsoons had failed; there was massive labour unrest and strikes; factories had shut down and the decline in production hurt the economy further. The then Prime Minister Indira Gandhi's younger son, Sanjay, had become the de facto power centre much to the dismay of all those who believed in democratic values; Sanjay's Maruti car affair had snowballed into India's Watergate; word of increasing government corruption spread to all corners of the country; and veteran socialist leader Jayaprakash Narayan launched his "Youth for Democracy" movement to "cleanse" the political system, sparking unrest among a large number of idealistic youngsters. Amidst all this, the one happy news was that the Indian cricket team led by Ajit Wadekar had triumphed 2-1 over Tony Lewis' Marylebone Cricket Club (MCC).

Still, more than these standout stories, it was the few years immediately before and after 1973 that made it an oddly remarkable year. In fact, judgements about these years were so widely contradictory that Sachin's year of birth would appear to be an accommodation for the warring factions of hope and despair in India's national identity.

In the parliamentary polls held in February 1971, Indira Gandhi rode handsomely to power with her slogan of *Garibi Hatao* (Remove Poverty). She was young for Indian politics, ambitious and confident, and appeared to symbolize a progressive India coming into her own. That image was further crystallized when, early in December 1971, India launched a war to liberate East Pakistan from the military dictatorship in West Pakistan. When the Pakistani forces surrendered in Dhaka to Lt General Jagjit Singh Aurora in less than a fortnight, Indira became strong enough to evoke slogans such as "Indira is India and India is Indira". One of her strongest political opponents and later India's prime minister, Atal Bihari Vajpayee, took the adulation into the realm of religion. He compared her to the Hindu goddess Durga, the slayer of evil forces.

In the middle of 1972, Indira Gandhi hit a new high. She signed the Simla Agreement with the then Pakistan President, Zulfikar Ali Bhutto that, importantly for India, had a clause saying India and Pakistan would in future refrain from use of force and resolve all issues bilaterally. Pakistan had sought to internationalize the Kashmir issue and this clause was seen to have cancelled out its demand for involving other nations in the dispute. Indira had by now emerged as a world leader of no mean stature.

However, hopes began fading soon thereafter. Growing political corruption coupled with Sanjay Gandhi's terror tactics resulted in a kind of fear psychosis across India. Indira refused to listen when Jayaprakash Narayan along with some other conscientious citizens and even some of her advisers and government officials warned her of the consequences of his behaviour. She heard rumour-mongers eagerly who fed her all kinds of tales. To begin with she was anyway hemmed in by the grave economic crisis of 1973 and even tried to cut government expenditure, but the nation's problems were ultimately overshadowed by perceived threats. Indira began her inexorable march towards acquiring absolute power, even if that meant a subversion of democracy. Meanwhile, Jayaprakash Narayan's movement gathered widespread support in 1974 and posed severe problems for her. So did the George Fernandes-led railway strike.

However, the entire country seemed to have temporarily forgotten its problems and welcomed India's foray into the nuclear age when, under Mrs Gandhi's leadership, it carried out successful nuclear tests in Pokhran in May 1974. But the demons did not leave Indira, and after the Allahabad High Court in June 1975 set aside her election to the Lok Sabha on grounds of unfair practices, she responded by imposing a state of Emergency in India. Opposition leaders were arrested, the press was gagged, and all dissent stifled.

In more ways than one, the story of Indian cricket in this period reflects the story of Indian democracy. For Indian cricket 1971 was the most glorious year. Sunil Gavaskar's Test debut coincided with India's first win against the West Indies. The young batsman from Ramesh Tendulkar's city of Mumbai bettered George Headley's record of maximum runs in a debut series. He got 774 runs at a baffling average of 154.80. After this victory, the team went to England and beat them on their home soil for the first time. B. S. Chandrasekhar, revered for his googlies, got six for thirty-eight and bowled out England for 101 on the fourth afternoon of the last Test at the Oval, leaving only 173 for India to chase. Ajit Wadekar, the then captain of the triumphant team, again from Tendulkar's city, and almost every member of his team became a national hero. The team got an incredible welcome on its return home. The flight was first taken to New Delhi for a meeting with the Prime Minister, and in Mumbai, more than a lakh people lined the route of the team's motorcade and waved jubilantly as the players journeyed twenty kilometres from the airport to the heart of the city. The 2-1 win against the MCC in 1972-73 was the third in a row.

But just a year later, in 1974, India's England tour turned out to be disastrous. At Lord's, India were all out for forty-two after England scored 629. Out of the three Tests, India lost two by an innings. The debacle continued off the field too. Captain Wadekar and one of India's star spin bowlers, Bishen Singh Bedi, had a major clash that affected the junior players; one Indian player was arrested for shoplifting, and the incident was seen as a national disgrace; Bedi was pulled up by the Board of Control for Cricket in India (BCCI) for appearing in a television programme in England; and the entire team was admonished when it arrived late for a reception held in its honour by the Indian High Commissioner. Ajit Wadekar, the biggest victim of the series, never played for India again. In almost every sense, India went from big hopes in 1971 to despair in 1975; and the year 1973 was the uncomfortable middle of a sad chapter. It seem to mirror poet Ramesh Tendulkar's darker portents more than ever before.

*

But the Tendulkars, of course, had reason to see things in a brighter light. They named the new arrival in their family Sachin, after the noted Hindi film music composer, Sachin Dev Burman, a favourite in the Tendulkar home. Sachin had three siblings: Nitin, Savita and Ajit, the last being eleven years his elder. All three were born of his father's first wife. After her death, Professor Tendulkar had married her sister, Rajni.

Ramesh Tendulkar hailed from Alibaug, a village 130 kms away from the island city of Mumbai. He came to Mumbai some time before independence to pursue higher education. While studying, he took up a job in the Modus Operandi Bureau of Mumbai police which was responsible for maintaining and storing the city police's records.

Although young Ramesh had to divide his time between his job and lessons, he won the Tarkhadkar gold medal at his Bachelor of Arts exams and the Na Chi Kelkar gold medal for his Masters in Arts from the University of Mumbai. After this he joined Siddharth College in Fort as a Marathi professor. Here, on his own initiative, he took extra classes for cricketers who could not attend lectures every day due to their playing schedule and didn't charge them anything. (Sunil Gavaskar maintains the professor was gifted with a son like Sachin because of what he did for these young cricketers.)

As a teacher, Tendulkar did not seek to mould students in his own image. He tried to help them see the world as it was, in all its gloom and beauty. Sachin once said that his approach towards his own children was pretty much the same:

> He never sat me down on his lap to tell me anything. It was his behaviour, his conduct that taught me a lot. I learnt from him that one must not be puffed up with pride in victory and one must not be crushed in defeat.[1]

After some years of teaching at Siddharth, Ramesh Tendulkar joined Kirti College in Dadar in Central Mumbai, where he eventually became head of the Marathi department (Sachin studied at the same college later). Fellow professors at the college remember him as a fair-complexioned man, slightly obese, with a wide forehead and unkempt hair. He was quiet and would not talk much even with those he knew. In the company of close friends, though, he would open up and chat for hours, 'emptying any number of tea-cups'.

To Ramesh Tendulkar's friends, what characterized him above all else was his lack of self-importance. He had no interest in academic positions and was unsuited to political ambition. His one passion was to spend his life reading the Marathi poets, V. V. Shirwadkar (a.k.a. Kusumagraj), Bal Kavi and the English poets Byron, Wordsworth, Shelley, Yeats and Eliot. He was so influenced by Kusumagraj's poetry that he named his first collection of poems *Manas Lahari* (Thought Currents) after Kusumagraj's classic *Jeevan Lahari* (Life Currents). Some of the poems in *Manas Lahari*, written in 1948-49, were published in a literary magazine in the 1950s, but the collection was brought out in book form only after Ramesh Tendulkar's death by his eldest son Nitin who, unlike the other sons Ajit and Sachin, took to literature. Many publisher-friends had tried to persuade Professor Tendulkar to bring out the collection earlier, but he had consistently frustrated their efforts.

Professor Tendulkar saw reading not as a passive exercise but as a dialogue with the minds of the past. The academic world is divided over whether a reader can understand an author wholly as he understood himself or must unavoidably make his own interpolations that make the writer's thoughts and sentiments unimportant. Tendulkar felt a reader could do both – understand an author in the light of his intentions and then construct one's own text, well beyond the author's control. His analytical study of Bal Kavi's poems, again published as a book only after his passing, is reflective of this attitude that mocks at both the traditional and fashionable academia.

Tendulkar's aesthetic instincts also drew him to music, films and theatre. He was so taken by these arts that he hated the idea of entering a cinema hall, a playhouse or a music hall just when a show was about to begin and leaving it the moment it ended. He believed in the atmospherics and wanted audiences to aid it. 'One must reach before a performance begins and wait for a while after it ends. An audience must participate, for the experience is incomplete if one does not take in the atmosphere,' he told his friends often. (One does not know about cinema-goers, play-goers or music aficionados, but lakhs of cricket lovers in stadiums across the world have religiously followed his principle whenever his own son, Sachin has turned out to bat.)

What made Ramesh Tendulkar all the more special to his friends was his sense of humour. A Marathi magazine called *Pradeep*, edited by poet Praful Dutt, had published Tendulkar's poems in some of its issues. The magazine shut soon afterwards. 'What else would happen (if they published my poems)?' Tendulkar had asked.

The professor would be away at work for most part of the day. So would his wife Rajni, who worked with the state-owned Life Insurance Corporation or LIC. So Sachin, the toddler, spent most of his time with his siblings and the maid in the house, Laxmibai Ghije. The maid, in fact, was the first bowler he faced in life. When he was two-and-a-half, she bowled to him with a plastic ball, which Sachin would hit with a *dhoka*, a wooden washing stick found in many Indian households that roughly resembles a cricket bat.

As he began to grow, Sachin showed himself to be a most impetuous child, and as unwieldy as the curly mop of hair he had at that time. He would not sit in one place for long and preferred running to walking. He always wanted to be out of the house, and on to the colony playground.

As a child, Sachin was also known to be a big bully. His close friend Atul Ranade, who met him in kindergarten at the New English High School, Bandra East, recollects:

I distinctly remember meeting Sachin first in junior KG. He had created a big chaos by holding a boy against a bench and beating him up. With his huge locks and strong body, he was a brattish, bullying character who always wanted to dominate proceedings. He was the kind of person who easily registered in the minds of others by his deeds. In both junior and senior KG, he stood out from among all of us little ones.

All of us used to fight during the break. Sachin once bullied a boy much older than him and thrashed him. The boy waited at the school gate with some friends at the end of the day, so that he could give Sachin a "reply". Sachin simply vanished. Nobody knew where he went.

This was the time Sachin started playing cricket with a tennis ball on the 30x30 yard playground in Sahitya Sahwas with other children in the colony. How was his first feel on the cricket bat? What was the grip like? How did his feet move? Did his batting show at all that he was a natural? These details are essential because we are looking at a four or five-year-old boy taking to cricket without the conditioning of experience or training, and sans any recall factor which eventually shapes the style of a cricketer. For these details we would have to therefore rely on Sachin's brother Ajit and his childhood friends like Sunil Harshe.

According to what they recollect, Sachin began by clutching the bat tightly around the bottom of the bat handle. So the "wrong" grip that later became a topic for much discussion was wrong from the word go. Like the grip, the batting too was instinctive, almost carefree. He had just about begun to watch batsmen on television but didn't copy anyone. His feet moved correctly most of the time. He was authoritarian with the ball in that he loved hitting it hard and ferociously and into the foliage in the colony. This was a most useful practice on the 30x30 yard playground, because there were hardly any fielders close to the foliage or the buildings. He could send the ball in that direction without fear of losing his wicket. If he plodded, there was always the chance of being caught close to the crease.

Sachin was luckier than many other boys playing cricket in Mumbai, for the surface on which he played his earliest game was even. He therefore learnt to sense overpitched, underpitched and good-length balls and adjust to their respective lengths. The surfaces of so many streets, street corners and so-called maidans in the city where boys often play their cricket are so rough that there are big holes all across the field, a major crack where a half-volley could land and ridges where the bowler may hope to put his good-length ball. Uneven surfaces have their own uses: they prepare a batsman for all kinds of playing conditions. But a player would rather play his first game of cricket on a sound surface, if only to discern correctly the basics about the variety of deliveries in a bowler's repertoire.

Sachin nevertheless also had to adjust to erratic bowling and unpredictable bounce in many a colony games as a result of some enthusiastic albeit amateur cricket. His brother Ajit noticed that even in those early years, Sachin made quick adjustments, had a good feel for the ball and judged its line and length well.

But cricket wasn't the only game developing into a passion; Sachin loved tennis just as much. As an eight-year-old he had a great fascination for John McEnroe whose legendary clashes with Bjorn Borg were then splashed across TV screens, and in 1981, Sachin sat glued before the small screen at home as McEnroe defeated Borg at Wimbledon in one of their more famous finals.

He celebrated crazily when McEnroe won, much to the chagrin of his brother Ajit and sister Savita who were rooting for Borg, and soon demanded from family elders a tennis racquet, a headband and two wristbands. He wanted to look like his idol. He had a McEnroe hairdo already, the other accoutrements would complete the image, he thought.

"McEnroe madness" has more than just anecdotal importance in the life of Tendulkar. Sachin seemed to have imbibed from the maverick tennis star the quality of raw aggressiveness, severity in dealing with opponents and a never-say-die attitude. Yet there was something McEnroe offered that was undesirable. His opponent Borg – offered just the opposite. Sachin left out the undesirable from his hero, and picked up the opposite from Borg – calm in the middle of a storm, a refusal to show the turbulence within. McEnroe often blew his top, shouted and screamed out his anger, frustrations and disappointments. Borg, during the course of their great rivalry, experienced the same emotions ever so often; he never brought them to the surface.

Sachin similarly has always remained poised and seldom made on- or off-field demonstrations of his displeasures and disappointments. There have been several occasions – for instance, the captaincy crisis, when he wasn't allowed to pick his team, the period after his father's death, when he returned to cricket immediately, and the ball-tampering controversy in South Africa – when his mental and emotional equilibrium was definitely put to test. There have been innumerable instances of sledging, especially by the Australians, not easy to digest for the most level-headed. But except for the odd encounter with England's ex-captain, Nasser Hussain, to protest against negative bowling tactics by Ashley Giles, Sachin has matched Borg's mental make-up all the way. A psychological portrait of Tendulkar must therefore have place not only for John McEnroe but also the Swede, Bjorn Borg.

*

Sachin was soon considered good enough to be part of the Sahwas' seniors cricket team. The reason: he batted aggressively, almost ferociously, hitting the tennis ball with abandon. Atul Ranade remembers how Sachin's batting in the colony once gave him two "stickers" on the left thigh. Both 'still stink.'

Sachin didn't talk much with the older boys; he was, like his father, an introvert. But the transformation that took place when he held the bat was like the transformation of a quiet musical score into a savage choreography of hard hitting. Or like the thunderous noise of the crackers that he burst in the company of his siblings and all other Sahitya Sahwas children when Kapil Dev's team defeated Clive Lloyd's at Lord's and lifted the Prudential World Cup in 1983.

With his love for outdoor activity and increasing enjoyment of the game, Sachin became something of a cricket zealot, and, for his family, a boy who showed determined rambunctiousness. He played all day in the colony, and when his mother called out for lunch or a glass of milk, he would go most reluctantly. When Rajni Tendulkar expressed concern over his non-stop cricket session, he would ask: 'Aai, ugach kashala tension ghetes? (Mother, why are you unnecessarily tense?)'

It is said that Sahitya Sahwas gave Tendulkar just the

environment he needed to begin his sporting endeavours. The spacious ground there is said to be crucial especially in view of shortage of playgrounds in a crammed city like Mumbai.

Former India batsman, Tendulkar's close friend, and now one of India's best known cricket commentators, Sanjay Manjrekar stresses the importance of *galli* (street) cricket:

> What's important for a young cricketer is to first enjoy the game a lot before he gets into serious cricket for schools and clubs. What I mean is playing *galli* cricket, with a soft ball, and playing it competitively. You know, when you are one of the main players. That's a nice way to start. It's important to realize you're enjoying it. Your mother's shouting from the balcony, asking you to come back, but you're enjoying yourself. During this time, you're gaining something valuable, you become street-smart and learn lessons in cricket competition. Your flair as a batsman and bowler develops more with a soft ball at that age than with a proper cricket ball. This is the ideal way to start cricket.
>
> I think this happened to Tendulkar and many other batsmen coming from Mumbai during the 1980s. It doesn't happen as much any more.

This is true. Good *galli* cricket gave Tendulkar the right foundations for a cricket career. Yet it could not have constituted the definitive push. There's a reason for this. Although the privilege of space is not easily had in Mumbai, *galli* cricket goes on just as vigorously, or even more vigorously, in other parts of Mumbai every day as it does in Sahitya Sahwas. It is played across the city with a passion often unmatched by cricket at a far higher level. So at a very young age, Tendulkar underwent the same experience that anyone anywhere in Mumbai, introduced to the game of cricket early due to the game's enormous popularity, would undergo.

So what, or who, was it that gave him the push? Tendulkar's coach, the legendary Ramakant Acharekar, who played a big role in shaping the little cricketer, feels that most of the credit must go to Sachin's family. Like Acharekar's assessment of Tendulkar's talent, this assessment too is correct.

There was room in little Tendulkar's life for all the things that are part of a child's world – nastiness, rebellion, a sense of reckless adventure. His "what-problem-I-got-no-problem" approach got bigger one day when, at age eleven, he thought of scaling a tree in Sahitya Sahwas to pluck mangoes with his friend Sunil Harshe. All the elders in the colony were then busy watching Dev Anand's hugely successful film *Guide* on State-run television, so the boys decided to make the most of the opportunity.

As Sachin climbed up, Harshe saw him go dangerously high for comfort. He asked him not to go too far. Tendulkar didn't listen, and as he tried to reach higher, had a bad fall. There was no major injury, but it hurt badly, and word reached Ajit Tendulkar of this "enterprise".

It was at this point that Ajit Tendulkar made a decisive intervention in Sachin's life. Enough of pointless adventurism; Sachin must now channelize his energies into something worthwhile, Ajit thought aloud. The eleven-year-old was told that since he was fascinated by cricket, it would be better for him to get into organized cricket practice. For this, he was told he would be taken to Shivaji Park, to the nets of noted coach Ramakant Acharekar. Ajit would request Acharekar to accept Sachin for the nets.

Less than a year earlier, Ajit had taken Sachin to the Wankhede to watch Richards. As Sachin walked toward Acharekar's nets in the company of his brother, the careless beauty of Richards' batting, and his callous indifference to bowlers, was fresh in his memory.

---

1 *Ekach Shatkar, Sachin Special,* 1998.

the city of cricket

> History is a social process, in which individuals
> are engaged as social beings... What seems to me
> essential is to recognize in the great man an
> outstanding individual who is at once the
> representative and the creator of social forces.
>
> — E. H. Carr, *What is History?*

> All things that are now happening have happened
> in the past, and will happen in the future.
>
> — Marcus Aurelius, *Meditations*

> Men and women are not only themselves; they are
> also the region in which they were born.
>
> — W. Somerset Maugham, *The Razor's Edge*

Why did Ajit Tendulkar think of cricket as the only possible vehicle
for disciplining his younger brother and giving him a sense of
direction? Why not any other sport, or any other activity, for that
matter? This question isn't satisfactorily answered by the sole fact
that Sachin was showing some promise in colony cricket. To take
this view would be gross over-simplification. There were other
reasons for his choice. Ajit Tendulkar, in his role as elder brother,
wasn't an isolated individual acting in a vacuum.

Sachin's brother, I reckon, represented Mumbai's middle-class
Maharashtrian society. It was from this standpoint that he
approached Sachin's problem: of increasing aimless mischief. We
must grasp this standpoint and see the social and historical
background in which it was rooted.

However, it's not my purpose to see only why Ajit Tendulkar, *in his own view*, acted as he did. If I did that, this would be an odd biography that follows the misleading "great-man" theory of history. Hardly does anyone all the time, or even very often, act from intentions of which s/he's completely aware, or which s/he's willing to swear by. Tendulkar's brother was no exception. He was the vehicle of a social group looking at certain means to improve its place in society. His act of taking his brother to Ramakant Acharekar's nets was determined not only by his conscious motives, but equally, by outside forces guiding his unconscious will.

These forces took shape as a result of a continuous accumulation of experience. And the experience itself arrived and acquired character as a curious mix of the four Cs: cricket, city, community and (a whole lot of) concern.

In the last two centuries at least, economic sustenance has been the main concern of an average Maharashtrian's life. In Mumbai in particular, the community's economic backwardness can be traced back to the mid-nineteenth century, when Marathi-speaking elite, like the Pathare Prabhus, were displaced by 'the more enterprising Bhatias and Banias'.[1]

Maharashtrians in the city chose early to involve themselves in occupations outside the industrial and commercial sector. Even in the textiles, tobacco and printing industries, which flourished from the end of the nineteenth century through the first half of the twentieth century and which had a good degree of Maharashtrian representation, Marathi-speaking people were involved mostly in manual labour. A survey in the early 1950s[2] shows that Maharashtrians lagged behind other communities staying in Mumbai in terms of occupational status and education. The percentage of Maharashtrians earning a middle to upper middle-class salary (500 to 1000 rupees per month) was conspicuously lower (four per cent) than people from the South Indian (7.9 per cent) and Gujarati (10.2 per cent) communities. As chemicals, pharmaceuticals, banking, insurance and other new service industries emerged after independence, Mumbai's Maharashtrians came to be employed in proportion to their population percentage (forty-three per cent) only in the lower-income brackets designating manual labour.

This was also the period in which the flow of migrants to Mumbai increased, and the Marathi population took a dip in a city it claimed, along with other competing groups, as its own. Not that Maharashtrians ever had a powerful majority. Even in 1881, they had a thin lead – 50.2 per cent of the city's total population. This rose, slightly, to 50.9 per cent in 1911. However, by 1931, the percentage had gone down to 47.6, and by 1961 it was 42.8. This decline can't be called a catastrophe but was enough to alarm a people facing financial anxiety in a booming economy.

On the political front too, Maharashtrians had never played a big role in Mumbai in the nineteenth century, though they were ironically in the forefront of the national movement.

This too was due to commercial backwardness. During the British Raj, voting rights were restricted to tax payers, and wealth, rather than numbers, determined political power. The representation of Maharashtrians in the Bombay Municipal Council of 1875 was a mere twelve per cent, though they constituted fifty per cent of the city's population.

However after voting rights were given to everybody in 1948, and especially after the creation of Maharashtra state in 1960, the political status of the Marathi-speaking people underwent a sea change. The gaining of political power led them to question their continued economic backwardness and evoked a desire for financial improvement.

It was at this time that cricket patronage came in, to help in more ways than one. But before we examine the nature and scope of that patronage, we must look at the course the game of cricket took in the city since it was introduced by the British.

*

The roots of Indian cricket are undoubtedly in Mumbai. In the eighteenth century, British officials first played the "recreational game" on a vast stretch of green on the southern tip of the island.

This stretch, where the Bombay High Court, the University of Mumbai and the Victoria Terminus stand today, was known to the British as the Esplanade Ground and to locals as the Maidan.

The Parsis of Bombay took up cricket, as an act of imitation, sometime in the 1830s. Official records say that the first Hindu to play the game was a Maharashtrian, one Ramchandra Vishnu Navlekar.[3] He entered the cricketing arena in 1861 and played a crucial role in the formation of the Bombay Union Cricket Club in 1866. The Parsis, along with the British [who looked at the sport as a medium for inculcating Victorian values in the locals and thus strengthening the Empire), gradually built a cricketing superstructure in the city. They set up a number of clubs, provided cricketing equipment and encouraged players. In 1877 some Marathi students of the Elphinstone High School started a Hindu Cricket Club. The Gujaratis, a community of traders, stepped in to give the club a sound financial base. From then on, Parsis, Gujaratis and Maharashtrians, in that order, promoted cricket in the city.

So far as the Maharashtrians were concerned, the promotion was helped in good measure by the fact that Lokmanya Bal Gangadhar Tilak, then one of the most prominent leaders of the Indian National Movement, didn't look at cricket as an alien sport. Tilak called for a boycott of foreign goods but never of cricket. On the contrary, at a public meeting, he praised Palwankar Baloo, a skilful practitioner of spin bowling, who played from the 1890s to the 1910s and often helped Pune's Hindus defeat the Pune European team.[4]

Tilak's praise may have had less to do with Baloo's cricketing skills and more with the fact that Baloo belonged to the Chamar caste, for the Lokmanya was trying to bridge the caste divide; but it certainly sent a message that cricket, despite its colonial origins, was indeed acceptable to the Indians.

The point was further driven home by the great social reformer and Tilak's contemporary, Mahadev Govind Ranade. Ranade garlanded Baloo at a public function in Pune after the bowler returned triumphant from Satara, having taken seven wickets against an all-white Satara Gymkhana squad. Then, two of Tilak's closest aides, Na Chi Kelkar and L. B. Bhopatkar, stepped in to promote cricket in Pune. They were followed by Tilak's political opponents: the moderate nationalist leaders, Gopal Krishna Gokhale and Wrangler R. P. Paranjpe. Gokhale and Paranjpe tried to popularize the game in both Mumbai and Pune.

Gopal Krishna Gokhale, considered the intellectual guru of Mahatma Gandhi, took over as leader of the national movement in the wake of Tilak's death. Gandhi was not at all fond of cricket. Nevertheless, cricket's association with nationalism slowly became real for his community, the Gujaratis, too and became evident when Ramesh Divecha, a prominent seam bowler, was arrested for participating in the Quit India Movement of 1942. As a result, legendary cricketer and one of the most prominent Gujarati spokesmen for cricket, Vijay Merchant, not only boycotted the trials for India's first ever Test tour to England in 1932 to protest British rule in India, he also told MCC's dignitaries at Lord's in his capacity as Indian vice-captain in 1946 that England should not believe an exchange of cricketers brought the two countries closer.

Yet, in Mumbai and elsewhere in pre-independent India, the promotion of cricket didn't quite make the impact it has today. It largely remained either a gentleman's diversion, a local prince's peculiar passion that moved him to fits of patronage or, at best, a diplomatic tool for the ruler and the ruled.

Cricket shed its imperial roots in the real sense after 1947, and the place to benefit most from this change, and to emerge as the centre of cricket, was Mumbai.

In India's financial capital, commercial establishments, big and small, had always keenly followed the Times Shield Cricket Tournament, meant for the working men, since its inception in 1930. With the passing of each year, the tournament attracted large crowds as the participating teams, "A" to "F" division, represented not only an impressive pool of talent which provided good entertainment to spectators but also attracted good publicity.

In the 1950s the Tatas, Mahindra and Mahindra and the Associated Cement Corporation (ACC), three of India's major business players, launched a cricketer recruitment policy, hoping that the involvement of their team in the Times Shield and their association with cricket and cricketers would bring in advertisement for their various companies. With more tournaments getting introduced in the city's cricket calendar, big banks – like the State Bank of India – and many other companies and firms too joined in the exercise.

This is where Maharashtrian participation in cricket took a turn. With the prospect of emerging economic reward and "job security" (a peculiar Indian term) cricket permeated deep into the middle, lower-middle and urban working classes. Earlier, players came mainly from south Mumbai: the elegant batsman L.P. Jai lived at Opera House, the Apte brothers were from Girgaum, Rusi Modi stayed close to Bombay Central and Meher-Homji was from Tardeo. Now, a northward shift happened, and Dadar and Shivaji Park, where the Marathi middle and lower-middle classes lived, became the hub of cricketing activity. Clubs like Dadar Union, Shivaji Park Gymkhana and many others gave a fillip to cricketing endeavours and not only began to set standards in cricketing excellence, they also allowed good players to play without paying any fees. This gave the economically deprived an opportunity to show their prowess on the field. And, as history and statistics have indicated, sportspersons from not-so privileged backgrounds demonstrate a bigger drive to succeed than those from affluent backgrounds.

The talents of the technically flawless batsman Vijay Manjrekar, pace bowler Ramakant 'Tiny' Desai, and Subhash Gupte, whom Sir Gary Sobers rated as the world's best leg-spinner, arose in the 1950s out of this approach to cricket – as a means of improving their economic and social status. Their names were held up as examples by thousands of others who began serious pursuit of the game.

Various public and private sector units now employed cricketers in large numbers, and even colleges like Siddharth, St Xavier's and Elphinstone took in cricketers with offers of "freeships" and other fringe benefits. As a result of this patronage, at least a few thousand Marathi-speaking cricketers landed jobs. The better cricket they played, the more quickly they were promoted at the workplace.

The statistics of Indian cricket soon recorded significant changes. In the 1930s, the national team had two Marathi-speaking players. In the period between 1946 to 1959, sixty-seven players in all were capped from across the country; out of these, nearly half – twenty-nine – were Maharashtrians.[5]

The competition to recruit established cricketers grew in the 1960s and continued through the Seventies and Eighties. Nationalized banks institutionalized the system of patronage by launching formal and widely publicized cricketer recruitment programmes. In the private sector, new entrants like Mafatlal, Nirlon and J. K. Chemicals came in to expand the network in a big way. The numerous smaller firms and companies that supported cricketers during this period have mostly gone unnamed, but their role was just as crucial, because they employed thousands of club cricketers, gave even the moderately successful player financial rewards, a "permanent job" and social mobility. Such firms also provided the necessary second rung of patronage, which made it easier for the top firms to hire top-level cricketers.

The question that arises is why, at that time, did such a system not come up in other cities of India. The fact is the process did begin elsewhere too, with the growing popularization of cricket. What made all the difference was that most banks and companies had their headquarters in Mumbai, and firms in other parts of India did not quite operate on the scale of those in the country's commercial capital. So, despite the Shiv Sena's fulminations against outsiders that played on the minds of Maharashtrians in the Sixties, the community did benefit from enterprising non-Maharashtrians who had set up base in the city.

The community had by now gained such a foothold in different aspects of the game that it acquired unquestioned dominance in Indian cricket. Mansur Ali Khan Pataudi, India's captain in the 1960s, said most members of his team spoke "Mahratti". Pataudi's successor as captain, Ajit Wadekar, and other members of his 1971 team that brought phenomenal cricketing success to the country, in fact, stood out as fine examples of the fruition of the whole process of patronage.

Wadekar's father, Lakshman earned a modest income as a supervisor in the railways. He felt he was "lucky" when all his four children got scholarships for their education. One of his sons, Ajit, was taken in by the State Bank of India as a cricketer: he not only went on to lead the Indian team, but retired as the bank's executive director.

Even more striking is the story of Wadekar's teammate Eknath Solkar. Indeed, it is the perfect symbol of the rise of the humble Maharashtrian cricketer from Mumbai.

Solkar's father hailed from Pavas in Ratnagiri district, where he worked in the fields of a landowner. When the family shifted to Mumbai, it went through considerable economic hardship. The hardship continued even as the father obtained work as a *mali* (groundsman) at the Hindu Gymkhana, one of five gymkhanas dotting the beautiful Marine Drive. Little 'Ekki' soon began operating the scoreboard at the gymkhana and took in his first cricketing lessons. When his playing talent became obvious, the gymkhana's members gave him cricket clothes and equipment. Solkar didn't even go to college, but thanks to an institutionalized system of support, played Test cricket. He now lives in Sportsfield, a plush apartment in Worli in South Mumbai built by the government of Maharashtra for eminent sportspersons.

The family of a Wadekar or Solkar didn't have any cricketing background, but as more and more Marathi-speaking people took to cricket, a cricketing tradition developed, and Sunil Gavaskar, the most illustrious member of Wadekar's team, came to exemplify that tradition. Gavaskar's father, Manohar played competitive cricket at the club level in Mumbai and introduced his son to the game. Sunil's maternal uncle, Madhav Mantri played an even bigger role. Mantri, during his childhood, studied under the streetlights and faced great financial difficulties before going on to represent the Indian team as a wicket-keeper in the 1950s. He set for his nephew an example of what could be achieved. Gavaskar's long-time batting partner, Ramnath Parkar grew up in the BDD Chawls of Worli, in trying circumstances. His father was a compositor in a press, and Ramnath himself didn't even get a chance to go to college. Yet, the city's cricket structure adequately nurtured and highlighted his talents. He eventually played for India. Parkar, significantly, was the first disciple of Sachin Tendulkar's coach, Ramakant Acharekar.

"Billionaire" Sachin Tendulkar therefore has the historical background of a Solkar struggling to get two square meals a day, a Madhav Mantri straining his eyes and studying in the light of streetlamps and a Ramnath Parkar going to Acharekar to ask not only for cricketing guidance but also for clothes and equipment. Tendulkar is today credited for bringing big money into cricket. This is true so far as the *extent* of money is concerned. But the fact is that Tendulkar himself is the product of big money coming into cricket – and vitally, Mumbai cricket – in the middle of the twentieth century. And he is the product of a desperate Maharashtrian's desire to get rid of economic anxiety. In a strict sociological sense, there would perhaps be no Sachin if Solkar's father had not taken the train from Ratnagiri to Mumbai and encouraged his son to play cricket.

Tendulkar is well aware that 'Mumbai has everything that can make a cricketer – a conducive atmosphere for the game, good grounds, talented coaches, seniors always willing to help youngsters, sponsors, and above all, a great love for cricket,' but I don't know if he is aware of the aforementioned social and economic aspirations. It is more likely that, like Gavaskar who said he considered himself an Indian first and a Maharashtrian later, and like some other cricketers from other regions who think along similar lines, Sachin is unaware of them. But he is undoubtedly influenced by the pull of these forces.

So was his brother, who dragged him out of the house one fine morning in 1984 and began the journey to Shivaji Park, where he would introduce Sachin to Ramakant Acharekar.

*

The cricketing structure in Mumbai had, by the year 1984, consolidated itself. Unlike cricket's earlier world capital Yorkshire, that hit rock bottom in the Seventies and Eighties, Mumbai had shown a great deal of resilience. Other Indian states had by this time qualified as good, even stiff, competitors. Pankaj Roy, Ambar Roy, Gopal Bose, Subroto Guha and Shute Banerjee had batted and bowled their hearts out and made Bengal the most powerful team of the East Zone despite the steady growth of Bihar and Orissa; Ghulam Ahmed, M. L. Jaisimha, Abbas Ali Baig, Abid Ali and Mansur Ali Khan Pataudi had blended the cricket of the princes and the masses, to give Hyderabad a respectable position on the Indian sports map; Gundappa Vishwanath, Brijesh Patel, Erapalli Prasanna, B. S. Chandrasekhar, Syed Kirmani and Roger Binny had guided Karnataka to a dramatic rise in the Seventies; C. D. Gopinath, Bharat Reddy, A. G. Ram Singh and Srinivas Venkataraghavan had brought to Tamil Nadu's cricket what Cho Ramaswamy, actor and political commentator, called the forceful Tughlaq touch; and the Amarnaths, both Surinder and Mohinder in association with an R. Pal, a Ramesh Saxena and a Bishen Singh Bedi, had often threatened to smash the icon of Mumbai to make Delhi India's cricket capital.

Mumbai did indeed suffer occasional defeats at the hands of the other provincial teams as cricket struck deep roots in different parts of India. But even when the icon was hit really hard, the odd thing was how only a few shards could be found on the floor. Mumbai's rank remained in place. Its team won India's foremost domestic tournament, the Ranji Trophy, fifteen consecutive times from 1958-59 to 1972-73, and even later Ranji defeats, aberrations at worst, couldn't do too much harm.

This was because a well-ensconced two-tier system was systematically generating immense talent. At the school level, there were two tournaments: the Giles Shield for junior schoolboys and the Harris Shield for seniors. The cricket played in these tournaments was fiercely competitive, for they acted as *the* platform for young cricketers to display their abilities. For adults, the Kanga League (for clubs) and the Times Shield were the two top titles around which other tournaments revolved.

These tournaments were responsible for the development of a strong maidan culture where "practice, practice and more practice" became a mantra, where players felt a keen sense of competition and pride in being associated with intensely fought cricketing encounters. The tournaments, in turn, fed and grew on the support of this culture.

The most unique of these tournaments, the Kanga League, came verily to mirror the city's cricket. It was played in the monsoon, when the outfield in a maidan would be squelchy, the grass grown beyond acceptable limits and the wicket dangerously full of cracks. To play under such conditions became a challenge for clubs and their players, and a lot of importance and prestige came to be attached to performances in the League. All cricketers in Mumbai worth their whites – whether they were Test, Ranji, "A" division or "G" division players – turned out for the tournament with a potent mix of earnestness and enthusiasm. The best of them, Sunil Gavaskar, underlined the League's importance like no one else did. He once returned to his home city early Sunday morning from a Test tour of England; at 10 am, he was all padded up and taking strike at the Shivaji Park for his club team, Dadar Union. Gavaskar, in doing so, highlighted another area of the city's cricket tradition: batting.

Vijay Merchant – scion of the Thackersey family, had begun the batting tradition in the early part of the twentieth century. He batted so well that the Maharaj Kumar of Vizianagram or 'Vizzy' as he was popularly known, one of Indian cricket's most scheming characters, impatient to control Indian cricket in the 1940s, offered Merchant's batting partner Mushtaq Ali a gold watch to run him out in a crucial Test match!

Vizzy and some of his acolytes had carried out a systematic smear campaign against Indian cricket's first superstar, C. K. Nayudu of Indore, saying 'Baahar se kaala, andar se kala, bada badmaash hai yeh Indorewala (His face is black/His soul the same colour/This man from Indore is a scoundrel).' Before Vizzy could shower any such racial slur on Merchant, England's C. B. Fry indulged in reverse discrimination and said he wanted to paint Merchant white and play him against Australia.

Merchant was a man of short height (like his successors Vijay Manjrekar, Sunil Gavaskar and Sachin Tendulkar). Like the other three, he too made up for its disadvantages with a refined technique, a sharp eye and good footwork. He defended and attacked with equal ease. Above all, he became famous for an exceptionally delicate late cut.

There is a story of how Merchant, many years after his retirement, took up the willow and decided to have a few knocks in the nets. A young fast bowler came roaring in and bowled a snorter just outside the off-stump. Merchant made an initial back-and-across movement, positioned himself for the cut and played it so fine and safe that were it not for the nets, it would have sailed over the slips for a four!

Vijay Manjrekar – the second standard-bearer of what writer Ramachandra Guha calls the Mumbai school of batsmanship – did much the same against that master of leg-spin, Bhagwat Chandrasekhar.

Guha writes that in one game, Chandrasekhar bowled one short to Manjrekar. The batsman put his left foot behind and readied himself for the cut, when the ball came in, viciously. It was the wrong 'un, and as the ball threatened to kiss the stumps, Chandra and the wicket-keeper virtually leaped up in triumph. What does Chandrasekhar then see? A split second before the ball could take the bails, Manjrekar's bat had intervened. He had executed a classic late cut, and the ball was running to the ropes. As Chandrasekhar looked on incredulously, Manjrekar went up to him and said: 'Good ball, Chandra. But not good enough for Vijay Manjrekar.'[6]

After Manjrekar's generation had passed, Sunil Gavaskar took guard for the Indian team. He had the unenviable task of facing up to the deadliest pace attack of all time: the West Indian quartet of Andy Roberts, Michael Holding, Malcolm Marshall and Joel Garner.

Where some of the world's most talented batters groped, Gavaskar got thirteen centuries against the West Indian pacers.

In the 1984 series against the Windies, Gavaskar had dropped himself down to the number four position to regain lost form. That made no difference in the Madras Test as he came in to bat with the score reading zero for the loss of two wickets. As he took guard, Viv Richards even ran up to him from the slips and said jocularly: 'Sunny, it don't matter whether you bat number one or four, man. The score's still zero.'

To make things more difficult for Gavaskar, Clive Lloyd's pacers began a continuous assault of shoulder-high deliveries. To say that he tackled them well would be an understatement. He cut the fast bowlers repeatedly and gracefully over the slips and got a career-best score of 236 not out. There were no snicks; all the cuts were played fine and accurately and placed properly over the slip cordon. The Windies didn't know how he could play the cut – that most fragile of shots – so well over and over again.

In the year 2001, another generation had taken over. Sachin Tendulkar was facing the world's then fastest bowler, Allan Donald, on a bouncy South African wicket. Donald and his bowling partners had a one-point agenda. Bowl chest and shoulder-high to the short man. Tendulkar cut them sometimes delicately, sometimes savagely, over the slips. Every ball that went in that direction was immaculately placed; when it bounced on to Tendulkar's face, he bent slightly backward, got his bat at the correct angle and caressed it; when it was a little less high, he bent down, smelled the ball, opened the face of the bat heavenward and sent the ball over the slips; and when the bowler bowled in the corridor of uncertainty on and outside the off-stump, the classic late cut came into play. Donald and company just could not work him out as he went on to score 155, regarded by Indian coach, John Wright as the best Test innings he has ever seen.

The South African bowlers thought they had done their homework. Before taking on Tendulkar, they had seen many video recordings to examine all perceptible flaws in his batting.

However, cricketers, like the rest of humanity, often take no notice of the past. This may seem obtusely theoretical or simply weird, but the fact is the South Africans hadn't seen Merchant, Manjrekar or Gavaskar's videos. If they had, they'd have known what Tendulkar could, all of a sudden, pull out of his hat.

TV watchers across the world that day marvelled at Tendulkar's cutting, and he must get the deserved appreciation for it. But the finesse was only partly his own; half of it was a historical given, an inheritance.

We think what we see on television has never been done before in cricket. But Tendulkar's batting proved what the Australian wicket-keeper of the 1930s, Victor Richardson, told his grandson, Aussie captain of the 1970s, Ian Chappell: 'Don't think anything in cricket is new, boy. It has all been tried before.'

The batsmen from Mumbai had, over the decades, also acquired a reputation for being *khadoos*. This word has no suitable English equivalent but suggests a blend of fixity of purpose, steely determination and finally a high degree of stubbornness that abhors surrender. These qualities came to the players courtesy the tough tournaments they played right from their schooldays. The troubled phases of Indian cricket ensured that they had to be further polished at the game's highest level.

So the national team had a Vijay Merchant and a Vijay Hazare[7] routinely stopping breaches that would otherwise allow an opposition attack to run through the line-up. These two were followed in the 1950s by Polly Umrigar, the last great representative of the city's – and country's – pioneering Parsi cricketers. As the decline of the Parsi community robbed cricket of other Umrigars, and the shift in Gujarati lifestyles from austerity to remarkable consumption denied Indian cricket any more L. P. Jais and Merchants, the Maharashtrian stepped into the saddle.

With India two down for zero against an English attack of Fred Trueman, Brian Statham and Moss at Lord's in 1959, in walked Vijay Manjrekar with a damaged knee and led a fightback with a stroke-filled eighty-five. Recovering fully from the knee injury two years

later, he took Ted Dexter's bowling side to pieces, setting an
individual Test score record for an Indian batsman with a masterful
189 not out in Delhi. In the Madras Test of the same series, while
the Indian batting collapsed around him, he got a faultless and
fluent eighty-five out of a total of 146 for seven. Luckily for the
Englishmen, he got out in what seemed the only way possible:
run out.

While Manjrekar – a man with a wider range of strokes than any
Indian cricketer before him – often ran out of partners, the Seventies
generation saw to it that three or four Mumbai players came together
to form the backbone of Indian batting.

Ajit Wadekar was a ruthless attacker but also enormously
stubborn. In one Ranji game in the early Seventies, Karnataka
skipper V. Subrahmanyam told his team to get a score of 300. That,
he felt, would be enough for two of Karnataka's, India's, and the
world's, all-time great spinners Bhagwat Chandrasekhar and Erapalli
Prasanna, to bowl out the Mumbai team. Karnataka got 350 instead.
Then, as one Mumbai wicket fell early, Wadekar went out and got
323 off his own bat.

Dilip Sardesai, originally from Goa, had settled in Mumbai and
learnt all his cricket there. He was forced to open the Indian innings
in the early Sixties and performed excellently against New Zealand in
1965. The decline began soon, and by 1969, he was being written off
as a liability. However, when Wadekar became captain in 1971, he
gave Sardesai the position he wanted to bat in. The result: in the
historic series against West Indies that witnessed the emergence of
Gavaskar, it was Sardesai who blocked all possible fold-ups of the
Indian batting with scores of 212, 112 and 150. He and Wadekar
gave the young Gavaskar much encouragement, and the "little man"
showed himself so defiant against a rampaging West Indian attack
that the Caribbeans wrote a calypso in his honour: 'It was
Gavaskar/The Real Master/Just like a wall/We couldn't out Gavaskar
at all/Not at all/You know the West Indies couldn't out Gavaskar at
all.' Another line – 'After me, the deluge' – would have suited
Gavaskar just as fine, for almost throughout his career, his dismissal

opened the floodgates and placed the Indian batting in the sphere of uncertainty. So long as he was at the crease, he saved the team from destructive bowlers like Lord Krishna had when he lifted the Govardhan mountain on a finger, and sheltered the people of Vrindavan from Lord Indra's anger.

From Gavaskar's very own Hindu Colony in Dadar emerged Dilip Balwant Vengsarkar. He took the blows of speedsters from across the world unflinchingly, and stood his ground whenever India needed him to do the job. 'Guts, guts,' was how Viv Richards described Vengsarkar's batting. For his courage, he earned the title 'Colonel', originally bestowed on C. K. Nayudu.

Sandeep Patil, Ravi Shastri and Sanjay Manjrekar were all born and reared in the same tradition. Patil was aggressive, a destroyer of the cricket ball; Shastri had limited talent but was full of guts, and Vijay Manjrekar's son Sanjay, was all class and correctness. Tendulkar and Vinod Kambli bore the same stamp of class and Sachin easily symbolizes the best in the city's batting tradition.

Gavaskar, Vengsarkar, Patil and Shastri were at the centre of Indian cricket, and the dominance of Mumbai was complete and continuing in the early Eighties when Tendulkar was learning his first cricket lessons in suburban Bandra.

There were many other batsmen, equally or less talented, who never made it to the national or even the Ranji team. These unsung heroes were the life-support of a vibrant cricket culture. There were also many sincere bowlers who could never earn as big a name as Subhash Gupte or Ramakant Desai, fielders who could never get the acclaim of an Eknath Solkar or a Ghulam Parkar and wicket-keepers who couldn't quite be a Naren Tamhane or a Madhav Mantri. But they kept the fire burning, the spirit alive, and the cricket going which was never less than top-class.

*

Of the many maidans that nurtured such quality cricket in the city, the one that exerted the most powerful influence was Shivaji Park.

Ever since it was thrown open to the public in 1925, Shivaji Park, located at the centre of the link between South and North Mumbai, had been more than a maidan. It had been a crucible of politics, cricket and culture. It was here that Mahatma Gandhi addressed huge crowds on more than one occasion in the 1920s, to fire the Indian imagination for the freedom struggle; it was here that Shripad Amrit Dange, from the 1920s to the 1960s, exhorted workers to unite in the name of Communism; it was here that George Fernandes built his reputation as a fiery trade union leader in the 1960s and 1970s; and it was here that political cartoonist Bal Thackeray launched the militant Shiv Sena in front of a two lakh-strong boisterous crowd in 1966.

The area around Shivaji Park was dominated by the Marathi middle and lower classes, so the essential ingredient of the park's ethos was a strong Maharashtrianism, represented, as it were, by the statue of Maratha hero Shivaji at one end of the maidan.

The sense of wronged justice felt by the community over the years across the city was strongest in this Mumbai locality. The ground thus became the platform for a desire to succeed, to gain a social standing, economic independence and a political presence, through cricket.

Most importantly, from the band of enthusiastic and committed cricketers here emerged two coaches who gradually gained a reputation for spotting, shaping and promoting young talent. Ankush 'Anna' Vaidya, the coach for Balmohan Vidyamandir, and Ramakant Acharekar, coach for Shardashram High School, set up their clinics on this ground for the simple reason that the schools they coached were located nearby.

Both also had their homes close to the ground, Anna barely a kilometre away and Acharekar three kilometres away, at Parel. The two spent most of their time on the Park's green and brought up a whole generation of dedicated and solidly professional cricketers.

The success rate of both coaches was equal during the 1970s and 1980s, yet Acharekar was lionized more than Anna because his own story, his devotion to cricket and the remarkable strides made by his pupils carried the unmistakable romance of risk-taking, which was secretly admired by a congenitally risk-reluctant Marathi society.

Anna Vaidya asked his young cricketers to get a solid education, so they would have something to fall back on if they did not succeed at sport. Besides, he looked at education as the steady handle in the complex weave of life.

Acharekar on the other hard believed in complete focus on cricket, to the exclusion of all else. If ever a pupil's crucial matches and crucial exams clashed, the coach would ask him to choose cricket over academics. He would be happier still if a youngster abandoned academics altogether in pursuit of cricket.

As a cricket fiend, he had lifted himself far afield from the other pleasures of life and had completely surrendered to the charms of the game, and he saw no reason why others could not do so.

Acharekar was born in Malwan, a village nearly 500 kms from Mumbai. When he was eleven, he came to Mumbai with his parents and, entranced by cricket, eventually got a job in the State Bank of India as a cricketer. Here, he played alongside Ajit Wadekar. As a wicket-keeper-batsman, he played only one first-class game, for State Bank against Hyderabad. 'This was in 1964, I got thirty runs,' he says.

Wadekar says of Acharekar:

> He was supposed to be the Don Bradman of "tennis-ball" cricket at Shivaji Park. He got a lot of runs in club cricket and was recruited in State Bank as a cricketer. His wicket-keeping was excellent, though he didn't shine as a batsman. He was studious about the game and looked more towards developing others' talent.

In 1967, when as a schoolboy, Ramnath Parkar, asked Acharekar for advice, he began coaching. That boy, an opening batsman, became the first of six Acharekar disciples to win a Test cap, and was also the first of the twenty-odd who would go on to play the Ranji Trophy.

Thanks to the efforts of Acharekar, Shardashram emerged as Mumbai's top cricket school. The only challengers to it were Anna

Vaidya's Balmohan, and Anjuman-e-Islam, which during the 1970s had started a refreshingly new Islamic current in Mumbai cricket that fused beautifully with the Maharashtrian mainstream.

Acharekar's style of coaching was non-transformational. He did not remake a player; he believed in development, in bringing out the cricketer within, which was, to him, like a seed waiting to sprout. The more a player practised and the more matches he played, the speedier would be the development of the seed into a full-blown tree. Many cricketers had more than a foretaste of the effectiveness of this method, both in unearthing cricket potential and in acquiring tangible benefits for career growth; it was almost as if he woke them up to the exciting possibilities of cricket, cricket and more cricket.

By the early Eighties, in fact, Acharekar had come to be seen as an underwriter of cricketing success. The perception all over the city was that most of his disciples went on to play the game at the highest level, and even those who didn't, at least played it well enough to get good, gainful employment.

---

1   S.M. Edwardes, *The Gazetteer of Bombay City and Islands*, Times of India Press, Bombay, 1909.
2   D.T. Lakdawala, *Work, Wages and Well-Being in an Indian Metropolis*, Bombay University Press, 1963.
3   Ramachandra Guha, *A Corner of a Foreign Field: The Indian History of a British Sport*, Picador, 2002.
4   Ibid.
5   Dr Richard Cashman, *Players, Patrons and the Crowd*, Orient Longman Ltd, 1980.
6   Ramachandra Guha, *Spin and Other Turns*, Penguin Books India, 1994.
7   Vijay Hazare was originally from Sangli; he moved to Pune to play cricket, and from there to Vadodara.

the schoolboy as cricketer

How can sesame oil be extracted Unless you press
the sesame seed?

– The Panchatantra

It was with some trepidation that Ajit Tendulkar approached
Ramakant Acharekar at his Shivaji Park nets.

The trepidation was in anticipation of an awkward question.
And as soon as he had introduced his younger brother to the portly,
round-faced coach and requested that he be allowed to attend nets,
the question was raised.

Had Sachin played with a proper cricket ball?

Ajit admitted he hadn't. The coach didn't mind; he asked how
old Sachin was, and whether he batted or bowled. 'He's ten, and does
a bit of both.' 'Fine,' Acharekar said, 'get him to the nets tomorrow
morning.'

The next day, Sachin went to the ground in a pair of jeans and
a T-shirt. He was asked to 'watch others at the nets'.

After nets, it was time for fielding practice. For this, Sachin was
roped in by Acharekar's assistant coach, Das Shivalkar. The boy had
never gripped a hard ball before; not that it created any obstacles in
catching and throwing the ball. Ajit watched from the sidelines with
a degree of relief.

Before the brothers left, Acharekar told Ajit that Sachin should
come wearing proper cricket clothing the next day.

Tendulkar batted for the first time in the nets the next morning.
Acharekar watched but gave no opinion, except to say the boy could
come for practice everyday.

The coach remembers:

> The first time I saw Sachin, he appeared to be like any other boy.
> In fact, I wasn't too happy because he tried to hit too many balls
> in the air. But when I watched him closely over the next few
> days, I could see he was middling the ball. He had begun to
> assess whether to hit a ball along the ground or in the air. And he
> hit the ball hard, was never defensive. The wristwork was good,
> so were the reflexes, the eyesight and the footwork. He was a
> natural cricketer.

A fortnight after Sachin's initiation into the nets, the coach decided
it was time for him to start playing practice matches. The beginnings
were bad. Tendulkar scored blooming zeroes in his first two games.

Some of his friends from Sahitya Sahwas had come to see him
bat. He was forced to give them weak excuses for failure. 'In the third
game, I scored seven. I thought I had achieved something,' Tendulkar
said years later.

However, he followed this up with scores of fifty-one, thirty-
eight and forty-five, and slowly began developing an appetite for
scoring runs. Of course the practice matches were a big help. He was
getting behind the ball better, was getting either fully forward or fully
behind, was driving correctly and cleanly with the full face of the bat
on both sides of the wicket and was enjoying the sound of ball on bat.

There are three near-indefinable things about batting: timing,
footwork and judgement. The reason I call them indefinable is that
their dictionary meanings are not up to scratch in the cricket sense.
Timing is a kind of ball sense, a physical and mental co-ordination
that enables a batsman to meet the ball at just the right moment.
This moment differs from player to player, and one who has plenty of
time to play his shots and who can actually play them late, even if it's
a nanosecond late than others, is the better player. Timing, as a
quality, can be developed and indeed has to be constantly looked
after, but an out-of-the-ordinary cricketer must begin with the
advantage of natural timing. Tendulkar, in his first few games,
seemed to show signs of it.

Footwork and judgement go hand-in-hand, for the one is dependent on the other. At the age of ten, Tendulkar had hardly any hesitancy about footwork. The movement of the feet at the point of delivery and beyond was quick and was based on sound judgement, which is – to put it in a rough way – sensing the ball's line, length, point of landing and bounce to make a corresponding response. This judgement has to develop to a point where it is more instinctive than deliberate. The more gifted cricketers, again, start off with a finer instinct than others. Little Sachin appeared to have that too – only the necessary, and necessarily arduous, process of its refinement had just about begun.

It was a rule in practice matches that a batsman who got fifty runs had to retire, so that others could bat. Such retirements began to get common for Tendulkar. This led to another development: Acharekar made Sachin a member of his own club, the Kamat Memorial Cricket Club. The purpose was not so much to play him even before he had made his debut at the school level, but to give him a feel of the atmosphere of club cricket. Absorbing the air inside a maidan tent is, after all, one of the nicest ways of introducing oneself to the rudiments as well as the intangible nuances of the game.

Tendulkar was easily enthralled by the milieu of maidan cricket. He practised rigorously in the mornings, from 6.30 am to 9.00 am, and whenever opportunity came his way, either played a day-long practice match or sat in the tent all through a club game, concentrating on the happenings in the middle.

School wasn't half as interesting. The New English School where his parents had put him wasn't too far from Sahitya Sahwas, but Sachin was never the scholastic type. He would rather be at Shivaji Park. In fact, after school hours, he would almost impatiently get back to the colony, and get all his friends together for a session of serious soft-ball cricket. There was also a practice session at home that he had made mandatory for himself. He had stuffed a stocking with a ball and tied it to a *rassi* (rope) that hung from the ceiling. He would play his strokes against the swing of the stocking. 'At home I hit a couple of thousand balls like this every day,' he says.

Perhaps the coach sensed the leanings. One day, he asked Sachin what he did in the afternoons. 'I play cricket with friends in the colony,' he was told. That was good, the coach said, Sachin must now attend the 4 pm nets too. The boy responded as if he were waiting to be asked. He turned up for practice on time, or even before the nets were put up in the afternoon, and left well after the sun had plunged into the sea waters behind Shivaji Park.

The school in Bandra was now the one big obstacle between morning and afternoon practice sessions. Acharekar found a solution to that too. He called up the Tendulkar residence one day and put a question to Ramesh Tendulkar: 'Can you shift your son to Shardashram High School? Sachin has a future in cricket.'

Prof Tendulkar discussed the matter with Rajni and Ajit and then asked Sachin. He said he would love to play cricket. At ten, he looked at it purely in terms of an ambition. He couldn't have considered the weightier question of making a career out of the game. That was for the family elders to do, and they too were in favour of the shift, thinking in clear cogent terms, that a boy averse to schoolbooks would do himself no harm in trying cricket as a route to success. In fact, if he indeed had it in him to go a long way, as the coach had suggested, the risk was well worth taking.

Thus, in the academic year starting June 1984, the name Sachin Ramesh Tendulkar appeared in the Standard Five students' list of Shardashram High School, Dadar.

Barely a few days after Sachin had begun answering the roll call there, Ramakant Acharekar took him along to buy a cricket kit. At the store, Sachin picked up a bat that was too heavy. Acharekar told him that his choice was wrong, but Sachin was exceedingly stubborn. The coach finally had to give in to his demand. When Ajit Tendulkar saw the bat, he said it was too unwieldy for a boy Sachin's size. 'I told him the same thing. He just doesn't listen,' Acharekar said.

Acharekar, though, had one problem with Tendulkar where he wasn't going to give in easily. He had noticed that Sachin gripped the bat at the bottom of the handle. This helped him play the pull or a full-toss effectively, but the coach foresaw difficulties. He felt that driving on the off would be tough if Sachin continued with this grip. First, he would play on the up. Second, he would lunge too far forward and overbalance. And, as he grew older, these problems would be compounded.

A change in grip was therefore suggested. Sachin tried the orthodox grip, both hands clutched around the middle of the handle. He floundered and struggled to stroke the ball. Without his knowing it, the hands repeatedly slipped down the handle.

The similarity with Sir Don Bradman, the legendary Australian brought to the world's notice only years later, began here, much, much before Tendulkar turned into a polished cricketer.

The Don too had an odd grip. A.G.Moyes, New South Wales' selector in 1926 and among the earliest to spot Bradman's potential, said this of his grip:[1]

> With most players, the handle runs across the palm of the hand
> and rests against the ball of the thumb. With Bradman, the hand
> is turned over so far that the handle presses against the ball of
> the thumb. As the grip tightens, the pressure becomes more
> intense. The left hand is turned so that the wrist is behind the
> handle... Some noticed this freakish grip and advised a change.
> Bradman would not hear of it. It had served him well and would,
> he believed, continue to do so.

Sachin Tendulkar hesitated to tell his coach that he couldn't help his so-called "strange" grip. However, Acharekar himself realized, in a few days' time, that Sachin was far more comfortable with his peculiar grip. The coach wasn't dogmatic; for him, the art of training was all about building on a player's nature. He had never tried to cast players in the same mould, and he saw no reason to inflict rigid rules on Tendulkar, so long as he packed a punch in his shots, kept his top hand locked at all times, moved the bottom hand swiftly according to the requirements of a stroke and looked towards harmonizing the bottom hand's power-giving capacity with the control provided by the upper hand. Plus, as Bradman would have said, the grip was serving Sachin well. He was getting runs. So the policy of intervention was abandoned.

In October 1984, it was time for the Giles Shield, the inter-school tournament for Mumbai's junior schoolboys, to begin. Acharekar told Sachin he'd bat number four for Shardashram. That was the most privileged position in the batting order, and the only thing that could have prompted the coach to give it to a boy untested and inexperienced in the rigours of school cricket, was a belief that Sachin would somehow fit in well. In fact, whether Tendulkar played for school or club, Acharekar made it plain that he would take no other position. Later, the coach didn't mind if Sachin played for clubs other than his own. 'Only make sure you bat two wickets down,' the boy was told.

Tendulkar played his first Giles Shield match against Khoja Khan High School at Azad Maidan in the heart of south Mumbai and scored twenty-four.

The innings however demonstrated that evolution was definitely under way. A batsman must always move to the off to play any shot. Sachin, with his upright stance, was making that movement. Since he was very small in height, anything pitched short of a length by a bowler came up well above his waist, and he especially delighted in pulling to the on-side deliveries that were pitched on the off-stump or even outside of it. In this knock, his off-side play stood out: out of three boundaries he hit, one was a square cut, one a cover drive and the third a straight drive.

When Tendulkar ended his second school game, the Giles Shield quarter-finals against Don Bosco School, there came a prediction that he would bat for India. This was from the umpire, Gondhalekar, who was impressed with Sachin's half-century. Forty of those runs had come in boundaries. 'You must be joking,' Acharekar told the umpire. 'This is the boy's first year in school cricket. There are many steps to be taken, many obstacles to be overcome.'

'Gondhalekar refused to backtrack,' coach Acharekar recalls.

After only five years, Tendulkar played for India, but sadly Gondhalekar was not around to see his words come true.

For all his opposition to the umpire's talk, Acharekar's subsequent action indicates that his own hunch wasn't very different. Shardashram were shot out of the Giles semi-finals, and Tendulkar was in the reserves for the Harris Shield, the tournament for senior schoolboys. So the schools' cricket season was over for him. Surprisingly, coach Acharekar at this point asked him to attend selection trials for the Under-19 summer nets conducted by the Bombay Cricket Association at the MIG Club in Bandra.

Tendulkar was a month short of twelve, an age at which nobody attends the Under-19 nets in India. The coach at the MIG Club, Dandekar, said this much to Ajit Tendulkar: 'It's too early for Sachin, he'll get his chances later.'

Tendulkar suffered one more such rejection at the start of the 1985-86 season, again after the coach insisted that he participate in a tournament generally not played by anyone less than sixteen years old.

Sachin had debuted in the Kanga League in June 1985 and got a measly five runs in his first game for John Bright Club in the "F" division. After the end of the monsoon and the introduction of a fresh cricket calendar in October, Ramakant Acharekar asked him to play the Gordhandas Cricket Shield – a tournament for clubs from Mumbai's suburbs – for the Hind Sevak Cricket Club. The club was managed by Acharekar himself.

A message was sent to the captain that Sachin should bat number four. Seeing Sachin's tiny figure, the captain left him out of the eleven, saying it was far too risky to play a twelve-year-old. Acharekar was furious; he told the captain to ignore his directive in the second game at his own peril. Sachin was taken in and got a quick thirty. At the end of the tournament, which the club won, he had received a special batting prize for his consistent performances.

He also got his first hundred during this season, in the Harris Shield quarter-finals against Don Bosco School. This paved the way for his selection for the Mumbai Under-15 squad.

Nets, practice matches, two major school tournaments and a slew of other competitions were increasingly making Tendulkar's cricket schedule a demanding one. The fact that he had to commute from Bandra East to Shivaji Park every day didn't help. Travel in the city's overcrowded trains and buses was taking its toll.

The Tendulkar family worked around this hurdle. Sachin was asked to shift to his uncle's residence, a stone's throw away from Shivaji Park. He was delighted; he could now really and truly eat, sleep and breathe cricket.

This was how his schedule soon read: at 7 am, he would be at the Park for nets; at 10 am, he'd either go to school or start playing a match (Shardashram was overly lenient with its cricketers, so it was more likely a match than school); during lunchtime, he'd rush to his uncle's home for a bite; after school, or at the end of the day's play, he was back to the nets for batting practice till 7 pm; and from there, he'd go back to his uncle's home and have a stiffly competitive game of table-tennis with friends before he had dinner and gave himself up to a good night's sleep.

His coach made the timetable more punishing. He laid down a rule: Sachin must play four matches a week.

That rule was observed more in the breach, for, far too regularly, it was four matches a day. If Sachin got out early in one game, Acharekar would put him on his scooter and take him to another maidan, where another game was on, and make him bat there. Sometimes Sachin would ride pillion from Shivaji Park to Azad Maidan or Cross Maidan in south Mumbai, a distance of about thirteen kms, to bat in his third or fourth match of the day.

Even where nets were concerned, Tendulkar often had to bat in four different places a day. The coach would ask him invariably to move to the net that had the best bowlers. This meant Sachin also batted in the nets of rival clubs and rival schools. Nobody refused Acharekar's request for batting practice for the boy, because the coach was highly regarded in the city's cricketing circles.

Sometimes, Tendulkar would get exhausted with too much batting practice. Acharekar would then place a coin on top of the stumps and announce: 'Anyone who gets him out will get this coin. If he doesn't get out, the coin will be Sachin's.'

'It was a big thing to get that coin for myself. I lost a couple of times, but I have thirteen coins with me. I haven't spent that money,' Tendulkar later said.

All the qualities associated with Tendulkar today – a remarkable quickness of eye, a powerful punch, superb wristwork, sound balance and exquisite timing – owe much to this rigorous training schedule of his childhood years.

*

Relentless practice had its immediate effects. Tendulkar had a dream run in the 1986-87 season. His school lifted the Giles as well as the Harris Shield, and his own contribution to the cause was 276, 159, 156, 123, 123, 197 and 150 respectively. Sachin was selected for the Mumbai Under-15 team for the Vijay Merchant Trophy, where he got 123 against Maharashtra in 140 minutes. This knock led to his inclusion in the West Zone Under-15 squad. He scored seventy-four against South Zone in the first game (but the West lost and were out of the tournament).

In the real sense, the name Tendulkar came to be associated with runs. Big runs.

Despite these performances, Sachin was not given the Best Junior Cricketer award, handed out by the city's cricket association every year. This was a major disappointment, because first, no schoolboy had scored half the number of runs he had that season, second, he was Mumbai's only batsman to get a ton in the Merchant Trophy, and third, he had top-scored for the West Zone Under-15 side.

When Sunil Gavaskar learnt of this, he dashed off a letter to Tendulkar. 'What was most impressive,' he wrote, 'was the way you batted alone when the others around you were not contributing much.' His last line was telling: 'Don't be disappointed at not getting the award. If you look at the award winners, you will find one name missing, and that person has not done badly in Test cricket!' Gavaskar had been denied the same award in the Sixties despite a string of big scores for St Xavier's High School.

Tendulkar shook off his disappointment and went back to assiduous practice. In fact, as someone who bowled regularly for the school team and rather fancied himself as a fast bowler, he turned up at Chepauk Stadium, Chennai, in October 1987 for the MRF pace bowlers' trial. The selected boys were to be coached by Australian pace guru Dennis Lillee. There, he was politely told that his built was too small for being a fast bowler.

However, this rejection helped Sachin Tendulkar. He realized that batting was his real forte and bowling a secondary passion, though the word passion could never quite be replaced by pastime or diversion.

'His passion about everything in cricket had to be seen to be believed. Even his talk centred around the game. It was as if cricket was the world, and the world was cricket,' Acharekar recalls.

He was also turning into an inveterate inquirer. He would ask Acharekar and his junior coaches, Das Shivalkar and Laxman Chavan loads of questions. Why did I get out? Why did the ball come up late? Where should my feet have been? Where do I play this kind of ball? Should I have left that one? Some questions – like those about why the ball swings and cuts – needed some knowledge of physics if the coaches were to give suitably satisfying replies.

Most of the questions he asked have today vanished from the coaches' memory. Indeed, they lasted no more than a minute or at the most a day in their minds. But these fleeting and forgotten questions underline the essence of any biography – that a person's character is illumined not only by moments of historical significance in his life, but just as much by incidents and events that are of a volatile and evanescent kind, those that quickly escape memory.

Details of just one day in the year 1987 illustrates how cricket was setting itself up as the very template of Tendulkar's character.

Sachin's schoolmate and Mumbai Ranji player Amol Muzumdar recalled how the boy, easily distinguishable by his curly hair, reached Shivaji Park at 6.30 am one day and batted in the nets for two hours.

After that, he played an inter-school game and was 275 not out at the end of the day's play. He didn't head home after that. He went to the nets again and batted for two more hours. He had batted, without anything in the nature of a decent break, for over twelve hours. 'Of course, at the end of it all, he devoured ten *vada pavs*,' Amol says.

The Mumbai Under-15 squad that went to Ahmedabad that year had a similar experience. The team reached Ahmedabad in the wee hours, and almost immediately after all the players got to their hotel rooms, they were in the throes of some badly needed sleep.

When manager Ramesh Kosambia did a round of the rooms to see if all was fine, he couldn't trace Sachin. He immediately informed the coach, and a frantic search was launched. As the "investigators" approached the terrace, they heard bat hitting ball. Tendulkar was practising alone.

It was no wonder that the difference between Sachin and other players his age – with the sole exception of Vinod Kambli, a cricketer we'll closely examine in the next chapter – was getting wider.

In one game against Balmohan High School at the Bengal Cricket Club's turf on Shivaji Park, Shardashram's Atul Ranade came in to bat at number six. Sachin was then batting at forty-seven. 'He just asked me to hang on,' Ranade says. In the two-and-a-half hours they were together at the crease, Ranade got eighteen not out, and Sachin got another 110.

Sanjay Manjrekar says:

> I had once gone to Shivaji Park Gymkhana to watch the Giles Shield final. Shardashram had bowled first, and the opponent team had got 400. I went up to the Shardashram coach and asked: 'Will you be able to chase that?' He said: 'Aapla ghoda aahe na! (We have our winning horse, don't we!)' Just the runs separated Sachin from the others.

During the same season (1987-88), Tendulkar pulled off a match that even die-hard Shardashram supporters had given up as beyond the scope of betting.

Anjuman-e-Islam had piled up 400 and in no time, reduced Shardashram to three for forty at the Azad Maidan. The target looked difficult; the surroundings, even more so. Over a thousand Anjuman supporters had circled the maidan and were shouting words of encouragement to their bowlers. Mumbai, despite its very big cricket reputation, was no stranger to violent crowds, and incidents of rowdyism, though not regular, couldn't be ruled out especially where a partisan crowd was present in some strength.

Gavaskar had faced a terrifying scene at the same ground during his college days. While he was batting for St Xavier's, a huge crowd came in to support rivals Siddharth College. Despite the crowd's constant abuse and verbal threats, Gavaskar carried his bat and won the game for his team. After that, the mob ran amok. Glasses were smashed, furniture in the tent was thrown about, and anybody seen siding with the opposition was roundly thrashed. Gavaskar and his team-mates had a vehicle waiting for them in anticipation of such trouble. They luckily escaped.

Amol Muzumdar, who walked in as the number five batsman to give company to Tendulkar that day, remembers: 'The scene was frightening. We had never seen so much of a crowd before, and even where cricket was concerned, we were in a spot.'

Those who witnessed Tendulkar's innings that day say it was arguably his best. While Muzumdar stood doggedly at one end, Tendulkar took charge and took the game away from the opposition. His innings had the stamp of determination: he watched the ball closely, defended all deliveries that called for respect, left all the tempting ones that had been deliberately fed to him, and punished anything bad that was sent his way. When he hit, he took no half-measures; he struck the ball with all the force at his command. The circle of Anjuman supporters was often pierced as the ball travelled along the ground like a bullet, forcing the spectators beyond the boundary to get out of the way. There was no gainsaying that the Anjuman bowlers bowled a good line and length – but they finally tired of Sachin's fierce resistance. When Shardashram reached the target, he was more than 150 not out.

Even Sachin's failures with the bat drew attention to the kind of reputation he was fast acquiring. In a match against St Mary's High School at Shivaji Park Gymkhana, he was out Leg Before Wicket for eleven. Parents of many St Mary's players had turned up to see the match. The dismissal sent them hurrying to phone booths; everybody was calling to inform that Tendulkar had been dismissed, cheaply. The St Mary's coach, former Ranji player Kiran Ashar, was indignant. 'We still haven't won, so can you hold your excitement please?' he cautioned in a studiedly unexcited tone.

Shardashram's toughest opponents, Balmohan Vidyamandir, once got Tendulkar out for zero at Shivaji Park. According to a player who then represented Balmohan, the news immediately reached the school premises, which was less than a Tendulkar hit away from the maidan. The school principal immediately announced over the intercom: 'We have got Sachin Tendulkar out for a zero. In celebration, I declare a half-day for the school.' Balmohan students in their uniforms rushed on to the maidan in hundreds. The successful bowler, one Vaidya, was lifted and paraded all over the ground.

However, Tendulkar's seriousness about cricket did not kill the child in him. He was undoubtedly under the spotlight but was as much a prankster as he'd been in kindergarten. Other children his age often thought they lagged behind him in cricketing talent, but in other respects, they could easily identify with him.

After every match that they played in one or the other corner of the city, Sachin and his close friend Atul Ranade would wait at a bus-stop to take the earliest available BEST bus home. If Ranade's bus arrived first, Sachin would pull at his kitbag and implore him to wait. '*Thamb re, thamb re, doosri yaeel* (Why don't you hang on, another one will come soon),' he would say. When his own bus came, he would, without the slightest compunction, quickly get in and go away.

Once, in a match in the prestigious Shatkar Trophy for junior cricketers, Ranade, who was part of the opposing team, fielded a ball sharply driven in the covers by Sachin. Sachin sneaked up to his friend during lunch-time and asked: '*Saalya, khara saang,* ball *tujhya hatat yeun chikatla ki tu kharokhar adavlas* (Rascal, honestly tell me, did you stop the ball or did it just get stuck)?' Ranade had to make the honest admission that he had not really seen the ball. 'Solid *goli hota* (It came like a bullet),' he said.

In the same game, Ranade took Tendulkar's catch at long-off after running a good ten to twelve yards. That led to his inclusion in the Mumbai Under-15 side. His friend offered "praise" soon thereafter: 'You made that catch look so good, you actually got into the Under-15 team!'

When the Mumbai Under-15 team toured Ahmedabad, Tendulkar, Sairaj Bahutule, who later played for India and Ranade shared a room. Unluckily for him, on one particular night, Ranade went off to sleep earlier than the other two. He woke up in the middle of the night with a burning sensation in his eyes. '*Aag, aag! Mee aandhala zalo!* (It's burning, it's burning! I've gone blind!)' he yelled. Sachin and Sairaj had put balm below his eyes. However, Sachin soon pretended that he was trying to help. He took his friend to the bathroom, washed his face clean and said: '*He* Nivea cream *mee tujhya dolyala lavto. Bara vaatel* (I'll apply Nivea Cream below your eyes. You'll feel better).' And proceeded to apply toothpaste on his friend's face!

Tendulkar was having fun on the field as well. In an inter-school game at Cross Maidan, he went berserk, hitting the bowlers all over the place. One such hit took the ball out of the ground and on to neighbouring Fashion Street, one of Mumbai's most crowded and congested spots. The ball was obviously lost.

As play was halted and the umpires called for another ball, Sachin went up to non-striker Amol Muzumdar. 'Do you mind playing the new ball?' he asked him. '*Masta* bat *var yaeel aani karkareet jaeel,*' Amol was told. That, translated into English, meant: 'It will come nicely on to the bat and go with a crack.'

Amol said yes but was baffled. A new ball is due only after a certain number of overs. Those overs had not been bowled. Besides, asking for a new ball was like giving the bowlers a weapon to fight with. A new ball leaps up and can swing uncomfortably enough for any batsman, however well set he may be. Sachin still persuaded the umpires. The umpires too, in a rather extravagant gesture to an upcoming cricketer, took the new ball.

The bowling captain was delighted. Here's our chance to get him out and then get the rest of them, he told his players. In the next ten minutes, his smile disappeared and Sachin's got broader. The new ball went to all corners of the ground with a terrific crack. Eleven minutes after it had been brought into play, it was lost.

When Tendulkar finally got out at an individual score of 183, every member of the fielding side, from third man to wicket-keeper to long-off, lay down flat on the ground, utterly exhausted and at the same time utterly relieved that the massacre was over. 'It was an incredible sight; I'd seen nothing like it,' Amol, who watched from the non-striker's end as the bowler collapsed dangerously close to him, remembers.

*

Tendulkar had now become the talk of the town, and the attributes of his batting style were discussed   seriously across the city's cricketing circles. The many descriptions of his batting had certain things in common. He's short and thin, people said. But he's strong. He begins his innings well. Has a lot of courage and confidence. Packs a lot of power in his shots. He's all bones, where the hell does the power come from? His eye's quick. His feet move correctly and smoothly. He walks down the wicket well and makes good strokes even off balls that are not easy to strike. He's determined and *khadoos*, but the idea one gets is, he is enjoying himself thoroughly.

The result: good news awaited Sachin in November 1987. His name was included in the thirty-six probables for the Mumbai Ranji Trophy team. In December, he was picked for the final fourteen but stayed in the reserves that year.

At one of the practice sessions held for the Ranji team at the Wankhede Stadium, Sachin received an equally big reward. Former Test player Sandeep Patil called out to him from behind the nets and asked him to come around. When he went up to Patil, Sachin saw that India's leading batsman Dilip Vengsarkar was conversing with him. 'Do you know who he is?' Patil asked. Tendulkar said 'yes' but was so much in awe that he couldn't take Vengsarkar's name. 'He wants to give you something,' Patil said. Vengsarkar gifted Tendulkar a new Gunn & Moore bat, but the sense of astonishment was so strong, that Tendulkar forgot to ask for Vengsarkar's signature on the willow. He had to be reminded of this by Patil. 'I still cherish that bat,' Tendulkar recently said.

A few months down the line, former Mumbai player Milind Rege and Hemant Kenkre proposed Sachin's name for inclusion in the Cricket Club of India's (CCI) team. The CCI, one of India's prominent cricket institutions, inducted a few promising youngsters every year into its squad as its "playing members". This allowed the youngsters to play in Mumbai's senior league and gain some valuable experience. Sachin's name was approved instantly, and to accommodate him, the CCI's then president Madhav Apte, a former India player, changed the Club's rules to allow a minor to enter the 'only for above 18' CCI dressing room.

Milind Rege later wrote:[2]

> When Sachin was inducted among the reserves of the Bombay team, many experts felt he was being rushed into big cricket. I felt the same. How wrong the so-called "pundits" of the game can be! We at the CCI decided to give this boy a feel of the "big" company. We did away with traditions by allowing a boy to use the club's dressing room... In difficult conditions of the Kanga League, Sachin played like a grown-up man. On a drying track Sachin was right on top of the ball. Even the seniors in the team fell by way of class.

The foundations of Sachin's career in product endorsements were also being laid around this time at the famous club. Hemant Kenkre, the then CCI captain, had been speaking highly about the little boy to everybody, including his would-be wife Varsha Bhonsle. Daughter of the legendary singer Asha Bhonsle and now one of India's most popular media columnists, Varsha had on a Sunday gone to CCI for lunch when she saw everybody engrossed in watching Tendulkar in a club game. He was belting the bowlers. The moment Kenkre moved away from the dressing room and sat next to her, she asked: 'Who's this boy? He's fantastic.' 'Oh, he's *Tendlya*,[3] didn't you see him at the maidan the other day...' She didn't need an explanation, because he had routinely bombarded her with adjectives on the boy's talent and *jigar* (guts) and predicted he'd be a star. She promptly told Hemant she didn't need his pitch; she could recognize a star.

Some time later, Varsha took charge of the ad campaign for her sister-in-law's tailoring business. The likes of singer Jagjit Singh, tabla player Zakir Hussain and Hindi film actor Jackie Shroff had endorsed their line of men's clothing; now, the search was on for a sportsman, and Varsha thought Sachin would be just right. Sachin had now graduated to playing Ranji but was still not a star. Hemant told her that; she insisted. He finally spoke to Sachin and only extracted a promise that when he became a star, he'd do an ad for him. Sachin was reminded of his promise when he returned from England in 1990 after scoring his first Test hundred. He responded quickly and delighted the product's designers and photographer Shantanu Sheorey by picking a black and a dark brown shirt; it would go well with his fair complexion. This was his first ad – and not Boost, which was his first popular ad – and perhaps the only one he has done for free. He was well aware of his star value by this time, and companies had begun to line up for his signature. However, it was the bond he had developed with his CCI captain that had prevented commercial considerations from intruding.

His position as CCI member gave him one more opportunity. That was to rub shoulders with international cricket players during an exhibition match in 1987. The moment was so remarkable that Sachin in fact ended up playing for Pakistan!

As part of the CCI Golden Jubilee celebrations, a Pakistan XI led by Imran Khan took on the CCI Golden Jubilee XI at the Brabourne Stadium, Mumbai. Imran was leading a full-strength Pakistan team that included Javed Miandad, Abdul Qadir, a very young Wasim Akram, Rameez Raja and Mudassar Nazar, among others. The CCI squad too had the likes of Mohammed Azharuddin and Roger Binny in its ranks.

The Pakistan manager had told CCI officials that they would need a few fielders in case some of their stars chose the hotel over the field in the middle of the match. So Sachin Ramesh Tendulkar and Kushroo Vasania, a former India Under-19 captain who had also been drafted in by the CCI as a "playing member", were among the few youngsters asked to be available that day.

After Pakistan were through with their batting and CCI's Chandrakant Pandit was belting the ball around late in the afternoon, Miandad and Qadir decided they'd had enough and said they would go back to the hotel. The Pakistan manager at this point approached Hemant Kenkre of the CCI, and asked for two reserve fielders. Kenkre looked around, saw Kushroo and asked him to go. Kushroo was recognized as a good fielder on the Mumbai circuit, so his choice was natural. While Kenkre and Mumbai Ranji player Shishir Hattangadi were looking around for a second fielder, the boy with the curly mop of hair went up to them and asked in his squeaky voice: 'Mee jaaoo ka? (Can I go?)' He didn't wait for Kenkre and Hattangadi to say yes. In a flash, he ran out on to the green and fielded for a good amount of time, as a member of the Pakistan team. He was in the same eleven as Imran, Akram, Rameez Raja and Mudassar Nazar.

Perhaps it is history's bizarre and stinging rebuttal of the two-nation theory and then five decades of hostility between India and Pakistan that the country's prized possession, Sachin Tendulkar, first set foot in the international cricket arena as a reserve fielder for the Pakistan XI.

After the match, Sachin and his schoolmate Marcus Couto, who later became an umpire, boarded one of Mumbai's Western Railway locals to go home. On the train, Sachin told his friend he was upset because 'the captain (Imran) had kept me too deep at long on.' He had tried to go for a catch, but the ball had been well beyond his reach. He felt robbed of a wicket.

It was because of this kind of intensity that, in spite of getting into the Ranji squad, Tendulkar allowed himself no laxity in the schools' tournaments. He scored more hundreds in 1987-88 than he had the previous year, including two triple hundreds. It was one of those triple hundreds that made the entire cricketing world sit up and take notice of Sachin Tendulkar.

---

1   A G Moyes, *Bradman*, published 1948.
2   *The Sportsweek*, 25-31 December, 1988.
3   Tendlya is an affectionate abbreviation of the name Tendulkar. Most players from Mumbai call him by this name.

the world beneath his feat

Now, as I keep devouring them, How long will the
supply last; That is the big question.

– The Panchatantra (A ravenous animal)

It's rather bizarre to look for the good in an act of mass murder. But any member of the 1988 St Xavier's High School team butchered by Sachin Tendulkar and Vinod Kambli during a world record partnership, including me, would have to have a heart of ice not to have shamelessly felt during that terrible time for our team, a certain eloquence.

I was in Class VII in 1988, batted number three for the Xavier's Giles Shield team and was in the reserves for the Harris Shield tournament. We got into the Harris semi-finals that year due to some good performances and under the able leadership of Sairaj Bahutule.

When news came that Xavier's were to face Shardashram in the semis, there was some apprehension in the school, for the time when one Sunil Gavaskar represented Xavier's had long disappeared, and Shardashram had acquired a great reputation in schools' cricket. To top it all, Sachin Tendulkar's name was hitting the headlines all too often, and matching him, headline for headline, and run for run, was his friend, Vinod Kambli.

Like Tendulkar, Kambli too was asked to move to Shardashram from his earlier school, Our Lady of Seven Dollars, by Ramakant Acharekar. Vinod had cricket in his blood. His father, Ganpat Kambli, a heavy-set, brawny man, was a fast bowler and hard-hitting batsman and had played the Times Shield in the top division. A factory worker, Ganpat Kambli lived with his family in a shanty at Kanjurmarg, a Mumbai suburb situated a long distance from Shivaji Park. So, after joining Shardashram, Vinod had to board crowded local trains during rush-hour every day, with a heavy kit-bag, to reach school and then Shivaji Park for practice. Not that he minded the ordeal; he loved cricket too much.

This common love for cricket led to the forming of a bond between him and Sachin soon after the latter switched to Shardashram. They found they got along well; they spent a lot of time together, discussing cricket, cracking jokes, sometimes – only sometimes – attending classes, and made big partnerships on the field.

They complemented and complimented each other in schools' cricket. A stylish yet marauding left-hander, Vinod scored nearly 3,000 runs in schools' cricket in the two years –1986-87 and 1987-88. While Tendulkar got 1,028 runs in 1987-88, Kambli's scores were 62 not out, 79, 100, 348 (the record partnership) and 13. In the Under-15 finals against Maharashtra in 1987-88, Kambli scored a match-winning 142 after Tendulkar got out for a duck; and in an earlier game against Baroda, he scored 89 against Tendulkar's 87.

At that time, Kambli seemed to know every Tendulkar score by heart. When he recalled Sachin's efforts, however, there was respect for a friend's talent and no bragging about personal highs.

Vinod and Sachin made their Kanga League debut together; Vinod in a dramatic fashion. Ganpat Kambli had gone to the secretary of a club to request him to play his son. The secretary took one look at Vinod and said: 'No way. The fast bowlers will kill him. I don't want to risk playing a child.'

The next Sunday, Vinod had gone to Shivaji Park to watch his friend Sachin play his first Kanga League game for the John Bright Club in the "F" division. The John Bright team was a player short, and the captain asked Vinod to play. While Tendulkar scored five in that game, Kambli scored a murderous eighty – against the same club that had refused him a place in its team a few days ago!

Acharekar said in 1988: 'Vinod is as good as Sachin. The two of them could easily be the best young batsmen in Mumbai and probably India today.'

This was more or less what everyone in Mumbai's cricketing circles thought of the two.

So, the apprehension of Xavier's' boys was justified.

Yet nobody could have remotely imagined the slaughter that lay in store for us. Tendulkar, then captain of Shardashram, won the toss against Bahutule on the Sassanian Cricket Club ground, Azad Maidan, and chose to bat. The opening bowler for Xavier's, Amit Sanghani, got the team early breakthroughs, and Shardashram were two down for eighty-four, when Tendulkar walked in to bat. At the other end was Kambli, not out on twenty-nine.

They started scoring at a rapid pace immediately. When Tendulkar was in the twenties, he edged medium-pace bowler Manish Walawalkar to first slip, but captain Bahutule dropped the catch and then shouted to the bowler 'Milega, milega (Don't worry, we'll get him soon.)' Some time later, Kambli was struck on the pads and the bowling side swore he was out; the umpire disagreed.

Once they settled in, Tendulkar and Kambli began striking the ball to all corners of the ground. Their drives were scorchers, and their cuts were like the repeated lashing of a whip, deadly and accurate. They hit with enormous power, and just as much contempt. Their outlook towards the opposition was sadistic, and at the end of the day's play, Tendulkar and Kambli were unbeaten on 192 and 182 respectively.

The funniest moment of the game took place on the second day. A medium-pacer from Xavier's, Shahid Saherwala, would always complain to captain Bahutule that he wasn't played in any game. He had been eventually selected for the semi-finals. After all the regular bowlers failed to make any impact against Tendulkar and Kambli, Bahutule brought him on.

The first ball was hit out of the ground by Kambli and was lost. Another one was taken. The next ball too was pulled out of the ground. And lost. Another one was taken. The third ball was hit just as far as the first two balls, but was retrieved. If the bowler was relieved that the ball had at least been found, there was another problem: it had been hit out of shape.

The bowler started his run-up for the fourth ball and stopped mid-way. He said he couldn't bowl; apparently, his leg was hurting. The captain and other team-members went up to him and realized the pain wasn't quite in the legs. Saherwala started crying. He couldn't take the humiliation any more. Finally, the captain issued a diktat: Saherwala *had* to complete the over.

Ramakant Acharekar had been in the maidan tent the first day and had watched the match closely. Due to work in office, he was going to stay away for the major part of the second day. But he had instructed his assistant, Laxman Chavan, to call him up regularly in office with the scores.

When Acharekar was informed by Chavan that Tendulkar and Kambli had completed their double centuries and the Shardashram score had exceeded 500, the coach instructed that the innings be declared immediately. If Shardashram declared, as Acharekar wanted them to, they would almost get a full day to bowl out the opposition. Also, Acharekar wanted Sachin to play a Giles Shield match the next day, so he didn't want this game to go into the third day.

From beyond the fence, Chavan waved to Sachin and Vinod to demand their attention. Both of them saw him and realized what he wanted to say, but thought he was trying to issue instructions on his own. They decided to ignore him.

Chavan grew desperate and moved all over the ground to attract their attention, waving his hands furiously till they hung limp on his sloping shoulders. He fidgeted, he paced, and writhed. He used all possible facial expressions, with features that twisted, stretched and finally slackened, reflecting his helplessness at his inability to get the boys' attention.

Sachin and Vinod still pretended they could neither see nor hear him. But they had their wits about them. While enjoying their batting, they sang Hindi film songs in the middle. Others in the Shardashram team were also watching the display of authoritarian batting: next-in-order batsman Amol Muzumdar, those who had _gotten out – openers Atul Ranade (who had scored forty-eight) and R. Mulye (eighteen) – and the tailenders were having a whale of a time.

Ranade recalls:

> While Sachin and Vinod batted, all of us were roaming all around Azad Maidan for nearly two days. I even went to the neighbouring Bombay Gymkhana and bowled a while in the nets. These two guys seemed to be into non-stop batting.

Amol, who stayed padded up for nearly two days, waiting unsuccessfully for a chance to bat, says:

> I was the next man in and therefore focused on things in the middle from the moment these two got together at the crease. They were not out at lunch on the first day. During this interval, I took a few knocks close to the tent to ensure my feet were moving. Then Sachin and Vinod went out again and returned, not out, at tea-time. In this break too, I took some knocks, because I felt a wicket could now fall any time. That wasn't to happen. Both continued to bat beautifully. Two of Tendulkar's strokes are still fresh in my mind. They were hit so hard and went so far, all of us in the tent joked: 'They'll have to take a scooter to get the ball back.' All Shardashram boys in the tent were having a nice time, joking and cheering.
> It was at lunch the next day that I realized they wouldn't get out. I then gave up hope of batting.

The mistake of having ignored Chavan dawned on Sachin and Vinod when they returned to the tent for lunch. From a phone booth in *khau galli*, a bylane opposite Azad Maidan, the two called up their coach at his workplace. He asked what the score was. He was told, 700-plus.

He was furious. 'Why are you still batting? Declare!'

Kambli made a request: 'Sir, I'm batting on 349.' 'Declare!' Acharekar screamed out again.

'Sir, but...'

'Give the phone to Sachin,' the coach said.

'Sir, but…'

'Just give the phone to Sachin!'

Sachin pleaded: 'Sir, Vinod needs one run to complete his 350, we'll declare as soon as he gets that.'

'Nothing doing, declare *now*.'

So declare they did and Shardashram finished at 748 for two, Tendulkar 326 not out (one six, forty-nine fours) and Kambli 349 not out (three sixes, forty-nine fours). Their partnership was worth 664.

That evening, Acharekar gave Tendulkar and Kambli what the Shardashram boys called, in their ingenuously descriptive prose, "*bamboo*".

Even today, Acharekar defends the roasting:

> There was no need to bat so long. Non-stop batting is pointless. You can score 400 or 500 runs each and the bowling side may still not get you out. Batting is about planning an innings. A team that knows when to declare is best. This is the lesson I wanted to give both.

Amol Muzumdar however has a different line:

> None of us were mature enough then to think of these things. We just enjoyed our cricket. And we watched Tendulkar and Kambli's innings with delight. They didn't play boring cricket; there was no miserly accumulation of runs. Their batting was aggressive, attractive and exciting. And Harris Shield matches were play-to-finish games, so time was not a constraint. They did nothing wrong by continuing the way they did.

As planned, Tendulkar was asked to play the Giles Shield game the next day, so Shardashram fielded with ten players as Xavier's, who had ended the second day at seventy-seven for three, were skittled out for 154 on the third.

Tendulkar and Kambli's performance received huge attention in the city and national media, but it was only a month later that it was discovered that they had created a world record. Their partnership was the biggest two players had ever had, for any wicket, and at any level of cricket. They had bested the earlier record of 641 runs, created in 1913-14 by T. Palton and N. Rippon for Buffalo River vs. Whoroughly at Gapstead, Victoria, Australia.

The world record helped Tendulkar and Kambli to get a foothold across the global cricketing firmament and, as both players today admit, helped accelerate their rise up the ladder. 'Because of the record, we could actually jump the ladder,' Kambli admitted later.

The "jump" took place in more ways than one, for Sun-Grace Mafatlal, a leading Indian corporate known for its patronage of cricket, soon offered a sponsorship to the Shardashram duo. Sun-Grace Mafatlal's chairperson Atulya Mafatlal announced that the company would take full responsibility for Sachin and Vinod's education and cricket expenses. This initiative, launched after much persuasion by Hemant Waingankar and Anil Joshi, the secretary of the Sun-Grace Mafatlal Sports Club, provided a big boost to the two boys.

*

In the next match, Shardashram were to play Anjuman-e-Islam in the Harris Shield final at the CCI-Brabourne Stadium. A good score there would be a fitting finale to a fantastic season. More vitally, it was an opportunity for Sachin Tendulkar to find a place in the Ranji eleven in the coming season. It did, and in just the way Tendulkar would have wanted.

If a batsman's maturity is determined by the way he organizes his innings, Tendulkar gave ample proof of it in the finals.

He came in to bat when the score was two down for thirty-five (one of the batsmen dismissed was Kambli). The wicket was slow; the ball didn't come on to the bat easily. It was crucial that at this juncture, a batsman put his head down, and bat judiciously, rather than bravely. Tendulkar did exactly that.

Former president of the Indian cricket board Raj Singh Dungarpur remembers the start well:[1]

Even as he was walking in to bat, the opposing team's captain put in place a long-on, a long-off and a deep-wicket. Everyone watching the game was keen to see Sachin's response to this field placement.

The first ball he played was thundered to long-off, the second thundered to long-on. He got singles off both. After this, he started checking his shot as he played to long-on and long-off and began picking two runs off every ball. Four such shots and he reached ten. My father, who had played with the likes of Jardine and Larwood and who knew his cricket, was sitting next to me at the CCI. 'This boy knows how to adapt. He'll make it big,' he said.

Tendulkar decided he would take no chances till the team had 400 on the scoreboard. He played along the ground till he was well set. Once the eye was in, the feet moving well and the ball meeting the bat's middle, he played a few uppish, yet safe shots, to get the field spread. That done, he began placing the ball toward fielders in the deep, and picked up ones and twos, not forgetting to punish the odd loose delivery. By the end of the second day, he was 286 not out, and Shardashram had crossed 500 for the loss of seven wickets.

Tendulkar reached his second triple hundred of the season early next morning. The news reached Dilip Vengsarkar, who was playing a Times Shield game for Tatas on the Parsi Gymkhana, about two kilometres away from Brabourne Stadium.

Vengsarkar had seen Tendulkar earlier at the Wankhede nets in December 1987. But this time, after he had heard that Sachin was 286 not out he appointed an "informer" to give him the boy's score at regular intervals. The "informer" would every now and then do the rounds from Brabourne to Parsi Gymkhana and pass on the latest position.

As he learnt of Tendulkar's 300, Vengsarkar felt like having a look at the boy's talent afresh. He abandoned his number four position for Tatas, put himself down at number six, and as lunch was called, took off for Brabourne.

Tendulkar had the ball, not the bat, in hand when Vengsarkar reached the ground. Shardashram had been bowled out for 590; Sachin's contribution being an unbeaten 346. An eyewitness told Vengsarkar, 'Sachin could have gone on and on if the side had not been bowled out.'

Vengsarkar began thinking on other lines. A score of 300 saps one's energy and overfills the fount of motivation. Tendulkar had taken the new ball into his hands and was bowling with a fierce determination. There was no sign either of exhaustion or complacency. In fact, he had taken two wickets already and had put his school on top.

Just as these thoughts crossed Vengsarkar's mind, many arms were raised; Tendulkar had beaten the bat again. Vinod Kambli, fielding at deep fine-leg, yelled encouraging words. Vengsarkar, seated in the pavilion, said in Marathi, '*Changla aahe!* (He's good!)'

---

1 Extracted from a speech at the C. K. Nayudu Hall, CCI, Mumbai, 4 December 2002.

tons of runs

Here is a genuine batsman, almost certain to go
far, and perhaps destined to be hailed, in time,
another star out of the East.

— Neville Cardus on young Duleepsinhji, when
he was being considered for the England team

Sachin Tendulkar had by now got so used to big scores, that getting
a mere hundred was a disappointment. 'A century didn't seem
adequate; I would feel upset if I didn't get any further,' he said,
recalling this period many years later. He also hated it if he couldn't
play cricket even for a short while. So it was with delight that he
received news in May 1988 that he had been selected to tour
England as part of the Star Cricket Club team. The tour was to begin
in June 1988, a lean month so far as cricket in Mumbai and the rest
of India was concerned.

Star Cricket Club was known to pick a team of Under-17s from
across the country for its annual England tour. The tourney had
acquired respectability because the club had, as its manager, Kailash
Gattani, a former Rajasthan all-rounder and a coach known for giving
youngsters good exposure in the grind of competitive cricket.

Playing in an English summer has always been an education
for cricketers from any part of the globe. So it was for Tendulkar.
The chief educator in England was the wacky weather. Sachin
experienced this on a day when he had a dream start, batting
under bright skies with the ball doing nothing spectacular. But
just as the batsmen were busy belting the ball around, clouds
appeared from nowhere, the temperature dipped and the ball started

behaving with a will of its own. In one day, a batsman had to bat under many different conditions, a sore test of concentration and adaptability. While fielding, Sachin would confidently get under a "skier" and position himself for a catch, only to realize in a moment that the ball was actually falling many yards beyond his right shoulder.

He had two more things to deal with. One, the tour was tight, with twenty-three matches packed in a month, and with just one day mentioned in the itinerary as "probably" a rest day. Two, he had developed a wart on the left hand between his thumb and index finger which stayed throughout the tour, making it tough to grip the bat. In spite of this, he got scores of forty-one, eighty-one, forty-four, sixty-three and seventy-three

In one game, he faced the kind of pace he'd never seen before. When he tried to play the bowler into the covers, the ball would go to gully because of sheer pace. This was indeed a surprise.

*

But there's no doubt that Tendulkar returned to India richer in experience and confidence, qualities that would come in handy as he took the plunge into big cricket. It was obvious by then that he would be included in the Mumbai Ranji Trophy team. But whether he would play or, like the earlier year, stay in the reserves was still a question. His enthusiastic supporters said the time was ripe for a transition to first-class cricket, but there were many others who warned against pushing him up too early.

In order to assert his claim to the Mumbai eleven, Sachin needed to get scores in the trial games played before the start of season between two teams of Mumbai probables. He took the "trials" by fire well, hammering Raju Kulkarni, then India's fastest bowler, on a greentop at Wankhede. He got fifty-five in the first game and forty-four in the second.

Milind Rege, then Mumbai selector, noted:[1]

> Every member in the team was delighted with the way Sachin
> batted. In fact, he was the only one to drive off the front foot to

Kasliwal, Kher and Sabnis, who work no indecent pace, as the
Wankhede practice wickets are fairly nippy.

But the then Mumbai skipper Dilip Vengsarkar knew the
difference between junior-level cricket and Ranji Trophy. He wanted
to know if the jump would be smooth for Tendulkar or not.

Vengsarkar's main worry was that to be hurt at a young age of
fifteen could have a devastating effect on Sachin's confidence. To
settle any doubts, Vengsarkar thought of testing the boy against Kapil
Dev. The Indian team was then practising at the Wankhede ahead of
a Test against New Zealand. Vengsarkar called Tendulkar to the nets
and asked him to pad up.

Kapil was brought on to bowl. Seeing the five-feet-two-inch tall
Tendulkar, he bowled the first few balls from a shorter run-up and
without full fire. When he sensed the boy's confidence, he took his
original run-up and bowled his typically lethal stuff. Sachin played
Kapil with great ease, and Vengsarkar gave the go-ahead for his
inclusion in the Ranji eleven.

Mumbai was scheduled to play Gujarat in the first West Zone
league game from 10-12 December 1988 at the Wankhede, so
Tendulkar would have the advantage of making his Ranji debut on
home turf. Even so, the pressure of peers and elders was
tremendous.

Throughout his childhood, Tendulkar had discouraged his
parents from coming to see him bat. It made him conscious, he said.
For the Ranji debut, though, he was to have an audience of not only
his family, hundreds of friends from Sahitya Sahwas and
Shardashram, but Sunil Gavaskar, Ajit Wadekar, Ramakant Desai,
Raj Singh Dungarpur (then chairman of India's selection committee),
Eknath Solkar, Sudhir Naik and Vasu Paranjpe. This was in addition
to Mumbai selection committee members: Naren Tamhane, Sudhir
Naik and Milind Rege.

Gujarat batted first and was bundled out for 140. At the end of
the first day's play, Mumbai had lost one wicket for ninety-five. On
day two, most spectators waited impatiently for Tendulkar, the

number four batsman, to walk up to the crease. His chance came a
few minutes before lunch, when Lalchand Rajput, captaining
Mumbai in the absence of Vengsarkar then playing a natural game,
was run out for ninety-nine. Surprisingly – and this odd sentiment
was to spread all over India soon – there was elation among the
crowd at the fall of the home team's wicket. They knew Tendulkar
was the next man in.

Close-in fielders crowded around the debutant and shouted
encouragement to off-spinner Nisarg Patel as he readied to bowl. The
first ball, bowled on a good length, was "smelt" by Tendulkar in his
forward defence. The second ball was identical and got the same
response. The third was a ploy by Patel to tempt Sachin to drive
uppishly. It was tossed up on the line of the off-stump, and Tendulkar
did drive it through the covers, for four. The next two balls were
deferentially defended, and as if to wipe out the accumulated
respect, the over's last ball was on-driven fiercely, between bowler
and mid-on, to the ropes. Lunch was declared thereafter.

After the break, Sachin cut loose, unleashing an array of
strokes, and reached eighty by the tea interval. Post-tea, Mumbai lost
three wickets in quick succession. There was fear that this would
upset Sachin's tempo. It didn't.

As Sachin reached ninety-five, a slip, point, cover, deep extra-
cover, long-off, mid-on, mid-wicket and square-leg all waited in
anticipation for him to commit a mistake. Left-arm spinner Bharat
Mistry had his plan ready: he was going to flight the ball high to get
Tendulkar out of the crease. The plan was executed to perfection till
the point of inviting him out. Beyond that, things went awry.
Tendulkar drove hard through the covers, forcing even deep extra-
cover and long-off to be bystanders, as the ball rushed to the
boundary.

The next ball, flatter and faster with an obvious intent to try and
get a confident batsman batting at ninety-nine LBW, was turned
behind square leg for a single. At fifteen years, seven months and
seventeen days, Sachin Tendulkar became the youngest Indian to
score a century on debut in the Ranji Trophy.

Ajit Wadekar, one of the keenest watchers that day, told me:

> I was tremendously impressed (with the way Sachin batted). He
> was the baby of the team, but it didn't show in his batting.

Mumbai selector Milind Rege noted:[2]

> What I like about Sachin is that he is comfortable in big
> company... After a couple of overs (after he came in to bat) came
> the new ball. As if to prove the folly of playing this young lad, the
> Gujarat bowlers were at Sachin's throat. (The way Sachin
> responded), Gavaskar, Solkar, Desai, Naik, Paranjpe and so many
> others nodded their appreciation.

Praise poured in from all sides. Comparisons with Sunil Gavaskar,
which can be disastrous for any young Indian cricketer, were made,
and there were predictions that Sachin would one day take his place
among India's batting greats. Tendulkar in his first domestic season
was exposed to many situations full of promise and, at the same time,
challenge.

The way he responded made it amply clear that in the crowd of
Ranji players, he would not be merely competent.

Crisis came calling in the very second West Zone league game
at Rajkot against Saurashtra. When Tendulkar came in to bat,
Mumbai were two down for zero. The boy loved aggressive batting
but here it was essential to build a partnership. Sachin curbed his
natural style and batted in the company of senior player Shishir
Hattangadi for two-and-a-half hours. When he finally got out for
fifty-eight, he and Hattangadi had together put up 133 and pulled
Mumbai out of the dumps.

However, in the second innings, all the pent-up ferocity
came to the fore, and he smashed the bowling all over the place.
Finally, he fell victim to his own uncontrolled aggression when eleven
short of a hundred, he slashed uppishly to point and was snapped up.
'Sachin gets carried away and cannot be curbed even by the non-
striker or by advice shouted from the gallery,' a newspaper report said
the next day.

Big-league cricket had taught him its first lesson: you can't have it your way all the time. The point was driven home further when he got out for seventeen in the third game against Vadodara. This game however proved that his first low score notwithstanding, Sachin's stature in the Mumbai team had already changed. Although Dilip Vengsarkar, Sanjay Manjrekar, Ravi Shastri and Chandrakant Pandit, all earlier away, had returned to the Mumbai team for this match, Tendulkar's batting position was retained at number four.

The next game against Maharashtra at Aurangabad demonstrated that the youngster had absorbed some lessons. He did not curb his attacking instincts, but the assault he launched was a controlled one, showing the bearing and temperament of an experienced man.

Maharashtra had in its team two pacers of potential: Salil Ankola, who was already being considered for the national team, and Gregory D'Monte, who had toured Zimbabwe as part of the India Under-25 squad. Ankola, in particular, was a bowler of tremendous promise. With a long run-up and fine acceleration, he could make the ball climb up nastily and move away. He bowled even better with the old ball.

Sachin showed him no mercy. In an innings of eighty-one, Ankola was driven repeatedly to the boundary. Most importantly, most of the boundaries were scored in the "V." The league phase over, with Mumbai ranking second in the West Zone, it was time to take on Hyderabad in the pre-quarters at Secunderabad. The wicket there was a vicious turner, and Hyderabad had three well-known spinners in offie Arshad Ayub, left-armer Venkatapathy Raju and leggie M. V. Narasimha Rao.

The dominance of spin was evident early as Ravi Shastri and Kiran Mokashi grabbed four wickets each to bowl out Hyderabad for 270. Mumbai were in a spot at seventy-nine for four at the end of the second day when Tendulkar came to the crease. A night-watchman had been sent ahead of him and had got out. Tendulkar stayed unbeaten at close of play along with Vengsarkar. When he returned to the pavilion, he made his displeasure known to team manager, P. K. Kamath. Kamath was asked why he had sent in a night-watchman. The next question was: 'Did you have no confidence in me?' The manager was stumped for words.

Since the team wasn't sitting pretty, wicket-preserving was called for the next morning. Tendulkar, accordingly, offered a straight bat. He had gauged the nature of the pitch well and had decided not to activate his instincts. Patient batting helped the pair of Tendulkar and Vengsarkar put up a fifth-wicket partnership of 118 that helped Mumbai squeak a slender thirteen-run lead. Mumbai ultimately recorded a six-wicket win to qualify for the quarter-finals against Uttar Pradesh.

In the quarters, Sachin was out cheaply in the first innings but showed in the second that he had strengthened his defences further. He batted nearly four hours for his seventy-five, ensuring along with the other batsmen that Mumbai piled up a score difficult enough for UP's batsmen to chase in the fourth innings.

It was time for the semi-finals where Mumbai was to face Delhi. If the Delhi team was without Mohinder Amarnath, Ajay Sharma and Sanjeev Sharma, the Mumbai team did not have Vengsarkar, Manjrekar and Shastri. However, Delhi had a formidable attack in Maninder Singh, Madan Lal and Manoj Prabhakar, so Mumbai had to make the most of its batting. Instead, Delhi made the most in the first innings, totalling in excess of 400. Mumbai lost wickets in quick succession. The one man who stood firm at one end was Sachin Tendulkar. He was sometimes defensive, sometimes belligerent but never reckless as he remained not out on fifty-eight at the end of the third day.

The main bowler to deal with was Maninder Singh. He had an injury on his ankle but bowled penetratingly enough to get a wicket every time a batsman appeared to be set. Someone was required to neutralize his spin, and Sachin was the only one who came close to doing that. In Maninder's first over, he hit him over extra cover for a boundary. After that, he stepped well out of the crease at regular intervals to punish the spinner.

On day four, Mumbai, 258 for seven, depended on Tendulkar to see the innings through to a respectable conclusion. Sachin had shown willingness to wait, but an hour into the morning, he ran out of partners. With the last man in for company, he tried to go for quick runs and holed out in the deep. Although he had top-scored with seventy-eight, his team lost and Delhi won the game on the basis of the first-innings lead.

The first Ranji season had turned out to be good for Tendulkar. At its start, many had said he was too young to be blooded. Midway, the Indian selectors had taken a decided interest in him and he had become a contender for the mid-1989 West Indies tour. Crowds had turned up at various Ranji venues to watch him play. Curiosity about him was growing by the day across India. And he had ended the season with 583 runs and scored an average of sixty-four.

And, to put things in perspective, he was still a little short of sixteen and appeared successfully for his Class X exams in March 1989, the same month that he battled against Delhi in the Ranji semis.

Soon after the exams, rather bang in the middle of a deserved break from cricket, Sachin was pulled out of home by noted coach Vasu Paranjpe and taken to the MRF Pace Bowlers' Academy in Chennai. As mentioned earlier, in 1987, Sachin had gone there by himself and had been rejected straightaway by Dennis Lillee. This time, he was going there as a batsman.

The legendary Dennis Lillee who had come down from Australia again to assess pace-bowling talent knew little of Tendulkar. For him, there was just a motley crowd of decent young batsmen that the bowlers could aim at.

One day at the Academy, Lillee set up a one-day game, arranged the field and told the bowlers where to bowl. A young pacer ran in to bowl and was hit out of the ground. The bowler was distraught and looked back at Lillee. He was told that he had bowled at the right spot. It was a good-length ball, only it didn't have bite. The next ball was slightly short. The batsman went on to the back foot and smashed it out of the ground again. Lillee told the bowler,

'That happened because he read you early,' and looked down at the batsman. He was very small and thin and obviously in his early teens.

A couple of overs later, Lillee went up to former Indian pacer and fellow coach at the Academy, T. A. Sekhar and asked if they had prepared a dead wicket. His answer was no. Lillee then examined the balls. They were new, shining and dream-like in their appeal for a fast bowler.

Finally he asked who the teenager was. 'He's Sachin Tendulkar. You rejected him two years ago,' Sekhar said. Lillee said he'd never seen him bat before. If he had, he couldn't have turned him down. 'No, no, you rejected him as a fast bowler,' Sekhar told him, laughing.

Lillee had a habit of standing close to the stumps at the bowler's end to examine the speedsters. He now went behind the nets and watched the batsman for some time. Not content with that, he took the ball in his own hands, asked Sekhar to do the same, and for the next forty-five minutes, the two of them gave Tendulkar everything: inswingers, outswingers, off and leg cutters, yorkers, super-fast deliveries, bouncers and slower ones. Sachin did get out a couple of times but Lillee was impressed. He thought the boy had come out of the 'baptism under fire' creditably. 'This guy will not only get runs, he'll get lots of them,' he told his fellow coaches, and at the same time cautioned against 'pushing the lad up too fast'.

*

Though Sachin was not selected for the 1989 Windies tour, Raj Singh Dungarpur, chairman of India's selection committee, said his name had indeed come up for serious consideration.

After the Indian team returned from the Caribbean crushed, and the tour to Pakistan, scheduled for late 1989, loomed large, Tendulkar became a topic for vigorous discussion again. The questions raised, in cricketing circles, the media and the streets and homes of India, were mostly about the desirability of exposing a sixteen-year-old to the fury of Imran Khan, Wasim Akram and company.

Just as these questions were being furiously tossed about at the start of the 1989-90 season, the Irani Trophy game was played between Ranji champions Delhi and the Rest of India. Sachin was included in the Rest of India team. It was important for him to make a success of the encounter, since the team for Pakistan was to be selected on the third day of this match.

Sachin, in fact, came in to bat on the third morning, when the Rest were struggling at 119 for four in response to a sizeable Delhi total. Pacers Atul Wassan and Sanjeev Sharma tried to rattle him. They were thrashed. Tendulkar, apparently unconcerned by the pressure of "selection day", began meting out similar treatment to Maninder Singh. The persistent left-armer eventually bowled a beauty and shattered Sachin's stumps just as he looked set for supremacy.

In the evening, a journalist called the Tendulkar residence in Mumbai to inform the family of Sachin's selection for the Pakistan tour. How his name was cleared is best told by the then chairman of India's selection committee, Raj Singh Dungarpur:

> The five selectors – G. R. Vishwanath, Naren Tamhane, Ramesh Saxena, Akash Lal and I – had no doubt about Sachin's talent. We knew he would one day play for India. But Tamhane (the West Zone man on the panel) and I were keen to play him straightaway. The point of discussion was, if he were selected now and he failed, would he be able to take the shock? Tamhane and I argued that if the boy succeeded, one thing was certain: he would serve Indian cricket for the next twenty years. This is a long-term investment, we pointed out. Still there was no consensus. Finally Tamhane got up from his seat and said: 'Sachin Tendulkar never fails. He is another name for success.' That sealed the matter.

As if in celebration of his selection, Tendulkar showed himself stubbornly independent from the rest of the struggling   batsmen of his team on the last day of the Irani Trophy game. He was not servile to the bowlers as he had been in some critical moments for his Ranji side earlier in the year. Instead he launched a full-fledged assault, reaching his half-century in a little over sixty balls. After a collapse reduced the Rest of India to 132 for six, Tendulkar had a 35 run partnership with Vivek Razdan. His own contribution to it: 33. When the ninth wicket fell at 209, Sachin was unbeaten at the other end with 89 runs to his name.

At this moment, Raj Singh Dungarpur made a critical intervention. The innings was to have been closed at nine wickets down, since middle-order bat Gursharan Singh had earlier retired hurt due to a fractured finger. Dungarpur asked Singh to pad up and give Sachin company; he didn't want the sixteen-year-old stranded a few runs short of a hundred. Gursharan gamely padded up, went out to bat and braved sixteen deliveries as Sachin grabbed the chance to reach his ton.

It was clearly a time for celebration. Sachin had, after first becoming the youngest Ranji centurion, also become the youngest to score a hundred in the Irani Trophy. And like the Ranji hundred, the Irani Trophy one had come on debut.

At the end of the day's play, an immensely proud Sunil Gavaskar went up to him and gifted him his own famous ultra-soft polyethylene batting pads. Gavaskar's act, in his own view, may have been plain encouragement, but from the point of view of Indian cricket, its history and its tradition, it was much more than that. It was an acknowledgement that Sachin had indeed upheld India's cricket tradition. He had seen tradition as a flowing river, not as a lifeless pool, and while demonstrating reverence towards it, he had become the new stream and the new channel that adds to the beauty and the vastness of the river.

Tendulkar had approached the hour of selection without a care in the world. The story of Gavaskar, who was appropriately a paradigm and an exemplar for all Indian batsmen, had been drastically different in a similar situation. Overcome by anxiety, he had gone to a see a film with a friend and another India probable Saeed Ahmed Hattea but was unable to sit through. On the journey back home in a Mumbai local, commuters recognized both Gavaskar and Hattea and expressed greater confidence in the latter's selection.

This had made matters worse. Back home, Sunil had played nervously with a cousin and had then offered to drop the cousin home when the telephone bell rang and uncertainty ended. The rest, as they say, is history.

Sachin, on the contrary, had blasted his way to a solid innings before Maninder got the better of him. The dismissal too did not make him edgy; he was nowhere close to a picture of coldness of course, but he had not really allowed the topic to gnaw at his heart, not even when the phone bell rang.

Gavaskar congratulated him on his selection and wished him all the luck. He knew more than anyone else that a debutant – in this case, all of sixteen years old – would need plenty of it on a tour to Pakistan, and then some more.

If the opportunity was big, the test was bigger.

---

1   *The Sportsweek*, 25-31 December, 1988.
2   Ibid.

the big test

Today is the first day of the rest of your life.

– Charles Dederich
(Hippie slogan of the 1960s)

What's a stern test for an Indian cricketer? Playing against Pakistan. What's sterner still? Playing against Pakistan, in Pakistan, before a hostile crowd. And what's sternest of them all? Making one's debut on a tour to Pakistan. The pressure of playing Pakistan in any situation can be enormous. India's cricket-lovers are notoriously unforgiving of cricketers who do badly against the old rivals, and hugely, sometimes disproportionately, appreciative of those who do well against them.

Cricket-crazy India may well forget all the bowling exploits of Venkatesh Prasad, but one ball of his that took Aamir Sohail's off-stump in the 1996 World Cup quarter-final is etched indelibly in its collective memory. Rajesh Chauhan the off-spinner may never be remembered as a bowler, but a sixer he hit to clinch a one-day final against Pakistan in the last over will be recalled for years to come. And Chetan Sharma's hat trick may already be forgotten, but a full-toss he bowled Javed Miandad in the 1986 Sharjah final is embedded forever on India's cricket consciousness.

History explains the bitter hostility between India and Pakistan and that's the reason why cricket between the two countries is seen as war minus shooting. Pakistan was carved out of undivided India in 1947 on the basis of a claim for Islamic nationhood championed by Mohammed Ali Jinnah. Though the partition of India did not exactly take place along communal lines – lakhs of Muslims stayed back – the two countries have had unending tensions between them in the last fifty-seven years. They have gone to war twice over the issue of Jammu & Kashmir and once over the issue of military dictatorship in what was known as East Pakistan (now the independent nation-state of Bangladesh). In the year 1999, after Pakistani army regulars occupied the territory of Kargil on the Indian side of the Line of Control in Kashmir, the two nations fought a mini-war. Again in 2001-02, India and Pakistan were driven to the brink of war after militants attacked the Indian Parliament in September and followed it up with a massacre in Kashmir.

The perpetual undercurrent of tension has affected cricketers from the two countries and even led to lengthy breaks in cricketing ties. In fact, Pakistani batting great Javed Miandad has in his autobiography written a separate chapter on cricket clashes with India titled 'Wars with India'. The title may do nothing to encourage those who want cricket divorced from politics, but it is not too far from the reality that cricketers from either side of the border have experienced while playing against each other over the decades.

Sachin Tendulkar's selection for the 1989 Pak tour, therefore, meant that he was up against a huge challenge. The tour could either make or mar his career, and more likely for a sixteen-year-old, prove nerve-wracking.

But even before team selection was done, Tendulkar watched from the sidelines a big showdown unfolding between Indian cricketers and the cricketing establishment. After the thrashing received by India at the hands of the West Indians, captain Dilip Vengsarkar publicly criticized his team members for their bad performance. This rankled the Board of Control for Cricket in India, which felt Vengsarkar was disowning responsibility. As if this weren't enough, six Indian cricketers, Vengsarkar and Kapil Dev included, went to the United States to play exhibition matches. The BCCI accused the players of violating their contract with the Board and slapped a ban on them.

The matter went to the Supreme Court, and the Chief Justice lifted the ban, saying the contract was loaded hopelessly against the players. The crisis ended but only after it had had its after-effects.

Vengsarkar declared himself unavailable for the Pakistan tour, and opener Krishnamachari Srikkanth emerged as the compromise candidate for captaincy.

Tendulkar wasn't involved in this fracas, but thirteen years later, he was to get embroiled, along with other team members, in a conflict with the Board over another contract. Seeing this episode from the sidelines perhaps gave him a reference point for the future.

Another reference point came along immediately after his selection. The Board and players disagreed on monetary terms for the Pak tour, and as a measure of protest, the players decided to give up their pay cheques from the series. However, the freshers of the team – Tendulkar, Salil Ankola and Vivek Razdan – were not included in this protest action. Tendulkar had been picked despite the argument of many that Imran Khan, Wasim Akram and others would have him for breakfast. His talent wasn't under question; his age, and its suitability for Test temperament, was. It would be fair to say that not only sceptics, even Tendulkar lovers were as anxious as they were hopeful about his performance.

One man whose anxiety levels were particularly high was Ajit Tendulkar, Sachin's elder brother. He even, in retrospect, admitted to a feeling of immense fear. Will Sachin get injured when facing the fast bowlers, he asked himself. To tackle the sense of nervousness sweeping through the entire Tendulkar household, Ajit told his parents, elder brother Nitin and sister Savita that Sachin was unlikely to play unless someone was out of form or injured.

But journalist-turned-commentator Harsha Bhogle called up the Tendulkar home on the morning of 24 November, the first day of the first Indo-Pak Test at Karachi, and broke the news that Sachin was indeed playing.

Tendulkar's score of forty-seven in his first appearance for India in a three-day drawn game against Pakistan Board Patron's XI at Rawalpindi had secured him a place in the Test. The Tendulkar family had not even expected him to be chosen for the Rawalpindi first-class game, so inclusion in the Test eleven was a surprise. In fact, Sachin had been picked over an established batter like

Mohammed Azharuddin. Azhar came into the eleven only after Raman Lamba reported unfit on the morning of the Test.

Sensing that the sixteen-year-old could be nervous on the eve of his Test debut, captain Srikkanth went up to him, sat him down and told him not to worry about his place in the team. 'You'll play all the four Tests,' the captain assured him. When Srikkanth approached him, the teenager was busy biting his nails; when he had finished speaking, Sachin simply smiled at him and went back to biting his nails.

The Test began badly for India. Tensions between India and Pakistan were high in late 1989; Kashmir was burning as a result of an armed insurgency; India was hurling charges of incitement and incursions from across the border; and there was offensive graffiti scrawled all over the walls of Karachi, the venue for the Test, denouncing Sindh's one-lakh-strong minority community. Hate spilled on to the cricketing green on the first day of the Test when a bearded man in a salwar kameez jumped the fence, rushed up to Kapil Dev, abused him, attempted an unsuccessful assault on Manoj Prabhakar and then caught Srikkanth by his shirt-front and tore his shirt.

Not a good spectacle for a sixteen-year-old to see on the first day of his Test career. But the next day, *The Dawn*, one of Pakistan's prominent newspapers, carried an astonishing report. Quoting a government-controlled agency, it said the intruder was no doubt an eccentric but, what a blooper, Indians, he was just trying to congratulate Kapil who was playing his 100th Test!

Cricketwise, too, India had none too good a time, with Pakistan ending the day at 259 for four and finishing its innings the next day at 409. Pakistan captain Imran Khan had scored 109 not out.

India was soon forty-one for four, with Srikkanth, Navjot Singh Sidhu (now a member of the Indian Parliament), Sanjay Manjrekar and Manoj Prabhakar scoring four, zero, three and nine respectively. This collapse happened in the middle of some typical late-night television highlights drama. Akram's first ball to Manjrekar, an inswinger, rose rudely, hit the batsman on the glove and fell just short of gully; Azhar was hit on the helmet by a snorter from the same bowler; Prabhakar came in and quickly edged Akram a little short of second slip; Azhar got into trouble again as he was dropped at third slip by Aamir Malik; and Shoaib Mohammed then dived at forward short-leg only to narrowly miss a ball awkwardly played by Prabhakar.

A most uninspiring sight for a boy out of school, all padded up and raring to go. Finally, exactly at 3.04 pm on 16 November 1989, Sachin Ramesh Tendulkar walked out to bat, the polyethylene pads gifted by Sunil Gavaskar flapping gently on his thighs and the Sanspareil bat, gloves, white helmet and arm-guard serving as his armour.

He watched Azhar "in misery" from the non-striker's end for one over till the strike he had dreamt of since he first went to his guru Ramakant Acharekar's nets was finally his.

First ball. Tendulkar, standing a few inches outside the crease, hands gripped around the bottom of the bat handle, drives Waqar Younis to point. No run. Imran closes in from cover, stands at shortish mid-off. Waqar bangs in a bouncer. Tendulkar ducks. Shows no sign of emotion. Imran goes back to cover. They want Sachin to go for the drive. He does just that, and is beaten comprehensively.

Waqar then pitches well up, and Sachin on-drives between bowler and mid-off. Four runs.

There are now four slips for Tendulkar, apart from a gully and a forward short leg, all waiting for him to make his first big mistake.

The next ball is short but speedy and nasty. Hits Tendulkar on his little finger. The glove is taken off, the damage assessed. All's well. Unfortunately, not for long. He's bowled by Waqar for fifteen, scored off twenty-four balls with two boundaries. Waqar, who was also making his Test debut at Karachi, says this of Tendulkar's innings:[1]

> I remember that match very well… who doesn't his debut Test! But what is etched in my mind is the fair amount of talk in the media about this batting prodigy from Bombay, around whom there were so many expectations in India. I remember bowling to him then and what struck me – and the other bowlers – immediately was the confidence exhibited by this teenager fresh

out of school. We treated him with some short stuff but he didn't
flinch – despite the pressure in the atmosphere that day.

Tendulkar did not sense half as much personal courage in himself as
Waqar thought he had shown. He has since said that he was beaten
by sheer pace in that innings. Akram gave him a personal welcome to
Test cricket with successive bouncers, and so often, the ball went
past his bat before he could complete his stroke. 'I was in terrible
shape. When I batted I did not know what was going on around me.
My feet were not moving, just my hands, and even those way outside
the off-stump that I was going for. I just felt out of place. I thought I
would never play a Test again,' Tendulkar said later.

He was indeed invaded by self-doubt. He wondered if he had
been able to cope with Test cricket. He felt in himself a deep
vulnerability. In the broad sweep of Test cricket, he was not among a
select band of debutants to feel so dejected. Cricket could evoke a
flood of historical associations for the restless stream of his
consciousness. But now that the great game has placed Sachin
among its very best, two personal associations are especially striking
for the historian. They are those of Don Bradman and Viv Richards.

On a humid Brisbane afternoon in 1928, the young "Bowral
wonder" Bradman had found himself taking guard against the touring
MCC on an eerily soft wicket, with the Australian score reading
seventy-one for five. He hit four fours but when he was only on
eighteen, he tried to put a ball behind square-leg and found himself
trapped plumb in front of the wicket. In the second innings, the turf
had worsened. It had become sticky. Bradman, reared on dry wickets,
had not batted on a sticky one earlier. He played the first ball
uneasily for a single and was out caught by Percy Chapman off the
second.

He had never felt worse while playing cricket than on his
Test debut, and the post-mortem done by others was no help either.
His teammate, Kelleway, said Bradman was not up to Test standard.
Even his ardent supporter, A. G. Moyes, thought his meteoric career
might have burnt out. Bradman was dropped for the next Test.

Recalled for the third, he got seventy-nine and 112 and never looked back.

Young Richards too found himself on a wet wicket in Bangalore, India, in 1974-75. He could not make head or tail of the Indian spin. After getting four uncomfortable runs, he played a sharply-turned ball straight into the hands of mid-on. In the second innings, he could not read Bhagwat Chandrasekhar's turn and gave an easy catch to gully. He had scored three.

Richards too went through acute distress. He first thought of his parents and thousands of Antiguan supporters whom he had disappointed. He knew they were constantly following the progress of the game at odd hours back in the Caribbean and felt worse. The other players told him the conditions were bad. Richards did not buy that argument. He thought he had been unable to meet the demands of Test cricket. In the next Test too, he started his innings hesitantly and came into his own only after seeing his captain Clive Lloyd take on the spinners at the other end and utter encouraging words to him between overs. He finally got 192 in that knock and from then on, became the best in the business.

Tendulkar was distraught and intensely annoyed with himself when he returned to the dressing room. He went up to teammate Ravi Shastri and said in Marathi: 'Mee khoop ghai keli [I was too impetuous].' Shastri said: 'Young man, you don't have to worry about anything. The fact that you are playing for your country at sixteen is good enough. Only one thing you must remember. When you are playing at the highest level, no matter how talented you are, you must respect the situation on hand.'

India ended with 282 in the first innings and was left to score 453 in the second for a win.

Tendulkar didn't get to bat in the second innings. However, he got to see a polished and composed 113 from friend and senior Mumbai mate Sanjay Manjrekar, who battled Pakistani pace for over 300 minutes. That innings was an educative experience for Sachin, for it redeemed India's honour in the game by first plugging the possibility of a collapse after skipper Srikkanth's early dismissal and then sending a signal to Pakistani bowlers that some Indian batsmen could stay frustratingly unruffled against fiery speed.

India finished at 303 for three, a respectable score for a team dismissed as no-hopers before the Test had started.

Before the second Test at Faislabad, Kapil Dev, into his 101st Test, was asked what he thought of the *bachcha* (kid) who was only into his second. Kapil said: 'He is good, but I have told him that instead of getting carried away after scoring thirty-odd runs, he will have passed the crucial test only after he has stayed out in the middle for at least a hundred overs. Only after that one can say he has graduated.'

Heeding both Shastri and Kapil's words, Tendulkar abandoned *ghai* (impetuosity) for maturity in the second Test. He walked in, again, in a tight situation. India, put in to bat, were 101 for four. Manjrekar was still batting, and Tendulkar's duty was to stay at the wicket, give him company and steady the rocky boat.

That duty was done. Sachin sneaked singles, sometimes by pushing the ball as close as silly point or just beyond short leg, and remained calm. If Imran thought a sense of restlessness would get the better of the youngster, he was proven wrong. So much so, that after Naveed Anjum was hit tidily past gully for four by Tendulkar, the Pakistan captain could take it no more. Hands on hips and cap tucked into his trousers at the back, Imran yelled at the slip cordon fielders, made dictatorial gestures with his left hand and curled his lips down and hard. Physiognomy experts could have told him his tricks weren't working.

What was worse for the Pakistanis was that while every Pak fielder and even Manjrekar was heavily sweatered on a cold day, Tendulkar was carrying on comfortably in just a half-sleeved shirt. That too, minus a vest!

Imran came in to bowl himself and tried to get rid of Tendulkar, but the boy stayed put. Between overs, notes were exchanged with Manjrekar on the obvious difficulties of playing out the Khan's overs.

At the end of the first day, Tendulkar was thirty-five not out, having stayed at the crease for 150 minutes. Manjrekar was unbeaten on fifty-eight, and the partnership was worth ninety-nine runs. Sachin batted for ninety-four minutes more the next day, and the partnership went up to 143. That day, Tendulkar drove one of Imran's balls for four, and as soon as Imran began to walk back to his run-up, there was applause. A puzzled Imran turned, checked the scoreboard. He then turned to look at Tendulkar and applauded. The sixteen-year-old's score read fifty-two – his first half-century in Test cricket, in his second innings.

Some time later, on fifty-nine, Tendulkar was caught plumb in front, off Imran. For a man who had firmed up his team's shaky position, he had a very dejected look as he walked back to the pavilion, head down. He had wanted to be there longer.

Later, Tendulkar measured the wicket-taking Imran's inswinger thus in his mother-tongue: 'Foot *bhar aat aala* (The ball swung in by a foot).'

Manjrekar said this of Tendulkar's effort:[2]

> I was surprised by his confidence when he walked out to join me in Faislabad at 101 for four. I advised him to play his natural game, only a little tighter. He was unperturbed by the fact that we had Imran and Akram firing in at him. This bowler is trying to do this, that bowler is trying to do that, I kept telling him (in Marathi). He was absolutely calm. For a batsman it is creditable. For a 16-year-old, incredible!

India totalled 288, and Pakistan put 423 on the board and declared after lunch on the fourth day. In the second innings, the Indian batting came into its own, Manjrekar following his first-innings score of seventy-six with a classic eighty-three, Sidhu and Prabhakar scoring half-centuries each and Azhar regaining form with a 109. Azhar, however, called for a single where there was none and ran out Tendulkar when the latter was on eight.

India batted till the end of day five, scoring 398 for seven. The draw demoralized Pakistan. They knew they could've scored 400-plus, which they did. They also knew India could have been bowled out twice in five days, but that knowledge didn't help transform things on the ground.

Manjrekar, one of the big obstacles in Pak's path, got bigger in the third Test at Lahore. The wicket was flat and made the game uninteresting except for scorers and statisticians who were kept busy by tall scores. Manjrekar batted for eight-and-a-half hours to get 218.

When he was well past his hundred, Pakistan's vice-captain Javed Miandad went up to Imran and told him that the new ball was due. Imran didn't take it. After Manjrekar completed his double century, Miandad again approached Imran and asked him to take the new ball. This time, an angry Imran said: '*Arre yaar*, I know the new ball is due. I'm not taking it now because I want to save it for that *chhotu* (Tendulkar) who's coming in next.'

The new ball notwithstanding, Tendulkar scored a confident forty-one before he was bowled by Qadir. India piled up 509 in its first innings, and Pak answered that with 699 for five. But a sleeping beauty of a wicket meant the game got nowhere near a result.

The fourth and final Test at Sialkot too turned out to be a draw. But it proved historic for Indian cricket in that it marked Tendulkar's real take-off in Tests. India batted first and got 324, Manjrekar top-scored with seventy-two and Tendulkar scoring thirty-five before being out LBW to Akram. Tendulkar batted with two fingers strapped together after being struck by a bouncer in this innings. The visitors, for the first time in the series, got a lead against the home side when they bowled it out for 250.

However, India faltered at the start of the second innings with an all-too-common collapse. Akram got rid of three batsmen – Srikkanth for three, Azharuddin for four and Shastri for nought – while Manjrekar was dismissed by Imran for just four. Tendulkar walked out to bat with the score reading thirty-eight for the loss of four wickets.

He again had to play the role of a stabilizer, this time in the company of Sidhu. This wasn't going to be easy, with Imran, Akram and Waqar at their nastiest. The three tried to get at Tendulkar in particular, constantly bouncing the ball at his shoulders or even higher. But Sachin took the short stuff cleverly and ensured that Pakistan's search for the fifth wicket became a protracted one.

Waqar, who didn't want it to remain that way for too long, especially after Sidhu had crossed fifty and Tendulkar thirty, bowled one snorter to Tendulkar that hit the bridge of his nose and drew blood. The story is best told in the words of non-striker Navjot Singh Sidhu:

> The ball rose awkwardly, struck Tendulkar's helmet and then hit his nose. The nose started bleeding. It was a pukey sight. I quickly called (the team physio) Ali Irani. I went up to Sachin as he placed a handkerchief on the nose to stanch the blood. I asked him if he could continue. Out came a squeaky voice: '*Main khelega* (I'll bat on).' Tendulkar took guard. The next ball from Waqar was thumped past the bowler for four.

The ball after that was slammed through the covers, for one more boundary. Everything was done with a minimum of fuss.

In fact, when Tendulkar was bleeding, some of the Pakistan fielders who surrounded him did their best to put fear in his heart with comments like: '*Bahut* cut *hua hai* (The cut is deep).' It did not work.

Sachin stayed at the crease for 195 minutes and, along with Sidhu, saw India through a critical stage. The two scored 101 together before Tendulkar was out caught behind off a ball by Imran for fifty-seven. India was 234 for seven when the Test finally petered out into another draw.

The books and statistics recorded all four Tests as having been drawn. But the fact was that India, the underdogs, had made the series their own. They had forced draws on a team that was expected to slaughter them. They had started badly in some games but recovered well to save face every time. In the final Test, in fact, they came out on top. Tendulkar's contribution in this Test was critical, because the gains of the whole Test series could have been cancelled out if he had surrendered to the relentless pressure of Imran and Akram when India were struggling for breath.

The injury in that Test had a profound bearing on Tendulkar's cricketing character. He was not lacking in guts. But what the injury, and his own response to it, did to him was remarkable. Tendulkar had been exposed to crisis situations earlier in the series. But when he got hit, he got to know what could be among the worst possible things to happen to a Test batsman in the middle of a crisis. More vitally, he learnt that even after taking such blows, he could carry on and take the battle to the enemy camp. A soldier is forever ready for battle, but when he enters battle, suffers an injury, then braves it and discovers he can still fight and damn effectively at that, his initiation into the battlefield is complete. Tendulkar's initiation into Test cricket was complete with that nose injury.

As far as one-dayers were concerned, surviving a leg-spinner of Abdul Qadir's calibre could be taken as proof of initiation. Tendulkar went a step ahead. He didn't just face Qadir; he roundly thrashed him.

The Tests over, the first one-dayer was scheduled between India and Pakistan on 16 December at Peshawar. However, it rained before the game, so the light was poor and the atmosphere hazy. Play was held up and appeared unlikely, but for the sake of the over 30,000-strong crowd, the organizers decided to convert the official one-dayer into a twenty-overs-a-side exhibition match.

The Pakistanis batted first and scored 157 for four. India seemed to be losing their way, with three wickets down for a little above eighty, when Tendulkar joined captain Srikkanth at the crease. The asking rate at this point was fifteen runs an over. Then took place a deadly assault on the deadliest spinner of the Eighties. The warm-up session took place in the second over of Mushtaq Ahmed. Mushtaq was hit for two sixes and a four by Tendulkar.

When this happened, master of guile Qadir went up to Tendulkar and as plain provocation, dared him to take him on the same way.

Tendulkar took him on in a manner that Qadir, and all those who saw the game, would never forget. The first ball was smashed for a six. The second one was hit over the bowler's head, again for a maximum. The third brought the third successive sixer. The fourth ball was hit for a four, and Tendulkar took three runs off the fifth. Sachin completed his fifty off eighteen balls as the over brought India twenty-seven runs. India couldn't score the seventeen needed to win in the last over, and Tendulkar stayed not out on fifty-three, but his short, sparkling, and in non-striker Srikkanth's words, "thrilling" innings proved extraordinary in more ways than one.

For one, Qadir was the world's most feared leg-spinner. With his dramatic hop, skip and jump run-up, he was an inventive bowler. He would bowl one ball three flights up, slip in a quicker one, bowl wide of the crease and skid in a googly, all in one over. A challenge thrown by him at a newcomer could not be taken easily.

For another, Tendulkar's repeated lifting of Qadir out of the ground was no slogging in a typical one-day situation. There was no stepping away and swinging of the bat on the horizontal plane. He produced clean hits with wonderful timing. He was in a situation where the best of batsmen are provoked to try and bridge the gap of runs with desperation. What Tendulkar showed was organized batting. He knew exactly what he was doing and went about his business with the intention of finishing off the match. In trying to do so, he tried to make the near-impossible possible. And though he couldn't pull off a victory for India, he left no one in doubt that for him, the realm of possibility was going to be very wide indeed.

In his first official one-dayer at Gujranwala, though, Tendulkar was out for zero, caught Akram bowled Waqar off the first ball he faced. Surprisingly, after this duck, he was dropped for the other two one-dayers.

The one-day series turned out to be farcical. Either the weather, or the crowd behaviour, was appalling. The Gujranwala game was crunched to sixteen overs due to bad light and was won by Pakistan. The Karachi one-dayer was abandoned after the crowd pelted stones at the Indian fielders and police had to resort to tear-gassing. The last game at Lahore was also reduced, to thirty-seven overs a side, due to bad weather. Pakistan won it by thirty-eight runs.

*

Tendulkar went to Pakistan as a "promising boy". However, with his batting, he proved he was more than a boy. The attack was undoubtedly strong, but he not only survived it but showed precocious talent. For starters, he quickly came out of the shock and horror of being hit in the face; stood up and smashed Waqar in the same over in which his nose had bled; then batted responsibly, sometimes even parsimoniously, in tight situations, like a seasoned Test player; showed excellent temperament and steady nerves. And finally dictated terms to Abdul Qadir.

He did play some airy shots to balls outside the off-stump, which was an occasional and clear betrayal of his age. But the company of the technically perfect Sanjay Manjrekar helped him immensely on the tour. In fact, he and Manjrekar would often stay up late in the night and play soft-ball cricket, even if the space available was just a little corridor. After they had together saved India in the Sialkot Test, they were seen playing their private game with a tennis ball outside the dressing room, apparently unmindful of a table full of biscuits that could be upset by one stroke.

Manjrekar told me:

> On the Pak tour, Sachin and I were two young cricketers getting a feel of the pressures of international cricket and helping each other out. I remember enjoying those moments, especially because Sachin was someone with whom I gelled. At most times I would talk to him as if I were talking to a kid, but when it came to cricket, it would be man to man.

Their friendship blossomed and benefitted Tendulkar, because Manjrekar was alongside him as a representative of the Mumbai school of batsmanship. That meant a lot of encouragement and inspiration. Manjrekar piled up a hefty 569 runs in the Test series at an average of 94.83 and provided the big-brother support to Tendulkar, who got 215 runs at an average of 35.83.

As the tour ended, captain Srikkanth said:

Sachin Tendulkar was the find of the tour. At Sialkot, he played a dream of an innings after we were in trouble at thirty-eight for four. Even after being hit on the nose, he kept going with scintillating shots. That is the hallmark of a great player.

Salil Ankola, Sachin's roommate throughout the tour, had something more to tell. One night in Sialkot, where both he and Sachin played their first Test, Ankola had heard some noise outside his room. When he went out to check, he saw Raman Lamba and Maninder Singh escorting Tendulkar by the hand, to his room. Sachin had sleep-walked to the corridor and was going around asking nobody in particular about a man from Malik Sports who was supposed to deliver his bats. Maninder and Lamba, who were hanging about, saw him and were perplexed. A sleepy Sachin caught the outline of two humans, did not quite recognize them but asked: '*Arre yaar, woh mere bats aaye hain, zara de de na mere ko* (My bats have come, please give them to me).' Maninder said: 'Sachin, by the way, it's 12.30 pm. Why don't you just go to sleep, we'll discuss it tomorrow.' Ankola pulled Sachin's leg no end the next day. The sleep-walker, of course, couldn't remember a thing. Ankola said the incident showed the boy's obsession for cricket.

Tendulkar said his Mumbai teammates Manjrekar and Ankola in particular had made him feel very comfortable on his first tour. He spent most of his time off the field with the two, had several conversations on cricket and learnt a lot.

The Indian team had meanwhile launched the Sunday Club during the Pak tour. The Club meeting meant an evening of pure entertainment, where a Maninder mimicked an Imran, a Sidhu imitated Yashpal Sharma, a Srikkanth did a catwalk and a Manjrekar sang noted Pakistani ghazal singer Mehdi Hasan's *Ranjish hi sahi*. Weird dress codes were enforced for these meetings to raise laughs, and some members had to wear lipstick while others had no option but to sport false beards.

At one such meeting, the sixteen-year-old member of the team was asked to sport a coming-of-age sign for men: a (false) moustache.

He was game for it and came wearing a thick one. But it was with his bat that he proved, on his first tour, that he had indeed come of age in Test cricket.

*

The Indian team was scheduled to leave for New Zealand in January 1990 – merely a month after its return from Pakistan – for a three-Test series and a triangular one-day series involving Australia.

Team selection for this tour turned out to be a shocker. In the name of preparing the team of the Nineties, the selectors dropped Vengsarkar, Shastri and Srikkanth and loaded the side with youngsters. Azharuddin was named captain and Bishen Singh Bedi the manager. Of those who made it to the squad, only Kapil Dev had toured Kiwiland earlier.

India went down ignominiously in the first Test at Christchurch that ended in four days. New Zealand batted first and scored 459. India was bowled out for a measly 164, Richard Hadlee and John Morrison running through the batting line-up. Hadlee had opened up the Indians toward the end of the second day; on the third, Morrison bowled a hostile spell to take care of the middle order. Tendulkar was one of his victims, out for zero, his first in Test cricket. He clumsily chased an outswinger that was well beyond the off-stump, got a snick and was caught by keeper Ian Smith.

Asked to follow on, India was all out for 296 and left the Kiwis a target of two runs to win. Hadlee picked up his 400th Test wicket in the second innings when he bowled Manjrekar. Tendulkar managed twenty-four runs this time but was again caught behind, off John Bracewell.

The second Test at Napier was ruined by bad weather as no play took place on the first and fifth day. But Tendulkar brought some excitement into the game with a powerful innings.

India, batting first, began miserably. Hadlee trapped W. V. Raman LBW first ball. Prabhakar and Manjrekar then steadied the boat with a partnership of ninety-two before Manjrekar left. Vengsarkar, flown in for the second Test, lasted two balls, and Azhar had his stumps shattered for thirty-three.

The score read 152 for four, when Tendulkar walked in to bat. Immediately on arrival, he played and missed twice. In one over, Hadlee tested him to the hilt, bowling continuously outside the off-stump. But Tendulkar didn't take the bait this time and prepared himself for a long innings.

Prabhakar got out for ninety-five and Kapil Dev scored four, leaving Tendulkar in the company of Kiran More. More began attacking the New Zealand bowling straightaway and gave support to Tendulkar with a fighting seventy-three.

Sachin cracked Hadlee past cover point, drove Morrison through the covers and, with more time spent in the middle, gained further supremacy. By the end of the third day's play, he had stood up to Hadlee and Morrison and got eighty not out. India's score read 348 for seven.

That evening, all talk focused on whether Sachin would be able to beat Pakistani Mushtaq Mohammed's record as the youngest Test centurion. Mushtaq was three months in excess of seventeen when he had scored his first Test ton, while Tendulkar, at the time of the Napier Test, was yet to turn seventeen.

The first ball of the fourth morning, bowled by Morrison, was driven through the covers by Tendulkar for four. The next ball was driven past deep mid-off, and Sachin ran four runs for it. He had come within twelve runs of bettering Mushtaq. However, he got carried away and hit the third ball in the air. John Wright (now the Indian cricket team's coach) at mid-off took a clean catch. Sachin had stayed at the wicket for 324 minutes.

Tendulkar returned to the dressing room and cried inconsolably, though the whole Indian team tried to comfort him.

In the third Test at Auckland, Tendulkar scored five in the one innings he batted. That Test was also drawn. New Zealand had won the series 1-0.

Sachin scored a duck in the first game of the triangular one-day series. He was dropped for the next match against Australia but came back in the third game against New Zealand at Basin Reserve. He scored thirty-six runs off thirty-nine balls, with five hits to the fence, and in Kapil Dev's company revived an Indian innings that was coming apart.

When New Zealand got their best bowler to tackle the youngster in the middle overs, he took on Hadlee with attacking shots all over the ground. The aggressive Kapil, in fact, eased off for a while when Sachin was blazing away at the other end, only going up to the youngster every now and then to caution him against taking too many chances. Thanks to the onslaught launched by the two, India finished at 221 and won an exciting game by one run.

India, however, failed to reach the final of the triangular series. The overall performance of the team on the tour had put paid to pretensions about "the team of the Nineties".

Tendulkar, though, generated a lot of curiosity in Kiwiland. His was one surname New Zealanders couldn't roll off their tongues easily, yet they found the idea of a sixteen-year-old playing Tests interesting. Local newspapers and magazines did many features on him, noting how he wasn't eligible to vote and how his father had to sign the contract with the Board as he, a minor, couldn't do so.

The great Richard Hadlee had the last word on Tendulkar. He said the young man had 'amazing talent' and the ability to hold his ground against "men" in tight situations.

1   *The Sunday Mid Day,* 1 September, 2002.
2   *The Sportsworld,* 27 December, 1989.

impact on england

The sharp edge of a razor is difficult to pass over. Thus, the wise say, the path to enlightenment is hard.

- The Katha Upanishad

India's tour of England in the middle of 1990 brought about subtle and significant shifts in Sachin Tendulkar's cricketing character. If, on the Pakistan tour, he had graduated in Test cricket, in England, he took the first step in linking himself to the world's finest players.

India left for England after exiting ignominiously from the Australasia Cup in Sharjah. It lost both its matches in Bukhatir country badly. Tendulkar himself played two very short and eminently forgettable knocks.

Indian captain, Mohammed Azharuddin commented harshly on Sachin's Sharjah failures, before the team left for England: 'He's playing too many shots. You have to push for ones and twos also, instead of trying to hit every ball for four. I've told him that you have to build your innings. You can't go for strokes from the first ball. But he will learn. He's only seventeen.'

The Indians were going to England in the second half of summer, so the ball wasn't expected to swing as much as it does in the first half, and the batsmen were expected to do well in conditions loaded in their favour.

They settled in easily. Sanjay Manjrekar carved out 158 in the second tour game against Yorkshire (for which Tendulkar was rested), and Dilip Vengsarkar, Azhar and Ravi Shastri too got among the runs in the early tour games.

Tendulkar got nineteen in the tour-opener against League Cricket Conference, but found his form with a fifty and a thirty in the third match.

A peculiar problem arose as India went into its fourth game against Kent. The touring team had one regular opener in Navjot Singh Sidhu, and one makeshift opener in W. V. Raman. Shastri and Manoj Prabhakar were stand-bys. With both Sidhu and Raman injured, and the team management unwilling to expose Shastri and Prabhakar – both vital bowlers – to the new ball in the warm-up games, a replacement was sought.

Tendulkar and wicket-keeper Kiran More offered to open, and had partnerships of seventy-five and sixty-six in the two innings. Sachin looked very good for his individual knocks of ninety-two and seventy.

At the end of the match, former England captain Chris Cowdrey did away with the stiff upper lip and commented: 'Young Tendulkar is staggering. There is no other word for him. It is very hard to believe he is only 17.'

Some more flowery prose flowed after Sachin rescued India in the sixth game, a one-dayer against Derbyshire. India had conceded 235 and was heading for a collapse when he turned the tables. He scored 105 not out off 149 balls and brought India victory in the last over by pulling one of the world's fastest bowlers, West Indian Ian Bishop, over the Queens' Park trees for a six.

Kim Barnett, the Derbyshire captain, called it 'an astonishing innings. Even the great players would have been proud of it.'

Yet that innings would never have been played if Tendulkar had not done some manoeuvring.

Before the Derbyshire one-dayer, India took on the Minor Counties in its fifth tour game. Sachin had done well in the matches he had played so far, and helped himself to an easy sixty-five against the Minor Counties too. During one of the breaks in that match, he went up to the Indian team manager, former Indian wicket-keeper Madhav Mantri, and said: 'Sir, I have played the fast bowlers here. Now I would like to play the West Indian pacemen.'

Mantri nodded and told the boy that if he continued to do well, there was no reason why he should not bat for India against the West Indies in the future.

Soon, the manager sat down with the selectors to pick the team for the Derbyshire one-dayer. It was selectorial policy to play all sixteen players in the initial tour games in order to allow everyone to get used to the English conditions. Thus, after every game, some players made way for others. Considering Tendulkar's string of decent scores, he was a prime candidate for "resting," and the selectors had almost made up their minds on his exclusion against Derbyshire.

However, they usually considered the opposing team's composition before finalizing the eleven. This time, as they were doing so, the name of Ian Bishop crept into the conversation before anyone else's.

'That was when I realized what Sachin had meant,' Mantri said in retrospect. The selectors were told of his wish. Luckily, despite the shenanigans that Indian cricket selectors have been famous for, no one saw the boy's oblique hint as a touch insolent. In fact, they were more than willing to give him a chance. This, according to Mantri, was because 'Bishop was young and at his nastiest best in 1990. No one would have been too keen to play him.'

The win against Derbyshire gave the Indians just the push they needed for the two one-day internationals. In the first, played at Headingley, they restricted England to 229 and chased the score comfortably, thanks to Manjrekar, Sidhu and Azharuddin's sensible batting. Tendulkar came in at number four and got out for nineteen, the only distinguishing feature of his short knock being a hundred-yard sixer, off veteran off-spinner Eddie Hemmings.

In the second ODI at Trent Bridge, Tendulkar came into his own. England put up a total of 281, the Indian bowlers lending a helping hand to the aggressive Robin Smith, as well as the technically correct Michael Atherton.

In response, both Vengsarkar and Manjrekar got fifties but with twenty overs left to go, India still needed 145. At this point,

Tendulkar, in the company of Azhar, began a crackdown. The two put on sixty-three runs in nine overs, Sachin scoring thirty-one off twenty-six balls. They found gaps easily, ran brilliantly between wickets, and refused to resort to any slogging. The English bowlers bowled a good line and length, but methodical batting brought India victory, with two overs to spare. Azhar was exhausted when he returned to the dressing room; his tiredness soon vanished as he was called on to receive the Texaco Trophy for the ODI series. The English media quickly sent out warning signals to the home team for the approaching three-Test series. They listed the qualities of every Indian batsman and of Tendulkar in particular. He was called Maradona for his curly mop of hair, and a headline in a paper screamed 'Teen Terror' in alliterative appreciation of his talent. Another paper said: 'At an age when our top youngsters are still trying to crack the local County second eleven, India's teen sensation, Sachin Tendulkar, is preparing to halt England's resurgence as a cricketing power.'

However, it was not Tendulkar, but England captain Graham Gooch who demonstrated a splendid resurgence in the first Test played at Lord's, from 26 July. Gooch and his Indian counterpart Azhar attracted all the attention during the Test, the former for his batting and the latter for his blunder and his batting, in that order.

Azhar won the toss and shocked everyone by asking England to bat on a wicket that promised lots of runs. Gooch, with his exceedingly high back-lift, brought the bat down with a crack and rattled up an individual score of 300 by the middle of the second day. Sir Gary Sobers' 365, the Test record for an individual batsman, looked surpassable, and the Indian attack looked utterly weak, but the long effort tired Gooch. He fell for 333, sparking a mini-celebration on the field by the Indians for the unjustifiable reason that he had not reached 365. Allan Lamb and Robin Smith too plundered the Indian bowling to get hundreds, and England declared at 653 for four.

The first task for India was to save the follow-on by reaching 454. Azhar rose to the occasion, scoring a spectacular 121. He reached his century in eighty-seven balls, with a Ranji-like wristiness and unChristian strokes that assaulted the orthodoxy of Lord's. Shastri, in his role as opener, got a composed century, and Vengsarkar was all class on his favourite ground, before he slipped a ball off the leg-stump into keeper Jack Russell's gloves.

Tendulkar did not help to keep the fight going. He took his chances as soon as he came in to bat, with the result that, when he was on ten, a ball from Chris Lewis went between bat and pad and hit the middle-stump.

The follow-on now looked unavoidable, but when India needed twenty-four to be able to bowl again, and last man Narendra Hirwani walked in to give Kapil Dev company, old warhorse Kapil, cool as his hometown Chandigarh in winter, struck four consecutive sixes off Eddie Hemmings and put an end to the anxiety-filled exercise.

A theory propounded by the ritualistic and Brahminical Hindu theoreticians says that a dip in the sacred waters of the Ganges is necessary for the expiation of all accumulated bad karma. Tendulkar, instead, took a dip at cricket's holiest of holies, and made amends for his batting indiscretion.

England was going along smoothly in the second innings, the score reading 250 for two, when Allan Lamb hit Hirwani high over the bowler's head, and well beyond mid-off and mid-on. The best anyone could have expected was an attempt at retrieving the ball. But Tendulkar, stationed at mid-off, set off in pursuit of a catch, his eyes firmly fixed on the ball. As the red gave in to the pull of gravity near the fence, he desperately thrust his hands forward, bent low and caught the ball in his right hand inches above the ground. He had run forty yards to take the catch.

Harsha Bhogle, writing then for *Mid Day*, called it "the greatest catch" he had ever seen.

Dilip Vengsarkar, not given easily to excitement, was overjoyed. He told his teammates: 'The next tour to England is in 1996. By that time, I think, Sachin will be the Indian captain. He will then tell everyone, "This is the ground where I took an impossible catch."'

The reflective strain of Hindu philosophy says that one must fulfil one's karma diligently and not aspire to the fruits of those actions. Tendulkar performed very diligently that day: the second effort was as good as the first one, but was quickly forgotten because, in pure statistical terms, it meant nothing. Its tangible result was the saving of one run, and the Englishmen scored so many of them against the Indians in that Test that the effort went largely unnoticed, and its fruits were non-existent. Tendulkar could only take solace in the feeling that he had done his work.

This is what happened: Sachin was fielding at deep square-leg. The batsman played the ball between cover and point, and ran a single. The cover fielder picked up the ball and quickly hurled it in the wicket-keeper's direction. But the throw was wayward. The ball went over the keeper's head. One run for the overthrow now looked easy. The batsmen, in fact, set off for it, but were halted in their tracks by the sight of Tendulkar. The sight was startling, because Tendulkar was not quite the distant little man at deep square-leg. He had anticipated shoddy throwing and had come all the way up to square-leg. He held the ball on the first bounce and saved a run. The batsmen were shocked.

England declared at 272 for four, leaving India 472 to win, a target never touched by a Test side in the fourth innings. The Indians went out as if in a procession, and the innings folded up at 224. However, Tendulkar, unlike his hasty first-innings display, batted patiently and occupied the crease for ninety-three minutes to score twenty-seven. He was out when Fraser brought one ball up beautifully from the good-length spot, and Gooch, at slip, took the catch.

In the break between the first Test and the second, India was scheduled to play a match against Gloucestershire. Here, Tendulkar blended good fielding with good cricketing manners. When Ian Greig lofted Ravi Shastri over deep mid-wicket, Tendulkar chased the ball and held the catch close to the boundary. He had his back to the umpires. There were hardly any spectators; he was the only one who knew he had just crossed the line. He could claim a catch. Instead, he raised both his hands to signal a six. A round of applause rang out from the entire Gloucestershire team, and it was not for Ian Greig's hit. Tendulkar the bowler was also introduced to Gloucestershire. Kapil Dev had a stiff neck and Venkatapathy Raju was already out of the tour with an injury, so Sachin opened the attack with Manoj Prabhakar. His spell turned out to be more than decent, for he bowled thirty-two overs and took three wickets. His victims were: one of the openers, the one-down batsman and the number five man.

Tendulkar was placed in a difficult position in the second Test at the Old Trafford, Manchester. India's batting was falling apart. In Sialkot, Pakistan, he had managed the rescue act with the support of other batsmen. No support could be had this time. He had to save the game on his own.

If he didn't remould the innings, India would lose, the series would be England's, and the third Test would only have academic interest. It was a test of Tendulkar's character and of his temperament, which Azhar had questioned before the start of the tour. It was also an apt setting to make history.

Though the Manchester wicket had turn, the Indian spinners failed to make the most of it. Gooch batted like he did at Lord's, and Atherton and Robin Smith used their feet brilliantly against the slow men and notched up hundreds. Indians again had over 500 runs to cover.

A shaky start wasn't new for the Indian batting line-up. The openers got out for nothing. Manjrekar blocked a collapse with a determined ninety-three, but after Vengsarkar was out cheaply, it was Tendulkar's job to give his captain solid support. The struggle was again on, to save the follow-on.

Azhar seemed to be in dazzling form, and was batting aggressively. It is not easy to curb yourself when your partner is blazing away at the other end, but Tendulkar took almost an hour to get his first run and, importantly, was not unsettled by the long, silent period out in the middle.

'I wanted to get off the mark, but I was not too worried about being on zero for so long. I had decided I would stick on at the wicket, whatever my score,' Tendulkar told the then *Mid Day* correspondent, Harsha Bhogle.

As Azhar raced to a hundred between lunch and tea, Tendulkar played a restrained innings of sixty-eight, and helped India not only to avoid a follow-on but to significantly reduce the deficit.

India got Gooch early in the second innings, but the breakthrough came to naught. Atherton, Smith and Allan Lamb crushed the bowling. England declared early on the fifth day, setting India a target of 408 to win.

The record for the highest run-chase in Test cricket then belonged to the Indians. At Port-of-Spain in 1975-76, Clive Lloyd had declared the West Indian innings and given India a score of 403 to get. India lost only four wickets and reached the target with seven mandatory overs to go; Sunil Gavaskar, Mohinder Amarnath, Gundappa Vishwanath and Brijesh Patel neutralized the bowling of Vanburn Holder, Bernard Julien, Albert Padmore, Raphick Jumadeen and Imtiaz Ali.

That, however, was no psychological advantage for the team of 1990. If India just batted out the whole day and drew the game, it was going to be a redemption of honour from the position it had drawn itself into.

Instead, defeat stared Indians in their face at the very start of the innings. The openers were Sidhu and Shastri. Sidhu was taken at short-leg for a zero. When the score was thirty-five, Shastri played a ball from Devon Malcolm on to his stumps.

Manjrekar hit Malcolm for three boundaries on the trot. Soon, his backlift got higher and higher, a sign of immense confidence. He reached his fifty with truly compact batting but while offering a forward defensive stroke to a flighted Hemmings' delivery, his bat went slightly ahead of his pads. The ball kissed the glove and went into the hands of the man at short-leg. India were 109 for three.

Vengsarkar had played some good shots in Manjrekar's company, and was now expected to carry the innings along. However, with the score still 109, he misjudged a Chris Lewis in-swinger, offered no stroke and was bowled.

Having seen two seniors get out one after the other, Tendulkar walked out into the middle, swinging his arms, looking for a brief moment at the sun, rehearsing the straight drive. If there was a churning in his stomach, his nonchalant appearance belied it.

Hemmings put in place a slip, a silly point and a forward short-leg and gave Tendulkar a nicely flighted half-volley. Sachin hit it with a flashing blade, through the covers, for four. Barely fifteen minutes later, Azhar, who was expected to play a captain's innings, though he had played two such innings already in the series, fell to a leg trap set by the off-spinner.

Tendulkar would have followed him soon. As Hemmings flighted one high in the air, he came down the pitch and, with no back-lift and no follow-through, hit the ball straight back at the bowler. Hemmings dropped a catch that had come at a comfortable height. Sachin was only at ten then. The lucky escape made Sachin realize that casual cricket was not the way to go. Now he set himself to building his innings.

Against Hemmings, he began to bend like a good disciple of Ramakant Acharekar and "smelled" the ball. Against Angus Fraser, who was getting superb away-swing and Devon Malcolm, who was getting the ball to cut either way, he became stern and vigilant, a picture of growing concentration.

When the total reached 183, his partner Kapil Dev, perhaps swayed by that magical figure that won India the 1983 World Cup, tried a wild swing that could be allowed only in the last over of a one-dayer, and was bowled. India was six down, and defeat, it seemed, was just around the corner.

Tendulkar thought the match could still be saved. His idea of a stiff and successful resistance stemmed partly from introspection, and partly from sound advice he had recently received from the man best equipped to offer it: Sunil Gavaskar.

Gavaskar, a television commentator for the series, told Tendulkar that he had been reaching out to the ball. That was not the thing to do on English wickets. 'These wickets are slower than Indian ones. Play your strokes a little late. If you play early, the ball wouldn't really have arrived, so you will play on the up and give a catch.' These words gave Tendulkar the solution to other technical problems too. He understood that if he reached for the ball, he was at risk of playing away from the body and even playing across the line. Both were dangerous things to do, and technically wrong. If he waited, he could get his body behind the ball, be technically sound and far safer. All this reworking could only be done with a strong supporting temperament. The policy of plunder would have to be given up for patience, he decided and brief, short-lived assaults would have to make way for a sustained search for runs.

That search was made with determination in the company of Manoj Prabhakar, who measured up to the task as ably as Tendulkar.

Both Fraser and Malcolm brought many deliveries on the off-stump to come up nastily, at shoulder-height, for Tendulkar. Sachin gave some of them respect, by moving back-and-across, bringing the bat down tidily and playing dead straight in the direction of the ball. At other times, he followed the direction of the ball, rocked on his back foot, and drove ferociously through the covers.

His confidence grew. Often, in the middle of dogged defence, bad balls get a polite reception. Tendulkar tore into the bad ones with ruthlessness. Anything pitched up was driven hard, anything on the legs was put away without any fuss, and balls that were short and well outside the off-stump, got full-blooded square-cuts, with Tendulkar getting right on top of the ball, and knocking it down severely to the ground.

At one point, Chris Lewis had four slips, a gully and a short-leg for Sachin. He bowled one ball wide of the crease and on the leg-stump. Sachin leaned on it and glanced it in the vacant fine-leg region for four. The next ball was outside the off-stump. Tendulkar went on the back foot, opened the face of his bat, and steered the ball at exactly the opposite angle from the previous one. It went between fourth slip and gully, for four. He was telling the opposition that he was also in control of behind-the-stumps strokes, on both sides of the wicket.

But the "V" is ever the favoured territory for the best batsmen in the business. After umpire Hampshire had called the last twenty overs, and Sachin had crossed ninety, Fraser figured out how. He bowled one on the good-length spot and made it climb. Tendulkar went on the back foot, got into a beautiful position and thumped the ball straight down the ground for four. As he completed the stroke, the follow-through of the bat was high, and the left elbow was just where the classicists would have wanted it: very, very high.

While the England team was now counting the overs left in which to try and bowl out the Indians – there were not more than eleven to go – Tendulkar had one eye on the overs, and the other on the runs needed for his first Test hundred. When he was on ninety-eight, Fraser pitched one up to him. Sachin drove cleanly past mid-off and ran three.

The entire Indian team appeared on the balcony, applauding, as Tendulkar quietly doffed his helmet, raised his bat, and displayed a faint smile. Sunil Gavaskar sprinted from the commentators' box to the dressing room balcony, to be among the applauders.

At 17 years and 112 days, Sachin Ramesh Tendulkar had become the second-youngest batsman to score a Test ton, a month older than what Mushtaq Mohammed had been when he became the youngest.

Tendulkar remained not out on 119, and Prabhakar, just as gutsy, on 67, as India finished the day at 343 for six. The youngest member of the Indian team had shown temperament, skill and strokeplay. 'He batted like an old pro,' England skipper Graham Gooch said. The slide had not only been stopped; the Indians actually found that they weren't too far from victory.

In England, the laws do not permit the offering of liquor to anyone under eighteen. But at Manchester, nobody could deny Tendulkar the champagne. There was tumultuous applause as David Lloyd declared him the Man of the Match.

Tendulkar was thrilled to receive the £500 award. The embarrassment on receiving a bottle of champagne and holding it up for the lensmen and the spectators, though, was clear on his face. He satisfied himself with a can of coke.

Sachin had been an absolute entertainer on the field. Now, it was time for him to offer some entertainment off the field, and entirely without intending to do so. After the prize distribution ceremony, most members of the Indian team got on to the bus waiting to take them to their hotel, except Tendulkar and Prabhakar. The two were delayed because, exhausted after their knocks, they had decided to take a quick shower.

Four women, namely, Mrs Kapil Dev, Mrs Navjot Sidhu, Mrs Manoj Prabhakar and Mrs Ravi Shastri, waited near the bus for Sachin to arrive. They wanted to congratulate him on his hundred. Since players' wives were not allowed entry into the dressing room, and since the hotel was too private a place to disturb him, they thought it best to meet Sachin before he got on to the coach.

However, as Sachin slowly approached the bus, his kit-bag slung over his shoulders, the four women burst out laughing and instead of congratulating him, went their own way, unable to control their giggles.

The Indian team manager was seated next to the bus driver. He heard the laughter and wondered what had happened. He soon found out. Sachin quietly entered the bus, slinked up to where Madhav Mantri was sitting, and asked him: 'Sir, may I sit here?'

Mantri looked up. The boy's face was full of embarrassment and lipstick marks. Everybody from grandmothers to little ones had kissed him. 'He had no option but to sit in front. He knew that if he went behind, all the players would tease him no end,' Mantri says.

A statement attributed by the English media to the other manager of the Indian team, Bishen Singh Bedi, embarrassed Tendulkar further. Bedi was quoted as saying that every woman in India, especially the middle-aged ones, would like to seduce Sachin. Bedi subsequently clarified that he had actually said every woman in India would like to "mother" him.

*

India had a good chance to win the third Test at the Oval. But it was blown by its inability to bowl out the opposition twice. In the first innings, Shastri and Kapil each scored 100, as India put up a total of over 600. England were bundled out for 340 and, forced to follow-on, had two days in which to save the Test. The Indians did anything but apply pressure, and when the fifth day's play drew to a close, England were 477 for four, David Gower not out on an imperious 157.

Tendulkar disappointed at the Oval. He was expected to carry along with him the lower half of the batting order. He came in and struck three boundaries but then thrust his bat clumsily outside the off-stump and gave a catch to slip. He however restored his dominance in a first-class match played against a World XI at Scarborough. Against a bowling attack comprising Mike Whitney, Meyrick Pringle, Roger Harper and Peter Sleep, he scored an unbeaten century, with seventeen hits to the fence.

At the end of the series, he had 945 runs at an average of 63. If this was proof that he was learning quickly, something else showed that he could soon be on the straight and narrow path to greatness.

The morning after he had put England out of the reckoning at the Old Trafford with a fighting hundred, Tendulkar went up to team manager Mantri and asked him if he had made any mistakes during the innings.

Mantri recounted that meeting as follows:

> Any seventeen-year-old who had just scored a Test ton against England, in England, would have been on cloud nine. In fact, anyone would have been proud of that knock. But Sachin wanted to know where he had gone wrong.

Sometime in the 1970s, another Indian batsman had asked a similar question. India was playing Alvin Kallicharran's West Indians at the Wankhede Stadium in Mumbai. The start to the Test was delayed because it had rained heavily the previous day. The wicket was wet and could have posed problems for the batsmen.

Kallicharran won the toss and put India in. The first ball bowled by Sylvester Clarke to Sunil Gavaskar proved just how bad things could be. Clarke hit the good-length spot, and the ball climbed up viciously for a batsman of short height. Any other man would have tried to save face and spooned a catch to the close-in fielders. Gavaskar somehow found enough time to get into position and offered a straight bat. The ball fell at his feet. Literally.

From then on, the little man was master of all he surveyed. In truly hostile conditions, he got a double hundred. Vijay Merchant, the grand old man of Indian cricket, watched the innings in his role as radio and television commentator. He was so happy that he dashed off a congratulatory letter to Gavaskar at the end of the day's play. Not content with that, he went up to Sunil the next morning and poured out more praise.

Gavaskar asked him if he had seen the entire knock. 'Yes, he had,' Merchant said. 'When I was on 197, Robert Philips bowled a bouncer. I hooked it uppishly to deep fine-leg. I got four runs. But Vijaybhai, I made a mistake in that stroke. What was it?' Gavaskar asked.

The hook has never been an easy shot. Not even for the enormously talented. This is not because it is difficult to execute, but because it is difficult to control. While playing it, a batsman first has to move back and across and, as the ball comes up to his chest, shoulder or even further up, he has to swing it somewhere between square-leg and the wicket-keeper. The right foot acts as a pivot, and as the batsman makes the swing, the body turns around in a semi-circle. By the time the stroke is completed, the batsman is, well, almost facing the wicket-keeper. The stroke is such that it can often be impossible to keep the ball down, so the trick is to play it in the air and yet away from any of the fielders. For this, control over the power of the swing is a must.

Gavaskar had not quite controlled the hook as he would have liked to. And that was weighing on his mind. Merchant tried to convince the man in pursuit of perfection: 'Sunil, I know (the mistake). But it was a long innings. One or two such strokes happen. Remember, you were tired, not physically but mentally.'

This was the standard set by the Mumbai school of batsmanship for Tendulkar.

By the end of the 1990 tour of England, Tendulkar was called "wonder boy" and even "run-der boy". Some said he was inexorably moving towards the path that Sunil Gavaskar and Bradman had trodden. His batting, fielding, application and his willingness to learn on the tour demonstrated that such a thing were indeed possible.

wonder down under

The tour to Australia changed me as a batsman,
particularly from the confidence angle.

– Sachin Tendulkar

Graduation in international cricket creates the need for career consolidation. This consolidation can't be easy for an Indian cricketer if the post-graduation course includes tours to Australia and South Africa, with a World Cup (in Australia and New Zealand) and a stint on the county circuit thrown in between.

The years 1991 and 1992 were therefore going to represent, for young Sachin Tendulkar, an awkward stage to handle before he could move on to the next. The physical symbols of this stage were the fast and bouncy wickets in Australia and South Africa and some dreadfully quick bowlers; its verbal symbol, at least as far as Australia was concerned, was sledging and full-blown on-field hostility; and its psychological symbol was a realm of pressure higher than the ones he'd so far seen.

As it turned out, this period in Tendulkar's career was distinguished by a precarious balance between order and anarchy, the result of a curious co-existence of brilliance and rashness in his batsmanship. He was, by turns, graceful and uncomfortable, utterly mean and wildly exuberant, squeezing in maximum concentration in one innings and sheathing his bat in a reckless garb in the other. He represented the pull of opposites, a clash of competing worlds in batting. Yet he matured and consolidated himself, because he had the focus and the understanding to look at this clash as a process of enrichment, not as an impediment. The foundations of this period of intricate evolution were, in fact, laid at home, and almost entirely due to domestic cricket.

India had two international commitments towards the end of 1990. They were: a one-off Test and three one-dayers against Sri Lanka at home, and the Asia Cup, also at home, featuring Pakistan, Sri Lanka and Bangladesh. After this, there would be a break of over eight months from international fixtures, enabling all the top players to play at the domestic level.

Tendulkar played in his first Test at home in November 1990. This was in Chandigarh, the hometown of legendary all-rounder Kapil Dev in north India. The hosts defeated Sri Lanka by an innings. Sachin scored only eleven, but was part of a winning Test team for the first time. It was an exhilarating feeling, and made up for the disappointment he felt at scoring poorly.

In the one-day series that was also won by the Indians, he acquired three more firsts to his credit. He got his first international wickets – those of Roshan Mahanama and Dammika Ranatunga – by bowling military medium-pace; his first one-day fifty, and as a result of that innings, his first Man of the Match award. He didn't do too well in the Asia Cup that was robbed of its sheen by Pakistan's last minute withdrawal, but scored a half-century in the final that India won.

Then it was time to turn out for the provincial team. All the other members of the national team did the same, and restored to domestic cricket the tang it lacked in their absence. The result was some terrific contests, which prepared Tendulkar for the tests abroad.

The semi-final of the Ranji Trophy, played between Mumbai and Hyderabad at the Wankhede Stadium, was one of the more educative experiences for the youngster. Mumbai batted first, and declared at 700-plus. Sanjay Manjrekar's contribution to the total was 377. He and Dilip Vengsarkar, who also got a hundred, provided for cricket-lovers the first enduring image of the game: the two of them took six runs in every over of left-arm spinner Venkatapathy Raju. Manjrekar would drive one ball to long-off and walk a single. Then Vengsarkar would lunge forward, push the ball to long-on, and walk a run. For the next two balls, the strokes would be reversed: Manjrekar would play to long-on, Vengsarkar to long-off. The result would be the same: one run, walked. The whole display was patronizing, as if the bowler should have been grateful that they weren't taking more than one run off every ball.

The second enduring image proved to be that of Sachin Tendulkar. Not of his batting, but of his dismissal. Sachin was going great guns, subverting the seniors' patronizing act for his own favoured sadistic version of batsmanship, and had succeeded in hitting Raju and his senior bowling partner, off-spinner Arshad Ayub, all over the place. In the middle of this enjoyment, Ayub bowled him a waist-high full-toss. It was brutally pulled for a four. Before starting his run-up for the next ball, Ayub asked the deep square-leg fielder to come up. The next ball was also a full-toss. Only this time, it was nearly chest-high. An impatient Tendulkar pulled it parallel to the ground, straight into the hands of the square-leg fielder. The deception was beautiful. A confident batsman had been tempted into throwing away his wicket. A promising player had been taught a crucial lesson: getting carried away could be costly. Curiously enough, Tendulkar's career has always wavered between recalling such mistakes and forgetting.

Making his Duleep Trophy debut for the West Zone in the quarter-finals, Tendulkar showed he had imbibed some of the lessons well. He was a picture of patience against the East Zone attack. By now known as a "100-ball-century batsman", he took 226 minutes to reach his hundred. After that, he cut loose and scored fifty-nine more in thirty balls, with nine fours and two sixes.

With this knock, he completed a unique treble: a century on debut in the Ranji Trophy, the Irani Trophy and the Duleep Trophy. The achievement was not merely statistical: the ingenuity of a Ranji, the pioneering cricket efforts in India of Iran's original inhabitants and the grace of Duleep, all seemed to have been fused into the personality of this young cricketer.

In the Duleep Trophy semis, Sachin faced a South Zone attack comprising Javagal Srinath, Anil Kumble, Arshad Ayub,

Robin Singh and Venkatapathy Raju, and got 131. His ton helped the West Zone secure a vital first-innings lead that saw them through to the finals. In the finals, he failed, and his failure explained the difference between the North Zone's 729 and the West Zone's reply of 561.

As if to make up for it, he came good in the Ranji Trophy semi-final against Delhi (82 and 125) and the final played in May 1991 between Mumbai and Haryana.

The Mumbai-Haryana match has gone down in history as one of the best ever seen on Indian soil. No one who either played or saw it at the Wankhede Stadium in Mumbai can forget it. Emotions ran high, pride on either side took a beating, and its restoration saw efforts that were truly heroic. The culmination of the contest saw Vengsarkar crying inconsolably, while a relieved Haryana team, led by Kapil Dev, applauded his and Tendulkar's efforts that almost took away the match.

Batting first in the final, Haryana piled up 522 and then bowled out Mumbai for 410. Tendulkar was out, LBW, to Chetan Sharma for forty-seven. Rather unexpectedly, Mumbai struck back, reducing Haryana to a hundred for five in the second innings. However, Haryana still reached 242 and set Mumbai 355 to get for the title. What made the target formidable was the required run rate – of over five runs an over.

Tendulkar joined his captain Vengsarkar at the crease when Mumbai was struggling at thirty-four for three. It was decided that he should go for the runs while Vengsarkar, who could step up the run rate at any time, would drop anchor and pick ones and twos. The youngster promptly began sending the ball to all the intimately known corners of the stadium. Kapil Dev had, only three short years earlier, been asked by Vengsarkar to bowl to the schoolboy Sachin, to test his maturity level. Now, as Vengsarkar stood at the other end, Kapil's deliveries went off the boy's bat like the Haryana hurricane overturned. Kapil's bowling partner, Chetan Sharma, was treated with as much disdain as Javed Miandad had once shown while hoicking him over mid-wicket for a six.

In forty-nine balls, Tendulkar reached his fifty. From there, he proceeded as if a hundred was a foregone conclusion. And indeed it would have been, if it were not for the mistake he made. After his fifty, he had scored another forty-six runs in twenty-six balls, when he went for a boundary to reach his hundred and holed out to Ajay Jadeja. His ninety-six, with five sixes and nine fours, had brought Mumbai back into the match and close to the title.

But there's many a gap between approaching victory and achieving it. Tendulkar left with the score at 168 for four. Vinod Kambli, who came in next, got out at forty-five. And then there was a virtual collapse. Vengsarkar alone batted with defiance. He looked like he would never get out, but when last man, debutant Abey Kuruvilla, joined him at the crease, Mumbai still needed fifty, and the chase appeared futile.

Vengsarkar challenged this futility, hitting Kapil Dev for some majestic sixes and fours, to bring Mumbai within three runs of the target, as Kuruvilla stood at the other end. It was a great exhibition of batting against a great bowler. However, when Mumbai were only three short of victory, Kuruvilla ran himself out in the pressure-cooker situation. Vengsarkar was left high and dry at the other end.

He had scored 139 not out, and had almost snatched victory from the jaws of defeat to restore his team's pride. But he was bitterly disappointed and cried like a child on his way to the pavilion, as indeed did many of the 4,000-odd partisan spectators at the Wankhede who gave him a standing ovation.

Tendulkar, who had put on 134 runs along with Vengsarkar for the fourth wicket, watched the 'Colonel's' final assault, awestruck. For him, this was the template of classic defiance, and of courage under fire. It would demonstrate its hold over his consciousness soon, in Perth, Australia.

*

That was some distance away, though. First there would be some rest and relaxation in the middle of major economic, technological and societal development. The development not only changed the face of urban, middle-class India, it eventually gave young Sachin Tendulkar's life and career a turn it would never otherwise have taken, and the game of cricket a push it would otherwise not have had.

Satellite television entered Indian homes in January 1991, with CNN broadcasting the build-up to the Gulf War. While viewers were, in April, still watching the aftermath of the war on their screens, STAR TV rained down five channels from the skies – Prime Sports, MTV Asia, the Chinese Channel, BBC World Service and STAR Plus.

In May, when Tendulkar was through with the domestic season, and resting before international cricket started again, the satellite boom was on in the real sense. This was a revolution for his country, for it ended decades of isolation. For urban and middle-class India, of which Tendulkar, his family and community were classic representatives, it was more than the opening up of skies. It was as if entire new worlds had been thrown open to them. The ordinary TV set had turned into a technicolour dream, and India had become a veritable bazaar of soaps, sports, sex, news, music and much else. Dinner-table laughter and suburban train arguments suddenly revolved around all the objects brought into homes by the changed skyscape.

For Sachin, the boom proved more significant than for most other Indians. With the spread of satellite television, the number and quality of TV advertisements shot up. Slicker and more stylish became the rule, and top companies began competing with each other to produce more visually attractive ads.

Satellite-channel-watching middle-class India was now the real consumer, for, along with the skies, the economy was also opening up. Thus, the search for brands was launched – and the name of Tendulkar naturally came up before those of most other Indian celebrities. Tendulkar soon emerged as a brand in his own right, and cricket programming on TV became so slick that even those in India who had no interest whatsoever in the game, turned to it. The Indian TV viewership for cricket soon beat all other countries, and India became the commercial hub of world cricket, and thus, its prime ruler. The result: in the last twelve years, many global one-day tournaments have been held only for the TV viewer in the subcontinent.

Tendulkar's status as star cricketer, and as a brand, increased a hundredfold because of the Indian middle-class fascination for cricket, and especially for cricket on television. The money he has attracted over the years thus owes a great deal to the money-power and the spending habits of the Indian consumerist classes.

Sachin definitely did not know in the middle of 1991 that things would turn out so well and so big for him and for Indian and world cricket. But he was well aware that his status, both as a middle-class Maharashtrian and as an Indian cricketer, was undergoing a sea change. Two of his actions during this period of transition bear this out.

First, as the potent symbol of a buying-power-driven middle-class that no longer took shelter under the umbrella of socialism, Sachin had bought himself a Maruti 800 in the year 1990. An earlier generation would not have relished the idea of driving car at age eighteen. This India was however different, and Sachin was its standing example. He had loved cars ever since he was a child; to own one and drive it around his big city was a dream come true. He took the car around Mumbai, drove it to match venues, and showed it proudly to friends.

The other action showed that along with the externals, the internals too were changing. Here, he was not merely the middle-class envoy; he was, chiefly, a celebrity, and he was getting accustomed to the role.

After Sachin had returned from his debut series abroad early in 1990, Savita Kirloskar, a photographer representing a leading Mumbai newspaper, *Mid Day*, had asked him for a photo session. He agreed. The session got off to a funny start. The debutant lenswoman didn't quite have a firm control over the camera, and the debutant Test cricketer was just as awkward with himself. He was self-conscious, out of his depth, and very shy. But he was anxious to co-operate. When the photographer put in a request, he put on an entirely new set of clothes, and once even stopped to ask her if he needed to wear socks for a shoot in the lawn.

Six months later, when Sachin returned from the tour of England, the same photographer went to his Sahitya Sahwas residence, along with a news correspondent. Tendulkar had changed. He was more at ease with himself, like the confident, emerging middle-class. All the discomfort he displayed was in an altogether different sense, the sense of being a camera-stalked celebrity. He came in twenty minutes late, his answers to the correspondent's questions were curt, almost abrupt, and he was eager to finish the whole thing as soon as possible. He was not uncooperative, but the invisible bond between the photographer and her subject no longer existed.

His own society was constantly underlining the change in his status. Less than a year after the advent of satellite TV, and a little before leaving for England to play county cricket for Yorkshire, Tendulkar, one day in Mumbai, drove his Maruti 800 from his Bandra home to the Gateway of India, the southernmost tip of the city. As he reached Gateway, he did not quite go up to the end of the queue for parking. He drove right up to a gate. Alongside Tendulkar was seated Nirmal Shekar, correspondent for *Sportstar*, one of India's leading sports weekly. A policeman, giving directions to car-owners, looked at Shekar and told him to "go behind and join the queue". Then, the policeman saw the man in the driver's seat. His eyes widened in awe. Within a moment, all the surrounding cars were asked to shift, and a special corner was created for Tendulkar's Maruti.

The fight for space is a perpetual one in Mumbai, whether it is space to live in, to stand or sit in a suburban train, to walk the footpaths or to drive or park a car. But when Tendulkar finally got off his vehicle, and everyone saw just whose car had been accommodated, all petty arguments, the lifeline of fast-paced Mumbai society, ended. Preferential treatment had introduced itself as a theme in Tendulkar's social biography. What an enduring theme it would be, was shown by later events, culminating in the Ferrari controversy.

*

In October 1991, India was back to international cricket. The first encounter of the season was against arch-rivals Pakistan and the West Indies in the Wills Cup in Sharjah. Tendulkar's friend Vinod Kambli made his international debut in the annual desert carnival. A middle-order bat, Kambli was inexplicably asked to open against Pakistan. He faced Wasim Akram and the other pacers bravely, to score forty on debut, and put up a good show throughout the tournament. With both the Pakistanis and the West Indians firing at him, there were times when he opened the face of the bat and, while trying to slice, got comprehensively beaten. There were moments when he looked pretty awkward doing that. Yet he raised the bar for himself and got decent scores.

If Tendulkar was disturbed that Kambli had been asked to open, he didn't show it. In the first match against Pakistan, he scored fifty-two not out, from forty balls. The push he provided towards the end of the innings helped India record a rare win against their old rivals. In the last league game against Pakistan, he got forty-nine, and won the Man of the Match award against the West Indies by picking up the wickets of four top-order batsmen. In the final, he was out LBW to Aaqib Javed, on the first ball he faced. With his dismissal, the bowler completed a hat-trick, and Pakistan went on to lift the Wills Cup with ease.

India had begun the tournament supremely confident, and had notched up three consecutive wins. Impressed by the rise of two talented Indian batsmen, Sanjay Manjrekar and Tendulkar, Javed Burke, chairman of Pakistan's selection committee had told Indian journalists, 'Your batsmen are simply superb.' Before the echoes of his statement could die out in the desert, India crumbled under psychological pressure in the final and returned home a demoralized side.

Pakistan was to tour India immediately after the Sharjah tournament, and the first Indo-Pak one-dayer was scheduled to be played at Mumbai's Wankhede Stadium on 28 October 1991. Members of the Hindu militant outfit Shiv Sena, led by Bal Thackeray, botched things up. Thackeray had vehemently opposed the Pakistan tour and demanded scrapping of cricket ties between the two neighbours on account of Pakistan's support to secessionist movements in Jammu & Kashmir. On 21 October, a band of Shiv Sainiks invaded the Wankhede pitch, poured oil on it and dug it up with sickles and old stumps. The incident created a furore, and Pakistan cancelled its tour for security reasons.

At the same time that sub-continental cricket was acquiring political and diplomatic overtones, cricket in South Africa was freeing itself from the fetters placed on it by the forces of bigotry. A disgrace called apartheid was on its way out. India had taken the lead in the early 1970s to keep South Africa out of international cricket, due to its apartheid regime. Late in 1991, India again took the lead as member of the International Cricket Council or the ICC, to demand the African nation's return to mainstream cricket. When the efforts paid off, and the ban on participation in world cricket was lifted, Dr Ali Bacher, the head honcho of South African cricket, decided to respond to the gesture by organizing a tour to India. The tour was hastily arranged as a replacement for the Pakistan tour.

After two decades of isolation, South Africa was to play three one-dayers in India in November 1991. It was not just a diplomatic coup; it was history. And history could not have asked for a better setting than the Eden Gardens, Kolkata, for its apt recording. The first one-dayer between India and South Africa took place before a 90,000-strong crowd in the West Bengal capital. The atmosphere was electric, and the spectators excited and exceptionally boisterous. All the South Africans with the exception of Kepler Wessels, who had earlier represented Australia, were making their international debut. They had never seen such a spectacle on a cricket ground.

Batting first, South Africa struggled to come to terms with the atmospherics and the Indian bowling side. They got 177 for eight in their allotted overs. But pace bowler Allan Donald, opening the Proteas attack, immediately made his presence felt to the cricketing world. India's top order was sent back in no time. With India looking shaky at sixty for four, debutant Praveen Amre – Sachin's senior at Shardashram High School – walked out to the crease. The junior schoolmate was at the other end.

Amre recalled the tense situation, which demanded a solid partnership for an Indian victory, and Sachin's response to it:

> The scene was daunting; almost one-lakh spectators were watching us. The first thing Sachin and I decided was that we'd call very loudly; otherwise the call would be inaudible in all that cacophony. We also decided we would try to hit the ball to the left of the fielders, because all their fielders were good and tactically it would help if we made them use their wrong hand. We sometimes ran even without calling, because the understanding between us was very good. The understanding was mainly because he and I had the same coach.
>
> Here I must mention a vital part of Sachin's batting. Some batsmen run their own singles quickly but don't take another's run with as much enthusiasm. Sachin ran my singles as if they were his own, and indeed he has always done this, no matter who his batting partner is. This attitude not only keeps the scoreboard moving, it motivates the other batsman.

The wicket was slow, yet the Shardashram boys adapted themselves well. They picked and punished the loose balls and ran their ones, twos and threes with a hunger then uncommon in Indian cricket. Both were not out when India reached its target. Almost in keeping with the nature of the occasion, Tendulkar and Donald shared the Man of the Match award.

Before Donald came to India, he had heard about Tendulkar and seen quite a bit of him on television. Australian pace bowler Craig McDermott had warned him that Tendulkar was going to be the best in the world, and Donald had every reason to take these words seriously. After he bowled to Tendulkar at the Eden Gardens, Donald confessed that Tendulkar was indeed difficult to deal with. A bowler needed extra preparation for someone like him. It wouldn't help if one just ran in and bowled, Donald said. A plan had to be put in place, and the line and length to be used against him decided a few days in advance.

India left for Australia immediately after the third one-dayer at New Delhi (it had won the series 2-1). They were to play five Tests Down Under. In the middle of the Test series, the West Indies would join in for the World Series Cricket one-day championship. And after so much cricket, there would be the biggest event of all, the World Cup.

Indian teams were known to do badly in Australia, but the 4-0 scoreline for the Test series turned out to be among the worst India has ever had. What the scoreline didn't say was that it could easily have been 2-2, were it not for some tactical mistakes, some bad umpiring and some terribly ruinous weather.

Tendulkar's reputation preceded his arrival in Kangaroo-land. The Aussie crowds were keen to have a close look at him. They had heard of a boy with prodigious talent setting the international cricket scene afire with refreshingly orthodox defences and exciting strokeplay. They knew that, for an eighteen-year-old, he had already shown some resilience in international cricket, and there was certainly no one of his age who could match his batting prowess. Yet they would pronounce their final verdict only after they had assessed his performance on the fast and bouncy tracks in their own country.

Like the other Indian batsmen, Tendulkar initially struggled on the lively wickets. The first Test at Brisbane was over in three-and-a-half days. Craig McDermott, Merv Hughes and Mike Whitney ran through an Indian batting order that looked rather formidable on paper. India had gone to Australia with three openers: Krish Srikkanth, Ravi Shastri and Navjot Singh Sidhu. Sanjay Manjrekar was number three, Dilip Vengsarkar on number four, Azharuddin at five, Tendulkar at six, Kapil Dev at seven, Manoj Prabhakar at eight, Kiran More at nine, Javagal Srinath at ten and either Venkatapathy Raju or Subroto Banerjee for number eleven.

Sachin Tendulkar scored sixteen and seven in the two innings

in the Test. The others were just as bad. Australia won the second
Test at Melbourne with eight wickets to spare. The Indian batting
caved in again. Tendulkar scored fifteen in the first innings, and just
as he had settled down in the second and reached forty, he went for
a wild shot and was caught in the deep by Allan Border.

He was distraught. The timing seemed to have gone wrong. The
ball wasn't finding the middle of the bat. And there were too many
miscued hits. At this point, "Mr. Gavaskar", as Sachin deferentially
called him, went up to him and gave him as benign a suggestion as
he had offered in England in 1990. According to Gavaskar's
diagnosis, Sachin was suffering the disadvantages of a batsman who
sights and reads the ball extra-quickly. He had, first, played from
memory the moment he landed in Australia. That would not help,
because the nature of Australian wickets was radically different.
Second, and this was where the chief disadvantage came in, he was
seeing the ball early and trying to go for it. Third, he was trying to hit
the ball too hard.

Tendulkar quickly understood the adjustments he'd have to
make. Indeed, according to Greg Chappell who first saw him bat in
the third Test at Sydney in 1992, this has been one of Tendulkar's
best qualities. 'He does sometimes struggle, but when that happens,
he starts thinking about it, listens to any sound suggestions and
comes back prepared,' Chappell says.

What Chappell has touched upon, but not really articulated, is
a lesson in sports psychology, in this case amply demonstrated by
both Tendulkar and Gavaskar. Professional sport is, in a major way,
about confronting doubt. Those who are introspective, like
Tendulkar, will face doubt more than most, no matter how much
talent they've got. At this stage in Australia, the eighteen-year-old was
indeed floundering. Although he did experience some interesting
stroke-playing, his batting had been anything but consistent. At the
back of his mind, he had perhaps started asking: 'When am I going
to score big again?' The moment this question is asked, psychology
begins to work its weave. There are two ways to negotiate its turns.
One is to say "awful", which is a nice way of submerging oneself in

maudlin sentiment, and turning on a flood of negatives. The other is to discard all the substitutes for intelligent thought. Tendulkar, for his own good, did the latter. He didn't retract into his shell. He told himself that a few low scores added up to some difficulty but not exactly a personal crisis. He listened to Gavaskar's advice and told himself that the next time he walked out to bat, he'd have a real go.

It helped immeasurably that Gavaskar was around to guide him in his run revival, like a fine guru. Gavaskar analysed the situation for the youngster, pointed out the changes that were necessary but did not overanalyse. He knew that would get a struggling batsman worried as hell, and getting bogged down by technique could be as bad for him as being riddled with technical faults. To this limited advice, he added something for effect. He asked Tendulkar to carry an adage in his head all the time. 'Form is temporary,' he said, overtly sounding proud of the cliché, 'class is permanent.' He didn't tell the boy that the cliché was founded in truth. For Sachin, the words resounded with steely conviction anyway.

The third Test at Sydney was a different story for Tendulkar and the other Indian batsmen. After Australia was bowled out for 313 in the first innings, the strength of the Indian batting line-up was made clear. Since the wicket was a turner, Australia had included in its eleven a young leg-spinner called Shane Warne. The debutant got the worst possible treatment from Ravi Shastri and Tendulkar and ended with figures of one for 150. The only wicket he had was that of Shastri – after he had scored 206.

Shastri repaired the damage caused by Sidhu's early dismissal with some truly obdurate batting. For some time, he had spirited support from Manjrekar and Vengsarkar. But it was his partnership with Tendulkar that truly flourished. The slow track was no hindrance to Tendulkar as he blazed his way to a hundred in 171 balls in the company of the experienced pro.

Frustrated by Sachin and Shastri's fightback, the Australians resorted to sledging. The young man was anxious to give it back to them. According to Shastri:

I had just reached my hundred and was having a verbal duel with the Australians. At the end of the over, Sachin came over to me and said in Marathi, '*Thamb, mazhya pan shambhar houn de (Wait till I get my hundred).*' And I said, with your brilliance, young man, you don't even have to do that. What happened then is history.[1]

When Tendulkar came close to his fifty, the spinners were on, and the keeper, the first-slip fielder and the man at silly-point became all the more offensive in their abuse. Sachin ignored it. As Allan Border pitched one short, he rocked on his back foot and cut the ball fiercely through the covers to reach his half-century.

Another shot was a pointer to his concentration that day. The tall, daunting Merv Hughes ran in, and, with his normal, quick arm action, bowled one that came slowly through the air. At the moment of release of delivery, Tendulkar's backswing was high. The bat remained suspended high in the air as Sachin read that the ball was coming on unhurriedly. As the ball came close to the perfect half-volley spot, the bat came down straight with astonishing hand-speed, and the red was thumped to the on-drive boundary with double the speed given to it by the bowler. 'What a shot!' exclaimed David Hookes, former Aussie opener and television commentator for the series.

Soon the bowlers tired of his impertinent ways. Proof of that was the ball that had helped him get to his hundred. Craig McDermott's body language said it all: he ran in wearily and completed his action as if he were going through the motions. The ball was going down the leg side. At ninety-eight not out, Tendulkar glanced it and ran a second run speedily. The helmet was taken off, the fist, tightened around the bat handle, was pumped twice into the air, and a faint smile emerged to signal satisfaction.

Tendulkar had become the youngest batsman to score a Test hundred on Australian soil. He was 18 years and 256 days old, as against the previous record-holder Neil Harvey, who had been 19 years and 121 days when he got his ton in 1948. Harvey had closely watched Sachin's Sydney innings. He was so impressed that after first saying 'brilliant performance, superb back-foot technique and good temperament,' he took the series of superlatives to an altogether higher level: 'He's the best player I have seen for ages... Given his ability and the number of Test matches they play these days, he could play 200 Tests before he's finished.'

Greg Chappell's prose was more measured: 'What the innings showed was that he is well-balanced not only as a batsman but also in the head.'

What set this innings apart from his Old Trafford hundred was that he himself decided its pace. He was aggressive against the bad balls and was, at the same time, composed enough to keep rotating the strike in order to allow his partner Ravi Shastri to have a go at the bowlers.

Tendulkar and Shastri put on 196 runs for the fifth wicket as India took a first innings lead. Rain unfortunately lopped off ninety-four overs of playing time, and at the end of the fourth day, India were 445 for seven. Tendulkar was not out on 120.

Azhar, however, declared only after the total reached 483. Tendulkar remained unbeaten on 148, getting 28 of the 38 runs added on the final morning.

Australia needed to get 171 to save an innings defeat. They ended up just about saving the match, at 173 for eight. Border led from the front with a fighting fifty-three not out. Since the ball was turning a lot, Azhar in his frantic search for victory, brought on Tendulkar to bowl. He gave it some gentle off-spin and got his first Test wicket in his first and only over; Merv Hughes was caught by Prabhakar, off Tendulkar.

India however narrowly missed victory, and Azhar came in for a lot of flak for the delayed declaration. It was said India would have been able to bowl the Australians out if the skipper had declared the innings at the end of the fourth day. This way, India would also have saved the precious ten minutes used up for the change of innings.

The WSC one-day series, also involving the West Indies, was played between the third and fourth Test. India's performance was unimpressive. It won only three of the ten matches it played.

Captain Azhar, in the middle of the Australian tour had meanwhile, refused to hold the regular post-match press conference because he was angry with the media's increasingly harsh criticism of his team's performance. After the team crashed out against Australia in the first of three finals, he not only relented, but also took a line that the press had still not taken up. 'We played the worst cricket ever,' he said.

When the second final too was lost, Azhar, himself under criticism from experts like Ian Chappell for 'irresponsibly lofting the ball to a grateful outfielder,' said: 'As far as batting is concerned, barring a couple of players, we have really done badly. We seemed to lack concentration.' He wasn't excluding himself. 'If only we had done half of what Sachin has done, the one-day series would have been a different story for us,' he commented.

Tendulkar scored over 400 runs from the ten games, the highest in the Indian contingent. In the first one-dayer against the West Indies, he was effective as a bowler. In a close finish, he had Anderson Cummins caught by Azhar in the slips leading to a tie, the first ever in one-day history for both teams.

In the second final, he first took a difficult catch and then effected a run-out by rocketing in a superb throw. During the chase, he had wickets falling all around him. He however, put his head down and played a sound innings of sixty-nine that took India within sniffing distance of a win. Australia's final margin of victory was only six runs. After the match, Tendulkar's eyes were full of tears. He couldn't sleep all night. He replayed the innings in his mind over and over again and fretted and fumed over the shot that had cost him his wicket.

By the next morning, he had found his equanimity. He told his teammates: 'I played that shot due to lack of experience. I'll make sure I don't make that mistake again.'

The Test series resumed after the triangular one-day tournament. The fourth Test was played at Adelaide. Like the Sydney match, this too would have been India's. But the umpires decreed otherwise.

Eight Indian batsmen were given out LBW, and most of these decisions were atrocious. The worst was had by Dilip Vengsarkar. As he stretched fully forward to Merv Hughes, the umpire raised his biased finger. A shocked Ian Chappell exclaimed on air: 'If that's out, I'm a Dutchman.' The Indian team manager, Abbas Ali Baig, sardonically said: he wanted to know if any changes had been made to the LBW law.

This kind of umpiring would have been enough to kill the resolve of any team trying to claw its way back into the series. Yet India came close to a win. In the first innings, Tendulkar bowled Mark Taylor for eleven and had Allan Border caught by Chandrakant Pandit for zero. His contribution was crucial in causing the Aussie downfall at only 145.

Needing 372 to win in the second innings, India fell only thirty-seven short. Azhar, who was going through a bad patch, dropped himself down to number six and asked Tendulkar to come in at number four – a significant shift in the batting order for the eighteen-year-old. The captain led the way with a gallant ton, and Prabhakar scored a gritty sixty-four alongside before being given out LBW, despite a big inside edge. McDermott then wrapped up the tail in no time. The series that could have been 2-2 was now 3-0.

The final Test at Perth was the final chance for India to salvage some pride. But the wicket there, Australia's fastest, has never been easy to bat on. Test cricket began at the WACA in 1970, and since then, the twenty-two-yard-stretch has been a fast bowler's fantasy-come-true. Dennis Lillee, Jeff Thomson and all the West Indian speedsters have wrought havoc there, forcing the best of batsmen to sweat and squirm in discomfort.

No matter how fast a bowler bowls, the laws of physics say that anything that strikes an object loses speed. So any ball has to lose a little pace as it comes off the wicket, though the nip on the wicket may very well assist its nasty bouncing, its deadly swing and vicious skidding. Perth is one of few wickets in the world that defies this law. The ball actually goes quicker off the wicket.

A fascinating story about Perth is perhaps told by the best all-

round cricketers of all time, Sir Gary Sobers. Sobers was captain of a
World XI team that took on Australia on this ground in 1971-72. The
World XI had scored a little over twenty for no loss the night before.
The next morning, everyone gathered in the dressing room to see the
openers continue. Lillee was the bowler, Gavaskar the batsman. On
the first ball, Gavaskar went forward, and the ball whizzed past his
head. All the members of the batting team went up to Sobers and
said: 'Captain, I'm batting at this position, I'm batting at that
position.' Sobers said they could do whatever they liked – as long as
they didn't take his own position, which was lower in the order at
number seven.

When Sobers walked out to bat, he saw that keeper Rod Marsh
was standing nearly thirty yards behind the stumps. So were the slip
fielders. As he approached the crease, he asked Ian Chappell: 'What
are you all doing so far back?' Chappell looked at him and said: 'You'll
find out.' The first ball that Lillee bowled to Sobers went straight past
his head. When Sobers looked back, he saw that Marsh was in mid-
air, and the ball had thudded into his gloves.

Most of the batsmen who've got runs at Perth have done so
through counter-aggression, whether it was Roy Fredericks in the
Seventies or Brian Lara in the late Nineties.

In the final Test between Australia and India in 1991, the hosts
batted first and got 346. India in reply, collapsed, thanks to Messrs
Whitney, McDermott, Reiffel and Hughes, all of whom would have
loved to roll up the track and carry it with them all over the world.
When Kiran More came in to join Tendulkar, the score was 159
for eight.

At this point, Tendulkar decided to counter-attack. As a rule,
before scoring runs, every batsman needs to get his eye in first.
Tendulkar, always partisan towards naked ferocity, had denied his
natural instincts initially, to give his innings the necessary breathing
time. He had taken the academic approach, nurdled the ball, picked
his ones and twos. Once the eye was in, and More was the only
proper batsman left for company, he thought the best risk
management at Perth would be through attack.

On a flat deck, a bowler has to slash his pace and focus on line and length alone. Here, there were no such inhibitions for the Aussies. Mike Whitney was hurtling forward, leaping into the air, letting go a throat-tickler and then swinging low for the follow-through. Craig McDermott and Paul Reiffel steamed in and gave it everything. And Merv Hughes was like Jeff Thomson. He just shuffled up and banged it in.

But Tendulkar took on each one of them. There was a crash here, a bang there, and a wallop another place. The assault had as much brawn and attitude as he could command. Sixteen boundaries were hit in two-and-a-half hours, as Sachin unleashed a brilliant range of strokes. When the bowlers pitched short or on a good length, and got the ball to leave him outside the off-stump, he went up on his toes and cut it with the full swing of the bat, keeping the body's balance intact. Anything anywhere close to the leg-stump was put away, either by leaning on to it or pulling it violently. Australians have always prided themselves on playing the hook and pull better than anyone else. Some of Tendulkar's pulls that day made them feel a bit on the inferior side. The half-volleys were sent back in the "V", and mostly well beyond cover, mid-on, mid-off and mid-wicket.

After he had whipped a chest-high delivery from Whitney through the covers, Australian commentator and one of the game's greats, Richie Benaud, said on air: 'It's a pity that an innings that deserved a crowd of over one lakh is being watched by such a small crowd.'

The bowlers' energetic actions turned ragged as Tendulkar pillaged his second fifty from fifty-four balls, with five hits to the fence. One of these boundaries, an electric on-drive off McDermott, helped him reach his century.

He had got 118 off 161 balls when he was caught at slip off Whitney. While he was at the crease 140 runs had been scored. Of them, only twenty-two had come off others' bats.

While he was on his way to the pavilion, the stylish Australian one-drop batsman Dean Jones went up to him and said: 'You are bloody good now, and you are going to be one hell of a player when you grow up.'

Anyway, the Indian innings soon folded up, and Mark Taylor gave the Indians 442 to score in the fourth innings for a win. Whitney bowled a hostile spell and made sure they didn't go beyond 141. Tendulkar made only five in the second innings, falling to Paul Reiffel.

His century in the first innings had not helped his team avoid another humiliating defeat in a disastrous series. Yet it remains one of the best knocks ever played at Perth. Tendulkar rates it very high among his Test hundreds, for the satisfaction of having tamed some of the best pacers on the world's nastiest wicket. What was also vital was that at a time when the Indian batting as a whole was on the back foot, with Vengsarkar reaching retirement stage, Azhar carrying on a suicidal streak with lofted shots and Manjrekar showing an astronomical run-out rate, he had saved the ship from sinking into the gluttonous sea of self-doubt.

*

In view of the drubbing it had received, India needed to do some fine-tuning before it went into the all-important World Cup 1992 campaign in Australia and New Zealand. Unfortunately, there was no time available for adequate stock-taking and repair. They had to play their first World Cup game barely a fortnight after the end of the Test series.

Despite their dismal performance in Australia, the Indian cricket team for the Cup had all the ingredients needed for a success story. Opener Krish Srikkanth had been brought back into the side. He could hit over the infield in the first fifteen overs. Shastri, who had gone back home after an injury in the Sydney Test, had also been flown in. He could take the singles and rotate the strike as Srikkanth went great guns. In the middle order, there were gifted stroke-makers: Azhar, Tendulkar and Manjrekar. They could keep up a good run rate and accelerate whenever necessary. The promising Vinod Kambli, dumped after the Sharjah tournament, had also been brought back along with Haryana's Ajay Jadeja. And Kapil Dev was just the right man for overs thirty-five to fifty.

Among the bowlers, Kapil had had a wonderful series against Australia. In the first Test, he had bowled three consecutive deliveries that could easily rank among the best in Test cricket. The first one was bowled to Allan Border. It pitched outside the off-stump on a good length, and swung in to rattle off-stump. The second was a superb outswinger. Pitched on an ideal length, it beat Dean Jones completely and escaped the stumps by an inch. The third one zipped in from outside the off-stump and crashed into Jones' stumps. It was cut and swing at its elegant best. Kapil had also earned his 400th Test scalp in the Perth Test when he trapped Mark Taylor Leg Before. He had notched up twenty-five wickets at the end of the Test series, his highest tally in a series abroad. Manoj Prabhakar too was displaying good maturity and shaping up well as Kapil's bowling partner. And young Javagal Srinath was beginning to hit the right spot. In Australia, where the grounds were big, and New Zealand, where they were small, spinners could be very useful. In Shastri and Venkatapathy Raju, India had two left-armers who could deliver.

The fourth World Cup in 1992 was special and different from the other three as it was to have day-and-night matches played under floodlights, with the players donning coloured clothes and two white balls being used from both ends. In addition, all nine teams would play against each other for the first time at the league stage, and a new rain rule had been introduced to protect the side batting first. The rain rule eventually turned a shocker, but it was first New Zealand captain Martin Crowe's turn to shock conventional one-day cricket thinking.

In the 1983 World Cup, the reigning champions West Indies had been humbled on the opening day by India, who were then seen as pushovers. The 1983 winners, India, were similarly defeated on the inaugural day of World Cup 1987 by Australia. Nobody expected New Zealand to do the same to Australia at Auckland on Day One of World Cup 1992.

Martin Crowe challenged all the previews that dismissed his team. He did not merely repeat history; he recreated it with innovation and enterprise. He first scored a hundred not out, to help his team reach 248. Then, after Chris Cairns had bowled the first over, Crowe tossed the ball to off-spinner Dipak Patel. The cricket world was taken by surprise. Patel had himself learnt of the strategy only at the end of the New Zealand innings. During lunch break, he had quickly hopped across to a neighbouring ground to turn his arm over in an impromptu net session. After all, like other spinners across the world, he wasn't used to gripping a glossy new ball in an international game!

Patel got just one wicket but gave away only thirty-six runs. Crowe set attacking fields for him even during the early overs, when there were restrictions on spreading the field, and ruined the rhythm of the Australians. Seven Aussie batsmen failed to reach double figures, and even David Boon's fighting hundred couldn't turn the match around.

The same day that the Kiwis carried out their shock treatment of the Aussies, India took on England at Perth. As mentioned earlier, Tendulkar had got on top of the Australian attack on this ground not too long ago. Against England, his timing, hand-eye co-ordination and instinctive placement suggested he was well on his way to doing the same. But Ian Terence Botham put the brakes on, and brought back to him several times over, the lesson that Arshad Ayub had taught him over a year ago.

Indeed, Botham versus Tendulkar summed up the game for many. Chasing England's 239, India lost two wickets for 63. Tendulkar and Shastri steadied the boat, and with thirty overs gone, India needed only a hundred-odd runs.

Tendulkar was batting fluently. With the match on the boil, Botham came on to bowl. In 1992, Botham had a very leisurely run-up. It was as if the England all-rounder was checking all the finer points of his plot to fox the batsman, before he let the ball go.

So far as Tendulkar was concerned, Botham first determined the intentions. They were, clearly, to finish the game with exuberant stroke-making. So Botham first gave him a half-volley outside the off-stump. Tendulkar, already well set, put his foot down and sent it through the covers for a four. The next ball was the ball of the tournament. Its length was again full. Tendulkar judged the length soon as the ball left the bowler's hand and put his front foot down. But as he launched into just the kind of drive he had played the previous delivery, the ball seemed to go away, gently. Placed on the same spot, it was a beautiful leg-cutter. Tendulkar bent forward and had committed himself to play. It was too late to take the bat away. The ball took the outside edge; the wicket-keeper said thanks. The old fox had won.

Soon after, Botham got Kambli to lob a catch to mid-on, and the rest of the batting crumbled. India finished eight runs short of England.

India's second match, against Sri Lanka, was abandoned due to rain. Young Kambli didn't want rain to affect his high spirits. He joined a bunch of colourful and attractive female cheerleaders along the boundary to keep himself and the crowd amused. Photos of his jig were published all over, and he later paid for his playfulness.

The third match was going to be crucial from the point of view of team morale, for India was taking on a powerful team, Australia. It turned out to be a terrific game that was ruined by the terrible rain rule. There was edge-of-the-seat excitement, sterling performances on either side, and some unforgettable moments. In the Australian innings, there was Dean Jones' strokeful ninety; in the Indian chase, there was Azhar's sizzling ninety-three, Manjrekar's graceful shifting outside the off-stump to superbly glance the bowlers for much-needed boundaries, and Kiran More's two sweeps to fine-leg that brought India tantalizingly close to the target. Similarly, Allan Border's direct hit that ran out a rampaging Azhar, the uprooting of More's stumps as he tried to go for a third boundary to fine leg and Raju's premature victory jump followed by his scramble to get into the crease as David Boon picked up Steve Waugh's throw and knocked off the bails were all more than just tense (for Indians) or exhilarating (for Australians) moments. They were perfect advertisements for the game of cricket.

However, the rain rule played spoilsport. Australia had originally set India a target of 238. After a twenty-one minute delay caused by showers, India was given three overs less to play (i.e., forty-seven instead of fifty). But only two runs were reduced from the target. That was because Rule 5.2 of the World Cup said: 'If, due to a suspension of play, the number of overs in the innings of the side batting second has to be revised, their target score shall be the runs scored by the team batting first from the equivalent number of highest scoring overs, plus one.'

This rule was framed with the intention of protecting the side batting first, which was usually badly hit in a rain-affected game. Unfortunately, it proved to be overly protectionist and left the team batting second at a gross disadvantage. For the side bowling first, it even became harmful to bowl a maiden, because that over would not be considered when the highest scoring overs were taken. South Africa, playing the World Cup for the first time in 1992, was done in by the rule in the semi-finals. One little shower at the Sydney Cricket ground, and they were given an unattainable twenty-one runs to get off one ball.

Meanwhile Tendulkar failed against Australia. A good innings from him would have reduced the burden on the Indian lower order, and as he always scored briskly, it would have been invaluable in a chase that went down to the last ball. Alas, that was not to be. He was out for eleven and Australia won by one run!

But both as a batsman and part-time bowler, Tendulkar played his role responsibly in the next match against Pakistan, at Sydney. He stayed not out at fifty-four, scored off sixty-four balls with a sense of controlled aggression. One particular ball bowled to him by Aaqib Javed was the highlight of the Indian innings. Aaqib ran in and turned his arm over with usual swiftness. Tendulkar read the slower one the moment it left the hand. It was slightly short, so he went on to the back foot, waited with a high backlift for the ball to arrive, and when it did, sent it soaring into the stands over mid-wicket. *Phekun dila* in Tendulkar's mother-tongue, and *phenk diya* in Hindi, are succinct descriptions for authoritatively middled lofted shots that clear the boundary.

With his strokes, Tendulkar raised the momentum of the Indian innings, which had begun in a miserable fashion with Srikkanth uncharacteristically getting five runs off thirty-nine balls. Azhar's gem of a thirty-two, and Ajay Jadeja's forty-six were crucial contributions from the early order but it was left to the team's youngest and seniormost member to take India to a fighting score. Tendulkar and Kapil Dev, between them, smashed sixty runs at seven an over, and helped India reach a total of 216.

The first two Pakistani wickets fell quickly, but Aamir Sohail and Javed Miandad tried to perform the rescue act. In the midst of this, there was another kind of excitement between Miandad and Indian wicket-keeper Kiran More. More was constantly shouting encouragement to the Indian bowlers when Miandad, known for his short fuse, was at the crease. After one such shout, Miandad lost his cool and did hysterical frog jumps in the middle to imitate More's leaps at the fall of each wicket. He was, as ever, symbolizing the rough edge of Indo-Pak cricket rivalry.

It was Tendulkar who brought back life into the bat-and-ball drama. Just when it appeared that the gritty Javed and the doughty Sohail were settling down to a big partnership, Sachin came along with his gentle breaks which resulted in Sohail being caught low at mid-wicket by Srikkanth. After Miandad was bowled by a Srinath yorker for forty, Pakistan's situation deteriorated, and India romped home by forty-three runs. Tendulkar won the Man of the Match award for his all-round performance.

The award was his again in the next game against Zimbabwe. It was only because of his eighty-one, scored off seventy-seven balls, that his team could reach 203. Despite a modest score India won, not because of good bowling, but the World Cup rain rule that victimized the opposition. For those who saw the truncated encounter, the most abiding memory was that of Tendulkar playing John Traicos, an off-spinner in his forties – more than double his age.

World Cups are, however, not won by individual efforts. The Indian team was clearly not in its element in the championship and soon bowed out, losing the next three games to the West Indies, New

Zealand and South Africa respectively. Against New Zealand, Sachin scored eighty-four after being let off early, but that couldn't help avert an Indian defeat.

What was significant was that Tendulkar had scored consistently in the World Cup, getting over 280 runs with three half-centuries at an average of forty-seven. Yet it had not been enough, because the team as a whole had not clicked. When Tendulkar had done well, most of the others had failed; when Azhar had regained his magic touch, the other batsmen, including Sachin, were not of much help; when Srikkanth looked fluent, his opening partner Shastri had been stuck; and when everybody had not done too badly, Kapil could not carry the tail-enders with him. The sorry tale repeated itself in the bowling and fielding departments as well.

The way the World Cup ended was interesting for cricket-lovers worldwide. Throughout the tournament, innovation was the theme, and Martin Crowe had led from the front in this regard. Along with the Dipak Patel experiment, he had made good use of the idea of hitting out in the first fifteen overs, when most fielders are placed inside the circle. Rod Latham and Mark Greatbatch, especially the latter, did some crazy hitting in the early overs and redefined attacking batsmanship in one-day cricket. The West Indies and England picked up the example of the Kiwis, and Brian Lara and Ian Botham gave their teams and the tournament more than just entertainment value with their superb pinch-hitting.

After all this, a team that played its one-day cricket in conventional fashion lifted the Cup. Though Pakistan would not have even qualified for the semis had the rain rule not showered its blessings, its cricket in the semis and finals was in typical Eighties' style. Chasing over 260 in the semis, they followed the principle that a team must keep its wickets intact till forty overs are bowled, and then go for the kill. Pakistan not only started slowly, their captain, Imran Khan, made forty-four from ninety-three deliveries. A young man from Multan, Inzamam-ul-Haq, took over when his team was 140 for four. He got sixty off thirty-seven balls and Pakistan strode into the finals. In the all-important game too, Imran and Miandad strung an unhurried partnership in the middle overs, helping their team reach 150 in forty overs. After that, the onslaught began, and Inzamam and Wasim Akram cobbled up ninety-nine runs for their team from the last ten overs, taking the total to a formidable 249.

Imran also did not make his bowlers do anything unconventional. Attack and aim for wickets, he told them, and he shuffled the bowlers intelligently. They delivered.

Get the basics right, work as a team, and you can turn the tables on anyone without doing anything unique. This was the writing on the wall, as Imran lifted the Benson & Hedges World Cup. India had blundered on its basics. For the youngest member of the Indian team, the post-grad course was turning out to be increasingly instructive.

As the pressures of international cricket were mounting, getting doubled and then redoubled by the team's continuing failures, and as the entire Indian team was facing a lot of music, a none-too-happy Tendulkar himself was taking recourse to music, his preferred mode of relaxation for much-needed relief. His teammates noticed that once off the field, Sachin loved to go back to his room and sit for hours tuning in to his favourite songs, mostly western pop. He did not like hard rock because he thought it was all noise. He opted for the expressive, throaty voice of composer-singer-drummer Phil Collins. From the singer's first solo album *Face Value* that features one of the most memorable contemporary pop songs, 'In The Air Tonight', to his band Genesis' 1991 album *We Can't Dance*, Sachin liked everything. Gordon Sumner, better known by his stage name Sting, was another favourite.

Despite his team's failure, Tendulkar had his wits about him. On a flight taken by the Indian team in Australia, he trembled and did a wobble walk all over the plane, to imitate an airsick Subroto Banerjee on a previous tour. His teammates were in splits.

Fortunately, unlike many Indian players, he did not neglect the basics even when he was off the field. Like keeping fit. He exercised without a break and, realizing he now looked like he was on the chubby side, in the early three months of the year 1992, lost nearly seven kilogrammes.

*

On his return to India after the World Cup, Tendulkar received an offer from English county Yorkshire, to be their first overseas player. He discussed the offer with coach Ramakant Acharekar and Sunil Gavaskar. The coach asked him to go ahead. So did Gavaskar, who had been one of the few Indians to play county cricket.

Yet, when Yorkshire Chief Executive Chris Hassell flew down to Mumbai in April 1992 and Tendulkar signed the $30,000 deal, the now nineteen-year-old was not merely following Gavaskar, Kapil Dev or Bishen Singh Bedi's footsteps. He was breaking new ground.

Yorkshire was the crowned capital of English cricket for most part of the twentieth century. 'A strong Yorkshire means a strong English side,' went the famous line, and like many other famous lines, it was based on truth. Giants like Wilfred Rhodes, George Hirst, Bill Bowes, Len Hutton, Hedley Verity, Maurice Leyland, Wally Hammond, Herbert Sutcliffe and Fred Trueman lifted the county to great heights, making it *the* team to be beaten in England and the symbol of a doughty cricketing spirit.

However, the decline began in the late 1960s, and despite the emergence of Geoff Boycott and his demi-god-like status for over a decade, the problems of infighting, a collapse of the team spirit and gossip-over-game came to a head in 1983 when Yorkshire finished last in the county championship.

All through the years of decline, Yorkshire stuck to its policy of not looking outside its boundaries for players. Other counties opened their doors as soon as county cricket was thrown open to players from other countries in the 1960s, and benefited immensely. Yorkshire's worsening performances meant that some good local players too switched to other, thriving, teams.

To pull Yorkshire out of the mess, the no-outsiders policy was finally discarded in 1992. Australian bowler Craig McDermott, then hot property in international cricket, was signed up for a three-year stint. He, however, withdrew owing to an injury. Geoff Boycott's immediate choice for replacing McDermott was Sachin Tendulkar. Although his proposal met with some opposition, as it was widely felt that Yorkshire's problem was a lack of class bowlers who couldn't bowl out other sides, Boycott refused to backtrack. His stubbornness, as also the lack of time to look for other players, saw Tendulkar's name through.

Tendulkar arrived in Yorkshire a nervous man. There was already talk that the xenophobic sections would try to make his life difficult: there was massive responsibility because he was breaking tradition; the expectations from local cricket-lovers were high; and the virtually non-stop cricket was not going to really ease the tension.

The fear of social rejection was still high when Sachin, having just about settled in the county, took his Honda Civic to a local gas station. The car had 'Sachin Tendulkar drives a Robert Bowett Honda' emblazoned across its side, so no one could be in doubt about who was in the driver's seat. An old man suddenly tapped on the window. Tendulkar shrunk back, nervously. The old man then extended his hand. 'Welcome to Yorkshire,' he said. Sachin shook his hand, and breathed easy.

As for his performance at Yorkshire, Tendulkar got a thousand runs in the season from twenty-five innings. His average of forty-six was more decent than exceptional. He got one hundred, against a Durham attack that included his tormentor in the World Cup, Ian Botham. Botham took his wicket here too but only after Tendulkar had set his side well on the way to the 262 runs it needed for victory in the fourth innings of a low-scoring match. In the Sunday League, which has forty-overs-a-side game, he got a ton against Lancashire. Yorkshiremen, who take special pride in defeating their neighbours, Lancashire, were delighted.

Despite rumours, racism did not ruin the atmosphere. In fact, at many venues, locals applauded when he walked out to bat. Ironically, it was the response of the sizeable number of immigrants from South Asia which was indifferent and sometimes even hostile. At a supermarket, Tendulkar had to hear quite a lot from a few antagonistic Pakistanis. He, in turn, did nothing to aggravate matters and generally behaved so well that people took him to heart.

Photographs of him wearing the traditional Yorkshire flat hat appeared all over and further warmed the atmosphere. But even in the middle of all this behaviour befitting the "propah" tradition-breaker, he was, somewhere, still a child. In the county club-house, he would wait for all other teammates to leave the shower and then lock himself in his cubicle for twenty minutes just to make sure that others didn't see his clumsy attempts to knot his tie.

In Yorkshire, Sachin lived in a beautiful bungalow in a small town called Dewsbury, near Leeds. The bungalow was shared by Vinod Kambli, who was playing the Bradford League for Spen Victoria. The two spent their evenings together, driving around in the Honda Civic and spending a lot of time with the family of Solly Adams, a millionaire and an ardent admirer of Indian cricket, who lived ten minutes away from Sachin's bungalow. Yorkshire has plenty of Indian restaurants, but the two buddies mostly preferred a pizza or ate at McDonalds. The reason: both loved eating non-vegetarian food, and Tendulkar in particular, who loved fish in all its varieties, found the Indian food there "lacking in spices".

The county season was cut short in August 1992 when the Board of Control for Cricket in India called Tendulkar back to play the Duleep Trophy. Yorkshire did not improve its position that season; in fact, it went a couple of places down. But Sachin's captain Martyn Moxon, Boycott and other Yorkshire legends like Trueman, Brian Close and Raymond Illingworth felt that he had done a fantastic job of breaking the ice on behalf of the "outsiders".

Tendulkar himself was a little disappointed with his performance but had thoroughly enjoyed the experience. He said: 'I never got going. Perhaps there was more pressure than I had first thought. I received a fabulous reception each time I came out to bat and I respect the people of Yorkshire for that. The guys in the dressing room were fantastic, the whole thing was good for my learning curve and I would play county cricket again if asked, but only if it did not encroach on the Indian itinerary.' Somewhere within, he knew the itinerary would not allow it.

Back home, some sort of frenzy was fast building up about Tendulkar. Even his eighties and nineties for Yorkshire were called bad scores. Nothing less than a Bradmanesque average was acceptable, where the young man was concerned. It was natural, therefore, that when India left for South Africa late in 1992, he was expected to get at least a ton a Test.

Reciprocating the grand gesture made by India the previous year, South Africa first sent out an invitation to the Indian team to play a Test series on its soil after a gap of twenty-two years. It was gladly accepted and the series was labelled the goodwill tour.

The Proteas, led by Ali Bacher, had trounced Bill Lawry's Aussies in 1970 and had been on top of the world when apartheid put a full stop to their Test cricket. On this trip however the one question asked repeatedly was: how would Azhar's boys fare against a team which had in it the supersonic Allan Donald? Moreover, how would Indians tackle Donald, Fanie de Villiers and Brian McMillan on South African wickets that aided pace and bounce?

The Indian captain, Mohammed Azharuddin, made it clear that the batting had to come good. He stated bluntly that all the batsmen in the side except Sachin somehow seemed to be taking their place for granted. They had to perform.

India had a new manager in Ajit Wadekar. He too stressed that there was no substitute to performing well. Yet what he saw initially from the team was little more than a display of goodwill. Of course the visitors were receiving a plethora of invitations from enthusiastic South Africans and overenthusiastic immigrant Indians, but the label 'goodwill tour' seemed to have been stretched a little too far. Wadekar later told me:

> Our team was young and talented. But the players were not focused in the middle. They had a lot of attractions and distractions. They accepted each and every invitation for the

evenings. I tried to change this. It was not easy, because it had deeply entered the players' system. Once, when I was telling the players to mend their ways, Kapil Dev protested and told me they were on a goodwill tour. I told him in front of the entire team that if he indeed felt that way, he should take the first flight back home. Slowly, all the players realized they needed to concentrate on cricket.

Sachin though was never really keen on going out for dinners. But he was often left without a choice, as the team members accepted all invitations. Ever the team man, he would be forced to tag along, against his wish.

Tendulkar's primary concern on reaching South Africa was to quickly learn all the adjustments that would be necessary on the wickets there. He shared this concern with his senior Shardashram mate, Praveen Amre, who was also part of the Indian squad.

Amre told me how Sachin and he prepared:

We first did a lot of homework on the practice pitches. Adaptation to foreign conditions calls for finer changes in technique, and that's what we tried to make. We would discuss the weight of our bats and whether it needed to be reduced to meet the ball more quickly. We would discuss how much we needed to shuffle, to meet the ball in time. Sachin and I shared a room quite often on the tour. He would all the time discuss cricket.

Both Tendulkar and Amre got into the thick of things early. In the festival match that marked the start of the tour, Sachin scored a hundred, and on the first ball of the first Test at Durban, bowled by Kapil Dev, he gladly accepted Jimmy Cooks' catch at third slip. On the second day of the Test, when he was not out on eleven, he played a Brian McMillan delivery behind point and took off for a single. Jonty Rhodes pounced on the ball, prompting the batsman to change his mind. Short-leg specialist Andrew Hudson, who had come up to the stumps, took Jonty's throw and clipped off the bails as Sachin desperately grounded his bat. The umpire at square-leg, South

African Cyril Mitchley, was in doubt. He looked up into the distance and marked out the shape of a box with his hands. The third umpire was at work. He took nearly half a minute to look at the close call and decided the batsman must go. Tendulkar had become the first Test cricketer to be given out with the help of the camera. The TV revolution that he had seen in his country the year before was changing the nature of the game itself.

Amre was thrust into the position of a rear-guardian in the Durban Test and responded by making a hundred on his Test debut. The Durban Test was eventually a draw, due to heavy showers. The second, at Johannesburg, was drawn by India, due to Tendulkar's batting and Anil Kumble's bowling, but not before some drama surrounding the same technology that had found its first scalp in the young batsman.

India put South Africa on the mat in the first innings at Johannesburg. The home team had crossed barely sixty for the loss of four wickets when Jonty Rhodes, batting twenty-eight, struggled to get into the crease as Javagal Srinath accurately threw at the stumps. It seemed to be a close case. Steve Bucknor, the neutral umpire for the series, declared him not out. The Indians pleaded with him to consult the third umpire. He would not. The replays on TV showed Rhodes was out. Eventually, Rhodes went on to score ninety-one and stretched his team's total to a decent 292.

India were two down for twenty-seven when Tendulkar walked in. In a short while, the scorecard read seventy-seven for four. Discipline and application were now needed to bring the team out of the rut. Tendulkar stood up to Donald and McMillan's relentless shoulder-length stuff for 372 minutes. Soon he reached his hundred and became the youngest Test cricketer to score a 1,000 runs in Test cricket. And when India were all out for 227, the scoreboard displayed nearly half the runs – 111 – against his name.

For the South Africans, batting had been defined by the likes of Barry Richards and Graeme Pollock. Both were attacking batsmen who had their careers badly affected by the international boycott of South Africa. In Tendulkar the South Africans saw someone in their mould. His hand-eye co-ordination and footwork were as exact as that of Barry Richards, and his through-the-line hitting, especially the short-arm punches, reawakened their cherished memories of Shaun Pollock. An imperious left-hander, Pollock had been known for his "see-the-ball-hit-the-ball" philosophy; the power in his shots was such that he had once left two Australian fielders at long-on and long-off stumped as he thumped a straight drive to the boundary just five yards away from each of them; and in an age not known for one-day cricket, he could find – even when he was in his early forties – a boundary an over with ease. The young Indian thus mirrored for the locals their own rich cricket skills and staked his claim as a good representative of the international cricket traditon: like Pollock, he kept his batting simple, hit really, really hard, had guts and was a pleasure to watch.

In the third Test at Port Elizabeth, Allan Donald bowled like a dream and took South Africa to their first victory since their return to Test cricket. Tendulkar was given out, caught behind, off the first ball he faced from Donald in the second innings. However, the ball had only hit his pad and Ravi Shastri, batsman at the non-striking end, dropped his bat in sheer horror.

After all the excitement and drama, the fourth and final Test was drawn with Tendulkar at seventy-three, the top-scorer for his team. India lost the "goodwill" Test series, and the South Africans announced to the world at large that they were still a power to reckon with.

Tendulkar's performance was disappointing in the seven-match one-day series, as was the rest of the Indian team's. His personal high was a thirty-two. In most of the matches, he got out to purely impulsive and impetuous strokes.

Once again it was time for introspection for the Indians as they flew back home. Azhar came under fire for his continuing failures as captain. He had even done badly with the bat in South Africa. A success-starved, cricket-crazy public now looked all the more to Tendulkar as possibly the only hope and example of accomplishment and triumph. If, in popular perception, the national team was a nonperforming unit that seemed to be on the losing side far too often, he seemed like the one performer who provided a terrific break from all the mediocrity around him in cricket.

The spotlight was clearly on Sachin Tendulkar and it started showing on the ninteen-year-old's face. He was now seen going to matches with a walkman's ear-phones firmly in place. On one occasion, this writer saw at the Wankhede Stadium in Mumbai, a crowd of clearly a few thousand waiting for over forty-five minutes after a match to see him perfecting his drives along the boundary line as a group of young bowlers turned their arms over. 'Sachin, Sachin,' the crowd bellowed, constantly trying to get his attention and begging him to wave out to them at least once. He was practising very close to the crowd and refused to give them so much as a glance despite their persistent pleading, but the look on his face revealed that he was extremely conscious of their presence. It wasn't as if he was not used to mammoth crowds turning up to watch him play and to the deafening noises in the middle of a match. But now things were going beyond that. Even when Sachin casually stroked a ball, a few thousand turned up to watch him and refused to leave till he himself disappeared out of sight. The numbers of such obsessive fans were drastically rising.

Sunil Gavaskar, realizing the immense faith reposed in him by the country, made a fervent public appeal to spare him the pressure. Yet there seemed to be no letting up. So the walkman became a regular fixture. So did Sting's album, *The Soul Cages*.

---

1   *The Mid Day,* May 2001.

the vice-captain as hero

He who is not courageous enough to take
risks will accomplish nothing.

– Muhammad Ali

Play the game for more than you can afford to
lose... only then will you learn the game.

– Winston Churchill

Do what must be done, disregarding everything
else.

– *The Mahabharata*

T he raucous Vinod Kambli brought good cheer to a brooding Sachin
Tendulkar early in 1993. Sachin loved Vinod's company, for he was
a chronic prankster and could beat back tensions and liven up the air
with his mere presence. He was also a confidant and a sounding
board. Just the man to have around when the pressure seemed to be
building up.

By now it became obvious that Sachin would have to assume
vice-captaincy of the national team. Mohammed Azharuddin was
being skewered for his captaincy and his poor batting form, and
Tendulkar's name was already being bandied about as the deputy-
in-waiting.

Don't delay his grooming as leader, those with an eye on the
future said. It was also obvious that Sachin would have to turn from
free-flowing stroke-maker to chief carrier of the team's batting
responsibilities.

For all the progress he had made in Australia, including the rise
from number six to number four in the batting order, he was still yet
another player in the Indian side. The job of guiding the Indian

innings still belonged to seniors like Dilip Vengsarkar, Ravi Shastri, Sanjay Manjrekar and Azhar. But, by the time India played the South Africans, the pressure of holding fort had passed on to him.

This wasn't an easy transformation. For instance, in Australia, Allan Border had said that if Tendulkar was eighteen, he was sometimes bound to bat like an eighteen-year-old. Border had asked that the boy be left alone to play his cricket. 'It is critical for him that he doesn't handle additional responsibility till he's much older,' he had stressed.

These words began to sound prophetic when Sachin showed a lot of impatience in the one-day series against South Africa late in 1992. It was as if the teenager in him were rebelling. When he was wrongly given out by umpire David Shepherd in the Port Elizabeth Test, nineteen-year-old Tendulkar's steely exterior collapsed, and television cameras caught not only the anguish on his face, but also the tears in the eyes. Would the boy, therefore, break out of the man's attire?

Well, the one thing the boy couldn't do was complain. His extraordinary quick transition from schoolboy to Test cricketer had cleared the way for rapid shifts and swelling demands. Yes, there was danger. He could get bogged down, withdraw into a shell and ultimately succumb. Luckily, he realized that though cricket was serious business, it didn't have to be grim. With this approach, through 1993 and 1994, he turned the situation to his advantage. He took calculated risks, made innovations and generated ideas, strategies and skills for his own and his team's advancement. In the entire process, Vinod stood solidly alongside, a friend in need indeed.

*

Kambli had had a poor World Cup in Australia, so when the Indian team left for South Africa, he found himself back in his home in the Mumbai suburb of Kanjurmarg. His reaction to his dropping was to score well in domestic cricket so that he could be selected for England's tour to India early in 1993. He made the series against

England his own, with explosive batting. And partnering him all along was Tendulkar.

All through the England series, Tendulkar batted with heightened responsibility, and was able to settle easily into the bigger role he was being asked to play largely due to the comfort of having Kambli at the other end. And Vinod's performance was spectacular; it considerably lightened his friend's sudden sense of burden.

Tendulkar watched gladly from the other end as Kambli, on his twentieth birthday, blazed his way to his first one-day hundred in the first one-dayer against England at Jaipur. India had lost three wickets for less than sixty, when the two of them came together at the crease. They stayed not-out at the end of the allotted overs; Kambli getting exactly a hundred, and Sachin eighty-two. India lost the closely-fought match when the English batsmen ran a single off the last ball, but Kambli was named Man of the Match. He got sentimental. 'I will never forget Sachin's birthday gift to me. It was his influence that helped me stay calm and reach my hundred,' he said.

However, both the Shardashram boys batted sloppily in the next one-dayer and didn't do much in four other one-dayers either, though India levelled the series 3-3. But in the three Tests that were played in the middle of the ODI encounters, there was no stopping them.

Tendulkar got a beautiful fifty in the first innings of the first Test at Kolkata, giving Azhar good support. Azhar had to score well and produce positive results if he hoped to stay as captain. He responded to the challenge by scoring a 182 that cleared the way for an Indian triumph at his favourite ground, Eden Gardens. Tendulkar too would have got a hundred, had it not been for – yet, again – a rash shot off a very wide Devon Malcolm delivery.

Kambli got sixteen in the first innings and eighteen not out in the second, as he and Sachin got together at the wicket to score India's winning run.

Chennai's M. A. Chidambaram Stadium holds the same appeal for Tendulkar that Eden Gardens does for Azhar. He has always scored runs there, and in a superb fashion. Shane Warne, whose leg-spinners were introduced to all corners of the ground in 1998, and

Pakistan, that nearly lost a high-pressure Test to Tendulkar's heroics in 1999, know of Chennai's special status well. Gooch's Englishmen were the first to be introduced to this, in February 1993. Tendulkar scored his first Test century on Indian soil at Chennai, in the second Test against England. The innings was a mix of style and reserve, calm and aggression. It was an indication that he was aware of, and sensitive to, new responsibilities, and was welcoming them with the right frame of mind.

The beginning of the innings underlined the new approach. Leg-spinner Ian Salisbury delivered a full-toss around middle-stump. Tendulkar squared up and did nothing more than gently push it into the vacant mid-wicket region. The ball rushed to the ropes. Former India captain Mansur Ali Khan Pataudi, commentating for television, said: 'He just pushed it but the ball sped like a rocket to the boundary.' Tendulkar had hardly sensed the pace and bounce of the wicket, when Salisbury and Graeme Hick, who was bowling off-spin, started giving him a taste of their generosity. Half-volleys and long-hops began to arrive almost at the rate of one an over. Tendulkar was merciless to both bowlers, and either variety of bad balls. Cover drives, on-drives and cuts and pulls became the order of the day. But just when aggression seemed to have got on top, there came a ball that truly tested his equilibrium. That ball defined Tendulkar's innings.

Hick pitched it a little short of length, on the off-stump, and Sachin went back, ready for a square cut. The ball unexpectedly straightened and came quickly off the wicket. Sachin had to change his entire physical position in a second. He got on top of the ball, and instead of playing a regulated square-cut *behind* point, he turned his wrists and stylishly rolled his bat over the ball, sending it rocketing *forward* of point, for a boundary. Neville Cardus once called a shot readjusted at the last moment by Denis Compton "delayed science". This was nothing less.

After the spinners were thrashed, fast bowlers Devon Malcolm and Paul Jarvis came on. Malcolm reared the ball up well, and Tendulkar gave him a straight bat and lots of respect. With Jarvis, it was a different matter. Jarvis had been Tendulkar's teammate at Yorkshire. Perhaps because of this, Tendulkar began to treat him as if he were at the Yorkshire nets. One chest-high ball was pushed behind the bowler casually. It went with astonishing speed to the boundary.

This push-drive has been an outstanding feature of Tendulkar's batting throughout his career. As the ball is pitched on a good length, Tendulkar just stands up. He hardly moves his feet, but the broad bat comes down on the ball firmly and authoritatively. Even then, the arc isn't too great, and often there is no follow-through. It is almost as if the bat stops all movement the moment it has hit the ball. The next thing you see is the helpless bowler looking blankly either at Tendulkar, or at the ball that's travelling far too fast. The final denouement for the bowler is the cover, mid-off or mid-on fielder's sluggish and resigned run to the boundary, to get the ball back.

Meanwhile, another Jarvis ball, short of length, was smashed with the full swing of the bat over the point fielder's head. A third, far outside the off-stump, was chased and reached only after the batsman had overstretched himself. Still, Sachin got it in the middle of his heavy bat and placed it immaculately through the covers for a four.

For one ball, however, he got his feet in a horribly wrong position. Jarvis pitched outside the off-stump, and Tendulkar tried to smash the ball through point, with his feet obstinately static. Everyone knew Tendulkar could get carried away and throw away everything with one rash stroke. Here, he just missed getting an edge. Surprisingly, unlike on many other occasions, the bad stroke acted as a wake-up call, and he was quickly back to his technically sound self. Malcolm had to bear the brunt for this. Two balls on the middle and leg, over-pitched, were delicately straight-driven past mid-on, for four. A third went through mid-wicket, the batsman leaning nicely on it, his head still and eyes glued to the ball, even when it touched the ropes. And, when Sachin was on ninety-seven, a half-volley from Malcolm was sent past the bowler, and down the ground, in style.

Kambli too began in imperious fashion and played confident strokes on either side of the wicket. The fast bowlers brought the ball up onto his rib-cage. He was up on his toes and glanced exquisitely. Tendulkar was at the other end when Kambli reached his maiden Test fifty. Soon after, though, Vinod got complacent, and casually tried to play a ball from Hick across the line. He was caught plumb in front.

Tendulkar's 165, Navjot Singh Sidhu's equally dominant century knock and Kambli and Amre's fifties helped India post a total that forced England to follow on and eventually suffer an innings defeat. From Sachin's point of view, the Test was also a personal victory. He had resorted to assault and battery just as he often had in the past. Yet what was noticeable was that he had discriminated between the accurate Malcolm and the other bowlers, and changed his game to suit their strategies.

The third Test was at Wankhede Stadium, the home ground for Tendulkar, Kambli and Amre. Tendulkar admitted that all three of them would be under some pressure before their own crowd. Kambli had no such anxiety. He dominated the Test with a dazzling innings of 224. Tendulkar had a 194-run partnership with him in forty-four overs, the left-hander playing aggressor and Sachin playing senior partner in the real sense, rotating the strike as much as possible, calming Kambli down when he looked impatient and talking to him at the end of each over to boost his confidence.

Tendulkar was clearly not as fluent as Kambli in this innings, and appeared to struggle sometimes to middle the ball. Yet he seemed happy with his seventy-eight, so long as it contributed to a valuable partnership with a valued partner. His good cheer at the end of the day suggested so.

As Sachin and Vinod chatted with one another after the end of the day's play, a photographer from a national newspaper, a friend of both, went up to them and asked for a shoot. Kambli, ever the mischievous one, said: 'I remember, when we got the world record partnership in school, you asked us to come over to your office so you could take pictures. You then sat us down in the office canteen and clicked away merrily. We didn't even get a *chaha* (tea).' He then turned to Sachin and asked, 'Right, Tendlya?' 'Barobar, *barobar* (Right, right),' Tendulkar said struggling through the uproarious laughter from all three. The relief was showing.

Tendulkar made a detailed analysis of Kambli's innings after the Test, which India again won by an innings. In that, he made it clear that the left-hander was truly easing the pressure on him. Tendulkar said:

> Vinod and I have played together through all the stages in our career: schools cricket, the Under-15, Under-17 and Under-19 Mumbai teams, Ranji Trophy and now Test cricket. Many people raised doubts about Vinod's ability earlier. He has proved them all wrong. I'm delighted about that.
>
> His innings at the Wankhede not only highlighted his talent, it was the sole reason our three spinners could go on the offensive and hand the Englishmen an innings defeat. An innings that clears the way for a Test victory is special. Vinod's 224 is just that.
>
> I've always known how talented Vinod is. Yet I must confess I too was surprised by his courage and determination during this knock. When he reached his 100, I saw him taking fresh guard. He did the same when he got to 150 and then to 200. What made me most happy was that, after getting out for 224, he came up to me and said: 'I shouldn't have got out.'
>
> Some of Vinod's cuts and drives were stunning. I too am an aggressive player, but when I saw his concentration while playing his strokes and realized that he was going great guns, I just decided to keep quiet and occupy one end of the crease. He was doing everything. He made my job easy.[1]

Ajit Wadekar, then manager of the Indian team, was known to be close to both Tendulkar and Kambli. In fact, he took upon himself the task of bringing out the best in Kambli, to the extent that the left-hander came to be called his favourite. Wadekar told me:

> Vinod was in tremendous form against England. No bowler could get him out. Sachin would love to see his friend get runs.

There was a tremendous bond between them. They used to hang around in my room, and everyone knew they were close to me. But it wasn't that Vinod was my favourite. My tendency is to look after a player who needs help and care. Sachin doesn't need looking after. That wasn't the case with Vinod. He had talent, as much as Sachin did. But he wasn't disciplined; he was wayward. It was only talent and nothing else. He didn't realize why discipline helped. I tried to help him. I didn't want his talent to go waste.

The Test series against England, pocketed 3-0 by India, was followed by a one-off Test against Zimbabwe at New Delhi. Kambli batted as if he were continuing from Wankhede and got a match-winning 227, falling only eight runs short of Sunil Gavaskar's 236, then the highest Test score by an Indian. Here again, Tendulkar, who got sixty-two, was involved in a century stand with him.

*

Prior to the England series, the Indian selectors had given enough indication that they were looking at Tendulkar as a candidate for vice-captaincy. They had asked him to lead an Under-25 India team that was to play England at Cuttack before the first Test. A foot injury did not allow Tendulkar to play that game. The selectors then asked him to lead a Rest of India team against England, in a three-day game at Vishakhapatnam, in the middle of the Test series. He had a peculiar experience in that game. There were some bowlers in the team he had not seen earlier in action, so he did not quite know how to manoeuvre the attack. By the time he had figured things out, the match was over; he wished it had been a five-dayer.

The selectors, though, were ready for their move. They made their decision and appointed Tendulkar vice-captain of the Indian team that was to tour Sri Lanka in June 1993. At the time of his selection, Sachin was only twenty years old, though unlike Tiger Pataudi who became captain by the time he played his third Test at age twenty-one, Sachin had already played twenty-five Tests.

There's a lot of importance attached to milestones in a person's life. However, India's cricket-crazy millions accepted Tendulkar the vice-captain, as if this was only one of the many milestones that had queued up for him for long.

The vice-captain's post in India is a titular one for a home series; but on a tour, it gains significance. He is part of the team management and often has to use managerial savvy in tackling team members. Sri Lanka was going to test the twenty-year-old's leadership skills.

Most members of the 1993 Indian squad had already turned out for India when Tendulkar was making his school debut. Yet the response of nearly the whole squad to his promotion was warm, in keeping with the phenomenal all-India sentiment.

Tendulkar got a chance to lead the side for the first time when flu forced Azhar off the field on the last day of the third and final Test. A draw appeared unavoidable in the final stages, but Tendulkar led aggressively, refusing to give up the fight. In the midst of that fight, he had to soothe nerves, as the umpires turned down some good appeals. That job was done satisfactorily.

The entire series was, in fact, marked by atrocious umpiring, which sparked a lot of tension between the two teams. Hardly any play was possible in the first Test, due to bad weather. In the second, at Colombo, Kambli got a hundred in the first innings and Tendulkar in the second; in the same Test, Tendulkar got a terrible decision in the first innings, and Kambli in the second. Tendulkar was given out caught at short leg when the ball had not touched bat; Kambli was given out caught behind when, again, the ball was some distance from the bat.

Tendulkar, deeply upset by this and other bad decisions, concealed his disappointment. Kambli didn't, and was reprimanded by match referee Peter Burge who in fact brought the two sides together at the end of the Test (which India won comfortably) and gave them a talking to, about conduct.

In the final Test, which ended in a draw, Kambli got another century and was involved in, what had by now become routine, a hundred-run partnership with Tendulkar. The understanding between the two young Indians baffled the Sri Lankans. They saw that Sachin and Vinod ran without calling each other. They just looked at each other and one knew from eye contact what the other was thinking.

Kambli carried his sparkling form into the five-nation Hero Cup played on Indian soil in November 1993. In the games leading up to the semi-finals, he got scores of seventy-eight, ten, fifty-five and eighty-six. Tendulkar's scores, this time, in contrast, were: twenty-six (not out), two, twenty-four and three. Sunil Gavaskar commented, as he had before, that Sachin was failing because he was again unconsciously lunging forward before the ball came on to the bat.

Sachin's failures attracted much attention, and people watched with interest and apprehension as India got ready to take on South Africa in the semi-finals at Eden Gardens, Kolkata. Tendulkar failed with the bat here too, scoring only fifteen. The wicket was slow and not easy to bat on. The Indians made things tougher for themselves. There were four run-outs, and except for Azhar who got ninety, no one looked good. The result was a total of 195.

The South Africans began far too watchfully, and were not really encouraged by the one-lakh-strong boisterous crowd that made even calling difficult in the din. Opener Andrew Hudson hung on at one end in a determined fashion. The other end was opened up. Hudson's partner, Kepler Wessels, was out cheaply, and Anil Kumble and Ajay Jadeja got two wickets each, to reduce the opposition to 130 for five. As hesitant stroke-making and indecisive running led to three run-outs, the required run rate climbed to eight an over. The powerful Brian McMillan and Dave Richardson finally fought back and got thirty-two runs in no time. When Richardson was out, the last over remaining, South Africa needed six runs to win.

The atmosphere in the stadium was a mixture of nervous excitement and tremendous expectation. TV viewers across the world saw senior members of the Indian team go into a huddle to decide who'd bowl the last over. Javagal Srinath and Manoj Prabhakar had given away too many runs in their last two overs, so the captain was not keen to bring on any one of them. Kapil Dev was an option; he had two overs left. But what one saw next was that suddenly, Tendulkar got hold of the ball to bowl. How did the ball land in his hands?

Ajit Wadekar told me thus:

> We had almost lost the match. At the end of the penultimate over, I sent out a message to Azhar that he (as captain), Kapil (as senior team member) and Sachin (as vice-captain) should discuss the situation. I said Kapil should bowl the last over since he's the most experienced bowler. When Sachin saw Kapil hesitating, he grabbed the ball and said he would bowl. I was shocked. Azhar just looked at me and shrugged his shoulders in sheer helplessness. The rest is history.

First ball. Tendulkar bowls a slow medium-pacer, just outside the off-stump, to Fanie de Villiers. He hits it through the off, gets one and tries to run a second. Salil Ankola throws from the deep, right into the gloves of keeper Vijay Yadav. De Villiers is run out.

Five runs needed from five balls. Last man Allan Donald is on strike. Tendulkar bowls full to him. Not one, but three balls in a row. Donald fails to connect, because Tendulkar is bowling so slowly, and with such definite loop, that the batsman can't figure out when the ball's going to reach. Donald gets one off the fifth ball.

Last ball, and hard-hitter McMillan needs to get four to win. McMillan has taken leg-stump guard. Tendulkar cramps him completely by pitching the ball between his bat and leg-stump. The batsman swings, gets an edge and runs a single as the ball goes down the leg side, unhurriedly. Tendulkar thumps his fists into the air to signal triumph. The entire team crowds around him to embrace him. Eden Gardens, and the rest of India, explodes with ecstasy. Sachin Tendulkar has created magic.

Before Tendulkar began the last over, quite a few team-members suggested to him that he bowl leg-spin. He rejected their advice and opted for leg-cutters. Tendulkar had a specific idea in mind. He knew the batsmen would go for big hits, so he thought it best to frustrate them with military medium pace where the ball would appear to arrive and yet not arrive. He had one concern too – that he might bowl a wide. That concern was aggravated when he ran in to bowl the last ball to McMillan. To his own satisfaction, he bowled straight. The last ball was also slightly quicker. Deliberately so, because Sachin knew McMillan, who had watched five balls from the non-striker's end, would expect it to be just as slow as the earlier ones. Sachin succeeded in unsettling McMillan with a faster one, and that too, pitched to perfection. It was intellectual cricket all the way.

As a matter of fact, for contemporary India, it was more than cricket. When things had almost been given up as lost, and when no bowler wanted to chance his arm in the fear that he would be blamed for defeat, Tendulkar had snatched the ball from others and insisted on bowling himself. By doing so, he was representing a courage that the majority of cricket-loving Indians admired, but were themselves hesitant to take in their own spheres of activity and their own roles as citizens because of an ingrained spirit of negativism.

Things were bad enough in India in 1993 and negativism as a whole had seeped into the very fabric of Indian polity. The politicians and the system as a whole had disappointed in a big way. The beginning of the year had seen communal bloodshed in many parts of the country over the Ayodhya dispute; the then Prime Minister, P.V. Narasimha Rao, had been accused of horse-trading to save his government in Parliament; the man accused in the biggest scam that shook the Indian stock market in 1992, the late Harshad Mehta, had said that he had given one crore to the PM, to buy Members of Parliament for the confidence vote; and a member of the judiciary had faced impeachment proceedings. Public spirits were therefore at the lowest ebb.

Winston Churchill's line that India was no nation, that it was just a geographical entity, seemed to have go deeply atched into the Indian psyche. At this point, it was refreshing for Indians to get a powerful jolt from a representative of a new India, who perhaps didn't even know what Churchill had said. Sachin Tendulkar, as the symbol of this new spirit, had turned things around with supreme confidence. He had reversed the popular line in the Indian national language Hindi, *Kuch bhi nahin ho sakta* (Nothing's possible) to *Kuch bhi ho sakta hai* (Anything's possible).

Even if a poll is held today in India to decide one pre-dominant image of national self-assertion from the volatile years of the 1990s, the image of Tendulkar taking up the white ball in the Hero Cup semi-finals and paving the way to victory will definitely prevail over all other images.

At the Hero Cup finals, India met West Indies and notched up a total of 225 for seven. Tendulkar got his highest score of the series – twenty-eight not out – and his friend, Vinod Kambli, top-scored with sixty-eight.

Tendulkar the bowler resurfaced in the finals once again. While Anil Kumble from one end claimed wickets with ease, Sachin took the prize scalp of yet another brilliant batsman, Brian Lara. Lara was batting on thirty-three and looking dangerous when Tendulkar bowled a quicker one that went through his defences and knocked the off-stump out of the ground. With the West Indies bowled out for 123, the Hero Cup was in India's kitty.

*

There's no doubt that Sachin's initiative as a bowler had fetched him the desired results. The initiative was fraught with too much personal risk, because it came at a time when he was not scoring runs. Failure with the ball would have invited more flak. For the sheer pluck he had shown, he deserved appreciation and he got it in full measure.

Almost unavoidably, and as one more price to pay for being Tendulkar, the appreciation soon got undermined due to the apprehension voiced over his batting form. The drying up of runs in one series was okay when it came to the other members of his team; he was expected to get runs every time he went out to bat.

He accepted he wasn't clicking with the bat. He was often in a dilemma, he said. He went out to bat in the thirtieth or sometimes the fortieth over. There was confusion on whether to stay put, or go after the bowling straightaway. He had tried playing shots and it had not worked, he said. The failures didn't result from a lack of seriousness, he pointed out. There were no problems with technique either. It was just that a few failures had added up, and that was making things tougher. All this was a result of deep introspection over his batting performance.

Suggestions then came that he could try doing for India what Brian Lara – not an opener originally – was doing for the West Indies. Lara batted number four in the Tests but had begun to open in the one-dayers. And he was getting lots of runs. Sachin was just as attacking as Lara, and would succeed similarly, it was felt.

Tendulkar too was thinking on the same lines. In fact, he and manager, Ajit Wadekar would often discuss the possibility of his opening and getting the maximum number of overs to deal with the bowlers. Time and again, the team management contemplated the move but did not make it, thinking it would be too much to risk Sachin's wicket early in the innings.

Finally, Sachin had to make the request himself. India left for New Zealand early in 1994 to play four one-dayers and a Test. The Kiwis won the first one-day international at Napier. India had to win the second, to stay in the series. India's opener Navjot Sidhu woke up with a stiff neck on the morning of the second one-dayer at Auckland. India was therefore in trouble before the match could begin.

Wadekar says:

> We had a real problem on hand when Sidhu reported unfit. Just as we were struggling to find a solution, Sachin came up to me and said he'd open. I told him we didn't want to sacrifice his wicket. He wasn't used to opening, I made it clear to him. He told me not to worry. 'I'll play the new ball well,' he said. Many people think I took the initiative of sending him in as opener. That's not true. The initiative was his own. I then discussed the matter with the captain, and we decided to let him open. Before going out to bat, Sachin asked me, 'Sir, how many runs do you expect from me?' I said a hundred, of course. 'The way you play, your hundred will be much quicker than anybody else's,' I told him.

Tendulkar narrowly missed his target, a hundred, at Auckland. Yet his eighty-two, scored off forty-nine balls, was much quicker than anyone else's. And it was an exhibition of murderous batting. New Zealand batted first and got the spectators terribly bored. In 49.4 overs, they got a measly 142.

Sachin walked out to bat with Ajay Jadeja and played the waiting game for the first three-four overs. Once the eye was set, the feet moving rhythmically, and the ball striking the middle, he went on a rampage.

Danny Morrison, then the fastest Kiwi bowler, had taken a hat-trick in the first one-dayer at Napier. He was taken for forty-six runs in six overs. Tendulkar got six boundaries off him, all through refined, orthodox shots, played almost casually but with amazing power. An exasperated Morrison finally bowled Tendulkar an unreachably high bouncer. That was banged in with utter desperation, and its sole motive was to ensure that Sachin's bat got nowhere near the ball. Gavin Larsen was then considered the stingiest of Kiwi bowlers. He was slammed for two sixes, and had to be taken off after his first two overs had cost the Kiwis twenty-four runs. Chris Pringle, Chris Harris and Matthew Hart received the same treatment.

Jadeja got out when the team's score was sixty-one. After that, it was Kambli who stood at the other end. The Indian captain and manager had told the batsmen that the score ought to be hundred by the twenty-fifth over. The hundredth run instead came in the thirteenth over. When Sachin got out at eighty-two, he and Kambli had put in over fifty runs together and brought India within sniffing distance of the target, which was not steep in any case. Every spectator on the ground stood up to applaud as Tendulkar made his way back to the pavilion after a majestic knock that had blown away all the accumulated boredom. His scoring shots went like this: "2,4,4,4,4,3,4,4,4,4,6,4,4,6,4,4,4,4,2,4,2, and 1". New Zealand captain Ken Rutherford, and even the two umpires, Chris King and Brian Aldridge, joined the gasping spectators in their applause.

The innings had a remarkable impact on cricket enthusiasts in New Zealand. Every game in the series thereafter saw a full crowd gathered in the stadium well before the start of play. Nobody wanted to miss out on a possible early onslaught by Tendulkar.

The one-day series was eventually levelled 2-2, and India clearly came out the winner because Tendulkar had emerged as an opener and showed he could frustrate the best of bowlers with early sabotage.

So one more initiative had worked. This one, in fact, had a long-term impact on his, and India's cricketing fortunes. He not only settled into the role of an opener capably but, with the passage of time, went on to get a record number of hundreds and other substantial scores from that position. He was pushed back to number four in 2002, but bounced back into the opening slot with a series of top-quality knocks in the 2003 World Cup.

Tendulkar's desire for constant innovation came to the fore on many occasions in the year 1994. He was now feeling more and more responsible for the team, and his thought processes were geared towards finding new ways for its success. Wadekar says that there were many times that he came up with ideas that were impossible to implement. For instance, during a practice session in New Zealand, Sachin went up to the manager and said he had a plan to cripple the Kiwis. 'Their team has a lot of left-handers. We'll pack the leg side with fielders and attack on the leg. They'll find it hard to score.'

Wadekar told him: 'That's okay, but one also has to bowl.'

As if in response, Tendulkar took a ball in hand, and bowled a few deliveries in the nets to try and show the manager how it could be done.

Wadekar's response was again realistic: 'You can bowl. What about the others? You have to consider the possibility of bowlers bowling wides, no balls, and losing their line and length due to such tactics.'

Wadekar later recalled:

> Sachin's ideas were much appreciated, but I had to sometimes tell him we needed to look at the team's strengths and weaknesses before going ahead with new things. But what I liked

was that he was so positive. Before a team meeting, he would
come up to me and share his ideas, so I could think them over
and then place them before the team. He would not come forth
in the team meeting. He didn't want to take credit for the ideas
he was generating. He just had the benefit of the team at heart.

All the hard thinking about the game, and efforts at improvement,
paid off when Sachin got his long-awaited first one-day hundred in
September 1994 against a strong Australian side in Sri Lanka.

Before India left to play the Singer Cup[2] in Lanka in September
1994, there was talk of how Sachin got off to flying starts and even
reached a good score, but failed to get to the three-figure mark due
to apparent haste. Many games were held out as examples of this
haste. A crucial game against Pakistan in Sharjah in the middle of
1994 stood out in the list and explained why he had still failed to get
a one-day hundred.

Tendulkar had had a rollicking start in this match, standing up
to the Pak pacers comfortably, and thrashing them mercilessly. He
reached his fifty in just over forty deliveries. Wasim Akram was hit for
a six that the bowler himself called "stunning". Tendulkar put his foot
down, took the ball from the middle-stump and hit it over mid-
wicket. But just when he had hit ten fours and three sixes and was
batting unstoppably at seventy-three, he went for a lofted shot
against off-spinner Akram Raza and holed out in the deep. When
Tendulkar was blazing away, Pak captain Salim Malik had feared the
Indians would get 280-plus. Finally, all they got was 219, which was
achieved by the Pakistanis without difficulty.

Tendulkar was never a self-perpetuating batsman. He was used
to taking risks and loved playing his cricket that way. However, he
would sometimes get out in crucial situations due to careless strokes,
and would come in for flak for lack of concentration. No one really
wanted him to bottle up his aggression. The only thing suggested,
and rightly, was that he should not be throwing it all away with his
own hands.

Sanjay Manjrekar, a crucial member of India's batting hierarchy
during Tendulkar's first five years on the international circuit, was a

privileged and close witness to Sachin's attacking batting style. He was unfortunately also a tormented observer of the young man's exasperating aberrations bang in the middle of some poetic batting. Manjrekar says:

> My partnerships with Sachin were often frustrating. The most frustrating was the one we had at Sharjah, against Pakistan. Pakistan used to beat us regularly at the time. I remember that in one game, Sachin and I were at the crease, and we were cruising along, all set to win the game for India. I told him it was just a matter of a couple of overs and we'd be through. The Pakistanis had dropped their heads and had given up. I remember telling him in the middle that we would be heroes back home if we won the match. Suddenly, out of the blue as it were, he played a wild shot and was caught in the deep. Our dreams were shattered. Pakistan came back into the game and we lost.

These aberrations were all right in the early part of his career. Now, as vice-captain and backbone of the line-up, his accountability was greater. Cricket was also rapidly gaining its existing high profile status in India. An example of how seriously it was being taken became evident when the Indian team once gathered at an airport terminal a few hours before flying off for an overseas tour. One of the team members cracked a joke, and everybody, including Sachin, burst out laughing. Out of nowhere, an angry man approached the players and, pointing a finger, yelled: 'It's not even four days since you lost. And you're shamelessly laughing.' The team had indeed lost a tournament two months ago, but was embarking on a new tour with renewed hope, enthusiasm and a necessary lightening of the spirit. Sachin and his teammates however realized that the cricket-lover still wanted them to be in a state of mourning; the defeat had hurt the follower so much.

Tendulkar luckily did not let worries show on his face as a result of such experiences. He only picked the most important lesson: do your bit for the victory; don't throw away your wicket.

Talking about Sachin's first century in ODIs in the Singer Cup contest against Australia in 1994, he hit Glenn McGrath, Craig McDermott and Shane Warne fiercely at the start. However, after reaching half-a-century, he slowed down. That meant that he was playing for the big one. Kambli, who himself scored forty-three not out, was at the other end as Sachin approached his first ODI hundred. He continually encouraged Sachin, asked him to punish the loose deliveries and play the good ones according to merit. Vinod held Sachin in a warm embrace when the latter reached his ton. The barrier had been broken, the critics silenced, and Warne, by this time the world's leading spinner, had been hit for fifty-three runs in his ten overs.

Tendulkar's Test scores were also getting better. He got a classy 142 against a Sri Lankan team that was walloped 3-0 in a Test series in India in the middle of 1994. This firmed up his average for the first time in the region of fifty, positioning him statistically in the company of the world's seventeen all-time best batsmen.

He consolidated his position there with excellent performances against the West Indies team that came to India late in 1994 for a three-Test series. Against an attack led by Courtney Walsh and Kenneth Benjamin, Tendulkar got 34, 85, 179, 54, 40 and 10.

His friend Vinod's run of successes unfortunately came to an end in the series against West Indies. Kambli got a mere sixty-four runs from six innings, and was made to jump up uncomfortably too often by Walsh, Benjamin and others who consistently bowled chest-high to him.

While Tendulkar soon went on to strengthen his position and indeed came out on top in international cricket, Kambli just as quickly lost his way, more due to his unruliness than anything else.

Vinod Ganpat Kambli had truly sucked himself out of the mires of circumstance and set his talent up for show. He was poor and lived with his parents and two brothers in a tiny shanty in the Mumbai suburb of Kanjurmarg. He struggled with his heavy kit every day in the overcrowded local train that he had to take to reach Shivaji Park for practice. He would mostly sit in the brake-van, along with the vegetable and milk vendors, the fishermen and fisherwomen, and other stray labourers who'd all be packed in like sardines, struggling with their heavy wares and the strong smell of fish.

He did not allow the economic deprivation to kill the fire within; he stoked it and brought amazing firepower into his stylish batting. Vinod was a "destroyer" of the cricket ball. Whenever Sachin batted in school, his attitude towards the bowler was: 'Okay, I take up your challenge. I'm going to hit you really hard.' Vinod's attitude was: 'How dare you bowl to me?' Between the two of them, aggression was a common quality. Vinod's was laced with contempt for the bowling. He was in the West Indian mould, the marauding batsman who enjoyed each one of his lethal assaults and enjoyed all the more when his flamboyant weapons got the other side down and out.

Sachin raced ahead of him and played the Ranji Trophy and Test cricket at a very early age. Vinod continued to score consistently and got into the Mumbai Ranji Trophy team also at the very young age of seventeen. It was only the comparison with Sachin's entry into the international arena that made it look late.

Kambli hit the first ball he faced in Ranji Trophy, from Bharat Mistry of Gujarat, for a towering straight six. Dilip Vengsarkar was then at the other end. He was stunned.

Vinod also began his Test career fantastically, and with a string of big scores against England, Sri Lanka and Zimbabwe, collected a thousand Test runs faster than any other batsman in the history of Indian cricket. In world cricket, only Don Bradman, Everton Weekes and Herbert Sutcliffe had done better in this regard.

Sachin was in fact asked if he was feeling the pressure owing to Vinod's runaway success. He rubbished the suggestion. 'I'm only too glad he's getting so many runs. There is no competition between us. We only complement each other,' he said.

Once, in a single over, Kambli hit Shane Warne for twenty-two runs. The final ball of the over was bowled well by the leg-spinner, and Kambli stretched fully forward to offer a forward defensive stroke. Sunil Gavaskar, then the coach of the Indian team, nodded his head vigorously in approval. Along with the runs, there were signs of developing patience as well.

Once firmly established in the Indian team, Kambli made the famous comment that while Sachin took the elevator, he had taken the stairs to success.

Yet success and stardom did not polish away his rougher excrescences. He cried copiously when India left the field due to a crowd disruption during the 1996 World Cup semi-final against Sri Lanka, but the schmaltzy sight did not pacify the selectors who took grave exception to his off-field behaviour. During the tournament, he woke captain Azharuddin in the middle of one night after a drunken brawl. It sent a wrong message, which was also wrongly taken. Kambli was dropped on disciplinary grounds, though his average in the Indian team was second only to Tendulkar's in the World Cup.

As for his game, much was made of his weakness against short-pitched bowling. Indeed he had a glaring weakness against the away-going delivery that was brutally exposed by the West Indians and other teams as well. But many others with more glaring technical flaws stayed longer in the Indian side. Some continue to do so. Kambli too would have stayed, if only he had said no to a lot of things.

Personally, he let himself slip away. He developed a drinking problem, spent more time at the J49 club in Mumbai than at the nets. Indeed, he often did not even attend net practice. For one Times Shield final in Mumbai, Kambli arrived at the ground fifteen minutes after the game had started. He was the captain of his team, and even that had apparently made no difference to him.

He loved the good things in life. Oddly, in a country whose middle and upper classes were by then known to spend generously, that could be something of a sin. His loud and colourful clothes, two flashy rings dangling from the earlobes, the thick gold chain around the neck, his in-the-vogue hairstyle and a little goatee, carefully cultivated, became topics for derisive comments. His love for loud music was ridiculed, and his general enjoyment of life was anathema to the conservative cricket establishment. The sparkling earrings were even exploited for their own benefit by tradition-worshipping political leaders, who told hugely-attended rallies that the studs were like those worn by the Peshwas, the eighteenth-century Maratha rulers known more for their extravagance and decadent ways than for governance. His independence of spirit was already causing some people excruciating headaches; he sadly gifted to them a host of real, solid arguments that they could use against him to put him down.

Vinod Kambli obviously needed guidance at every point. Many people didn't know how to deal with him. Wadekar, during his tenure as manager, found the right formula. With patience and sincerity, he forged a relationship with Vinod on the basis of a warm, friendly attitude. Acting the opposite of a taskmaster, he made him aware of his capabilities and taught him to put performance over everything else. After Wadekar went, there was no one to give him that kind of special treatment.

When Tendulkar became captain in 1996, Kambli was picked over Sourav Ganguly for the Sahara Cup against Pakistan in Toronto. His selection invited charges of nepotism against Sachin. 'I have no friends on the field, only off it,' Sachin replied.

Vinod got dropped again and got back in the team in 1998 only to suffer a horrendous ankle injury while fielding as a substitute against Zimbabwe at Cuttack. His foot did a 180-degree turn and, to make things worse, he fell on top of it, bringing his whole body weight to bear on it. The result was a fracture, a dislocation and two torn ligaments. As Vinod writhed in pain on the field, Tendulkar ran up to him, had one look at his twisted ankle and, shocked, buried his face in his hands.

'The injury had a big psychological impact on him. It must be still playing on his mind. That was the biggest blow to his career,' Wadekar told me. What also made a lot of difference was that when he was first left out of the Indian squad for the 1996 tour to England, Rahul Dravid and Sourav Ganguly came into the side and cemented their places for the long haul.

Kambli did return to the Indian team for a brief while in 1999, 2000 and last in October 2001, but in his coach Ramakant Acharekar's words, he was by then into *"adam tadam* batting", meaning, wild and reckless batting. He somehow seemed unable to play the ball down. The year 2001 also saw the emergence of two solid players in the Indian team: Virender Sehwag and Yuvraj Singh. Two more places were gone.

It is unlikely Kambli will make a comeback again. He will be missed by world cricket, because for all the negatives, he was a man of cheer, colour and so much spontaneity. He and Tendulkar were once batting together in a school game at Mumbai's Azad Maidan. Up at the striker's end, Vinod, who was about to take guard, spotted, through the corner of his eye, a kite in the air. Cut off from its umbilical cord, it was flying across the field, sinking. Banishing the thought of getting ready to face the next ball, Vinod hurriedly took off his gloves and got hold of the kite's *manja* (string). He first tugged at the string to find out what adjustments the kite needed before it could be flown. It appeared to be in fine shape still. So he yanked the *manja*, made the kite shoot up and began flying it! He had an expression of delight on his face and a trace of melancholy, perhaps because he had no wooden *phirki* to untangle more *manja* and send the kite soaring higher.

Tendulkar first watched unbelievingly from the other end, and then broke out into uncontrollable laughter. He had not seen anything like this in an official game and was not likely to see such a thing in future at least from any other cricketer, anywhere. Kambli soon won for himself a resounding slap from coach Acharekar, back in the tent. Tendulkar, though, couldn't get over it for a long, long time. He still calls it the most hilarious incident he's ever seen.

Cricket today is filled with cold, zombie-like men. By and large an aggressive lot, they abuse, stare menacingly at the opponent, clench their jaws and behave as if the field is a war zone. Cricket needs humans with the quality of colour, liveliness, a certain lightness of spirit and a touch of vulnerability. Kambli could've provided all this. Many teams playing India still wonder why Kambli isn't in the team. Only he can answer that.

Commentating on television during the 2003 World Cup, Vinod Kambli called Sachin and Sehwag 'Ram' and 'Shyam'. Kambli was the original Shyam. But unlike the Shyam (Krishna) in the great Indian epic *Mahabharata*, he didn't quite mix his colour with a steadfastness of resolve.

---

1 *Ekach Shatkar*, 15-31 March 1993.
2 India, Sri Lanka, Pakistan and Australia competed for the Singer Cup, the first big one-day tournament to be held in Sri Lanka.

Whose bat is best?

I have been up against tough competition all my
life. I wouldn't know how to get along without it.

– Walt Disney

The best is the enemy of the good.

– Voltaire

The technical brilliance of Sunil Gavaskar, the casual attitude of Sir
Viv Richards, the silken grace of David Gower, the streetfighter
sensibilities of Javed Miandad and the bulldog tenacity of Allan
Border defined batsmanship for an entire generation of cricket
watchers throughout the 1980s.

While Gavaskar in his heroic last Test innings at Bangalore in
1987 laid down for the nth time a batting benchmark, the other four
continued playing into the early Nineties but made their exits from
the scene after the first three years. They had done their jobs as
torch-bearers. It was now for a new set of batsmen to take over. This
meant not merely being proficient but setting the standards and
determining the highest levels to which the art of batting could go.

The game's followers had begun their search for replacements
well before each one of these top five faded out. They got Tendulkar
in their frames as soon as he appeared on the scene in 1989. While
they zoomed in for a closer look during the first few years of his
career, he steadily grew in stature. By the time he exploded as an
opener in one-dayers, he had legitimately staked his claim for entry
into the elite category.

A left-hander from Trinidad, Brian Charles Lara, emerged on
the world scene in 1992 with a magnificent double hundred against

Australia and announced that he was in the same league, and seriously posed stiff competition to Sachin.

In the same year, a lanky Pakistani from Multan, Inzamam-ul-Haq, walked imperiously on to the wicket in the World Cup and won it for his country, declaring that Sachin and Lara had both better watch out for him.

A couple of years after Lara and Inzy had firmly entrenched themselves in the international arena, there was consensus in the cricket world that they along with Sachin were the world's most exciting batting talent. The Mark Waughs, Aravinda de Silvas and Jayasuriyas were of course around, but their craft was revealed in its full splendour only a couple of years later, and even then, they were said to be *nearing* Sachin and Lara's levels with their spectacular successes with the bat. In 1994, Inzamam though was believed to be in step with the Indian and the West Indian.

The shortlisting of the three youngsters – Lara was twenty-five in 1994, Inzamam twenty-four and Sachin twenty-one – inevitably led to comparisons. A debate was launched: whose bat was best? It became an engrossing debate soon, because the strengths of each player was substantive. Tendulkar's story was such that had it been the work of a writer's imagination; it could've been dismissed as too fantastic and improbable by many. Ranji debut at fifteen, success against Imran Khan, Wasim Akram, Waqar Younis and Abdul Qadir at sixteen and then continuing successes marked by a high level of consistency. Soon as he touched twenty, he had also become the man around whom the entire Indian batting revolved. He seemed able to do everything – play flowing strokes, launch a savage assault, graft for runs or just stay put. He could demonstrate orthodox technique, but if the situation so demanded, could take a good-length ball from outside the off-stump and hoick it over mid-wicket. The trouble was that he did not quite carry the innings through to the end. Just when it appeared he'd take the game away, he would chuck his wicket.

This was where Lara appeared to be scoring over him. By the time Lara came to India late in 1994, he had got only three Test hundreds. Yet all of them were, to put it mildly, big. Unlike Sachin, he wasn't happy if he reached the century mark. He wanted to go on. At Sydney in 1993, West Indies were two down for hardly anything in response to an Australian total in excess of 500 when Lara walked out to bat. His team had badly lost the second Test at Melbourne just a few days ago, and the West Indies record at the SCG was nothing to boast about either: they had last won here sixty years ago, and out of the eleven tests played on the same venue earlier, they had surrendered eight.

As was obvious, a twenty-three-year-old playing his fifth Test was expected to feel the heat. What Lara instead proceeded to do was plain slaughter. The line 'hitting the ball all over the place' is often used by commentators slackly, for want of a better description for a good innings. Lara brought out its real meaning. Aussie captain Allan Border, who watched haplessly as even a greyish cloud cover couldn't stop the left-hander, said: 'For sheer crisp hitting of the ball into the gaps, it was as good an innings as you'd ever see.' Rohan Kanhai of the West Indies, one of the most elegant hitters of all time, called it one of the greatest innings he had ever seen. 'Back foot, front foot, timing, placement, against both spin and fast bowlers. He was marvellous.' When he was on 277, he was dismissed in what appeared the only way possible. He fell short of his crease as Carl Hooper sent him back on a call for a single at cover.

In the second Test of the 1994 series against England, Lara set the Bourda ground at Georgetown, Guyana, alight by scoring 167 in 210 balls. Though nobody in the crowd knew, Lara was throughout the innings troubled by an itching in the eye that needed drops. Doctors said it was a condition that sometimes took care of itself and sometimes called for a minor surgery. Lara had first felt the problem in the first Test at Jamaica. He had had difficulty in picking up Devon Malcolm's bowling and had to be removed from the slips. He dropped two catches, both of which had come into the pit of his stomach. Yet he missed nothing in his masterful knock. Even after he got to a hundred, he looked not satiated but hungrier.

In April 1994, in the fifth Test of the same series at Antigua, he shattered Sir Gary Sobers' record for the highest individual Test score. That innings of 375 too had its origins in a crisis. Two days before the Test began, the Windies had suffered their first defeat at Kensington Oval in fifty-nine years, and Lara himself had got out in a reckless fashion when the situation called for discipline. He came in for a lot of criticism for his extravagant shots. Lara had a bigger responsibility at Antigua because his captain Richie Richardson and vice-captain Desmond Haynes were not playing.

The West Indies were eleven for one when he came out to bat. In a few minutes, they were twelve for two. England's two fast bowlers, Angus Fraser and Andrew Caddick, were looking good. They could run through the West Indian line-up. England's plan was to bowl short to Lara and force him to swivel and give a catch at square-leg. They knew that was the only shot he played without adequate movement of the feet, and that was also the only one he hit in the air. So they sent in a good amount of short stuff. He initially revealed a straight bat. The moment he was confident that he was sighting the ball well and his feet were moving right, he brought out the pull, the hook and a range of drives. There were many glorious back-foot drives straight to the ropes, and he pierced the field beautifully, placing the ball in the smallest of gaps between mid-off and extra cover.

It is true there wasn't much in the wicket, but the outfield was so slow that it held up the most powerful of shots. It blocked Lara's strokes too but even when beyond 300, he ran his twos and threes with determination.

As Sir Gary embraced Lara after his record was broken, he said the Trinidad youngster was the only modern cricketer who had looked capable of besting his own 365, made way back in 1958. Just six weeks later, Lara blasted his way to a 501 on a county ground.

Lara was ruthless with all types of bowling, and the enormously high backlift notwithstanding, had elegance of movement and the gift of timing. His batting was also laced with a subtle tenderness, a tenderness associated only with the styles of batting princes like him and Sachin. Above all, Lara had shown the ability to curb his fits of energy; he could be relied upon to ensure the team's challenge wouldn't get buried. Compared with Tendulkar , Lara gave bowlers very few chances. Tendulkar often said of himself that sometimes he would just hit the ball, see it in the air and walk back dejectedly, wondering why, all of a sudden, when he was doing so well, he had to do that silly thing. In case he went past hundred, Sachin would take too many liberties.

Lara's three innings were a study in contrast. At Sydney, he had not allowed the bowlers anything. Yes, he was dropped once, but that was when he was on 172, and the stroke he had played then was a cruel and ferocious cut off Merv Hughes that Steve Waugh couldn't hold on to. Finally, the Australians saw him depart only after he tried a suicidal run.

With all the irritation in his eyes in the Guyana Test, he saw the cherry like a football. The keeper got a stumping chance well after he had crossed his hundred and made a mess of it.

The Antigua knock that lasted thirteen hours was chanceless and also nearly flawless. Jack Russell was Lara's closest observer from behind the stumps. He noted Lara's little deviations from correctness on his way to 375. When the third new ball was taken, Lara played a risky shot over the covers. Russell said that if Alec Stewart had been fourteen feet tall, his hand might have reached the ball. When England had taken off their slips, Lara had deliberately edged one, and Russell had touched it with the tip of his finger. For two balls that were very short and wide, Lara could not keep himself from playing the square cut. Both times, he hit under the ball. There was also a shout for a catch at first slip, which Russell said was 'out of sheer desperation'. Two times, Lara was beaten on to his pads, and once, without really intending, he played a ball in the air on the on-side. That fell a long distance away from any fielder. 'Faultless,' Russell finally said. 'We have perhaps seen the perfect innings, forget about it being the biggest.'

The Pakistani youngster, Inzamam-ul-Haq, who was competing with men of such class, had single-handedly turned around the 1992 World Cup semi-final. He had walked into a tense situation to face an inspired New Zealand side. Imran Khan and Salim Malik were already back in the pavilion, but Javed Miandad was still at the other end. In his company, Inzamam carved a sparkling sixty off thirty-seven balls. He also scored a valuable forty-two in the finals that Pakistan won, leading Imran Khan to suggest that he would soon be the world's best batsman.

Timing and skilful wristwork were the essence of Inzamam's batting, and he had a knack of finding gaps with flamboyance. Talented he was, no doubt, but he was certainly not in the same league as Tendulkar and Lara. That was because he played far too casually, often not bending enough, and not bringing his bat and foot together. He did not shuffle as much as a batsman needed to in order to get in the line of the ball. Apart from causing a host of technical problems, this made him a perpetual LBW candidate. Besides, he was anything but athletic, a terrible runner between wickets, and remains so till date. Although it is to be conceded that he remains one of the most attractive batsmen in the world today, there is a pretty sharp difference between the good and the great. Despite creating ripples of excitement by his batting prowess early in his career, Inzamam, sadly for world cricket, could not cross the divide in all these years.

The excitement created by him still wasn't half as enormous as the one whipped up by the other two men when the West Indies arrived in India late in 1994. The idea of a Sachin versus Lara battle for the first time in a Test series was so attractive that the media promptly labelled the whole series a "Tendulkar-Lara" showpiece. Watch out for the Trinidadian hero, the Indians were warned from the day Lara got his world record. Watch out for the little fella from Bombay, the Caribbeans were told from the day Tendulkar destroyed the New Zealand attack in Auckland.

The thrill of comparative scrutiny entered even the Indian dressing room at the start of the series. Wadekar told me:

> The bug of comparison had hit the dressing room. Our players would regularly discuss Sachin and Lara's similarities and differences. Sachin heard everything but would not

bother. He did not allow the talk to affect him. He focused on
his game.

The highest Lara got in that Test series was ninety. He didn't
score much in the one-dayers either. Tendulkar, in contrast, was in
fine form. In the Tests, he got a 179 at Nagpur. An encouraging sign
in view of the future was that he was deeply unhappy at having
missed out on a double hundred and said so in unambiguous terms.
In Mumbai, he scored eighty-five when the Indian batting was
crumbling around him on a difficult wicket. The track was so bad
that some West Indian batsmen were wearing chest guards even
against spinners. Tendulkar went in to bat in the second innings
when nobody except his Mumbai mate Sanjay Manjrekar seemed to
have a clue about. Sachin played aggressively, driving, cutting and
flicking the nigglingly accurate Walsh and giving leg-spinner Dhanraj
such a charge that he had to be taken off before he bowled too many.
Sir Gary Sobers called it one of the most impressive innings he had
seen. In the long run too, he got the better of Lara, largely because
of his unwavering focus on the game.

Lara, on the other hand, found success and its attendant
demons hard to fight. His story in the ten years since his world record
has been similar to that of an average Indian cricket lover. He has
either been too high or too low, hardly ever in the middle. Whenever
he's batted with complete focus on his game, he's been unstoppable
and a match-winner in every sense of the term. But his frequent
skipping of tours, his emotional entanglements, the psychological
problems that forced him to consult a psychiatrist, the inexorable
pull of pressure and so many other factors have deprived cricket of
what could've been a "greater" Lara. The contrasting approaches Lara
and Tendulkar took to their lives and cricket in the two years, 1994
and 1995 were in themselves sharp pointers to what was in store for
each one of them.

Lara's problems began almost the moment he played a pull to
the square-leg boundary to surpass Sobers. Within minutes the
Antigua press box was flooded with calls from many organizations

wanting to hand over cheques to him. When he went home to Trinidad the next week, the gifts came in an avalanche. The national airline offered him free travel till he covered 3.75 lakh miles. A walk in Port-of-Spain was named the Brian Lara Promenade. Along with a car and free calls on his mobile, he was gifted a lovely plot of land right in front of the Queen's Park Savannah. And the country's highest award, the Trinity Cross, was his.

When he headed for Warwickshire a few weeks later, there was a 50,000 pounds contract waiting for him. In England, Lara became the top story for the media hounds, and his 501 contributed to things getting further out of hand. Every move of his was scrutinized in a way usually reserved for British celebrities. If he went to dinner with a woman, it hit the headlines. If he had a headache, it was on the news pages. If he smiled, it made for a good photograph and if he frowned, there was always a speculative story waiting to be done. The Madame Tussaud's panel decided to "immortalize" him in wax and place his figure alongside those of Viv Richards, Nigel Mansell and Severiano Ballesteros in the Garden Party area of the exhibition.

Soon Lara was carrying two mobile phones in London (according to a Caribbean writer, an unconfirmed three). He had two lines at his Birmingham flat. Apparently, all the phones rang all the time, and he'd be busy talking to Trinidad, Florida, South Africa and some other place at the same time. Everyone and his/her uncle and aunt wanted a piece of Brian Lara.

Sobers saw the danger and sent out warning signals. He said Lara now did not have to worry about his batting. That would look after itself. He had to see that he was not exploited. He needed to carefully handle the glory, the hero worship, and above all, the windfall in terms of money. Sobers had belief in Lara's intelligence, but he asked him to be on his guard with "bandwagon-jumpers" who would praise him one day and be the first to put him down the next.

Lara, alas, slipped. The runs came infrequently, there were conflicts with the team management, he pulled out of tours for personal reasons and there were constant reports of fallouts with his captains. Things came to a point where he scowled: 'Cricket is ruining my life.'

How did Tendulkar treat the same period? For him, like for Lara, 1994 had been what Richie Benaud muttered while describing Lara's cover drives, 'shimply shuperb.' He had had a dream start as opener in the one-dayers, had got his first one-day hundred and had performed excellently against the West Indies. Sure, international status had not come to him with as sudden and unrelenting an aggression as it had for Lara, but since his Test debut, Tendulkar in India had had all eyes turned towards him no matter where he went and all cameras focused firmly on him. All his activities were watched closely. Lara's case became an odd one because it was the first such case outside India. In Tendulkar's country, successful cricketers from the national team had no option but to face the harsh glare. And the one who emerged a superstar at a very young age in an era of TV was subjected to even stricter scrutiny.

Towards the end of the year, Tendulkar got down to addressing some of the most crucial concerns about his cricket. He acknowledged he was throwing away his wicket just when he had good chances to make big scores. He had to pay better attention to building his innings, he conceded. He had already in the one-dayers started slowing down after reaching half-a-century, he pointed out. In the Tests, he had to get substantial counts. 'I must not just get big hundreds, but double hundreds and maybe triple hundreds if it is possible,' he thought out aloud after he got 179 against the West Indies at Nagpur.

When he got three zeroes in a row – the first in the Singer Cup final in Colombo and then two in the first two one-dayers against the Windies – he made it clear that he had played rashly, and that no youngster should follow what he did. He had got a hundred in the earlier game, so in the Singer Cup final he had suffered from an overdose of confidence, he said. He had underestimated his opponent, which was a terrible thing to do, and had tried to hit over the top. In the first one-dayer against the West Indies, he had got a truly good ball. In the second one, he said, he was impatient to get off the mark because of the two blobs he had accumulated. He chased a ball that was far away from the off-stump. He should have left it, he just had to stay there for a while and things would have been all right, he felt.

While Lara one day, shockingly, picked up his cell phone on the ground when fielding for Warwickshire, Tendulkar too got talking in the middle. Without the phone of course. Sometimes, he got talking to the number ten or eleven batsman to learn from him a few lessons about his own batting. He was asked why he took the views of the last two batsmen. They were playing international cricket for a while, he said, they may have perceptive observations to make, they could perhaps see things that he couldn't about his batting. It was important to listen, he stressed, though the final decision to act on suggestions was his own.

If Sobers was saying a word or two to Lara, Gavaskar in India was consistently talking tough to Sachin. In the matter of his dismissals owing to rash shots, Gavaskar severely criticized those who said 'Sachin should be left alone.' Should we all be happy with Sachin blasting four consecutive boundaries and then getting out trying to hit one more boundary off the next ball, he asked. Why should people be happy with sixteen runs when he could score '100 more, 200 or 400 for that matter?' Every Tendulkar run meant more pleasure to those watching, so the more the merrier, he argued.

Gavaskar said players like Lara and Tendulkar could not be asked to give up their aggression as that would be like killing their basic instinct. But Sachin needed to be choosy with his shots and not get carried away by previous strokes. He needed to put a price on his wicket, and given his talent, that could not be less than the three-figure mark.

The Little Master shrewdly used an example that Sachin would understand best – that of Sachin's childhood idol, John McEnroe. McEnroe had won only as many titles as Mats Wilander. But if it was universally accepted that McEnroe was more talented, how would the ratio be allowed to remain? The fact that the equation existed meant that McEnroe had not made full use of his capabilities, he had been carried away by things that incensed him. Therefore Tendulkar needed to marry his innate genius with logic. After all, nobody wanted just flashes of brilliance from Sachin but solid performances. Tendulkar accepted that "Mr. Gavaskar" was right, and most importantly, that he was saying all this for his own good. He would try to work on all the things suggested, he assured Sunil.

Given its normally punishing annual schedule, India did not play much international cricket in 1995. Yet Sachin seemed to have worked on those suggestions. After the series against the West Indies ended early in 1995, there was a triangular one-day series at home with the Windies and New Zealand as also with some other teams. He got two centuries in that series, one against each opponent. In April of 1995 India went to Sharjah again for a triangular tournament, with Pakistan and Sri Lanka as their opponents. He scored a hundred in a league game against Lanka and in the final against the same team that India won by eight wickets, he got forty-one. In Sharjah, Tendulkar became one of the youngest in the world to get 3,000 runs in ODIs.

Soon he returned to India to play the Ranji Trophy. He had missed it the previous year, when his team won the title after a ten-year gap, because of his international commitments. Appointed as Mumbai captain, he helped his side retain the trophy by scoring a hundred in each innings of the final against Punjab. The first ton came in eighty-three balls, the second in sixty-six. In all, he got five centuries from seven innings in the Ranji Trophy at an average of 122.28.

Lara meanwhile had carried a very moderate Trinidad & Tobago team to victory in the Red Stripe Cup in 1994 almost entirely on his own. He had scored three hundreds in the tournament, and all of them had been in keeping with his high-scoring targets – above 150. However, instead of repeating it the next year, he seemed to be losing his moorings.

In India, before the Ranji final, Mumbai played the Wills Trophy one-day final against Haryana. Given fifty overs to get 263, they reached the target in the thirty-seventh over, losing only one wicket. Tendulkar had scored 116 of those runs.

New Zealand toured India late in 1995 but most of the matches were interrupted by rain. Sachin got only one fifty in three Tests and one in five one-dayers. India won the Test series 1-0 and the one-day series 3-2. A slightly younger Tendulkar might have been unduly perturbed by some ordinary scores against his name. Not any more. He said he had taken note of his mistakes. The vacillating balance of body weight had caused a bit of bother, but 'All I need is one big innings to sort things out.' Torrential disturbance in the face of failure is the recipe for further failure. The better approach was to find out the little adjustments that were going wrong. And set them right.

After all, cricket was all about approach.

Tendulkar's approach in the Kiwis' early tour game against Mumbai had itself pointed to his increasing maturity. That match was held under peculiar circumstances. Soon after the New Zealand team touched the Indian shores, their manager Glenn Turner had wondered if the team could last five days against the hosts in three Tests. There was more to that remark than met the eye. It was more cautious than self-deprecatory. He did not want to make fancy declarations but wanted a potentially good team to focus more on the field. It was also suspected that the shrewd Turner wanted Indians to become absolutely complacent before the Kiwis laid their trap.

The New Zealand-Mumbai contest was to be followed by the first Test. Mumbai had three Test players in Sachin Tendulkar, Sanjay Manjrekar and Vinod Kambli respectively. The Kiwis wanted to get a good feel of them, and give them a bad time, before the big games.

For Sachin, the New Zealanders placed three men on the boundary and kept bowling on middle and leg. They wanted him to step out and hit over the top. He was aware of that option but thought it unnecessary. One, it would be a clear response to a trap. Two, he wanted to get some practice against the visitors, and three, he wanted to face all their bowlers before the Tests. So he hung around and had a quiet but comfortable stay in the middle for thirty-nine. He timed the ball well, took ones and twos and played within himself.

By now, captain Azhar was so convinced of Tendulkar's dependability that he began to hand over more and more responsibility to him. Azhar admitted he was leaning a lot on the vice-captain. At all training camps, in particular, he left the supervision of the team to Sachin along with coach Ajit Wadekar. Sachin made sure that nobody deviated from the fitness regimen, Azhar said.

*

As had happened with Brian Lara, Sachin too was now offered real big money for his iconic status. He had been introduced to the head honcho of WorldTel, the late Mark Mascarenhas, by common friend Ravi Shastri at a Bangalore pub. This was sometime in the second half of 1995. In October 1995, Mascarenhas asked for and obtained exclusive rights to the Tendulkar name for five years. The deal signed with Tendulkar was then worth $7.5 million, which translated into Rs 31.5 crore, and later reportedly renewed for twice the amount.

Indian sports followers were aware that tennis champs on the global circuit pocketed a million dollars as appearance fees and that some heavyweight championship boxing bouts were worth a hundred million dollars. They also knew that golf and motor racing could boast of sums that looked overly inflated. But they had seen nothing like this in their country, not even in its most popular sport, cricket. When Ravi Shastri won an Audi as Man of the Series in the Benson & Hedges World Championships, it was seen as a momentous gain. If, at the end of Kapil Dev's career, some businessman declared that he would give the bowler a thousand-odd rupees for every wicket he had taken, it was considered an extraordinary amount. Tendulkar's deal represented for India a step beyond the most fertile unimaginable.

In the same year, Indian chess player Vishwanathan Anand had won half a million dollars after he lost in a title match against Gary Kasparov. That was the highest an Indian sportsperson had made as prize money in an event. Here, it was not prize money, it was money for the potential marketability of the name Tendulkar. Mascarenhas said he wanted to cultivate the name into a "corporation".

Sachin's status as India's most popular sportsperson and hero of everyone from the bicycle-buyer to the Mercedes owner was no doubt at the core of WorldTel's decision to bank on him, but the deal had as much to do with the spread of satellite TV and cable links, the astounding rise in adspend among corporates in India and the increasing influx of multinationals who were more than willing to pump in huge amounts to tap an exploding market of a consumerist middle class. Before he signed the contract, Sachin was already endorsing six products: Boost, Pepsi, Gillette, Action Shoes, Bajaj, Band Aid and VISA. That number was expected to shoot up significantly.

Would this record deal affect Tendulkar's cricket, was the question raised across India. The plainly envious said he wasn't worth so many zeroes, the genuinely concerned said he ought to keep his head intact, his feet on *terra firma* and concentrate on cricket, and those who knew him closely, said the money would increase his drive. The cynical pointed to the performance clause in the contract. The simplest condition was that he had to be in the Indian team. That could possibly bring in pressure.

Tendulkar's response to the riches was markedly dissimilar to that of Lara. He did do a lot of advertisements and now even appears to be overexposed in ads, but he wasn't swept off his feet. Of course, unlike Lara, who didn't have a steady family life after his father's early death, Sachin had a stable and strong middle-class family background that gave him a certain value system and a rootedness that would help him hold ground. But money can do the weirdest things to the sanest and most securely rooted humans, and Sachin was after all human (Matthew Hayden was also not around then to call him God).

Among other things, Indian cricketers have often been criticized for their obsession with money earned through endorsements. Cricket lovers and the media have often felt that endorsements have a direct impact on their performance as the ads can distract them from their real calling. One of Sachin's key achievements is that he has proven wrong the assumption that the more the endorsements, the more a cricketer is likely to lose his form. Of all of Indian cricketers right from C.K. Nayudu, who as the first superstar Indian cricketer did ads way back in the 1930s, he has done the maximum number of endorsements, almost, as said earlier, to the point of overkill. His game, instead of plummeting or suffering to any extent, has only gotten better.

That, apart from his cricket, is the biggest advertisement for Sachin Tendulkar.

*

Still, just as Lara has lessons to learn from the Indian, he has lessons to teach him too. Much to the delight of cricket lovers the world over, Lara did not simply fold up. He faltered, fell, and recovered himself. This cycle ran its length quite a few times. Then, in 1999, a new life in cricket began.

Lara returned to the Caribbean a leader of a team thrashed 0-5 in South Africa. He was appointed captain on probation for the first two Tests at home against Steve Waugh's Australia. In the first Test in his hometown Port-of-Spain, West Indies collapsed for a disgraceful fifty-one in the second innings. The second Test was in Jamaica, and the crowd there weren't too happy with him, because he had succeeded local boy Courtney Walsh as captain. Australia got 256 and West Indies appeared to be crumbling at four down for less than forty when Lara re-emerged. He got his first fifty in 140 deliveries but then launched a frontal attack. When he played the ball that got him his hundredth run, scores of delirious Jamaicans ran on to the ground to congratulate him, never mind if he replaced Walsh as skipper.

There were many superb hits in his knock of 213 but two balls underlined its character. Glenn McGrath brought one up nastily, striking Lara on one side of his head. He lost his balance and fell. There was a feeling of shock all around. He got up and cover-drove McGrath with such a sting, the ball went hissing through the grass to the boundary. It was spirit all the way, and it helped his team to level the series.

In the next Test at Barbados, the West Indies, asked to get 308 for victory, lost three quick wickets on the fourth evening. Lara was then two not out. When the score read 105 for five on the final day, Lara decided the only way out was to step up the gear. His bat became a flashing blade. Jimmy Adams stood at the other end for a long time, but when Curtly Ambrose came to the crease, two wickets were left and there were sixty runs to get. Gentle giant Ambrose defended for over sixty minutes as Lara went berserk. Close to the target, Lara edged but the ball went just past Ian Healy's gloves. Ambrose was out and Walsh arrived when seven big runs were still needed. Walsh survived a beautiful in-swinging yorker and many other balls. A no-ball and a wide helped. Finally, Lara sent one through the covers and delightedly ran to his teammates, bat in one hand and stump in another, for a collective, emotional embrace.

That score of 153 not out is widely regarded as one of the best knocks in a chase ever. In the same year, Tendulkar played a heroic innings against Pakistan at Chennai. It was a similar sort of situation, and like Lara, he knew he couldn't make a single mistake because his was the only wicket the opposition wanted. He fought doggedly, but when backache caused trouble, blew it away. The target was too close then; the others proved incapable of reaching it.

Lara meanwhile contined to be in superb form and established total supremacy over Muttiah Muralitharan in Sri Lanka in 2001. Where others were scared of dealing with his off-spin, Lara laid Muralitharan's wide variety of balls to waste at Colombo on his way to 221. The off-break, the floater, the arm-ball, the top-spinner, were all read from the bowler's wrist. Lara stepped out and lofted the ball over and over again, cut cruelly and swept regally.

He got 688 runs in the series, yet the West Indies lost all three Tests. This was education for those who complained that Sachin's score did not often lead to an Indian win. Firstly, the statistics said something else altogether, and in one-dayers in particular, India has won eighty per cent of the matches in which he has got hundreds.

But Lara's performance against Sri Lanka was a classic example of how one batsman could dominate so completely throughout a series and still land on the losing side.

Later Lara led the West Indies to the biggest successful chase in Test history, that too against a powerful Australia, in 2003. And in September 2004, when nobody really expected it, he led the West Indies to a stunning victory in the Champion Trophy against a formidable England side led by Michael. Although he didn't score much in the thrilling final that showcased the true Caribbean Spirit, his captaincy and fielding were instrumental in inspiring his team. Lara took a splendid low catch at short mid-wicket to dismiss danger man Andrew Flintoff at a crucial stage of the match, and in the end over ran out centurion Marcus Trescothick with a direct hit. If the two had stayed, even the splendid ninth-wicket partnership between Courtney Browne and Ian Bradshaw would'nt have been enough to save the Windies. Lara is once again undoubtedly back at the top, with a string of big hundreds and double hundreds and a world record of 400 in Test cricket, and is again a strong challenger to Tendulkar.

That is great news for cricket. Not only is Lara a treat to watch, he and Tendulkar can only push each other. Their skills are such that the pushing can possibly bring out spectacular things from the blade of each. For a start, Lara's many momentous innings can be a reminder for Tendulkar that he has still not got a truly big innings in Test cricket. It has been long overdue. And his match-winning hundreds are the other lesson that, however unreasonable the demand, when the innings rests on your shoulders, don't give away your wicket once you're on and on full flow.

*

If Tendulkar's head was in the right place after five years of uninterrupted success and a fresh, lucrative commercial deal, so was his heart. In May 1995, he married Dr Anjali Mehta, a paediatrician who practised at a state-run Mumbai hospital. A gold medalist in medicine, Anjali belonged to a family that was part of the crème de la crème of Mumbai society. Her father, Anand Mehta, was a business magnate and a sportsperson. He had played bridge for India. Her English mother, Annabelle Mehta, was known for keeping the family's philanthropic traditions alive with her involvement in charity work. Besides, the family had a rich background of entrepreneurship and education. It counted among its own India's culture czarina, Pupul Jayakar.

Sachin had begun dating Anjali in 1990. When they first met, she didn't have a clue about cricket, though her father was (and still is) something of a cricket fiend; when they got married, he said she followed cricket, but 'only a little, not much'.

Because of Sachin's status, their dates were sometimes an exercise in hiding. He once put on a false beard, pulled a hat over his head and took her to the cinema. There, his beard slipped, and he was mobbed.

Anjali was brought up in an atmosphere of affluence that was absolutely unlike anything that the intensely middle-class Maharashtrian and suburban Tendulkar household had known. Yet the ethos of culture and education had rooted her in reality. She struck up a rapport with down-to-earth Sachin immediately. Having lived all her life in a bungalow in the downtown and elite Breach Candy locality of Mumbai, she had no problems shifting after marriage to suburban Bandra in a flat just below that of Sachin's parents. 'He can be a normal person in this colony (Sahitya Sahwas). He moves around easily, mixes with the children as well and still plays cricket with friends,' she said of his comfort levels there. They lived in Sahitya Sahwas till a couple of years ago, when they shifted into a plush one-floor apartment at the classy Le Mer building in Bandra West that has Bollywood actress Aishwarya Rai among its other occupants.

Oddly, when they decided to tie the knot, Sachin asked Anjali to speak to *his* parents about it. In a largely patriarchal Indian society, it is generally the other way round. It is the boy who goes to meet the girl's parents, and "asking for the girl's hand in marriage" is the near-mandatory method of beginning a long and complex process that leads to matrimony. Here Sachin was, unintentionally, breaking new ground because of his shyness.

The wedding, held at the Jewel of India Hall, Worli, turned out to be the most-talked-about social event not only in the city's but the nation's calendar. Banners congratulating the couple were put up at various corners in Mumbai, and TV channels, newspapers and magazines went ga-ga about the young cricketer's start of a new innings. A leading satellite channel offered Tendulkar a huge sum to telecast the wedding live. He was told, rather pompously, that it would rival the marriage of Charles and Diana in 1981. He turned down the offer. Even a feverishly excited media were asked to keep off. However, after a last-minute intervention by a senior sports journalist from the city, press photographers were allowed a very short session on the hotel's lawns during the reception of one of the most celebrated couples in the history of Indian cricket.

don of a new era

Stripped to the truth, he was a solitary man with a
solitary aim.

> – R.C. Robertson-Glasgow
> on Sir Don Bradman

He bats just the way I did.

> – Sir Don Bradman on Sachin Tendulkar

'**S**ix balls from me, ten runs to win,' Javagal Srinath shouted, before
Sachin Tendulkar could begin his "last round" at the India nets.
A batsman's "last round" is generally a simulation of a slog-overs
situation, where he tries big hits. These contests are at once serious
and great fun, and they make net practice beneficial in the real
sense, in that they prepare both batsmen and bowlers for matches.

Sachin was used to hearing these words from his friend, Srinath
who was known to all as a fast bowler with a grand inner core, a man
who measured success in terms of efforts and not results. He joined
the Indian team in 1991, when Kapil Dev was still around, but four
years down the line, had become the spearhead of the attack. One of
the enduring tragedies of Indian cricket is that he and Sachin never
really fought a duel in domestic cricket, as symbols of Karnataka and
Mumbai cricket. They made up for it, however, with their all-too
frequent fights in the nets.

Sachin accepted the challenge with a broad grin. When the six
balls had been bowled, he walked off with a grin getting broader by
the minute. Srinath's unhappy face said it all as he had grown
accustomed to losing these fights that Sachin simply loved. But the
great trier that he was, he never shied away from taking on the best
batsman in the world. He knew that even if he lost, there were

lessons to learn. Besides, with the biggest event in international cricket approaching, these sessions with a world-class fast bowler were extremely important for Sachin too.

The quadrennial World Cup was to be played in India, Pakistan and Sri Lanka early in 1996. Well before it began, connoisseurs as well as casual cricket watchers analysing the chances of the various teams were unanimous about one thing: if India was to reach Lahore for the finals and lift the Cup, one man, aged twenty-two, had to fire all the way through the tournament.

This wasn't a healthy reflection on Indian batting which also boasted of a Navjot Singh Sidhu, an Azharuddin, a Vinod Kambli, a Sanjay Manjrekar, an Ajay Jadeja, a Manoj Prabhakar and a Nayan Mongia. Yet the load of expectations that Tendulkar now had to carry was real and considerable. He had been an exuberant youth when he played his first World Cup in 1992. He had averaged forty-seven for a struggling side then. This time, he had to up that average and add some more.

Captain Azhar wrote in his syndicated column a good three months before the championships that Tendulkar had to help India win the Cup. After others echoed this sentiment, former India captain Krishnamachari Srikkanth said the demand was unfair, for others in the team had to do their jobs as well. Nobody, at least in India, was willing to listen.

Of course there were valid points to be made vis-à-vis India's possibilities for a win, and many people raised them nicely and well. They argued that the story of India's Cup challenges had not been a pleasant one since Kapil Dev's team brought the Prudential Cup home in 1983. In 1987, India had messed up a strong chance, and in 1992, the team had struggled to stay afloat in Australian conditions. There was never any strong belief in an Indian team playing a major tournament abroad. In 1996, the World Cup had come back to the sub-continent. The wickets were familiar; the crowd was crazily supportive. That could camouflage a lot of chinks in the Indian armour. The team too, wasn't as lacking in ability as it appeared to have been in 1992. Again, in 1992, the team had lost miserably against Australia before its Cup campaign began. In contrast, the three years leading up to 1996 had been decent for Indian cricket. The team looked stable if not dazzling. And there was an improved, and supremely confident Sachin. He had to take charge, and the others had to play around him.

This logic, in all its soundness, was forced to be secondary to an overriding national emotion, and Sachin had to look at that. The Indian cricket fan's mindset changed fundamentally in 1983. For every World Cup after that, the average Indian fan thought his team *had* to win. Anything less than that was unforgivable, no matter if other teams were stronger or played better on a given day.

Tendulkar started India's campaign in keeping with the expectations, with a run-a-ball century against the freshers, Kenya, in the first match at Cuttack. Given 200 to win, India won by seven wickets.

The Cup challenge well and truly began in the second day-and-night encounter against the West Indies at Gwalior. There was again talk of Sachin vs. Lara before the match. Fielding first, India got Lara out, caught behind cheaply, and then bowled out the Windies for 173. Whoever thought this total was undersized had to do a brutal reality check soon. The West Indian speedsters sent Sidhu and Jadeja back for nothing.

It was now Tendulkar's job to steady the boat and guide the innings. He began confidently but when he had barely crossed double figures, he glanced uppishly to square-leg. He was dropped. When he reached twenty-two, he tried to pull one and top-edged. The ball went high into the air, close to the crease on the on-side. Every Indian who saw its vertical progress, panicked. The dismissal looked certain, and with it, the end of the Indian chase. Windies keeper, Courtney Browne positioned both hands right to receive the ball, but when it finally responded to the force of gravity, it went through his two humongous gloves, and fell to the ground. A deafening roar went off across the ground and in millions of Indian homes and restaurants, where people had their eyes glued to their TV screens. Moments of tension in cricket are many, but several Indians will still swear that for them, there were few so lingering and so relieving in the end as this.

Chastened, Tendulkar put his head down for a big score. Captain Azhar was looking solid at the other end and together, they fashioned just what their team needed – a good partnership. Azhar was done in by the desire to hit Carl Hooper over long-on for a six. He connected, but the ball went a little squarer than he had intended – into the hands of the deep mid-wicket fielder.

In came Vinod Kambli, and batted coolly alongside his schoolmate until a mix-up, rare between the two of them, led to Sachin's run-out. He had scored seventy and put India on course, but his dismissal again raised doubts about whether India could get the forty-odd runs still needed for a win. They did, and one of the highlights of the remainder of the innings was a pull by Kambli that sent Ambrose's sizzler over square-leg and into the stands. It was one of those copybook shots cricket experts could recommend to a beginner. It came off the middle-of-the-middle, with the batsman's body positioned perfectly for the pull, and it was struck in an imperious Caribbean style. The West Indians were certainly alarmed. India won with a degree of comfort, and chief comforter Tendulkar was given the Man of the Match award, his second in succession.

The next match brought in its wake the second best compliment Tendulkar has ever received in his career (I rate the one by the bookies, where they said a match was "on" only after he got out, as the best; of which later). India was to meet Australia in its most crucial league game, at the Wankhede Stadium in Mumbai on 27 February 1996. Wankhede was lit up for the first time for this day-night clash; the capacity crowd that had turned up wanted one man, who was playing in his hometown, to illuminate it a great deal more.

It was a visitor, Mark Waugh, who shone first. Just a few days earlier, he had got a hundred against Kenya. He got a hundred here too, with his carefree elegance and wristwork. A strange decision by Azhar to bring on left-arm spinner Venkatapathy Raju very early in the innings helped the Australians tremendously. Waugh and his opening partner, skipper Mark Taylor, effortlessly and repeatedly hit Raju to the ropes and into the stands.

Fortunately for Azhar's team, quite a few Aussie wickets fell in quick succession in the end overs, and their total read 258, a good one, but much less than what they had earlier threatened to make.

India lost Jadeja in no time, and in his second strange move of the day, Azhar sent in Kambli at number three. This despite the fact that in the earlier game, the left-hander had made a dashing thirty-plus at his usual number five slot and stayed not out till his team reached its target. Kambli was clueless, and the opposition in turn exploited his mental state. He was castled for nothing.

From the other end, Tendulkar saw the two depart and decided that a do-or-die approach was now best suited for the crisis. Australia was in any case a team forever on the offensive, both in word and deed. They had a powerful attack comprising Glenn McGrath, Damien Fleming and Shane Warne. And once they were on top, they really turned the screws in. A counter-offensive seemed the only way to ward off impending disaster and get on top; otherwise, they were going to swallow it all up.

So he turned his bat into a sword. He cut Fleming behind point and past a diving third-man for four, drove McGrath straight past a diving mid-on for four, and hit a McGrath half-volley through the line, over mid-wicket, for yet another four. One McGrath ball was pulled violently, and this writer was not the only one at the stadium who didn't see it before its breathtaking progress had been punctured by a banner beyond the ropes.

McGrath was even then best in the business for his line and length. Neither helped him as Sachin took twenty-seven off two overs. Once in those two overs, McGrath had a caught-and-bowled chance. As I re-read the previous sentence, it is evident to me how a cold, accurate description of cricket can sometimes be misleading. It was technically a chance. The ball was hit so hard, it could only have stuck, no one could've *caught* it.

There is hardly a technical flaw in Tendulkar's batting, and the stamp of his batting excellence is that he bats in the "V". For one so perfect, it is amazing how he plays the cross-batted shot effectively and – yes, this is a contradiction in terms – cleanly and correctly. Many technically sound batsmen have been forced to do the same by pyjama cricket, but where Tendulkar stands out is that he, the natural aggressor, plays it boldly and exceedingly proudly.

Sunil Gavaskar infused self-belief into Indian batting and pulled it out of the morass of inadequacy that a colonial hangover had sunk it into. Gavaskar was a classicist. He gave batting an Indian stamp while keeping its most ancient and most charming traditions alive. Tendulkar plays as straight as Gavaskar did. He preserves and enhances all the charm associated with correct batting. And then, in an assertive Indian step ahead, he suddenly yanks it out of its superstructure like Vivian Richards did. With a cross-bat. Richards did it in his Caribbean way; Sachin does it like a swordsman from the Indian warrior tradition. For balls that make him feel it wouldn't work, he quashes the textbook theory, hits across the line, often repeatedly, and tries to bang a fine bowler off his line and length just when he looks in a position to knock him down.

This is a blend of physical and psychological warfare Indian cricket did not have earlier. Gavaskar was the Jawaharlal Nehru, Gopal Krishna Gokhale and M.K. Gandhi of Indian batting. Like Nehru, he was polished, haughty with opponents on the field and temperamental if provoked. Like Gokhale, he stood like a wall and showed the path. And like Gandhi, even his aggression – and there was so much of it despite the wrong impression that he was defensive – was non-violent. Sachin is Bal Gangadhar Tilak, Vallabhbhai Patel and Subhash Chandra Bose, all rolled into one. He will brook no niceties if they hinder self-assertion.

Fast bowler Shane Lee, brother of Brett Lee, got a taste of Tendulkar's devilish cheek at Wankhede. He pitched one a little short. Sachin put his foot down and whacked the ball straight over his head – with a cross-bat. After the raw aggression, there was a subtle touch that put the ball in the same place. Shane Warne bowled his first ball short. Tendulkar went on the back foot and lifted it with his bat apparently powerlessly. It bounced once and slammed into the sight-screen.

Warne was driven and swept with total control by Tendulkar and his partner Manjrekar. Manjrekar intelligently put the ball into the gaps and rotated the strike, allowing the younger man to run riot.

Ultimately, Sachin reached his fifty in forty-one balls. When he once swept Warne, I tried to follow the ball and couldn't see it. In a moment, I heard a loud thud on the ropes. One of the sponsors' boards had been hit very, very hard – with a sweep!

One of the keen watchers of Tendulkar's batting that day was Sir Don Bradman. He sat glued to the television set at his Adelaide home and, in the middle of the innings, called out to his wife Jessie and asked her to have a look at the Indian youth. 'He bats just the way I did,' he told her. Bradman was not given to overstatement. He had watched closely, and had thought that Tendulkar's technique and shot selection matched his own. (After this, the Don sought every opportunity to watch Tendulkar. The last he saw him was in the 1999 India vs. Australia Test series.)

When Sachin reached ninety, the crowd held its collective breath in anticipation of a ton. That did not come. He stepped out for a big hit off Mark Waugh, who saw the initial movement and sent the ball down the leg-side, out of his reach. Keeper Ian Healy did the rest.

After he was out, all Indian hopes rested on Manjrekar. However, Steve Waugh, that faithful combatant, rose to the occasion as ever and got Manjrekar out caught behind for sixty-two. Things just fell apart after that, and sixteen runs was the final gap between the Indian and Australian totals.

Tendulkar continued his attacking mode in the next match against Sri Lanka. He cut and glided the ball behind square on the off-side and paddled and whipped it behind square-leg on the on-side. In front of the wicket, he drove without reservations. He danced down to Muttiah Muralitharan and hit him over long-on for a six. When fast bowler Pushpakumara bowled one outside the off-stump in the slog-overs, he shifted outside the line, bent a little and smacked the ball again over the long-on for a maximum. When he was run out for 137 in the last over, commentator Tony Greig said: 'Sachin Tendulkar, take a bow.'

India had posted a strong 271, but that wasn't enough for a rejuvenated Sri Lanka who were chasing remarkably well in every game in the Cup. Their openers Sanath Jayasuriya and Romesh Kaluwitharana, who revolutionized batting in the first fifteen overs in this tournament, reached fifty in the fifth over, and a solid middle order comprising Aravinda de Silva, Arjuna Ranatunga and Hashan Tillekeratne built on the foundations and saw the side through.

Against Zimbabwe, Sachin got a paltry five, his first failure of the Cup. Kambli scored a ton and led India to victory.

This World Cup tournament was special as it was the first to have quarter-finals due to the participation of twelve teams. Since four teams were new to the world stage, there was hardly any question about which eight would qualify. For India, the quarter-finals became very special. They were to play Pakistan, at Bangalore. Luckily for them, Pakistan captain Wasim Akram was out of action. He had reported unfit with an injury and Aamir Sohail was to lead in his place.

Those who played that game for India say that when they first took a round of the Chinnaswamy Stadium, in Bangalore, for their warm-up, the ground let out a roar they had never heard before. That roar coursed through their veins, and they told themselves they just could not lose.

The performance was a reflection of that same feeling. India batted first and got 287 for eight. Tendulkar got a spirited thirty-one before playing on to the stumps. Sidhu displayed controlled aggression for his ninety-three. After he had crossed seventy, he suffered a toe injury but carried on in pain. Azhar scripted a wristy little nugget before being beautifully caught behind; Kambli made a solid twenty-four and looked so good that an alarmed Imran Khan, in his role as TV commentator, kept repeating, 'He's middling the ball, Pakistan must get him out,' before Vinod had actually done anything; and Ajay Jadeja set the stadium alight with two towering sixes off Waqar Younis and splendid hitting in the slog-overs.

India's innings over, Pakistan openers Aamir Sohail and Saeed Anwar started as if they had taken a cue from Sri Lankans Jayasuriya and Kaluwitharana who had made the Indian bowling look pathetic in an earlier game. They crossed eighty in the first ten overs, and even after Anwar was out for a personal forty-eight, the mood not only in the stands but across India was sombre because everybody knew how India usually gave up much before a match was over.

Soon Venkatesh Prasad turned things around. Aamir Sohail hit him for a cracking four through the covers and, having completed the shot, pointed belligerently to the cover region to indicate where most of his balls were supposedly destined to go. The crowd was deathly silent, and Sohail's gesture was shown more than twice on television screens as Prasad went up to his bowling mark. Sohail was in a mood for massacre. The next ball disturbed his furniture, and the crowd rediscovered its booming voice as if in an instant.

While Anwar and Sohail were blazing away, Imran Khan was making disapproving noises in the commentary box. He said they seemed to be in a tearing hurry, and that was not a healthy sign. His fears came true when the dismissal of the two put a strain on the other Pakistan batsmen, who did not prove up to the mark. India won comfortably, and the celebrations that followed across the country were fit for a World Cup final triumph.

The Bangalore victory made the Indian contingent smug. A few days separated the quarters and the semis, yet the high was such that manager Ajit Wadekar had to remind the team that the World Cup was still some way away.

The semi-final against Sri Lanka was to be played before a one-lakh-strong Eden Gardens crowd at Kolkata, a factor that would weigh in favour of the Indians. The wicket at Kolkata, though, was bad and was expected to deteriorate as the match progressed. Shockingly, Azhar, on winning the toss, chose to field. The idea behind the decision was negativistic and reactive. It underlined that even a so-called "high" did not help remove Indian cricket's sense of self-doubt. Sri Lanka had chased astonishingly well throughout the tournament, so the Indians wanted to prevent them from batting second. So, first, there was a defeatist assumption that, if they batted second, the match would be theirs. And second, there was appalling disregard for the nature of the wicket. That too, a wicket that promised extensive corrosion in the second innings.

Surprisingly, India had a wondrous start. The danger men of the tournament, Kaluwitharana and Jayasuriya, were out in the first over – the right-hander caught at third man and the left-hander falling to a leg-slip trap. Now the Indian team and its management were more than convinced that the decision to field first was correct. Even after Aravinda de Silva and others got in and gave momentum to the Lankan innings, the Indians did not realize they needed to set a field to check the runs on this kind of a wicket. Lanka finally went up to 251.

The deception for the Indians was thorough. Because, so long as Sachin was at the crease during the chase, the wicket's surface did not seem to have changed enough to create trouble. Sidhu was out early but before the end of the first ten overs, Sachin had hit one four each through point, cover, extra-cover, mid-off and mid-wicket. In fact, he and Manjrekar coasted along and took the total to ninety-eight in twenty-three overs.

Muralitharan was of course a class apart but both Sachin and Sanjay noticed that even Kumara Dharmasena, innocuous at his best, got the ball to turn drastically and jump in his first over. Dharmasena had a great smile on his face when he finished his over, as if the turn had indicated a win for his team. The deterioration was now happening quickly, but the batsmen reckoned that so long as they kept up their partnership, there would be no trouble.

Then disaster struck. Jayasuriya, coming on to bowl in place of Muralitharan, bowled one down the leg-side to Tendulkar. The ball hit his pad and he stepped out of the crease for one-tenth of a second. In that time, keeper Kaluwitharana picked up the ball lying close to the stumps and took off the bails. The Lankan openers had failed with the bat. In concert, they got the wicket that cleared their path to Lahore for the finals.

Soon after Sachin was out, Manjrekar tried to sweep Jayasuriya and was bowled round his legs. Azhar spooned the easiest catch in

the world, World Cup or not, to Dharmasena. Srinath, promoted over
Jadeja to give company to Vinod Kambli, was run out for six. Jadeja
literally searched for the ball for ten deliveries. On the eleventh, he
was bowled round his legs by Jayasuriya. Mongia left for one, and
Ashish Kapoor for zero.

It was all over for India as they were 120 for eight. As defeat
looked imminent, the Kolkata crowd turned violent. Water bottles
and soft-drink cans were thrown into the playing arena. When the
shelling refused to stop, match referee Clive Lloyd led both teams off
the field to give the crowd time to calm down. The teams returned
after half-an-hour. But just as Muralitharan got ready to bowl the
second ball of his unfinished over, the missiles rained down again.
Now ground officials reported that there were glass bottles too. That
was the end of it. Lloyd called the teams back and declared the
match awarded to Sri Lanka by default. Kambli cried on his way to
the pavilion but that was consolation neither for the irate crowd nor
for other Indian supporters who had seen an awful collapse.

Ajit Wadekar, then manager of the Indian team, told me:

> The wicket was unprepared and unfit for any level of cricket.
> Only Sachin could get runs on a wicket like that. Once he got
> out, I really had no hope.

And then added:

> We were playing wonderfully in the Cup, like one unit, had all
> the confidence in the world and thought we had the Cup in our
> pocket. We had a plan against Sri Lanka. We wanted them to bat
> first because they were good chasers. We also bowled them out
> cheaply, but the wicket deceived us.

If the wicket was unfit for *any* level of cricket, surely the team
management knew that batting second on it would be hell, and that
even a reasonable total would be tough to chase?

India had a realistic chance of lifting the World Cup. Had they
got through, there was every possibility they could beat the
Australians in the final. A reactive rather than a pro-active approach,

and disrespect to the sacred piece of earth that determines how a game goes, and how one has to play, brought to an ignominious end an otherwise bright pursuit.

Lanka skipper Arjuna Ranatunga, who went on to lift the World Cup, was asked after the triumph if there was a moment in the entire championship when he felt the Cup could slip away. He said the partnership between Tendulkar and Manjrekar in the semi-finals was the only time when such a thought had crept into his mind. Luckily for him, things took a positive "turn" soon.

A distraught Kapil Dev said after the semi-finals that Tendulkar appeared to be in his 'usual best form' against Sri Lanka before he got out and the match was lost. 'Usual best form' was a contradiction in terms, but in this case, it made sense. Tendulkar ended up as the highest run-scorer in the Cup, with 523 runs at an average of eighty-seven. But the prize he was expected to win for India had gone elsewhere.

*

Barely two weeks after the World Cup, India, Pakistan and Sri Lanka were in Singapore for a three-nation one-day tournament. After the World Cup all the teams were very exhausted.

Though Tendulkar would much rather have been at home, he made as much use as he could of his relative anonymity in Singapore. There was nearly no cricket-playing nation where a crowd did not gather around him. This place, despite being a former British colony, was an exception. In the evenings he got to move about liberally in the famed shopping centres of Orchard Road. The big malls were like an open house for him, for he loved to buy T-shirts and enjoy culinary delights. One day, he was walking along a food outlet, happily certain that nobody knew him, when a man seated at a table by the roadside who looked like a local waved out to him. Sachin smiled to accept the greeting. The anonymity had ended in a non-cricket-playing country too. And he had contributed to it with his first hundred against arch-rivals Pakistan.

At that time, apart from appreciation and adulation for his art, he also generated some off-the-field discussion. For the first time in his career, he was fined twenty per cent of his match fees for an oversized MRF logo on his bat. MRF, it was then reported, paid him Rs 1.5 crore annually.

Meanwhile, the Indian team once again bowed out before the finals but had more cricket coming its way. From Singapore they went to Sharjah, where they were again to play Pakistan and a third team, South Africa. India lost its first game against Pakistan, but the next match against them was Tendulkar's.

Runs came from his bat as water bursting from a main. The Pakistanis blocked the off-side to try and prevent him from scoring. He hit relentlessly on the on-side as if he relished the yawning gaps there. It made no difference that most of the balls were pitched on and outside the off-stump. Waqar Younis, Aaqib Javed, Ata-ur-Rehman, Saqlain Mushtaq and the new Pakistan captain Aamir Sohail were all unable to stop the flow, and Rehman in particular was repeatedly smashed between mid-on and mid-wicket. Sachin either put his foot down and hit him through the line or played short-arm pulls.

Indian captain Azhar was occupied more by off-the-field matters on this tour and often left on-field management to his deputy. Tendulkar took to moulding himself in keeping with his altering profile. An example of this was had in the middle of his knock. Pakistan had got debutant opener Vikram Rathore out cheaply. But then Sachin and Sidhu had taken the Indian score to 200 by the thirty-ninth over. Sachin took the single that was to be India's 200th run, and there was applause in the crowd. He checked the score, looked back at Sidhu and asked him to stay there and not get carried away: the team needed the two of them.

Tendulkar carried on smoothly till the forty-fifth over. Then he decided to open his arms. Waqar Younis read his intentions beautifully and slipped in a slower one. The batsman swung and hit it straight down the throat of the mid-wicket fielder. Azhar continued the thrashing and took twenty-four runs off the last over by Ata-ur Rehman.

Pakistan's response to India's (then) record score of 305 was 277 all out. Tendulkar bowled with an expression of quiet fury throughout and bagged two wickets with his leg-cutters. After he had sealed the win by trapping last man Saqlain Mushtaq Leg Before, he angrily told the batsman where to go and received a warning from match referee Ranjan Madugalle for his outburst.

Sharjah was a time for mood swings. During one match, Ajit Wadekar distributed a leaflet in the press box announcing he was quitting as manager. So long as he held the post, he said, he would be missing out on a higher ranking at the State Bank of India. When Sachin returned from the field and got to know, he went to the press box, tore the press release into two and said, 'Sir's not going anywhere, he's not going anywhere.' He relented only when Wadekar told him how his promotion at the workplace was at stake.

The issue of the outsized MRF logo also cropped up a second time. Madugalle handled it sensitively, talking to Tendulkar like an elder brother and avoiding any sermonizing. The words were well taken, and Sachin walked in with a bat minus the MRF logo.

After losing the finals in Sharjah to South Africa, India left for England to play three Tests and three one-dayers. Tendulkar had come of age in international cricket on the 1990 tour of England. He was now going as vice-captain who had done a fair bit of leading already.

India went through a torrid time at the start of the tour. They not only lost the one-day series but also Navjot Sidhu, who walked out of the team after a conflict with Azhar. Though many people accused him of that, Sidhu did not take the decision in a moment merely because he was left out of a one-dayer. Discontent had been brewing for some time, Sidhu's communication channels with his captain had been muddled, and he saw no way out. His going was both drama and tragedy. Drama, because it brought to the fore all the internal dissension in the team. And tragedy, because it robbed India of a fighter who had been the hero of the World Cup quarter-finals against Pakistan and, with Tendulkar, co-architect of the team's record total against Pakistan in Sharjah.

The tragedy was compounded by India's disastrous performance in the first Test at Edgbaston. In the first innings, they were bowled out for 214, and after England took a lead of nearly a hundred, they played themselves into a similar mess. The only one who put up resistance was Tendulkar. He played an innings of such class that the Edgbaston crowd was in raptures.

The wicket at Edgbaston was a test of a batsman's technique and staying power. There was movement off the pitch, and the bounce was unpredictable. As far as Sachin was concerned, he did not have anything to prove on a tough wicket, but the adaptability, temperament and strokes he showed gained a special meaning in view of the low morale experienced by Indian cricket and sealed his status as the world's best batsman.

He belted the bowlers with refined strokes, not one of which was out of the one-day basket. He found gaps despite the wicket's weird behaviour. At one point, England captain Michael Atherton spread the field to block his boundaries. Tendulkar almost scoffed at that field setting with a delicate glance that had the entire stadium clapping.

His partners deserted him one by one. He was out ninth when he tried to hit a Chris Lewis bouncer into the stands and Graham Thorpe, running backwards from mid-wicket, took the skier. Once he had returned after scoring his ninth Test ton, England quickly wrapped up the match. Chris Lewis later said: 'It was nice to get Tendulkar. To score those runs on such a wicket must surely mean he is a very good batsman. Cricket is all about being positive. I bowled positive and he batted positive. It was good cricket.' Tendulkar was deeply upset by the lack of application shown by the other batsmen, and there was widespread criticism from all quarters of a team that wanted one batsman to carry the team forward.

However, application was not the only problem. The ill-effects of having Tendulkar around were also beginning to tell on some Indian batsmen as they began to blindly emulate him. Most experts have maintained that it is tough to bat in the same team as Tendulkar and alongside him, because the others begin to wonder why they can't try his ways and even when they do, fail miserably.

One of the victims of this fix was a man of superb technical skills, Sanjay Manjrekar. When he started, he was pure perfection, and his style was, like Gavaskar's and Vishwanath's, made for the poets. For the first few years of his career, he was skilful at batting with Tendulkar. He would intelligently pick ones and twos while Sachin would go ballistic. As his Mumbai senior, he would routinely advise Sachin on what to do.

Slowly, his technique changed. He brought his right hand down, close to the bat shoulder, thinking he'd be able to deal with the quickies better this way. This was not in imitation; he just felt like trying it out. But while Sachin had a naturally unorthodox bottom hand, Manjrekar's unnatural adjustment made him unconsciously open the face of the bat and get caught in the slip cordon. The grip also robbed him of the punch to play front-foot strokes. His second move, that happened in a confidence crisis and amid a growing self-imprisonment-by-technique, was not unconscious. His temperament was still such that his father, the illustrious Vijay Manjrekar, would have been proud (without telling him so), and he batted perfectly all right with every batsman other than Sachin. When he batted alongside Tendulkar, he appeared to be trying what his junior Mumbai partner was doing. It is human to want to match your batting partner, but the problem was that their styles were different. Manjrekar's focus was technique, so naturally he would not find it easy to show the lavishness that a stroke-player like Sachin did. As the runs dried up for him, he seemed to be trying Tendulkar's tactics when batting with him. Unfortunately he missed out on an easy mantra given to him by Gavaskar: you don't have to be aggressive, just be positive. Having Tendulkar at the other end often made him forget that.

This writer is an admirer of Manjrekar, so however unjust it may sound, allow him to hold this against Tendulkar. But this is more than an emotional response. It is an indicator of how an increasingly confident Tendulkar could sometimes impact Indian batting, without his really knowing it.

When in England, Tendulkar also heard of the praise showered

on him by Bradman, and encouraged by that, went on to dominate
the rest of the Test series with scores of 31, 177 and 74. It set a right
example for youngsters Rahul Dravid and Sourav Ganguly, who made
their debut in the second Test and came up with gritty performances.
Both the second and third Tests were drawn.

On the third day of the last Test at Trent Bridge, Tendulkar was
asked to lead the side, as Azhar was unfit. He led for two days, all
through the England innings. His captaincy was closely observed by
all, because Azhar was already under fire and it was only a matter of
time before he was asked to step down.

Azharuddin had failed repeatedly as batsman and captain and
seemed to be severely troubled by personal issues. Especially after
the World Cup, things had been dreadful for the team he led. Manoj
Prabhakar had carried out a diatribe against the establishment and
against Azhar in particular. That had spoiled the atmosphere even
before the team for the Singapore and Sharjah tournaments was out.
Then, Vinod Kambli was dropped apparently for disciplinary reasons,
but there was no official word on the matter. When Sidhu pulled out
of the team, the turmoil reached a height, and reports from England
left no one in doubt that the sudden development was actually a
culmination of dissent. Personally, too, he had set an embarrassing
example. He had abused a photographer for clicking a picture of his
with Sangeeta Bijlani, who he married later. He was out on the
streets with her, so it wasn't exactly a private moment, and he had
forgotten that a public personality – that too, the Indian captain,
arguably holder of the second most important job in the country –
could not ask to be left alone. Associations of photographers had
protested, and it was manager Wadekar who prevented the matter
from snowballing by arranging a meeting between Azhar and the
lensman. Azhar shook hands with his victim, but grudgingly. He had
come into the Indian team a shy, modest, down-to-earth boy who
played beautiful cricket. He was now seen as snooty and
supercilious. Sandeep Patil, who took over as manager from Wadekar
for the England tour, also said in his report that Azhar seemed to
spend less time with the team and more with his new-found love.

Azhar had kicked up a storm around himself, and it was almost sure to claim him as its victim.

Hence the extra attention on the deputy holding fort. Tendulkar was supposed to set an attacking field because India had scored over 500 in the first innings. Instead, he took a defensive approach and actually reduced the pace of the game for which he won a lot of criticism.

Why did he feel the need to be defensive? He had felt that both Atherton and Nasser Hussain had got hundreds, so the possibility of an Indian lead had already become thin. At that point, he did not want the England team bowled out quickly. If that happened, India would have to bat a little too early, he said. The prospect of India batting early was fearful for him, because – and he did not say *this* – except for him, no one had shown any diligence, concentration and application on the whole tour. This was how he analysed the position of each: Vikram Rathore was not fit to bat; Manjrekar and Mongia were supposed to open the innings, and both were struggling for form; for Ganguly and Dravid, it was only the second Test match; and Azhar was injured and rather badly out of form. If India lost two quick wickets, there could've been trouble, he thought. Tendulkar later said that the two days he led made him aware of the ordeal he'd have to face if he became captain.

He was soon to find out that the two days weren't so bad, compared with what lay in store for him.

the captaincy crisis

Uneasy lies the head that wears the crown.

– William Shakespeare, *Henry IV, Part II*

In his first stint as captain of the Indian cricket team, Sachin
Tendulkar internalized a longstanding principle of his country's
cricket: it is not a person, but a force deployed by a group of
individuals that calls the shots. That force is intrigue, and one of the
more intriguing things about it is how an individual, even if he's the
most acclaimed cricketer in the world, can find himself completely
powerless to fight it.

The story of Indian captains before Mansur Ali Khan Pataudi is
a dismal one but can be summed up with a single example: in 1958,
India had four captains for a series against the West Indies. Pataudi
infused unity in the team and that process was taken forward by his
successor Ajit Wadekar. In the final analysis, Wadekar typified the
uncertainty surrounding the post. He received a rapturous welcome
after a victorious tour; three years later, his house was stoned after a
bad series, and he was forced to sneak into his home city to avoid
public anger.

Sunil Gavaskar, Bishen Singh Bedi and Kapil Dev had a relatively
better time. Yet their phenomenal personal successes (each was
ranked among the best in the world in his area of specialization) and,
in the case of Gavaskar and Kapil, a few standout victories
notwithstanding, they never reached the levels they'd have liked to
conquer as leaders.

That was because, like those who went before them, they were given little resources, zero back-up, no words of assurance about their tenure and had a sword dangling forever over their heads. The team would often be divided along regional lines; public expectations, especially after 1983, were unreasonable; and in Indian cricket, there was no concept of grooming a captain. Every Test was like a final exam; you were as good as your last match. A slight dip in personal form could mean the end of it all. The co-operation of teammates too, didn't come naturally, and you had no time to win them over and build your side, because almost all your time would be spent dealing with men of intrigue in the establishment. They just loved your state of unease.

At the start of Tendulkar's first phase as skipper in August 1996, all of the above was a constant, as it had been during Mohammed Azharuddin's term. And there were some more issues to handle, which Sachin's predecessor had already faced.

The volume of cricket had increased so much in the Nineties, that Indian spectators had become suitable candidates for the National Geographic Society's basic education programme. Cricket in India had turned into a TV sport, where one saw an unending stream of matches, day after day, without so much as a decent break. The TV viewers, whose numbers were shooting up phenomenally, expected their team to win every day. The combination of the magic on screen and the daily matches made them lose geographic awareness. No matter if you played in Sharjah one day and in South Africa the next, your performance had to be ditto. Variations in wickets, weather, ground conditions, etc., did not count, and you were not given time to adapt to the changes. Because, for the viewer, the changes didn't exist. Everything was part of that little box, as if cricket was being played on a fourteen- and twenty-one-inch stretch.

This distinction in cricket perception was crucial during Tendulkar's first phase as captain, that lasted a little over a year. India squeezed in more cricket in this period than it had ever played in such a time frame earlier. The result was an overall disappointment that did not look at all the factors weighing on the team, and a wealth of opportunities for the selectors and others in the set-up to play games. Tendulkar has had many firsts to his credit in international cricket. However, in the matter of Indian captaincy, he scored a negative first: he became the one to move fastest from a position of public acceptance, to that of disapproval. One year was all it took for it to happen.

In his case, one year was too abrupt for a denouement. He was, after all, the so-called wonder boy and saviour of Indian cricket. In the end, that image fed unreal expectations and made his and his team's failures all the more unacceptable. The rise and fall is nothing short of a case study in the vagaries of Indian cricket.

He started out in such a position that he had almost no reason to bear in mind that being captain of India was substantially different from being captain of any other national team. On 8 August 1996, his place at the helm was announced for the three-nation Singer Cup in Sri Lanka and the Sahara Cup against Pakistan in Toronto, Canada. At twenty-three years and 171 days, he had become India's second and the world's seventh youngest captain.

There was no debate on the decision, only nationwide approval and the expectation that it was now up to Tendulkar to recreate his magic as captain. Indian cricket desperately needed to look up, and it could do that if it had a strong captain either leading from the front, or pushing the squad from behind. Tendulkar's image was that of a decision-maker. His act of grabbing the ball to bowl in the Hero Cup semi-final had brought his leadership qualities to the forefront. He did not hesitate to take charge, made moves that looked risky but were in the team's interest, didn't flinch from the sight of defeat but tried to turn things India's way; his behaviour on and off the field was inspirational, and his performance so far had never been any less than good.

As captain of the Indian team, his first experience of the whims of selectors a constant in Indian cricket, came immediately on appointment. He was given hardly twelve hours to join the selection committee for picking the team. Instead of thinking about the kind of team he wanted, he had to rush to find a seat on a plane. This was his time to reflect on the combination he'd prefer and plan for the future. The Board of course had its own ways.

Sachin got a hundred in his first match as skipper. This was in the Singer Cup, against Sri Lanka. India failed to enter the finals, but that did not diminish the overall warmth for him. His early efforts had become obvious. He was encouraging teammates on the field, was listening to their ideas, strategies and concerns and was leading by example. The Indian captain's relations with the media, that had broken down after Azhar turned uncommunicative, had also been restored. Sachin was speaking, on behalf of a team.

India obtained a 2-1 lead against Pakistan in the Sahara Cup in Toronto and then slipped up to end 2-3. Even that did not affect the euphoria displayed for the new captain. He had scored a match-winning eighty-nine in the first match and failed in the other games. The failures didn't seem to matter, because the signs were positive. Pakistan captain Wasim Akram said Tendulkar had shown an attacking streak, and he deserved praise for it. After their return from Toronto, India were to play Australia in a one-off Test for the newly-instituted Border-Gavaskar trophy. In the interregnum, there would be the Challenger Trophy between three teams of India probables at Mohali in Punjab. The tournament had been launched to allow India's most talented players to compete with each other and give the aspiring ones a chance to showcase their abilities against those already in the team.

Five members of the Indian team asked the Board for permission to skip the tournament. Their request was turned down. Tendulkar, on the other hand, drove home the point that a demanding international schedule did not mean one had to change one's attitude to domestic cricket. The matches were not being shown live on TV. Financially, there was nothing to gain. The crowds at Mohali also weren't big, because they had only a week earlier had their fill by watching the Sahara Cup. Sachin, by now India's richest cricketer and the world's top batsman, however played the Challenger with the passion he was known for on the international stage.

He was angry with himself when he was out Leg Before to medium-pacer David Johnson in the first match. He fought back by slamming two hundreds and with partnerships of 189 and 190 with Rahul Dravid and Sourav Ganguly respectively. Azhar played the first match and then opted out for "health reasons". Javagal Srinath, however, was another senior who played straight from the heart. The two were adjudged best batsman and best bowler for the tournament. He's leading not only the team, but also Indian cricket as a whole, the pundits said of Tendulkar.

Three more quick successes seemed to justify that praise. India defeated Australia at New Delhi to win the Border-Gavaskar trophy, went on to lift the Titan Cup and then pocketed the three-Test series against South Africa at home 2-1.

Sachin scored only ten in the Test against Australia. He made up for it with three fifties in the league phase of the Titan Cup. He also got the only half-century scored in the Titan Cup final, which India won comfortably against South Africa.

In the Titan Cup, India fought back after being routed 0-3 in the league phase by the South Africans. That fightback was credited, rightly, to Sachin's statement that urged some of his players to be more committed. 'There is contribution from everybody in the South African team. We are playing for India. Everybody should realize the significance of playing for the nation. If the top order does not get the runs, the middle order should strive hard. I don't know what's wrong with us,' he said.

The South Africans were in superb form and were expected to crush India in the final at Mumbai. Tendulkar had a different way of looking at it. Before the final, he said: 'The South Africans haven't been tested. They are a good side, but like all other international teams, under pressure things can happen to the batting. You just have to be able to bring them to that position.' This was aggression, and it had its impact. India, scoring 220, bowled out Hansie Cronje's team for 185. Tendulkar had a hands-on approach from the moment the South Africans began their chase. He got the team together before the first ball was bowled for some encouraging talk, and was restlessly energetic on the field, running to the bowler almost once every three balls, asking for opinion from everybody and setting attacking fields.

His batting suffered in his first full Test series as captain at home against South Africa. In three Tests, he managed just one fifty. Despite some complaints, he wasn't too disappointed: the result of the series was 2-1. India had won the first Test at Ahmedabad, lost the second one at Kolkata and come back in the third at Kanpur to defeat South Africa by 280 runs.

His leadership and Srinath's firepower were responsible for the shock that Hansie Cronje's team were given in the first Test at Ahmedabad. On a turning track, South Africa was sixty-five for four and they appeared to be well on their way to getting the 170 runs needed for victory. They were playing to a plan – to smother the spin of Anil Kumble and Sunil Joshi. It seemed to be working. At this point, Tendulkar brought Srinath back into the attack. Srinath bent his back and bowled the South Africans out for 105. A shocked Cronje admitted his team was not mentally prepared for the move Sachin had made.

The captain had, in a way, almost guaranteed Srinath's effectiveness with a few suggestions, and the bowler himself acknowledged that.

Srinath always worked extra hard for his team, yet success had eluded him so often that he had come to acquire the (rather unfair) tag of a luckless bowler. Tendulkar gave a thought to his problems and told him before the Test series that he needed to alter his length. Srinath usually bowled a length that was ideal for a fast bowler. However, on Indian wickets that were unfriendly to pacers, the ball never reared up as expected, so the ideal length would strangely mean that the deliveries ended up being short and the batsmen could belt him. Sachin told him to bowl a little fuller, so the batsmen would be caught in two minds and the balls that would rise would do so suddenly .Srinath tried that and became unplayable.

A final one-dayer, the Mohinder Amarnath benefit match, was forced on the South Africans at the end of the series. Cronje complained his team was tired; the International Cricket Council nevertheless gave the game official status. The Indian captain regained his batting form in this match, getting his first ODI hundred at his home ground, the Wankhede. His local crowd did him no favour by disrupting proceedings in an imitation of the Kolkata crowd. After Azhar was given out caught behind, the electronic screen on the ground showed the ball had brushed his pad strap. For the East Stand spectators, this was reason enough to start throwing plastic packets filled with water on the ground. Play was held up for twenty minutes. Tendulkar was batting on ninety-one when the disruption happened. The Mumbai crowd, that was supposed to know its cricket, was changing, and the Mumbai boy was none too happy about it. Five years later, he would also not be too happy about the hundred, because investigations into match-fixing revealed sordid details about that game.

At that moment, though, the hundred further livened up things for him and his team. He had won his first Test and one-day series as captain at home, his batting had finally come good, Srinath was firing despite a sore shoulder, the other bowlers too were contributing, and there was hope for the tour of South Africa that India now had to undertake.

The record books, as statistics go, concealed a lot about the South African tour. They said India lost the three-Test series and the subsequent triangular one-day tournament. The fact was that the team rose from the ruins and put on a fight that put a scare in the minds and hearts of the opposition.

The beginnings were in tune with tradition. India usually loses the first Test on a tour, because it plays the big game before adequately acclimatizing itself to foreign conditions and wickets. This is because of the schedule decided by the Board. It is the world's richest Board, and it seems to think that preparation in unfamiliar conditions is not half as important as profits.

In this case, India played only one three-day game before the first Test at Kingsmead, Durban. The wicket for the three-dayer was as slow as they come in India. The one for the first Test however, Tendulkar said, was among the fastest he had seen.

India set a new record in ignominy at Durban. After being bowled out for a hundred in the first innings, they posted in the second lowest total against South Africa in cricket history: sixty-six.

Here, Allan Donald bowled the ball of his career to dismiss Tendulkar. Sachin had smashed to the boundary two consecutive half-volleys served by him after lunch. For the third ball, Donald came from wide of the crease. The ball pitched on an ideal length outside the off-stump and came in sharply to take the off-stick. Tendulkar's bat had not even come down fully when the ball went through.

The second Test at Cape Town drew home another truth that has often escaped Indian cricket: in a five-dayer, you have to play well not in two or three sessions but from the first day to the last.

For a few hours in that match, Tendulkar and Azhar dominated the opposition attack in such a way that the result – a 288-run defeat – seemed almost unfair even to the South African crowds. They put on 222 runs in forty overs, with Azhar's wristy flair at its best and Tendulkar demonstrating sensibleness, control and power. Local partisans on the ground cheered every stroke by the two, as they took sixty runs off Lance Klusener in six overs. Donald said Tendulkar at 169 looked "unstoppable", when Adam Bacher took a blinder off a hook shot. For the rest of the match, the Indians, as usual, were at the receiving end.

A 0-3 result was now a distinct possibility, especially in view of a touring Indian side's propensity to surrender like a guest loath to mortify the host. Tendulkar however was insolent. '*Ek test tari ghenaar aamhi* (We will win at least one Test),' he told journalists in Marathi at the Natal nets. Then, like he had done before the Titan Cup final, he pushed the South Africans into a psychological corner. 'Anything can happen in cricket. Who thought we would be all out so cheaply in the first Test. We can put the South Africans under pressure in forty or fifty overs. It's a funny game,' he said, again obviously referring to Cronje's team's weakness when under pressure.

His idea seemed to be working when South Africa, needing 357 to win in ninety-five overs, were struggling at seventy-five for five before lunch on the last day. Just after lunch, showers caused by a thunderstorm forced the teams to go off the field. Play was held up for nearly two-and-a-half hours. The Indians were now itching for a win. The umpires had decided to restart play at 3.30 pm because the absence of a super sopper had slowed the drying up. Half-an-hour before that, Tendulkar and Kumble went to the ground, checked the outfield, came back and told the umpires that they would take the field. 'We are willing to risk injury and no one should be blamed,' the Indian captain said. So play resumed at 3.15 pm.

When South Africa were 228 for eight and four overs still remained to be bowled, the umpires called off play again due to poor light. India narrowly missed a victory. 'If we could not force a win it was because of the stoppage of play for two-and-a-half hours. Srinath and Kumble had found their rhythm. I am disappointed I could not bowl Srinath and Prasad after tea because of the light conditions,' Sachin said later.

In the one-day tournament, India's entry into the finals depended on its run rate in the last league match against Zimbabwe. When Tendulkar won the toss and decided to field, the equation was: no matter what the target, India had to make it in 40.5 overs, otherwise Zimbabwe would go through.

The target: 241. That meant they had to score at least six runs an over. Tendulkar had batted in the middle order in the Tests, his slot as opener handed over to Rahul Dravid. But strategy was at work here and he was back as opener for the one-dayers, which made all the difference in this deciding match. As he launched an offensive in the first fifteen overs, Zimbabwe's bowlers, Heath Streak, Eddo Brandes and John Rennie ran out of ideas. As frustration overtook the fielders, Sachin repeatedly stepped out, took the ball on the bounce and cut it over the infield. He pivoted, pulled and consistently beat the fielder placed at long leg. The outfield had thick grass, but when he hit along the ground, the power in his shots made the ball travel. When the field was spread, the run rate began to drop but he and Rahul Dravid ran hard and took the graph up again. His hundred off ninety-seven balls, backed up by Dravid, Jadeja and Robin Singh's grit, ensured that the target was reached an over in advance.

Obviously, Tendulkar set off panic in the South African camp in the finals. He had to fire if India were to reach a reduced target of 251 from forty overs. After Sourav Ganguly's early exit, he shook Donald and company with a bombardment of blows. Donald, bowling at 145 kmph, was pulled over mid-wicket for a six, and Shaun Pollock was served a forcing stroke forward of point as the shot of the day. His shot-making stirred the defensive Dravid into similar action. They took the run rate to nine an over before a Tendulkar flick landed into the hands of the fielder at short fine-leg. He had got forty-five in thirty-three balls. Finally, India fell a mere sixteen runs short, Dravid getting an impressive eighty-plus and keeping up the momentum that he and his captain had generated.

Dravid, then just a year into international cricket, thanked Tendulkar for the confidence he had given him. 'Sachin took me by the shoulder after the Durban Test and told me he wanted me to bat at number three (Dravid had earlier opened in the five-dayers). He told me what he expected from me. He said I would get a long period as the number three batsman. Opening is the work of a specialist. I opened the innings in the Tests by chance. I'm essentially a middle-order bat and I would like to stay there. It was nice to know I would be batting at number three, because then I could mentally prepare myself.'

There was appreciation back home over the way India had, after a terrible start to the series, battled its way back in the third Test and the one-dayers. Though the South Africans had won, India had come out as the real winners. Among several other things, the rapport the new captain had struck with his players was appreciated a great deal.

Despite popular perception, Tendulkar was upset. He felt that tantalizing possibilities of a triumph had ultimately been buried beneath the scorebooks in South Africa. However, he determined to make amends in the Caribbean, where India was to go immediately after their return from Cronje country for five Tests and four one-dayers.

*

It was at this time that the oft-repeated image of Indian cricket

Sixteen-year-old Sachin Tendulkar makes his Test debut against Pakistan, in Pakistan, November 1989. He said he was beaten by the sheer pace of Wasim Akram and Waqar Younis in his first Test innings.

Below: In only his fourth Test at Sialkot, Pakistan, Tendulkar was hit on the nose by a rising ball from Waqar Younis. He bled badly, but when asked by batting partner Navjot Sidhu (second from left) if he'd like to go in, only said, 'Main Khelega' ('I will bat on'). The next ball was hit past the bowler for four.

In England, 1990. Even at seventeen, Sachin was not conscious of his small frame and saved the Old Trafford Test for India with a fighting debut hundred.

Right: With his idol, Viv Richards.

At Sydney, 1992, with Dilip Vengsarkar. Sachin got a hundred in this Test and followed it up with another ton on the world's fastest track at Perth, thus establishing himself as the mainstay in the Indian batting line-up.

They amassed runs together since childhood, and in a happy coincidence for Sachin, close friend Vinod Kambli was at the other end when he reached his first one-day hundred, against Australia in the Singer Cup in Sri Lanka, 1994.

Brian Lara lets Tendulkar have the honours in 1994, the year in which the debate on who's the better bat began. That question is still not settled, and a real answer can perhaps be found only when we look back a decade later.

Below: This camaraderie with Mohammed Azharuddin (standing, with wife Sangeeta Bijlani) ended soon after Sachin became Indian captain in 1996. Sachin later told authorities probing the match-fixing scandal that he felt Azhar did not give in 100 per cent during his captaincy.

Tendulkar reaches his hundred in the Chennai Test against Australia, March 1998. He dominated the Aussie attack all through this series.

Below: Australia captain Steve Waugh congratulates Tendulkar after the latter had single-handedly taken India to victory in the Coca-Cola Cup in Sharjah, April 1998. Soon after this handshake, some members of the Australia team, led by Shane Warne, lined up in the Indian dressing room for Sachin's autograph on their T-shirts.

Top (right): Tendulkar dominated Shane Warne so completely in 1998 that modern cricket's finest leg-spinner said he had 'nightmares of Sachin just running down the wicket and belting me back over the head for six.'

Top (left): The memory of this Test innings, against Pakistan at Chennai in 1999, still haunts Tendulkar. He got a superb hundred battling intense back pain but left the task of reaching the victory target unfinished.

Below: When the match-fixing controversy broke out in the year 2000, the cricket world was keen that Tendulkar, seen here with South Africa's Hansie Cronje who was at the heart of the scandal, should speak on corrupt practices in the game.

Below (right): A packed crowd at Eden Gardens, Kolkata, hurled stones on to the field and disrupted play after Tendulkar was controversially run out in a Test against Pakistan in 1999. The then ICC chief Jagmohan Dalmiya (extreme right) then asked Sachin himself to intervene and calm the spectators.

Shane Warne and Mark Taylor in the slips will agree that this pull is perfect for the coaching manual. The head is still, the eyes are firmly on the ball even after it has been struck, the body is beautifully balanced and the wrists have been rolled in such a way that the ball stays down.

Below: Sunil Gavaskar left the commentators' box and went down to the boundary line to congratulate Tendulkar as he walked in after equalling Gavaskar's record for the most Test hundreds (34) against Bangladesh in Dhaka, December 2004.

authorities, known among other things, for cynicism, obduracy and insularity, came to the forefront.

Gearing up for the West Indies tour, Tendulkar believed that India could beat the opposition with a good measure of spin bowling. At the meeting to select the squad, held at the Cricket Club of India in Mumbai, he asked for an off-spinner to tackle the many left-handers in the Windies team. The selection committee, which has traditionally held Indian captains by the scruff of their neck, refused. Furious, Sachin walked out of the meet and went home.

A picture of the meet carried by the national media the next day reflected the happenings beautifully. The picture showed the selectors, India coach Madan Lal and BCCI general secretary J.Y. Lele (who was present as convenor) sitting around a table, discussing keenly. Tendulkar was at the same table but his body language was entirely different from that of the others. While the others were relaxed, he was stiff, and his expression pensive, like that of a man under enormous strain. His face was turned away from everybody, to the wall on the left. He was blankly examining the paint, and nervously chewing the nails on his left hand.

Sachin protested that his views had been ignored though he was the one who was to lead the team on the field. As per convention, Indian selectors have never liked a captain who speaks his mind. As word of his protest reached, they heard it with a conspiratorially keen ear.

The Indian team proceeded to West Indies and hardly two days after they landed in Jamaica, Javagal Srinath was forced to pull out of the tour due to a shoulder injury. He was to be the biggest threat to the West Indies batsmen; with him gone, India's chances had reduced considerably. Tendulkar had seen the signs earlier and warned that such a thing could happen due to a badly planned schedule and an excessive dose of cricket. Srinath had earlier withdrawn from the one-off Test against Australia due to a hurting shoulder and come back for the home series against South Africa and got a match-winning six-wicket haul at Ahmedabad. The pain had obviously stayed due to the gruelling schedule, so Tendulkar had played him only in the Tests and one-dayers in South Africa and in none of the tour games. On the same tour, Srinath had thrown underarm from the outfield, yet had led the attack in every sense of the term. But the problem had aggravated, leading to a rotator cuff tear. He also had a whippy action, which did not help alleviate pain. 'I hope it does not happen, but if Srinath or Venkatesh Prasad break down in the West Indies, we are going to find it very tough,' Sachin had said before the start of the tour.

His fears had now come true. 'It was a blow that left us stunned. It was unfortunate we lost him at the start of the series. He was much needed here because it is always tough to play the West Indies,' he said on Srinath's departure, with a voice reflecting deep worry.

He now felt handicapped by the team which seemed forced on him. The Indian team had been left with only two specialist bowlers: Venkatesh Prasad and Anil Kumble. Sunil Joshi and Dodda Ganesh were around, but they had not made it to the eleven regularly so far; and Abey Kuruvilla (whom Sachin had pitched for) was making his debut. Under these circumstances, Tendulkar felt he was being robbed of a chance to defeat the Windies.

The selectors for their part went a step further. As a replacement for Srinath, they sent Noel David, an off-spinner from Hyderabad who had struggled to find a place for himself even in the provincial Hyderabad eleven; he was suddenly propelled into the national squad. Tendulkar was unnerved, and the media carried reports on how he lost his head on hearing of David's appointment and asked 'Noel Who?' The selection of Noel seemed deliberate. You wanted an off-spinner. We've given you one, still you can never be sure whether to play him or not, the selectors seemed to be telling Tendulkar. It was a petty and tendentious act, overplotted and overacted.

Six years after the controversy, the selectors may have acquired the tag "former", but their justification for the move has to be quoted here because it is telling. In the wake of the Abhijit Kale bribery controversy in November 2003, which led a former Ranji player to rake up the Noel David episode, journalist Ehtesham Hasan of *Mid Day* spoke to the then selectors, Kishen Rungta (Central Zone),

M.P. Pandove (North Zone) and then Board secretary J.Y. Lele to get their views on David's selection.[1]

According to Lele, Tendulkar had sent a fax to the selectors from the Caribbean saying that either Kanwaljit Singh from Hyderabad or Tushar Arothe from Vadodara (both leading spinners on the domestic circuit) be sent as replacement for Srinath. Pandove said the issue was old and therefore, 'I don't remember what had happened.' Rungta on the other hand first contradicted Lele: 'There was no fax. It was an emergency, Tendulkar spoke over the phone and asked us to send an off-spinner. It was a unanimous decision.' Then he became sarcastic and said: 'Tendulkar is a big star and a busy person, so I don't think he was aware of the names of some of the good performers at the domestic level. That's the reason he said "Noel Who?"'

Draw, draw, defeat, draw and draw. That was how the five Tests against the Windies went. The last two draws were brought about by rain. The first two draws were genuine no-results.

The West Indies dominated the first Test at Kingston. The Indians expectedly took time to get used to the conditions but nevertheless did not lose, for once. Tendulkar said this was the first time since 1989 that an Indian team had not been defeated in the first Test of a series abroad. Statistically, he was in the wrong. The first Test in Sri Lanka in 1993 had been drawn. Logically, he was spot on, for less than an hour of play had taken place in the Lanka Test.

The second Test at Port-of-Spain, the slowest of West Indian wickets, saw the Indian batting dominating, though Tendulkar did not get a hundred. The defeat in the third Test at Bridgetown, Barbados, bang in the middle of the draws, stood out. It was truly the centrepiece of India's cricket calamity on the tour.

India, in response to the West Indies' 298, took a twenty-one-run lead, Tendulkar showing the way on an unpredictable wicket with a ninety-two embellished by classic back-foot drives. When the West Indies were bowled out for only 140-plus, India had to get 120 for a win. At the end of day three, India were two without the loss of any wicket. The possibility of a rare overseas victory was getting real.

The wicket had deteriorated in three days, so it was important for the Indians to get a decent start on the fourth morning. Their final score was eighty-one all out, an indicator of shocking surrender. Even a bad wicket could be no excuse for it. A pack of cards may have looked like a fortress before the Indians that day. Navjot Sidhu – back for this series after the punishment he received in the wake of his controversial pullout – got a nasty one that hit him on the glove and landed in the hands of gully; Azhar had his stumps rattled; Tendulkar was caught by Lara at slip off an Ian Bishop out-swinger; and V.V.S. Laxman ended up as "top-scorer" with nineteen runs to his credit. Brian Lara, captaining the West Indies for the first time after Courtney Walsh reported unfit, had to use only three bowlers to bring about the destruction: Ambrose, Bishop and Rose. A fourth one wasn't even needed.

'I can't believe we couldn't make even 120,' the Indian captain said in disgust. He knew the defeat would go down as one of the darkest and most humiliating in the history of Indian cricket. Whenever a team is chasing a small total, a tiny partnership is all it takes for the opposition to start panicking. Nobody tried to string a decent partnership; no one attempted to raise his game. Team manager Madan Lal went to the extent of saying that a team that couldn't chase 120 deserved to be punished.

There was immense curiosity in the Caribbean about Tendulkar the batsman-turned-captain. He had not been picked for India's previous tour there in 1989, though as India's most promising young batsman then, he had been a strong contender for a place in the team. This was the first time West Indians were seeing him in flesh and blood. The name Sunil Gavaskar is taken with high regard in that part of the world. The Caribbeans respect their pacers, so they have special status for the man who stood up to the battery of Andy Roberts, Malcolm Marshall, Michael Holding, Joel Garner, Colin Croft and Vanburn Holder, among others, without a helmet and took thirteen Test centuries off them. Sachin was seen as his successor in the Indian batting tradition. They were therefore keen to have a closer look at him.

Sachin did not get a single century in the five Tests, though he got close to one thrice. That was odd for a batsman of his consistency. His knock of ninety-two in the first innings at Barbados was fluent, but his eighty-eight in the first Test at Kingston was sketchy. He had a tough time middling the ball and was in fact caught plumb in front of the wicket on the second ball he faced, when the umpire ruled in his favour. Even that eighty-eight was scored in over 300 minutes, agonizing for an amazingly quick scorer. He justified the slowness of that knock, saying that he would rather get a sluggish eighty than a quick twenty or thirty and that he had to bat cautiously on slow wickets where close-in fielders were backed by a deep point. In the final analysis, an average of fifty-seven from the series, second only to Dravid's in the Indian team, was nothing short of good. But the average could not hide the stresses and strains that were now telling on his batting as nobody else was willing to take the responsibility for scoring runs and shaping an innings. The third one-dayer against the West Indies was an outstanding example of the way things were worsening.

The count was 1-1 as the two teams went into the third of four ODIs at St Vincent, so the psychological advantage for the last game would naturally lie with the team that won this one. The Indian batting folded up as if it were striving to provide a one-day parallel to the Barbados Test disaster. Responding to the Windies score of 250, they reached 157 before losing their second wicket. All they needed was sixty-eight off sixty-five balls, with eight wickets still in hand, when the crash began. They were all out for 231.

Tendulkar turned purple. He had taken precautionary measures and instructed the batsmen not to play airy shots. Nobody listened. At the end of the game, he said: 'I can only give them instructions that they shouldn't be hitting in the air. I can't bat for them.'

Azhar, in particular, played a casual, careless shot that sent the ball straight into the hands of cover. He was supposed to play the central role in the chase and ensure that the others played around him. Instead, he openly flouted the captain's instructions and played as if he were in catch practice.

All through the Windies series, Azhar batted so shabbily, it appeared that he was unconcerned about batting. He was the seniormost batsman in the team and it was expected of him to bat responsibly and deliver in at least one match. The third Test and the St Vincent one-dayer had of course called for a good innings, but even otherwise, the less-experienced and middle-order batsmen needed solid support from a senior. Dravid, Ganguly and Laxman had only played a few Tests between them in 1997. Sidhu, following his 1996 England tour fracas – with Azhar himself – had not been in the team until the West Indies tour. So Azhar should have been playing the elder statesman's role. Tendulkar narrowly missed three hundreds in the Tests and got good scores in the one-dayers. He too needed Azhar's help in moulding the Indian innings. No help was however obtained. Every batsman goes through a bad patch, but the strokes Azhar played on the tour had carelessness written all over them. He had thrown away his wicket more than once.

The activities and attitude of the selectors and Azharuddin now intercut the story of Tendulkar's captaincy in a more absorbing fashion.

Sachin got a rather deceptive break from tensions when Azhar was dropped for the four-nation Independence Cup to be played in India in the summer of 1997. Azhar had stretched himself too far with his pile-up of silly dismissals, and the selectors said they were dropping him for his lack of commitment. To add to that, the Indian media around this time began to vigorously splash stories on the involvement of bookies in Indian cricket. There was more than an insinuation that Azhar's bad performance was due to his links with bookies. Not that many believed this theory as a turbulence in personal life was said to have affected his form more. However, three years later the story took a dramatic turn.

Tendulkar slammed a century in the first match of the Independence Cup against New Zealand and appeared to put all friction between him and the selectors behind with total commitment. However, India did not put up a good show in the tournament. Pakistan opener Saeed Anwar got a world record 194 at Chennai against them. Tendulkar's decision to allow him a runner had a key role to play in that giant knock. Anwar had been unwell before the match began. His class and absolute domination of the

Indian attack notwithstanding, it is impossible that the exhaustion and fluid loss he suffered in the Chepauk heat and humidity would have allowed him to continue the way he did with a runner.

Failure to reach the finals of the Independence Cup brought harsh criticism for the Indian team and its leader. This was what the selectors were waiting for. Two of them, Shivlal Yadav and Sambaran Banerjee, now went to the media and said they had made up their mind to sack Tendulkar.

Tendulkar retained his post for the Asia Cup in Sri Lanka (July 1997), but only just. The selectors spent an hour debating his fate and eventually voted 3-2 for him merely because they could not come up with a better alternative at the time.

Before his re-appointment was announced, Tendulkar had said that India had just about begun its efforts to build a young team. He spoke in detail on the phase of transition the team was going through. Most of the players who were part of the team in the early Nineties – Dilip Vengsarkar, Kapil Dev, Ravi Shastri, Krish Srikkanth, Manoj Prabhakar and Kiran More – had gone. Two experienced and reliable batsmen, Navjot Sidhu and Sanjay Manjrekar, had been in and out of the team. If Azhar, Kumble, Srinath, Mongia and he were excluded, from among the others, Ganguly, Dravid, Prasad and Rathore had made their international debuts only the previous year (1996) and Laxman, Kuruvilla, David Johnson, Dodda Ganesh and Noel David were rank freshers. Plus, Sidhu had returned to the team not before the West Indies tour, and Srinath had had an enduring injury that culminated in his missing the Windies tour.

If this was an explanation for the Indian performance, it was also a request to give the team time to settle down before it could be expected to work wonders. Tendulkar cited the example of the Sri Lankans who painstakingly built a team of youngsters in the early Nineties that eventually lifted the World Cup. He said Sanath Jayasuriya had taken close to a hundred games to prove his ability. The selectors had persisted with him and with Aravinda de Silva, Arjuna Ranatunga, Asanka Gurusinghe, Roshan Mahanama and Hashan Tillekeratne, and the results had been marvellous.

The concept of team-building has seldom been accepted by Indian selectors and even a large section of Indian cricket followers. They have even baulked at anyone who touches on the subject. The selectors did not like Sachin's long-term interest theory. What appalled them most was that he was setting sights on the future when they were actually planning to sack him. Of course they never gave him a chance to build a team; even for the Asia Cup, they did not give him the team he wanted.

He had wanted Vinod Kambli and Nayan Mongia and got into a major fight at the team selection meeting in Bangalore as four of the five selectors – Shivlal Yadav, Sambaran Banerjee, Kishen Rungta and M.P. Pandove – strongly opposed these names. During the argument that lasted over two hours, Sachin lost his composure more than once. The only person who backed him was chairman of the selection committee, former India fast bowler Ramakant Desai. Sachin said Kambli had played a gutsy knock against Pakistan at Chennai, and Desai pointed out that Mongia was the best keeper in the country. But they had more than denial coming their way. They were handed a shocker: Azhar, dropped a few weeks ago for what the selectors themselves called 'lack of commitment and lack of interest in the game', was brought back, and Saba Karim was taken in as wicket keeper.

Tendulkar spoke out again, violating for the nth time the sacred code that the Indian captain had to be a mindless zombie. 'It's a B-grade team, and it has been imposed on me,' he told the media. He said the captain had to be given the team he wanted since he was the one who got all the criticism. 'But I'm powerless,' he admitted. Out of sheer despair, he also said he was not dying to remain captain; the selectors could relieve him of the job if they didn't allow him his prerogative on the cricket field – the team composition.

The selectors stored these statements in memory, for future reference and action.

The Lankans demolished India in the Asia Cup final. After that, India had to play three ODIs and two Tests against Lanka. Lanka won the one-day series 3-0, and Tendulkar's two hundreds in the two drawn Tests were overshadowed by a Sri Lankan record total of 952 for six at Colombo. Jayasuriya and Roshan Mahanama put up a record partnership of 576 for the second wicket.

Tendulkar was over-defensive and did almost nothing to break their partnership. Sure, the wicket was what he would call *paata* (flat) and the Indian bowling had its limitations, but there seemed to be a sense of resignation in his captaincy that day. His usual aggressive gestures, his penchant for innovations and his love for strategy were nowhere to be seen. His natural self was such that he would often relish the thought of devising and employing tactics to disturb a comfortable batting pair. He was instead a picture of unnatural quiet.

Was it because, on the field, he was not sure of the combination he had? The question was relevant because, off the field and briefly away from the team's responsibilities, it was the same old Tendulkar on fire.

He would frequently play table-tennis with the team of Indian journalists in Lanka. The rule laid down by him was that there would be no discussion on cricket, so he could take his mind away from it. The journalists initially set down their own rule: they would only play doubles, because individually, Sachin was far better than any of them. They relented when he offered to play singles with a disadvantage. His opponent would have to get eleven points, while he would have to get twenty-one. This rule would generally be in place for a few games. Then, he would reduce the points to six for his opponent. He would still win most of the time. Also, he could play table-tennis with either hand, with the same ease. And he even boasted that he had once defeated the Gujarat state champion.

The Jayasuriya-Mahanama onslaught, however, had snuffed out the stiff competitor within him.

While India were playing in Lanka, former Pakistan captain Rashid Latif created a sensation in the cricket world by alleging that four Indian players – Mohammed Azharuddin, Nayan Mongia, Venkatapathy Raju and Navjot Singh Sidhu – were involved in betting on cricket. He soon backtracked, saying he had been misquoted. The media was by now unwilling to let go of the subject.

Manoj Prabhakar had claimed in a newsmagazine that a teammate had offered him twenty-five lakhs to throw a match against Pakistan in Colombo in 1994, and the press was following up that story with a series of articles on betting and match-fixing. As public opinion in India veered towards suspicion, the Board of Control for Cricket in India set up a one-man inquiry commission to probe the match-fixing and bribery allegations.[2]

In this atmosphere heavy with intrigue, India went to Toronto to play the second annual Sahara Cup against Pakistan. They were expected to lose, just as they had the previous year. But surprisingly they won four games out of five. Tendulkar got a fifty only in the last match. He said he wouldn't bother about his form if his team was winning. 'These wins against Pakistan have been the most satisfying in my career,' he said. India had missed the services of Srinath, Prasad and Kumble at Toronto (Pakistan too didn't have Wasim Akram and Waqar Younis. On wickets that helped seamers, Tendulkar bowled young Sourav Ganguly extensively, calling him his 'secret weapon'. The boy from Bengal got fifteen wickets in the five matches, a good amount of runs and won the Man of the Series award. A year ago, some people in Kolkata had expressed anger against Sachin for choosing Kambli over Ganguly for Toronto. The same section this time expressed its appreciation of the way he had used Ganguly both as bowler and batsman. The next challenge was also against Pakistan, in Pakistan. India lost two of the three one-dayers played there, and Tendulkar's poor scores were one of the reasons for the defeat.

As expected, there was more to the series than bat and ball. In the second one-dayer at Karachi, Sachin had to take his team off the field for a while after stones were hurled at Nilesh Kulkarni, Debashis Mohanty, Ajay Jadeja, Vinod Kambli and Sourav Ganguly. After the first two incidents of stone-throwing, a disturbed Tendulkar was persuaded by match referee Ranjan Madugalle and Karachi's then commissioner of police Mir Hussain Ali to continue play. After the third incident, he put his foot down. The top cop appealed to him not to go in, but Madugalle gave all support. The Pakistan media criticized Tendulkar's move. 'He should have been diplomatic and should not have decided to take his team back,' *The News* said. 'The incidents may have been minor, but I did not want my batsmen to get injured,' he said in defence. When India batted, the same Karachi crowd was happy to see Tendulkar's cameo innings of twenty-one and the strokeplay of Ganguly and Kambli. They were shaken when Rajesh Chauhan hit Saqlain Mushtaq for a six in the last over and left in a mood of despair after India had won.

On this tour, a Pakistani journalist who was obviously well-informed about the conflicts in Indian cricket asked Tendulkar about the desirability of having Azhar in the team. He did not get the expected answer. 'Do you know his (Azhar's) record? Please go and check his Test and one-day record,' an annoyed Sachin said. He had felt the need to stand by his teammate.

A frantic cricket calendar meant that immediately after they returned from Pakistan, India would play three Tests at home against Sri Lanka, then fly to Sharjah for the four-nation Champions Trophy and then fly back home to play three ODIs against the Lankans.

As the first part of this schedule – the Tests against Lanka – was unfolding, the Indian media was again abuzz with talk of a "definite move to sack Tendulkar". The 5-3 result against Pakistan in the two series had apparently come as a hurdle, but *The Week* quoted a national selector and a BCCI official as saying that a section of the Indian Board had given its go-ahead for his removal as captain. The same magazine said that a powerful lobby of bookmakers who couldn't cut ice with Tendulkar had started dangling the carrot of money in front of the selectors to ensure they gave him the stick.

The move was confirmed when, just before the team flew to Sharjah after drawing all three Tests against Lanka, the president of the Indian cricket board, Raj Singh Dungarpur made a desperate phone call to the national selectors from London to tell them that Tendulkar must not be sacked.

The selectors were still powerful enough to dictate the batting order. They told him to bat lower down the order because he wasn't getting runs. He did, and got scores of ninety-one, three and one.

In fact, the sitcom turned curiously tragic in Sharjah. India's three straight losses were degrading enough but they were outrun in their indignity by Azhar's suicidal streak. In the third game against West Indies, India was chasing 229 when Azhar, on arrival at the wicket, began to run like he were impatient to get out. He went for runs that simply weren't on, and while attempting one such suicidal second run, fell short of his crease. He had scored four (the team folded up for 188). He had done pretty much the same thing in an earlier match against Pakistan too. Geoff Boycott, Sunil Gavaskar and Mark Nicholas, commentating for television, said they could not believe what they were seeing; it was, according to them, the height of irresponsibility.

Following the outcry, the selectors summoned Azharuddin and had a closed-door meeting with him. 'Azhar has been reprimanded, and pardoned,' selection committee chairman Ramakant Desai told a packed hall of journalists after the meeting.

Azhar's bad form continued in the one-day series against Sri Lanka. At the end of it, that is, just a few weeks after the reprimand, he was named captain of the Indian team!

Tendulkar had voiced his desire to step down after the third one-dayer against Lanka. He wasn't allowed to. The reason: the selectors wanted to sack him and declare that they had sacked him.

On 1 January 1998, Ramakant Desai told the media that the selectors had been debating a change in captaincy. On 2 January, when he announced the sacking at a press conference, he said there had been no "pre-determined" move and that Tendulkar had to go because his batting had suffered.

The press meet soon transformed the sitcom into a melodrama full of double-talk. Desai began: 'There was no pre-determined move to sack Tendulkar. But we felt that the extra burden of captaincy must not continue to affect his form in the one-dayers. That will be a disservice to Indian cricket.'

Although the "bad-form-in-one-dayers" argument was absolutely correct, the media questioned the claim that the change was not pre-meditated. Desai was told by the journalists that two selectors had spoken on the intended sacking in July 1997, before the Asia Cup. He was reminded of Dungarpur's telephone call before the Sharjah tournament asking selectors not to remove Tendulkar, and his own statement made a day earlier – 'We had been debating a change in captaincy' – was read out to him.

He was stuck for words, so another selector Kishen Rungta took over. He was asked about the doubts raised over Azhar's commitment and the dressing-down he had received for that. Rungta said there were no doubts about Azhar's commitment, and that he was summoned by the selectors for a pep talk. 'We wanted to boost his spirits which seemed to be rather low after many negative things were spoken and written about him,' he said. A few weeks earlier, Desai had told a press meet that Azhar had been reprimanded. The English dictionary did not quite say that a reprimand meant boosting of spirits. Rungta pointed out that as a 'last-ditch attempt to avoid the unpleasant step of sacking Tendulkar, we asked him to bat lower down the order in one-dayers. But he got only two scores of fifty-plus in six innings. We were therefore forced to take this step.' Desai had earlier denied that it was the selectors who had asked Tendulkar to bat lower down. Rungta was now affirming it.

Desai finally lavished praise on Tendulkar: 'We have tremendous respect for him. Nobody since Gavaskar has got so much admiration from everybody. Unfortunately, the selectors could not reach any other conclusion for his batting failures in one-dayers but that they were due to the problems of captaincy... The selectors have gone on record appreciating his sportsmanship, his habit of taking all the blame on himself. He is one of those who keeps up the fight. Very few captains put their heads on the block as he did, but we want him more as run-scorer than as captain.'

Desai was right about this. It is true the selectors held a firearm to Sachin's head, never gave him the team he wanted, spiked him whenever possible, and didn't even allow him to resign; it is true seniors like Azhar did not play the role he expected them to play; and it is true the overdose of cricket in his first year as captain was dreadful; Indian cricket had never had such a crammed schedule earlier. But it is also true that Tendulkar had, only a few months after assuming captaincy, become a deeply worried man, partly because of the responsibility and partly because of the shenanigans.

The ubiquitous record books however showed conflicting conclusions. For one-dayers, they were bad, and for Tests, they were good. He had led India in fifty-four ODIs and averaged thirty-seven, which was meager by his standards. India had also lost thirty-one of those matches. In contrast, in seventeen Test matches, he had averaged forty-five and had got four hundreds and four fifties; India had won three of those Tests, lost four and drawn ten.

But reality often emerges once we have statistics out of the way. His batting had indeed been affected; its manner had changed. Where earlier he had more than a shot to one ball, he was now hesitant about playing freely; where earlier he would destroy and sometimes even be reckless, he now seemed to be taking the other extreme of unnatural defence and over-caution; where earlier he was a youngster full of life on the field, with a pleasant countenance that suggested a bundle of optimism, captaincy had made him look depressed.

There is such a thing in nature as a two-headed turtle. Each head of the turtle controls the two legs on its side. Often the right head says 'retreat,' while the left one says 'advance'. The heads fight over food and seldom agree on anything. While batting, Tendulkar the captain sometimes appeared to match that freak specimen in nature.

---

1   *Ekach Shatkar*, 15-31 March 1993.
2   India, Sri Lanka, Pakistan and Australia competed for the Singer Cup, the first big one-day tournament to be held in Sri Lanka.

the golden year

It's all about winning. It's all I really care about.
It's the only thing and everything. I'm obsessed.

– Pete Sampras

I wanted some of my best performances to come
against a strong team like Australia.

– Sachin Tendulkar

Stepping into the nets in full batting gear, Sachin Tendulkar carved out a scruffy patch outside his leg-stump and asked three leg-spinners to put the ball there. They did, and for two hours and more, he put his left leg out and hit the ball in the curve between mid-on and square-leg. He bent and drove the ball, swept, he went down on a knee and smashed it, and he came down the wicket to knock it out of the ground.

This done, he asked the bowlers to give him flippers, top-spinners and googlies. He played, missed, swept, hammered, struggled, was bowled. He continued till he felt tired. Next day, he was back and trying more of the same.

This was in Mumbai in January 1998, a few weeks before Australia's tour to India for three Tests and a triangular one-day series. The Aussies had by this time acquired the title of "the team of the '90s", and though Glenn McGrath and Jason Gillespie weren't coming, they had in their ranks Shane Warne, considered the world's best spin bowler. He had, since his dreadful debut against India in 1991-92, baffled batsmen the world over with deceptive flight and a startling amount of turn generated even on unhelpful tracks.

Well before the Australians arrived, the series was labelled the Tendulkar vs. Warne contest. In press meets, Tendulkar was asked pointed questions on the imminent clash. He gave a stock reply: it was not Tendulkar vs. Warne, it was India vs. Australia. This wasn't true. Tendulkar had indeed been thinking of Warne more than anyone else in the Australian team. He had watched Warne on television, demolishing South Africa in 1997-98 and had decided he'd make the leg-spinner his target. This was intended as a psychological ploy; if "unplayable Warne", as he was called, was hit badly early in the series, it would unnerve the Australians and give India an edge.

He put the ploy to work in the first tour game: Ranji Trophy champions Mumbai vs. Australia, played at Mumbai's Brabourne Stadium.

After Australia declared their innings at 305 for eight, and Mumbai opener Sulakshan Kulkarni was out for a blob, Tendulkar came out to bat. He began comfortably, giving sound company to the other opener, left-hander Amit Pagnis who appeared to be relishing the Aussie attack. Mark Taylor soon brought on Warne, and Tendulkar readied himself.

As the second ball whirred out of Warne's wrist, Tendulkar put his foot down and slapped it hard, sending it soaring over long-on. From then on, all the strokes he had tried out during those assiduous practice sessions were played with deadly intent and deadlier power. While in the practice sessions, the ball had often been blocked by the nets, it now either cut the grass savagely on its way to the long boundary or sailed smoothly beyond the ropes.

Pagnis too got into the act, carting Warne for four boundaries before falling to Paul Wilson for fifty. As Sanjay Manjrekar, playing his final first-class match, joined Tendulkar at the crease, he was treated to a fine spectacle. Warne was hit for fifty runs in his first spell. When he came on to bowl again, twenty-eight runs were taken off him in seven overs. In his third spell of only three overs, Tendulkar, now in the company of Rajesh Sutar, took thirty-three runs. During this last spell, Sachin did a repeat of his first sixer. It was as if the bowler had come full circle: he had tried one ball, then tried many others in vain, and finally bowled the first type of ball again, with the same, crushing, result.

One would think that the shots played in the arc from mid-on to square-leg were similar. They weren't. They were like the images of a single planet captured by the Voyager: many in number, and each one of them revealing in its own right.

The seam of the ball that left Warne's hand was known to whirl in intricate choreography like the rings of Saturn. That created fear in the hearts of batsmen the world over. The Voyager had a special eye: it could make out the small rings within the big ones, in this case, the stitching on the seam, and decode the image, that is, read the ball. Then the eye co-ordinated with the hands, and the piece of willow made a colossal primordial collision with the ringed planet, either tipping it on its side along the ground or hurtling it into the air with an active volcanism till it went into the stands and ended up a mere blotch in space.

Bowling sixteen overs in all, Warne gave away 111 runs, his most terrible figures ever. Tendulkar reached fifty in forty-six balls, a hundred in ninety balls and went on to score his career's best of 204 not out in Mumbai's total of 410 for six declared.

What was worse for the Australians was that they were bowled out for 135 in the second innings and suffered a humiliating defeat at the hands of a first-class team. Tendulkar's knock had set the tone for the series and put the Aussies back in more ways than one.

The first Test was played at Chennai where Sachin led all the way, playing one of the most memorable knocks of his career. In the first innings, he seemed like a man in a hurry. He hit Warne's first ball for a four and then, in the same over, launched into an extravagant drive. The ball took the edge, and Aussie captain Mark Taylor at slip lapped it up.

Australia, batting second, acquired a seventy-plus lead, and though the visitors would be the ones to bat last on a deteriorating track, India had to put up a fighting score.

Tendulkar walked out to bat when the fourth day was half-over and the wicket had worn a lot. The fast bowlers were operational, and the ball was keeping low on and outside the off-stump. A couple of balls escaped from beneath his bat. So he began to adjust his strokes at the last moment to meet the sliding deliveries. He sliced some balls cleverly for runs and in fact succeeded in striking a few ferocious forcing strokes off the back foot.

Warne and off-spinner Gavin Robertson too were not allowed any benefit from the track. Warne bowled round the wicket and into the rough, bad news for any batsman. Tendulkar sent the ball repeatedly in the arc between mid-on and square-leg and was now looking menacing. He took balls from outside the off-stump and played them against the spin, over mid-wicket. Anything short on the off was cut cruelly. Warne desperately tried the googly and the flipper, without success.

Soon Sachin reached his hundred but not before giving wicket-keeper Ian Healy a workout. Mark Waugh was bowling gentle off-breaks on the off-stump. He cut him fine on more than three occasions, playing the shot at exactly the moment it appeared that the ball was going through to the stumps or hitting his pads for an LBW case. Each time, the ball slipped tantalizingly past Healy's right glove.

Yet the definitive marker of that innings was a ball he did not play at all. Warne had pitched it into the rough; it turned and rose spitefully to waist height. Tendulkar was on the back-foot and near-committed to playing it down defensively. He sensed its nastiness and dropped the bat at the final moment. The ball went past his glove. Had it not been for that adjustment, it would have hit the glove and ballooned into the hands of the keeper, or to the slip or silly point. Rahul Dravid had been out in exactly the same fashion a little while earlier. Sachin had watched that from the other end, and while batting, he had done what Dravid, after having played extremely well, couldn't. Sometimes, it's a fraction of a second which separates the very good from the great.

Tendulkar's 155 not out helped India declare at 418 for four and bowl out Australia for a 179-run victory.

It was more than evident that the Chennai Test had swayed India's way only after Tendulkar got going; the second one, at Kolkata, was however one-sided. India won by an innings and 200-plus runs after getting a big first-innings total. Azhar scored his near-mandatory, and classy century at his favourite ground, and Navjot Sidhu, Dravid and V.V.S. Laxman all got near-hundreds. Tendulkar again left Warne desperate during the course of his seventy-nine, making it clear he was judging his flight, direction and turn easily.

The result of their contest was unchanged in the third Test at Bangalore. Though Australia salvaged some pride by winning the Test by eight wickets, Tendulkar scored 177 with three sixes and twenty-nine boundaries.

The loss of captaincy seemed to have given him some sort of release. He was batting like a liberated child, and Australia, as a collective force, seemed to be stimulating him like nothing else.

In the Pepsi three-nation ODI series (Zimbabwe was the third team) after the Tests, he shocked the Aussies with his bowling skills too. In the first one-dayer at Kochi, he broke a steadily building partnership between Steve Waugh and Michael Bevan. The two were threatening to successfully chase a sizeable score when he flighted a leg-break to Waugh. Trying to drive against the spin, Waugh got a leading edge that sent the ball back into the bowler's hands. Sachin celebrated like a child-juggler, tossing the ball excitedly from one open palm to the other, a wicked smile playing on his lips.

Bevan tried to come down the pitch. Sachin saw this and sent a faster one down the leg-side, leaving it to the keeper to complete the formality. Navjot Sidhu was in the habit of teasing Sachin that he bowled well in the nets, from a distance of sixteen yards; in this one-dayer, he ended the Australian chase by pocketing five wickets from – Sidhu's laughing admission – twenty-two yards. He had even missed a hat-trick.

Tendulkar was back as opener for the one-dayers. Azhar on reappointment as captain had restored his position and had put his foot down when some people opposed the move. That was further liberating, and he celebrated it in the second league-game at Kanpur with an innings that Steve Waugh called "great". India was given 222 to chase, on a track where the ball kept low. Tendulkar decided the best policy was to reach the ball and play through the line. He scored a hundred with seven sixes, breaking Kapil Dev's record for maximum sixes in an innings by an Indian,[1] and took India through to the finals.

The way he went about it, commentator Harsha Bhogle said on air that though the boundary line was a landmark on the field and every cricketer treated it as such, Tendulkar seemed to have no concerns about it. All his seven sixes were towering, but two stood out. The first one was against off-spinner Gavin Robertson. Sachin came down the pitch in a relaxed manner and gave the ball a forearm push. The ball hit the billboards. When Darren Lehmann was purveying left-arm spin, he bowled one on the legs outside the leg-stump. Tendulkar played it inside out, over extra-cover, for a massive six.

Australia beat India in the finals and felt they were finally out of trouble. They weren't.

If there was a prize for putting oneself in a tight spot, the Indian team, of any era, would win hands down, provided its equally unpredictable neighbour Pakistan didn't do anything worse. The team in the second half of the Nineties was especially volatile: brilliant one day, breathtakingly inept the next. When it wasn't at either extreme, it would find the odd midpoint of uncertainty. Three days after the home series, Azhar's team arrived in Sharjah for the tri-nation Coca-Cola Cup – Australia and New Zealand were the other teams – and found itself facing one such common predicament: Australia had already qualified for the finals; in the last league game against them, India had to either beat them or better New Zealand's run-rate to be the second finalist.

Tendulkar plundered the Aussie attack, scored 142 in 131 balls and took India through to the finals. These are the bare facts about a knock that has gone down as one of the finest in one-day cricket. These facts may create an impression that consistent attack was the theme of his batting, and many who have actually seen the game, have felt the same, because the obvious can also be obfuscating.

Cricket, however, is like God; it exists in the details. And the details here are eye-openers. They do not merely shed light on the term "cricket sense"; they are, rather, incontrovertible proof that the game is played more in the head than on the field.

Tendulkar's battle against the Australians began when they were batting first. Mark Waugh was timing the ball fluently in the middle overs along with Michael Bevan, picking ones and twos with stunning regularity. When Sachin was brought on to bowl, India badly needed to break through. Waugh had crossed eighty, his team was 170-odd for three, and with many overs to go, they looked set for a 300-plus total.

Sachin saw that Waugh was so confident, if he nèeded to stretch out and drive, he would. That could create room for error. So he bowled a textbook flighted leg-break that landed outside the off-stump. Waugh took the bait and drove, only to slice the ball into the hands of Sourav Ganguly at cover-point.

Sunil Gavaskar was live on air. He said: 'They always want him to do magic with the bat. Tendulkar here has done magic with the ball too.'

Then Sachin rocketed in a throw to run out the other Waugh, Steve. His third act was the message-for-the-evening-to-unfold. He was stationed at long-on for the last over. Bevan hit a cross-batted shot to him and ran a single. Bevan's partner Shane Warne started out for a second. Tendulkar saw this and, from long-on, threw the ball straight into keeper Mongia's hands. Warne had to scamper back into the crease. Aggression would be met with aggression, Sachin seemed to be telling the opponents.

When the chase began, he launched the kind of planned blitzkrieg that could alone subdue a hardnosed opponent who had put up 284 on the scoreboard. The target to qualify vis-à-vis the run rate was 254. 'One of the top three batters would have to get a hundred,' Ravi Shastri said on air as Tendulkar and Ganguly strode out to the crease. Gavaskar noted: 'Sachin is a positive thinker, he'll be looking to get 285, not 254. He knows he's got to get a big score, and he might begin to bang the ball straightaway.'

With exactly this aim, Tendulkar took guard and had what can be called a patently false start in the first few balls. The Sharjah wicket did not have too much bounce, so a man bent on aggression might be induced to put his front foot down all the time before launching into expansive strokes. This could be dangerous, for it would mean blind neglect of the merit of a ball and, for the perceptive and accurate Aussie speedsters, a quick detection of the batsman's seriously suicidal propensities.

On the very first delivery that he faced, Tendulkar came on to the front foot before Damien Fleming had released the ball from his hand. That ball was struck to mid-off. The same premature movement was made for the second ball, which was glanced for two. For the third, he put his foot down the third time, slashed, and missed. The fourth was a well-directed bouncer; it made him duck. The bouncer helped, because Tendulkar realized the mistake he was making by committing himself on the front foot. He now decided to first pick the line and length and only then attack.

His attack began, in the real sense, in the sixth over. Michael Kasprowicz let go a slower one, an off-spinner. Tendulkar picked it up, came down the track and hit a cross-batted shot over mid-wicket for six. The next ball was banged in short. It was pulled over square-leg for another six. His prudent decision to respect the line and length and only then commit himself had brought him the two sixes, the first off the front foot and the second off the back, in two consecutive deliveries. Because of those two hits, India had jumped from sixteen for no loss in 5.4 overs to twenty-eight for no loss in six overs.

The first Indian wicket – Sourav Ganguly's – fell in the ninth over, and Nayan Mongia came in as one-drop bat, ahead of Azharuddin. Tendulkar asked him to stay on the wicket and carried on with his agenda. Next Kasprowicz was glanced for a four. As the ball crossed the ropes, the Aussies hurled a string of "compliments". Tendulkar's response was a defensive back-foot stroke that sent the ball through the covers, for yet another four.

He had his chances. He would have been out if one throw had

directly hit the stumps, and he was once dropped by Kasprowicz, although off a no-ball. Yet his sights were set on the target. As Mongia co-operated by hitting over the top for some useful fours and a six, he went up to him time and again and mentioned one word: stay.

Warne again came in for special treatment. As soon as he started his spell, one of his deliveries was picked up from around the off-stump and dabbed to deep fine-leg for two. Then there was a rare Tendulkar sight: a flat-batted cover-drive off the leg-spinner. The flat bat made the shot look like the lashing of a whip, and indeed it was just as harsh; in Indian cricket parlance, it would be called a *chaabuk*.

The partnership between Tendulkar and Mongia was broken in the twenty-second over, the same over in which Sachin reached his fifty. Mongia hit into the hands of mid-wicket, and Azhar followed him back in the pavilion six overs later when he edged a near-wide on to his stumps. Ajay Jadeja, who replaced Azhar, was also out in no time. The scoreboard suddenly read 138 for four.

When India had added a few more runs and the thirty-second over was about to begin, cricket found a new interrupter. So far it had known rain, bad light and rowdy crowds. Here came a sandstorm. Rivulets of sand flew across the desert floor, forcing most people on the field to hunker down. The umpires crouched low, their eyes slammed shut, and the Australians covered their faces with their caps. Tendulkar's body language however was different. He stood impatiently at the crease, bat firmly in hand, his eyes narrowed but not shut. The teams finally had to go off the field. India were at this point 143 for four, had not hit a boundary in ten overs, and the runs had slowed down.

When play restarted after a sixteen-minute break, the target stood revised – 133 to win, and 95 to qualify, from fifteen overs.

In Tendulkar's words, this was the strategy his team planned during the break:

> We discussed the situation in the dressing room. It was decided
> that I would bat through the innings, while V.V.S. Laxman (now
> his batting partner) would take risks and play strokes.

Unfortunately Laxman couldn't connect too well. We were
pressed for time as well as overs. So the two of us decided in the
middle that I would go for the strokes.[2]

Tendulkar unleashed a new attack. In the first over after resumption
of play, Kasprowicz tried a slower one. He was hit over his head and
in front of the sight-screen for a maximum.

Steve Waugh, a bowler of tremendous intelligence who almost
always delivered in a crunch, was flummoxed by sharp tactics.
Tendulkar deliberately started playing him off the front foot each
time. He wanted Waugh to bowl short. When he did, Sachin stayed
back and pulled the ball over mid-on for a four.

In another over, he played Waugh entirely off the back foot,
whether the ball merited it or not. This forced Waugh to pitch it up
in the next over. When he did, Tendulkar hit him over his head for
yet another four. He was systematically getting a boundary almost
every over.

By the fortieth over, India needed forty-two to qualify.
Tendulkar was already past his hundred and was seeing the ball big.
Overgenerous strokes could have emerged from his blade, but an
evolved Tendulkar used judgement. When Waugh bowled one on the
off-stump that was not easy to put away, he played a cheeky angled-
bat shot to third-man for four. In another over he noticed the fine-leg
fielder was inside the circle and aptly got in the line of a ball that was
on off-stump and paddled it over short fine-leg for a four. The bat
angles for both the cheeky strokes had been accurate; he was
marrying intelligence with hand-wrought elegance.

There was passion too. When V.V.S. Laxman said no to a call for
a single, the gentle giant from Hyderabad was shouted at. '*Bhaag na!
Pura ho jata tha* (Run! We'd have got it),' he was told. When the forty-
first over ended, India needed twenty-four to qualify. Sachin and
Laxman got into a huddle. Sachin clearly wanted to go for a victory.
He later said:

> At first we were trying to qualify. However, that evening, I was
> finding the middle of the bat most of the time, and even the

strokes I hit in the air were clearing the field. So I told Laxman:
'We'll win the game and give the Aussies a big psychological
blow. This will help us in the final, because they will know that
no matter how much they score, we can chase.'[3]

The first ball of the forty-second over was sent into the stands; on the
second, Sachin was dropped on the boundary by the deep mid-
wicket fielder who lost the ball at the last moment and conceded
four. After this, Damien Fleming was smashed over long-on and deep
into the crowds. In the next over, India had qualified.

Wanting to finish off the game as quickly as possible, in the
same over, Sachin made room for himself outside the leg-stump and
hit over the covers for four. Before he could wrap things up, however,
he got a dubious caught-behind decision. Everybody at the ground
stood up and applauded as he made his way back to the pavilion after
almost handing down a lesson in sports psychology to the Australians.
The lesson was driven home even after he was adjudged out. He
noticed, when he was on his way back that he was walking with a Viv
Richards-like swagger. While the other lessons had been deliberate
and well thought-out, this one was near-involuntary, a case of the
aggressive unconscious assuming complete control. He had never
walked like this before, he said.

India lost the game from there, but his 142 had taken them into
the finals, where they could make amends. Most important, the
psychological implication of his innings for the Aussies was that it
made them feel like losers. Their sentiment was reflected by coach
Allan Border: 'Hell, if he stayed, even at eleven an over he would
have got it.'

When, two days later, he walked out to bat in the final, the roof
of the stadium was nearly taken off by the roar of a breathless crowd.
They were expecting him to do just what he had done in the previous
game, with a result in favour of his team of course, and they felt there
was a good reason for their expectations: the date for the final was 24
April 1998, Tendulkar's twenty-fifth birthday.

There was another birthday boy: Damien Fleming. He was on
the other side, and he along with the other bowlers was going to have

a go at Tendulkar to defend a once-again formidable Australian score of 272.

Tendulkar had his same batting attitude, head on; even so, there was a subtle difference from two days ago. He had earlier been Viv Richards; now, he was like Pete Sampras, his modern-day favourite among tennis players.

Tendulkar never tired of telling his friends how he liked Sampras' controlled aggression and how he marvelled at his consistency (in 1998, Sampras was busy maintaining his number one rank for the fifth year running, a world record).

The similarities between Sampras and Sachin are striking. Like Sachin, Pete was a child prodigy, and started playing tennis at seven. If the child cricketer invoked Richards and Gavaskar, little Pete too had legends as idols: Rod Laver and Ken Rosewall. Like the Indian, he was a driven young man, obsessed with his game. He hated losing. By his early twenties, he had quite a few Grand Slam titles under his belt, as Sachin his hundreds, and he was earning millions in endorsements (much more than a cricketer could hope to have). Significantly, by 1998, people had stopped comparing Sampras with his peers; they were discussing his place among the all-time tennis greats. Yet his behaviour on and off the field was as impeccable as Tendulkar's, and he had stayed away from all the dangers and pitfalls created by his growing status.

Sampras' standout quality was his quiet intensity on court *throughout*. Tendulkar too burned on the inside, but his intensity could still be hijacked in the middle of an innings by his impatience and desire to be swashbuckling.

In the final, Tendulkar took the Sampras approach: look at the innings as an evolution, and integrate your game in such a way that the opponent fails to target just one point causing the whole edifice to come down.

In the first three overs, Tendulkar got to play merely one ball as Sourav Ganguly took most of the strike. The crowd was roaring for Sachin, and seeing too many balls from the other end could, for all his experience, unnerve him.

That did not happen. He had come out with the aim of dominating not five, ten or even twenty-five overs; he wanted to dominate the whole quota and take his team to the target. Ganguly was striking the ball well and getting good runs. So Tendulkar began to work his way around for ones and twos. He nudged, he late-cut, he push-drove gently; he found the gaps without much difficulty.

After Ganguly left, Nayan Mongia kept up the momentum and helped him keep a cool head. Next man Azhar did the same. Azhar and Sachin, in fact, strung a fine partnership. The Indian captain, who was a superb runner and a Carl Lewis in comparison with the other two batting partners, enabled quick-footed Tendulkar to convert many singles into twos.

It was not that Tendulkar did not attack. When Shane Warne went round the wicket in his sixth over, he greeted him by dancing down the track and lifting him over long-on for a six. The mantra, however, was integration. The very next ball from Warne was on the leg-stump and tempting. He just pushed it along the ground, and where the Aussies expected him to take one, he ran for two. It was sensible cricket. Even the inside-out shots were played with equanimity, and the smashing was calm yet cruel.

The all-out violence of the India vs. Australia home series returned only after the fortieth over, as India inched close to the target. Warne was straight-driven and cover-driven brutally, and Kasprowicz was hit on the roof.

When India were twenty-five short of the target, Sachin got a second successive false decision, this time for being before the wicket. He was not out on two counts. First, the ball had pitched outside the leg-stump. Second, when it went across and hit the pads, it had missed the off-stump. Gavaskar said sardonically on air that it was after a long time that the ball had hit his pads; he had been middling it all the time, so perhaps he was given out for not middling.

Tendulkar walked off with displeasure written all over his face. The bad decision though, came too late to threaten the course of the match; India won by six wickets, with nine balls to spare. Tendulkar had got 134 off 131 balls, with twelve fours and three sixes, and snatched the Coca-Cola Cup.

Cricket can be a strange leveller. In the ODI series in India, the home team had won all league games before Australia beat them in the finals. In Sharjah, Australia won all the league games; India took the final.

The two memorable desert knocks took Tendulkar to a new level in international cricket. The Sampras parallel became more remarkable. First, the financial rewards were improving, though they weren't close to tennis standards. The tournament sponsors announced a special 2,000 pounds award for his hundred in the final league game. After the final, he got a thousand dollars for hitting the highest number of sixes in the tournament, five hundred dollars for most sixes in a match, a thousand dollars for fastest fifty, twenty-five hundred dollars as man of the final, an Opel Astra for being player of the Cup, and a share of the ten lakh rupees award announced for the Indian team by Board president, Raj Singh Dungarpur.

Before the final, Sanjeev Gupta, then marketing head of the Coca-Cola company, had promised Mark Mascarenhas that he would give Sachin a Mercedes 500 if India won. Mascarenhas asked Gupta if the promise stood even if India won without Sachin doing much. 'Yes,' Gupta said. When the agent communicated the word to Sachin, he said: 'I will win the Merc tomorrow.' He did.

Second, and more important, comparisons with his peers nearly stopped; everybody was now discussing Tendulkar's place among the all-time greats. And the position they approved was lower only to that of Sir Don Bradman.

Steve Waugh said his batting had shown that 'in history, he will go down as second to Bradman.' Richie Benaud said he had never seen better batting in one-dayers. Sanjay Manjrekar said Tendulkar had taken the definitive step towards becoming the second best batsman in the history of cricket. Tony Greig said he was the nearest thing to Bradman there could be. And Shane Warne called him amazing and unstoppable.

When the Indians were having a gala time in the dressing room after the final, Warne walked in, took off his T-shirt and asked Tendulkar to sign it. 'Whom do you want it for?' Sachin asked. 'For me, of course,' Warne said. When he went off, Sachin saw that five other Australian players had lined up with their T-shirts, for the same purpose. People who played the toughest cricket on earth were showing their respect for him.

Tendulkar had since the start of the year played ten matches against Australia in both formats of the game. He had got a double hundred, five hundreds and two half-centuries from those. His average: 113.

*

With that Bradmanesque average, he was now ready to meet the master himself. And Sir Don gave him a chance to do so very soon. On the occasion of his nintieth birthday, Bradman invited Tendulkar and Shane Warne to his Kensington Park home in Adelaide. The big day, 27 August 1998, was to be marked by a dinner in Bradman's honour for over one thousand people. The Don decided to keep away from it. He decided to have a quiet morning with his children and grandchildren, and in the afternoon planned to meet the two modern-day cricketers he appreciated the most.

Both Tendulkar and Warne, dressed in suits, were nervous as they shook hands with the Don. But Tendulkar said Bradman quickly put them at ease, striking up an absorbing conversation that lasted an hour. He told Tendulkar that he was the modern era's best bat and placed him in the same league as Sir Gary Sobers, Barry Richards and Arthur Morris.

Tendulkar meanwhile was keen to ask Bradman questions. He began by asking Bradman about his initial movement. Bradman said he moved back-and-across to fast bowlers and got on to the front foot to spinners without committing himself totally. Asked about his psychological preparations for a big match, the Don answered that when he was in Adelaide, he would attend to his work as stockbroker for three hours before he went to the ground. When the day's play ended, he would return to his work for a few more hours. If he were playing away from Adelaide, he would take a long walk before and after the match.

Bradman, eager to find out more about Tendulkar, asked him if he made any movement before the ball left the bowler's hand. Sachin's answer was 'I-don't-know'. The Don said that he thought Sachin surely had some movement, otherwise it would be impossible for him to play the shots he did.

When Tendulkar told him that he had been coached, the Don expressed surprise. That surprise was because, he said, just like him, Sachin's left elbow did not point to mid-off when he took guard. A coach would always tell his pupils that the elbow *had* to face mid-off.

Bradman had first said in 1996 that Tendulkar batted like him. His opinion stayed unchanged till the time of his death in 2001 but, always a reticent man, he never really explained why he felt so. This is unfortunate because Bradman was an excellent analyst; his books, especially *The Art of Cricket*, are regarded as classics in cricket. In the final chapter of this book, I have done a detailed comparison of the two. After all, Tendulkar's position in the rich history of the game cannot be determined without such a comparison. However, while we are on the subject of Tendulkar's domination of the Australians in 1998 and his subsequent visit to Adelaide on Bradman's invitation, we must look at Bradman's supremacy over Indian bowlers and his journeys to India.

Exactly forty years before Tendulkar collared the Australian attack at home and in Sharjah, the Don gave a similar treatment to the Indians. During India's tour of Australia in 1947-48, he scored 715 runs in the Tests, with four hundreds, at an average of 178. His total count against the Indians was 1,081 runs (with six hundreds) at an average of 135.

It was during this series that Bradman scored his hundredth first-class century. When a film of that knock was shown in England, the famous cricket writer R.C. Robertson-Glasgow said: 'At that historic statistical moment, when Bradman was about to go from 99 to 100, there was the Indian bowler (G. Kishenchand) trying to deliver the ball with one hand and applaud with the other, a feat that is beyond the most enthusiastic practitioner.'

Prof D.B. Deodhar, known as the Maharishi of Indian cricket, covered the tour for an Indian newspaper. He wrote: 'Bradman, when at 50, could confuse our attack and after a century could rout it to the fun of the crowds (Tendulkar appeared to do just this to the Australians in 1998). He could have easily established some more records against us if he had meant to, but, as one critic put it "he threw away his wicket possibly to avoid the slaughter of the innocents."'

The Indians were indeed considered "innocents" and starters in Test cricket in 1947-48, though they had played their first Test in 1932. Their tour to Australia was not expected to bring in any profits, but Bradman gave all his support for it, saying the 'interests of the game should not be subservient to finance'. He was of the opinion that while Test cricket between England and Australia would always blossom, 'it cannot remain in isolation and will be materially strengthened if other countries can match their skill'. So he felt it was his duty to 'assist the less mature cricketing countries to the highest level of play' and all through the 1947-48 tour, attempted to help the Indian players. The Indian players found him 'extremely cordial and friendly'.

For all this, Bradman never really visited India in spite of a number of invitations that went out to him regularly. The Indians could not fathom why he did not come, but their regard for him remained the same. Bradman also never visited the Caribbean islands, South Africa or even New Zealand, so the Indians couldn't complain too much.

That does not mean he did not set foot on Indian soil. He did have two stopovers. Two months after India's tour ended, he was on his way to England for the last time when the liner carrying the Australian team docked in Mumbai for a few hours. A large number of his fans waited at the pier to greet him and his side. Bradman was unwell and decided to rest in his cabin. The crowd however would just not disperse without seeing him. Finally, he emerged on the deck and waved to the fans, who waved back excitedly.

The second stopover was in Kolkata in 1953, when Bradman and his wife Jessie were on their way to London. A team of Indian cricket board officials and local cricketers received the couple at Dum Dum airport, and a photograph of the occasion shows a garlanded Bradman smiling broadly in recognition of the warm welcome. The smile disappeared soon. Hundreds of cricket lovers had gathered at the airport to have a glimpse of him. They broke through the police cordon, and the Bradmans had to be taken away hurriedly in an army car. So Bradman also shared a not-so minor problem with Tendulkar: the problem of being mobbed wherever he went.

If Tendulkar was thrilled with the honour of meeting Bradman, he had a major national honour coming his way back in India. He became the first cricketer to win the Rajiv Gandhi Khel Ratna, India's most prestigious award for achievement in sports. The award, worth one lakh rupees, a plaque and a scroll of honour, was given to him by the then President K.R. Narayanan at a special function on 29 August 1998.

Along with him, there were two other Indians who won big awards in the year 1998. One of them was scientist A.P.J. Abdul Kalam, the father of India's missile programme and currently the President of the country. He got the Indira Gandhi award for national integration. The other was Amartya Sen, who won the Nobel Prize for Economics.

Awards and accolades notwithstanding, there was no doubt that in pure cricketing terms, Sachin had made significant paradigm shifts during the year, both for himself and his team. When the year ended, the statisticians showed that he had rattled up a hell of a lot of runs, making it his best year in international cricket. In the Tests, he had averaged over fifty, and in one-dayers, he had scored close to 1,900 runs with nine hundreds that took him past Desmond Haynes' record for the maximum one-day centuries. However, it was more the manner in which he had gone about making those runs, and the results he produced for his team with initiative and ingenuity, that justified the word paradigm. Apart from the Test and ODI series against Australia at home and the Sharjah tournament, there were many other intense efforts that marked him out as the chief flag-bearer of Indian cricket and attracted the highest possible attention for him at the international level.

At the very beginning of the year, he had given the team the stimulant of self-belief that it very badly needed. In January 1998, India had played Pakistan in the best-of-three finals in the Silver Jubilee Independence Cup in Bangladesh. India took the first final (Sachin got sixty-seven in forty-four balls, belting Saqlain Mushtaq, the major bowler on a slow wicket, out of the attack), Pakistan the second (he scored just one), and in the decider, Pakistan set India a target of 315. No team had ever chased such a large score in one-dayers till then. A breezy start was a must if the improbable score was to be reached. Tendulkar, just back to the opening slot under Azhar's captaincy, approached the chase with a mix of zest and bombast.

Saqlain, who came on to bowl early in the innings, was again belted. By the time Sachin was out in the ninth over, he had got forty-one off twenty-six balls, and India had reached seventy-one, just the platform they needed for a spirited chase. More significantly, the opposition had been rattled by the onslaught and put on the defensive. Ultimately India overtook the target in the penultimate ball, registering a historic victory against its arch-rivals. When the winning hit was made, everybody in the Indian team was seen jumping in the dressing room, as if something unimaginable had happened to the entire team.

The Dhaka innings was the foundation on which India approached an almost unbearably busy annual cricket schedule with a degree of self-assurance. In the final analysis, they had a record five one-day tournament victories, a one-day series victory against Zimbabwe and a Test series triumph against Australia at home. Most of the victories were either at home or in places like Dhaka and Sharjah, which had similar conditions, and this did take away some of the glitter even if the team was certainly far more consistent than it had been in 1997. Yet the fact remained that many of its conspicuous weaknesses remained hidden because Tendulkar most often took on the opposition all on his own, and the weight he bore considerably eased the pressure on the rest of the side.

A good example of this was the final of the Nidahas Cup in Sri Lanka (played in June-July 1998). Tendulkar and Ganguly (who was increasingly proving to be a reliable opening partner) smashed the Lankan attack before the Colombo crowd and put on a world record opening partnership of 252. Although Sachin got 128 from 131 balls, India still had to struggle to defend its total of 307.

The "lone ranger" image was further strengthened as the year progressed. When India met Australia in the third quarter-final of the ICC mini-World Cup played in Bangladesh towards the end of the year, India, batting first, was reduced to eight for the loss of Ganguly and captain Azharuddin. Tendulkar realized he would have to carry the innings on his shoulders, and the best way to do it against the Aussies was to match aggression with aggression. The Sampras influence had by now prefixed the word 'controlled' before aggression, so Sachin decided he would not hit in the air early on but play his strokes freely nevertheless. The result was 141 from 127 balls. Australia began their chase of the Indian total of 307 spiritedly and looked comfortable at 145 for two when Tendulkar was given a chance to turn his arm over. He got Steve Waugh caught and bowled and then dismissed three more: Michael Bevan, Damien Martyn and Brad Young, ending with figures of four for thirty-eight as Australia were all out for a little more than 260.[4]

One of the worst victims of Tendulkar's single-handed domination of a whole season was Zimbabwe's Henry Olonga. India returned to Sharjah late in 1998 for the Coca-Cola Champions Trophy also involving Sri Lanka and Zimbabwe. In the match before the India-Zimbabwe final, Olonga got Tendulkar out off a sharply-rising delivery. This dismissal was much discussed in the run-up to the final. The pace bowler later regretted all that discussion, for Tendulkar got back by smashing 124 runs in the final. Olonga bowled six overs in all and was taken for fifty runs. It must be mentioned here that he bowled exceptionally badly and gave too much width, helping Tendulkar to have easy swings off almost each ball.

This match is remembered mainly for the statistics and the crazy hitting, Sachin reaching his fifty in twenty-eight balls, his hundred in seventy-one balls and along with Ganguly chasing Zimbabwe's total of 196 in record time. But Tendulkar's attitudinal change in the middle of his knock was the most surprising aspect of it all. He was having wild swings and had just crossed his fifty when he skied one and the Zimbabweans dropped an awfully easy catch. His recklessness ended with that stroke. As decided earlier, he did play aggressively but not with abandon. This was quite unlike the Tendulkar who was known to fall an easy prey to temptation.

Similar adjustments were starkly highlighted in the MCC vs. Rest of the World match played at Lord's on 18 July 1998 to mark the 150th birth anniversary of the legendary Dr W.G. Grace. Though it was an exhibition game, twenty-two of the world's top cricketers participated in it, each putting in his best and most serious efforts. Tendulkar's batting in this match was a mix of the mundane and the extraordinary. Early on in the innings, he often played and missed, chased balls outside the off-stump, tried not-so good heaves to the leg side, got inside edges and mistimed some strokes. It appeared to be an off day, but even on such a day, he stayed composed and got a hundred against an attack comprising Glenn McGrath, Allan Donald, Javagal Srinath and Anil Kumble.

What was more refreshing for Indian cricket lovers was that he was also instinctively challenging some of the conventional attitudes in Indian cricket. After the Sharjah tournament in April, India played what was seen as an entirely avoidable triangular one-day series at home involving Kenya and Bangladesh. Most of the players were aware of the punishing schedule that lay ahead and were glad to skip some of the games. However, when Tendulkar was rested, he was furious and spoke his mind to the authorities concerned. Then, after flying from one corner of the globe, Kuala Lumpur (where India had gone to play the Commonwealth Games amid conflict between the BCCI and the Indian Olympics Association) to the other, Toronto, for the fifth Sahara Cup game against Pakistan, he got a nice, unruffled seventy-seven. From there the team flew out to Harare for a three-ODI series. There again he stood out with a hundred.

He had thus wielded his willow through the year with power, elegance and above all, cricketing acumen. The results for the Indian team were obvious, and his personal position next to Don Bradman too was confirmed.

It was during this golden year, when Tendulkar trailed clouds of the highest glory and began to acquire an aura of invincibility about him, that his deification began in India (Matthew Hayden spelled out the word God, when he saw the scenes in India in 2001).

However, for bowlers across the world, he was the opposite: a confirmed fiend and a tormentor. One of the bowlers he respected very much, Shane Warne, led the others in confessing after a harrowing 1998 experience: 'I'll be having nightmares of Sachin just running down the wicket and belting me back over the head for a six.'

---

1   Kapil Dev had hit six sixes during his knock of 175 against Zimbabwe in the 1983 World Cup.
2   *Ekach Shatkar, Sachin Special,* 1998.
3   *Ibid.*
4   India lost the semi-finals of the mini-World Cup against the West Indies.

troubled times

Life is not a continuum of pleasant choices,
but of inevitable problems that call for strength,
determination and hard work.

– An ancient Indian saying

The start of a new year, 1999 and a difficult phase in Sachin Tendulkar's career, was marked by a zero he scored in the first of the five one-dayers against New Zealand in New Zealand. Excessive cricket had not deterred the Indian cricket establishment from sending the team to Kiwiland at the fag end of 1998 for three Tests and five one-dayers. The Tests had been played before the ODIs, and in the second Test at Wellington that New Zealand won to take the series 1-0, Tendulkar had got a fighting hundred. So nobody really seemed to mind the naught, and there were no alarms either when he got twenty-three, forty-five and five in the next three one-dayers (he missed the fifth due to a wrist injury).

That was because one of the biggest cricket events for India and the world was not during but *after* the New Zealand tour. Pakistan was coming to India, after twelve years, for a two-Test series that was to be followed by the Asian Test championship (also involving Sri Lanka) and a triangular one-day series. Cricket lovers across India and Pakistan, and those in other cricket-playing countries like English cricket writer, Mike Marqusee, who felt the absence of India-Pakistan cricket undermined the Indian sub-continent's claim to be the game's new powerhouse, looked forward to serious cricket. Since Imran Khan's team had played absorbing cricket in India in 1987 and India went to Pakistan in 1989 for a series that came to be known more for Sachin Tendulkar's Test debut than anything else, there had only been sporadic bilateral cricket between the neighbours, played mostly on neutral soil, and just one short Indian tour to Pakistan, in 1997. Pakistan's 1991-92 tour to India had been cancelled due to political tensions, and Indians had thus far been largely deprived of the sight of the new-generation Pakistani stalwarts like Wasim Akram, Saeed Anwar and Inzamam-ul-Haq.

There was of course unpleasant political drama and thuggery preceding Pakistan's trip to India. The perpetrators were the same ones who had dug up the Wankhede wicket in Mumbai in 1991 and caused the cancellation of that tour: the Shiv Sena. Their method was similar this time too, only the scene of excavation shifted to New Delhi's Feroz Shah Kotla Stadium, which was supposed to host the first Test. In a pre-dawn attack, the Sainiks stormed into the Kotla Stadium with an army of newspaper correspondents and camerapersons, and ruined the pitch. The Sainiks in Mumbai, not to be left behind, ransacked the Indian cricket board's office at Churchgate and, apart from smashing quite a few trophies, did considerable damage to the Prudential World Cup that Kapil Dev's team had proudly brought home in 1983. Serious questions now arose about whether the tour would take place at all. They were settled only after the leader of the then ruling Bharatiya Janata Party and India's Home Minister L.K. Advani rushed to Mumbai and persuaded his ally, Shiv Sena chief Bal Thackeray, to call off his party's "agitation" against the tour.

The harm caused to the New Delhi wicket meant that the venues for the first and second Test had to be interchanged. Chennai would now host the first Test, and New Delhi the second, so officials there would get enough time to restore the pitch.

Chennai was Tendulkar's favourite hunting ground, and the stage could not get bigger – an Indo-Pak Test on home soil after more than a decade – for a player to put up a fine and memorable performance. In the event, the Test turned out to be an exceptional advertisement for Indo-Pak cricket, and an agonizingly unforgettable chapter in the life and career of Tendulkar. He did come up with a very fine performance, but in a few crucial moments, it became entirely ineffectual.

The first day of the Test belonged to India's gifted leg-spinner Anil Kumble, and the second to Pakistan's equally gifted off-spinner Saqlain Mushtaq. Kumble pocketed six wickets and made sure that the visitors were bundled out for 238; Saqlain picked five and limited India's lead to a meagre sixteen. One of Saqlain's victims was the diminutive batsman the Pakistanis wanted out before anybody else. Tendulkar tried what was correctly termed an "ambitious shot" by the Indian media off only the third ball he faced, and was scooped up at gully by Salim Malik.

After sub-continental spinning prowess, it was the turn of sub-continental swing to make its presence felt. Venkatesh Prasad took six wickets as Pakistan in its second innings crashed from a comfortable 275 for four to 286 all out. Tendulkar, with his gentle spin, contributed to the team's cause by picking the wickets of Pakistan's two most important middle-order batsmen: Inzamam-ul-Haq and Yousuf Youhana (in the first innings too, he had trapped Youhana Leg Before when he was fifty-three and looked set for a big score).

India was left to get 271 to win the Test. Only three days of the match were over yet, so time was not a constraint. The wicket had turned considerably from day one; that was something the Indians had to watch out for, especially because the opponents had a talented spinner in Saqlain. Regardless of the way the match went, one thing was clear: it was going to be a stiff contest and a critical examination of both the famed Pakistani bowling attack and the much-commended Indian batting line-up.

Even on a spinning track, the likes of Wasim Akram and Waqar Younis never ever took a backseat, and not in a prestige match in any case. In the fourth over, when India had merely got five on the scoreboard, Waqar got rid of Sadagoppan Ramesh, who had scored a comfortable forty-three on his home ground in the first innings, and in the sixth over trapped V.V.S. Laxman for a duck plumb in front of the wicket. If six for the loss of two wickets sounded bad, eighty-two for five sounded fairly disastrous. Without too much fuss, Akram and Saqlain had between them demolished Rahul Dravid (ten), Mohammed Azharuddin (seven) and Sourav Ganguly (two) as Sachin Tendulkar held up one end.

What India now desperately needed was, as before, a solid partnership. Besides, it was absolutely necessary that Tendulkar should stay at the crease till the end. Until now, he had looked sturdy though wickets had fallen quickly at the other end. Fortunately for him, and for the Chennai crowd that had been shocked into silence, Nayan Mongia, who came in at the loss of the fifth wicket, appeared, from the word go, decisively responsive to the need for forging a partnership.

Tendulkar was not known for playing sheet-anchor in the manner of a Sunil Gavaskar or a G.R.Vishwanath, but here he had to show total application and carry the innings on his own if India was to stage a fightback. With Mongia keeping one end firm, he brought out his own mix of Gavaskar-like intensity and obstinacy and Vivian Richards-like rage. The stubbornness was reserved for the good balls, the rage for the bad ones. He straight-drove a decent Akram delivery for four. The bowler's eyes followed the ball as it rushed to the boundary. When it crossed the ropes, Akram thrust both his hands into his head and puckered his forehead. It was, for one of the greatest bowlers of all time, a very rare expression of helplessness. The very sight of Akram running in full steam to bowl to Tendulkar was one of the most beautiful in the game, and the Chennai crowd got to see plenty of it that day. What made the encounter special was the enormous respect that the two had for each other. Tendulkar was aware that the Pakistani was the best pace bowler of his time, and Akram acknowledged that the Indian was the number one batsman in the world.

Tendulkar played two sweeps off Saqlain and Shahid Afridi with the power normally reserved for his cover-drives, and the umpire once had to quickly get out of the way when he stepped out to Saqlain and thumped the ball straight. There was a quiver of excitement in the Chennai crowd as the strokes were balanced with dogged defence from both the batsmen and the innings progressed well beyond what had earlier looked like a near-hopeless situation. The sign of real revelation and hope for them was that Tendulkar was building his innings steadily.

However, there was one disturbing sight here: Tendulkar was frequently clutching his back, as if in pain, and was having difficulty with the follow-through to his strokes. Not that it stopped him in any fashion. After he crossed eighty, Tendulkar hit four fours in an over off Saqlain. In that same over, he let himself go as he stepped out and inside-edged, but wicket-keeper Moin Khan missed the catch and the stumping too. A few minutes later, Sachin glanced Saqlain beautifully to complete his hundred, and the M.A. Chidambaram Stadium erupted in ecstacy. India now looked closer to achieving the target of 271.

Suddenly Mongia did what was clearly indefensible. He slogged Akram mindlessly, spooning a catch to Waqar Younis at mid-off. At this point, India needed fifty-three to win. But Pakistan had still not found the opening they wanted. Sunil Joshi walked in and proved a reliable partner, adding valuable runs with Tendulkar as the score approached 250.

Tendulkar's back spasms were, in the meantime, getting worse, and just twenty-odd runs short of the target, he began to look urgently intent on finishing off the game before the pain got unbearably excruciating. He hit two quick fours, prompting non-striker Sunil Joshi to walk up to him in the middle of the Saqlain over. The scoreboard then read 254 for six. 'Dekh lena (Be watchful). You have to hang in there,' Joshi told him. 'But,' according to Joshi, 'I knew something was coming.'

That "something" was nothing short of a disaster. The very next ball, Tendulkar stepped out to Saqlain, tried to hit him over mid wicket and top-edged. As Wasim Akram took the catch at mid-off, Pakistan's coach Javed Miandad got out of his seat, clapped thunderously and did everything short of a jig. He knew, the Pakistan team knew, and so did the Chepauk crowd that fell completely silent. The fact was that the rest of the batsmen were not up to it to score the seventeen runs needed for India's victory. Sunil Joshi, Anil Kumble, Javagal Srinath and Venkatesh Prasad got four runs between them, and India crashed to 258 all out. It was to Pakistan's credit that they were relentless in applying pressure even when Tendulkar was blazing away, and completed their job swiftly once he was out of the way.

For Tendulkar, it was one of the most distressing experiences of his Test career. He had given a splendid demonstration of batting, and many were reminded in the middle of his knock, of Sunil Gavaskar's masterful innings of ninety-six against Pakistan at Bangalore in 1987. That knock had not prevented an Indian defeat. Nor did Sachin's, but the vital difference was that Gavaskar had not made that momentary slip-up that made a wonderful effort go waste. What made the Chennai throwaway worse was that it was Tendulkar who had reintroduced the element of contest into the Test after the seedbed for an Indian collapse was ready.

Gavaskar commented on the debacle without circumlocutory mildness. 'Never leave something that you can do to someone else,' he said, leaving no one guessing whom he was referring to. He could talk straight because he was the prime torch-bearer of the batting tradition Tendulkar had inherited, and could empathize with the physical pain that Sachin was going through at the time.

Tendulkar was mean while deeply hurt by the Chennai defeat and made a frank acknowledgement that he had left the task unfinished. 'I should have reached the target myself,' he said. 'I was hitting the ball well but when the strain aggravated, I could not go ahead with the follow-through. Every time I attempted, the pain increased.'

According to Sanjay Manjrekar, the defeat still troubles Tendulkar:

> Whenever we are discussing India-Pakistan cricket, he invariably goes back to the Chennai Test and to what could have happened if he had stayed on. He knows he could have finished the game, and he knows that if he had, it would have been one of the best Test innings of all time.

Drama was an intrinsic part of an Indo-Pak series, and after the Chepauk cliffhanger, it unfolded again on a grand scale first in New Delhi, where the second Test was played, and then in Kolkata, the venue for the inaugural Test of the Asian Test championship, an idea mooted by the then president of the BCCI, Jagmohan Dalmiya, involving India, Pakistan and Sri Lanka. While at the Feroz Shah Kotla in New Delhi, Anil Kumble was at the heart of the action, picking up all ten wickets in Pakistan's second innings to wrap up a convincing Indian victory by 212 runs. Tendulkar, after doing little in Delhi (six and twenty-nine respectively), returned to centrestage in Kolkata again, this time not due to the runs he scored but due to a sensational first-ball dismissal and then a controversial run-out. In both instances, the man pitted against him was the same: Shoaib Akhtar.

After Pakistan was bundled out for 185 in their first innings at the Eden Gardens, Kolkata, India made a decent start and were doing well at 147 for one, when "Rawalpindi Express" Shoaib Akhtar castled Rahul Dravid. Tendulkar came in, as usual welcomed by a roar from a crowd that was in excess of one lakh. Before he could bring his bat down to meet the first ball, it went through his defences and knocked middle-stump out of the ground. The dismissal created quite a stir because the pace generated by the bowler was exceptional even in the light of his country's rich fast-bowling history. That was the ball that launched Akhtar's career in the real sense.

In the second innings, Akhtar the fielder created obstacles for Tendulkar. Tendulkar played Wasim Akram past mid-on and set out for three. While charging to the bowler's end to complete the third run, his eyes were fixed firmly on the ball hurled back by substitute Nadeem Khan. Akhtar, who had come in from the off and stood behind the stumps to receive the throw, was therefore blocked out of his view. He banged against Akhtar at the edge of the crease and, with the impact, his grounded bat was momentarily thrown into the air. It was the wrong moment for him, because it was at this point that the throw directly hit the stumps. The third umpire, K.T. Francis, came into play, and he declared Sachin out.

The huge Kolkata crowd saw the run-out as more than a consequence of accidental collision. They felt Akhtar had played foul and deliberately blocked Tendulkar's path. The crowd began to holler, and in less than a minute, paper missiles began to rain down all around. Sachin's own disappointment on being given out was visible, and instead of going straight to the dressing room, he walked into the Trans World International (TWI) TV room to watch the replay along with match referee Cammie Smith. He shook his head unbelievingly as he saw the dismissal.

Before Azhar, the new batsman, could face a ball, the stone- and bottle-throwing went out of hand, and Pakistan captain Wasim Akram led his team off the ground. The match was interestingly poised at this juncture. India, needing 279 to win, were after Tendulkar's removal three down for less than 150. And this was only the fourth day. A result was a certainty, unless of course crowd behaviour prevented any further play as it had at the same venue during the World Cup semi-final of 1996.

Fearing a repeat of the 1996 situation, ICC chief Jagmohan Dalmiya, very much a son of Kolkata, asked Tendulkar to walk around the stadium along with him to try and calm the crowd. This worked and after an hour-long disruption, play restarted. Unfortunately there was another disruption on the final day when, needing sixty-five to win with four wickets in hand, the home team lost three wickets in quick succession. Dalmiya this time put his foot down, for he knew that continued crowd trouble would not only mean greater loss of face, there was a very real chance that the beautiful ground in Kolkata would be boycotted by the entire international cricket community. So the men in uniform were sent in hot pursuit of the trouble-makers. The police crackdown continued for close to three hours, and the stadium was emptied of spectators. The final Indian wicket fell at 231 with nobody except the media, the assembled policemen and state association officials watching.

Debate and discussion on Sachin's run-out rumbled on for a long time after the Test, and even today, the dismissal is resuscitated. It is amazing how biased cricket can be in favour of the batsman. It is perfectly all right if a batsman runs craftily and doesn't allow a fielder a view of the stumps he's aiming at. Not only can a fielder then not see the sticks, he can't even attempt a direct hit. Such cases are held out as examples of the runner's intelligence. But, on the other land, if a fielder does something similarly crafty, as Shoaib Akhtar appeared to have done in this case, it is called unsporting.

Sadly Pakistan soon did something that could justifiably be called unsporting. When they met Sri Lanka in the final league match of the Test championship, their place in the final was already secure. India's Test with Sri Lanka at Colombo a few days ago had ended as a high-scoring and dull draw (Tendulkar was one of the high scorers with a hundred), so if Pakistan conceded some bonus points to Lanka in this Test, India could be effectively blocked out of the finals. That is exactly what was done, and though Pakistan won the final against Lanka by more than an innings, that act took off much of the sheen from the triumph.

*

If Tendulkar's dismissals had generated a lot of talk, his back pain had led to a much more widespread concern. Immediately after the Chennai Test, the state of his injury eclipsed debate on whether the Indians could make amends in the second encounter at New Delhi or not. While all he said was 'I am okay,' he was clearly feeling the effects of the pain during the practice sessions before the second Test, and a vacillating team management had made him go through two trials before finally declaring him fit. His presence was of course considered crucial if India had to level the series, and Raj Singh Dungarpur, the then chief of the Indian cricket board, betrayed the common sentiment when he said: 'If it is humanly possible, Tendulkar will play.' That, he said, was borne out of his conviction that Sachin was more committed than any other cricketer he had seen, but it was above all else a desperately worded statement.

Sachin had played the second Test and after that the Asian Test championship too, yet the pain had indeed aggravated since he had first felt it under the blazing Chennai sun. One of the doctors who examined him during the Delhi Test had in fact said he had looked "very tense". Few things could, after all, be more serious for a sportsman than an injury, and probably nothing could be more important for an international cricketer than the once-in-four-years World Cup, which was barely four months away (June 1999, in England). The Indian Board meanwhile disregarded repeated complaints of fatigue from all the team members and squeezed in two more tournaments before the World Cup: a triangular ODI series at home in March, with Pakistan and Lanka as the other two teams, and another tri-series in Sharjah in May, with Pakistan and England as the other competitors.

Tendulkar opted out of both these tournaments to give himself some rest, so he could be fit for June 1999. This was the first time in ten years of international cricket that he was sitting out of a full series due to an injury. He later said he should not have played on regardless of the pain, because he was at that time not even aware of the exact nature of the injury. As a weary Indian team lost both the ODI tournaments, Tendulkar flew to England to consult a specialist. A little before he left, in March, he received another national honour.

This time the award was bigger than the Khel Ratna that he had won the previous year. It was the Padma Shri, India's fourth highest civilian award (the top national honour is the Bharat Ratna, and demands to give it to Tendulkar were voiced vociferously by some Members of the Indian Parliament after he was adjudged Man of the Tournament in the 2003 World Cup). There were thirty-three other recipients of the same award that day, plus fourteen who won the second highest civilian award, the Padma Vibhushan, and another fourteen who were given the third best civilian award, the Padma Bhushan. Yet, as in so many other nations, it was the sports hero who drew maximum applause.

At this function, a pleased Tendulkar told mediapersons that he felt his back was getting better. Doctors in England too gave a positive verdict and so did the Indian cricket establishment. Finally, he was declared fit for the World Cup. The announcement came as a huge relief not only to cricket-obsessed India but to other cricket-playing nations too.

A World Cup in England was bound to send Indian hopes soaring, for it was there that India had caused one of the most stunning upsets of all times in 1983. Sixteen years and three World Cups had passed since, and twice, in 1987 and 1996, India had reached the semis before giving it all away. With the Cup going back to England, Indian cricket fans felt there was every reason why it could be again lifted at Lord's by their own captain. The team's one-day performance in 1998 had been encouraging. Over the turn of the year in 1998-99, the team had not done too well in New Zealand and had gone down dreadfully against Pakistan and Sri Lanka at home and Pakistan and England in Sharjah. The difference between 1998 and the first half of 1999, the Indian cricket followers reckoned, was the absence of Tendulkar. India had won five one-day titles in 1998; Tendulkar had played the pivotal role in reaching the team to the finals, and in each of those finals, he had scored a century. He had not been able to get a fifty in the four one-dayers he played in New Zealand. However, India had levelled the series 2-2, so that performance was seen as an aberration at worst. In the home ODI series against Pakistan and Lanka and in Sharjah, he had not played at all, and that "explained" the defeats. It had been nearly forgotten that cricket was a team game (unfortunately the story of Indian cricket is lined more with individual heroic efforts than a confident team combativeness, so it was nearly inevitable that the lone-ranger psychology at the height of Tendulkar's powers should lead to apotheosis – further, the team in 1999 was nowhere close to being a close-knit unit). So it was, as in 1996, time again for him to 'win the World Cup for India'.

The build-up to the tournament saw unprecedented hype in India. The media went to town showcasing India's chances at the World Cup, and it was big boom time for the advertising industry which was buoyantly optimistic about cricket and its biggest brand –Tendulkar's ability to influence consumer choice. The industry spent an amount in excess of two hundred crores to try and cash in on the event. It was a reflection on the kind of profile cricket had acquired in the country by 1999 that even audio cassettes and music video albums featuring leading stars of the Hindi film industry exhorting the Indian team to blast the others out of the tournament flooded the market. The entire impression created by the corporate frenzy was as if all cricket-playing countries were getting together in England for the sole purpose of handing over the Cup to India at a ceremonial dinner. A get-together of Kapil Dev's 1983 squad members was also organized, which was not surprising, and given the general atmosphere, it wasn't further surprising that a festival match was planned in Mumbai, pitting the 1983 team against the one freshly picked for England.

Tendulkar batted earnestly in the exhibition match and top-scored with a hundred. As a rule, he took exhibition matches as seriously as official ones.

A benefit match played in Dadoji Konddev Stadium in Thane city (adjoining Mumbai) for former Mumbai Ranji player Ravi Thakkar in May 2001 is a case in point. Tendulkar had agreed to play, but came down with high fever on the eve of the game. He nevertheless travelled forty kilometres from his house to Thane and told Thakkar: 'I'm unwell and really struggling, I'll just bat first (he was aware a crowd of 15,000 had gathered at the stadium primarily to see him, and he didn't want to disappoint) and then leave home.' Then he put on two sweaters and, running a high temperature, batted in the searing summer heat for a good thirty overs, to score ninety runs.

For the World Cup, India was placed in Group A along with England, Sri Lanka, South Africa, Kenya and Zimbabwe, while Group B had Pakistan, Australia, New Zealand, West Indies, Bangladesh and Scotland. On the basis of a complicated points system, the three leading teams from each group would go to the Super Six stage, and from there, the top four would go to the semi-finals. For India it turned out to be a case of semi-stasis. The team got into the Super Six with great difficulty and, once there, went out of the reckoning quickly enough. However, for the Indians and for

Tendulkar, the central moment of the tournament was not so much the end of the pre-Cup publicity bubble but an incalculably more difficult reality: a tragedy and its aftermath.

India lost the first game against a truly strong South African side in spite of getting a total of 253, which was anything but small in English conditions. The match was close, as South Africa needed twenty-seven in twenty-six balls, but then Lance Klusener, one of the real stars of the tournament, made it a no-contest by hitting three fours in three balls and driving his team home with more than two overs to spare.

The next match was against Zimbabwe at Leicester on 19 May, a strong chance for the Indians to get their first few points. At around 10:30 on the night of 18 May, just as the team was ready to go to bed, coach Anshuman Gaekwad got a phone call. It was from Mumbai, and it was to tell him that Tendulkar's father, Professor Ramesh Tendulkar had died of a heart attack. He was asked to break the news to Sachin, but found himself in an extremely difficult position and instead approached Sachin's wife, Anjali, who was in London at the time with daughter Sara. According to Sachin, 'When my wife told me at Leicester that he had died, I could not believe it. My first thought was that I must go home.' He, Anjali and Sara got on to the first flight to India early on 19 May. The other team members got to know the news only after they woke up. There was shock all around.

In India Tendulkar's personal tragedy took on a public dimension. There was a feeling of a heartfelt and deep concern for the young man who had lost his parent, someone he was very, very close to. Whenever he was asked how he could keep his feet firmly on the ground despite having enjoyed enormous success, a huge popularity and substantial wealth, Tendulkar would point to his father's teachings, which were not strictly teachings but more an unconscious revelation of character and integrity in everyday life. He seemed to look to his father's example before every move he made. There was thus a clear understanding of how much he would be affected by the tragedy. Yet a question that looked wholly inappropriate at the time instinctively cropped up in popular consciousness. That question, raised with a genuine sense of apology, was: would Tendulkar, now on his way home, be able to return to England for the World Cup?

Before Tendulkar could even land in Mumbai, and in the midst of the Zimbabwe match that turned out to be another shocker of a close finish in favour of the opposing team, the question was being put to the Indian coach Anshuman Gaekwad. He told the media: 'We must wait for the funeral before we can even start thinking of asking him. I will be in touch with him.' Prof Ramesh Tendulkar's funeral was held at Dadar's electric crematorium very early in the morning to avoid any media intrusion. Only Sachin's family and close friends were present.

Almost immediately after that, he decided to fly back to England. India's third game was against Kenya, and they had to win not only that but also the next two games against Sri Lanka and England if they were to reach the Super Six stage. Tendulkar landed in London the day before the Kenya game and, at the airport itself, was surrounded by mediapersons.

How was it that he had come back so soon? He said: 'My mother thanked me for returning home but then insisted that I return to England immediately after the funeral. She said that is what my father would have liked me to do.' He further said: 'The whole country wanted me to play. The World Cup is very important to India, so I completed the necessary rites and took the first available flight to be here with the team.'

The team did not expect him to be back so soon and was moved by the gesture. Gaekwad spoke on behalf of the other players: 'We'll do everything we can to keep his mind occupied.'

Sadagoppan Ramesh had opened the batting for India in Tendulkar's absence and had done well, so captain Azhar decided to retain him and put Sachin down the order against Kenya. The move generated much debate, for Azhar had become the favourite whipping boy by this time. There were repeated and impassioned calls in India from cricket experts and the general public alike to remove him as captain. Much of the blame for India's dismal performance so far, and the visibly dipping morale of the team, was placed squarely on his shoulders. And his reticence once again seemed to be going against him.

Tendulkar came in to bat in the twenty-third over, with the score at ninety-two for two. India did not lose a wicket after that, as he and Rahul Dravid broke a few records in their partnership and took the team's total to 329.

Tendulkar got off the mark by threading the ball between long-on and mid-off for an attractive four. He was relatively quiet till he had crossed twenty, figuring out the nature of the wicket because Martin Suji in the first few overs had shown excellent late movement. After that there was a typical Sachin show on display. A reverse-sweep went like a square-cut to the ropes, a lofted on-drive hurried the ball into the stands, and when the power of the bottom hand took a backseat, the top hand moved like a violinist's on his bow and explored several angles and pierced gaps. The strike rate was in keeping with his record: the first fifty in fifty-four balls, the second in thirty. When he reached hundred, he looked up at the skies, as if paying a tribute to his father. 'I just looked there... it's tough to explain what I felt,' he said. When the innings ended, he was not out on 140, and as he and Dravid made their way back to the pavilion – Dravid's hundred was equally good but was overshadowed, and he didn't mind it one bit – the normally reserved Azhar came down to the edge of the boundary to give the two a pat on the back.

While accepting the Man of the Match award after an easy victory, an emotionally charged Tendulkar repeated what his mother had told him and dedicated his century to the memory of his father. He admitted the century wasn't his best but added, 'under the circumstances it was special.' Although the century had looked easy, it wasn't. 'It was difficult to concentrate. In the middle, strange feelings would sometimes creep into my mind. I surely felt that my father was up there, watching. The feeling was strong,' he later said. Even as India won against both Lanka and England and entered the Super Six, he admitted to reporters that he was finding it hard to focus. 'I find it tough to believe I won't see my father again. I can't digest that fact. After tours, the first thing I did was to go home and spend time with my parents. I find it hard to face the fact that with him gone, I won't be able to do that.' He said he was 'still confused'. On the one hand, he felt he should be home with his family; on the other, 'I know how much it means to them that I should be here, doing my best for India.'

Before the second Super Six game against Pakistan (Australia trounced India in the first one, with Sachin getting out for a zero), he hoped he would get one more hundred, for he was 'sure that when I walk out at Old Trafford, my father will be watching over me'.

Though by now it was highly unlikely that India would advance to the semis, the tension of a normal India-Pak game was taken several notches higher because of a war that had broken out at the India-Pakistan border. Pakistani troops had surreptitiously entered the Indian territory of Kargil, in Jammu & Kashmir, and captured the snow-capped heights, and Indian soldiers were engaged in driving them out. The war finally got over in end-July with India regaining the heights, but only after thousands of its soldiers had died.

Although India kept up its record of winning against Pakistan in the World Cup (as it had done both in 1992 and 1996), Tendulkar did not get the hundred he wanted. He scored forty-five and was annoyed with himself when he got out.

Soon India crashed out of the tournament after being defeated by New Zealand in its final Super Six match. Its performance had been eminently forgettable except for Tendulkar's hundred against Kenya and the win over Pakistan. Tendulkar himself had not had a great World Cup, yet for India's cricket lovers, his team and the Indian cricket board, it was more than enough that he had returned without the cricket authorities placing any kind of pressure on him. The very act of returning, and the diligence he showed in spite of obvious difficulties, won him appreciation. On the whole, the Indian team's disaster was overshadowed by the Kargil conflict, for national attention was almost entirely focused in that direction. Cricket, at least temporarily, was not top priority.

Kapil Dev was one of the leading Indian personalities who went to Kargil to meet the soldiers fighting from the worst possible position: they were in a valley, facing an avalanche of attacks from the other side's troops perched atop the mountains. Kapil had strongly condemned the Shiv Sena's violence earlier in the year and spoken passionately in favour of India-Pakistan bilateral cricket. Appalled by what he saw in Kargil, he advocated snapping of cricket ties with Pakistan. After Tendulkar returned from the World Cup (a time when Indian soldiers were well on their way to regaining the lost heights), it was unavoidable that he should be asked a question on this delicate issue. He endorsed Kapil's words. 'So many have died. The wounds are far too fresh to consider normal sporting relations,' he said.

For Sachin Tendulkar the second half of 1999 was as bad as the first half, and it began by him receiving a "surprise" at a rather short notice by the selectors. The World Cup performance had left the Indian cricket establishment staggering. The defeat was much criticized but the man who expectedly bore most of the brunt of popular discontent was the captain. Azharuddin's personal form had left much to be desired, and his distance from the other players, borne of his unwavering hands-off approach, was complete. He was accused of tactical blunders, and most pointedly, of not winning. And a captain who didn't win could hardly keep his job in Indian cricket's scheme of things.

The selection committee's meeting to appoint the captain for all international fixtures up to September that year (the committee's term ended the same month) was to be held at Nagpur on 28 July. Tendulkar's name as a likely replacement   naturally came up for discussion in the public sphere, but reports in newspapers and magazines across the country clearly said that he wasn't keen on taking up the responsibility again. This was true. His first experience had left him disillusioned, and he didn't want the same old problems cramping him all over again. The names of Ajay Jadeja and Sourav Ganguly were therefore also bandied about in the media.

A few days before the selectors could meet, the chairman of the selection panel Ajit Wadekar, also a resident of Mumbai, went to

Tendulkar's Bandra residence. Tendulkar was busy playing table-tennis then. He left the game and sat down with Wadekar. After some initial casual talk, Wadekar brought up the subject of captaincy. Tendulkar said he was not "mentally prepared" for the job. Wadekar did his best to persuade him but his answer remained the same, though he did not speak up aggressively against the suggestion.

As Wadekar was about to enter the Vidarbha Cricket Association's building in Nagpur on 28 July for the selectorial meet, newspaper correspondents asked him how long it would take to decide. 'Should be quick, let's see,' he said smilingly. The five selectors[1] emerged from the meet only after close to two hours, and the BCCI secretary Jaywant Lele announced to the media that Sachin Tendulkar had been unanimously chosen as captain. Wadekar stressed that hardly any discussion had taken place on Sachin's name. 'It took only two minutes for us to decide on Sachin,' he said. So why did the meeting last so long? That, the selectors said, was because they were informally discussing coach Anshuman Gaekwad's confidential report on the team's World Cup performance. Wadekar said everybody had been 'of one voice on Tendulkar' because 'he is the best man for the job, he will be around for a long time, and he gets along well with all his colleagues. What we are looking at is the future.'

Word had been going around for some time that Mohammed Azharuddin was one of the reasons Tendulkar did not want to take up the captaincy. He had been shocked by Azhar's curious style of attacking batting during his first stint as captain, it was said. Wadekar was asked about a comment ascribed to Tendulkar, that he wouldn't be skipper if Azhar were in the team. 'He has not gone on record or told us anything like that. At least I haven't heard that. That's not right,' he said. Tendulkar's first phase as captain had not been a successful one. Would it be different this time? 'Sure, he is now more mature and confident and experienced,' Wadekar stressed.

Captaincy had therefore been thrust on Sachin Tendulkar. The BCCI president Raj Singh Dungarpur had ratified the selection committee's decision, but what about the man himself? Well, he had disappeared, a little like Miss Froy in Alfred Hitchcock's *The Lady Vanishes*. Neither the selection panel, nor anybody from the cricket board, nor any journalist was able to get in touch with him. Even the selection committee's message informing him of his appointment, as Jaywant Lele said, had been 'recorded by the answering machine at his residence'. Some said he could be at a friend's place in Mumbai, others said a family bungalow in Lonavla might be the place, while others pointed to Puttaparthi, the abode of the spiritual guru Satya Sai Baba (whom Sunil Gavaskar too worshipped ardently). It was all ill-informed guesswork, and didn't help.

A full twenty-four hours after the announcement, Tendulkar re-emerged in Mumbai and declared that he would hold a press conference the next day, while a relieved Raj Singh Dungarpur announced that Sachin had accepted the captaincy. The suspense however had still not ended, and expectedly, the media was present in such full force the next day that at the Cricket Club of India's hall a little before the press conference was to begin, Tendulkar arrived from the rear entrance and spared everyone greater inconvenience. He soon disappeared behind a wall of cameramen and photographers, and they had to be requested to move aside before proceedings could begin. Nobody blamed them for their scramble though, for they were capturing on camera a man who had made himself inaccessible for some time. And the expression on his face was telling as he sat behind the microphones. He was tense. 'First of all, I am sorry for this delay. I was not in Mumbai and only arrived last night,' he began. He said he had learnt of his appointment quite a few hours after the rest of the country had got to know. 'Then I saw it on the news,' he said.

Then the barrage of questions began. Wasn't he unwilling to lead? Had the selectors forced it on him? 'I was not mentally ready. I had told everybody concerned, the BCCI president, the chairman of the selection committee, that I wasn't very keen on accepting the job at the moment. For the last two years I have only thought of playing for India. But now that it has been given to me, I accept,' he said. He made a good attempt at explaining his hesitancy. 'You normally expect the vice-captain to be the next captain. Ever since I lost the captaincy (early 1998) I have not been vice-captain. So I wasn't thinking of it. It was different in 1996. I had been vice-captain for a long time, so I was prepared to become captain. This time I wasn't.'

Other questions too were tackled tactfully. About the youngsters (most of them his own age), he said they were playing well and named Dravid and Ganguly in particular; about Nayan Mongia's catch being adjudged the best in the World Cup, he said he was 'happy' (Mongia's peculiarly impulsive hit in the Chennai Test was fresh on his mind); about the team, he said he wished the selectors would give him the players he wanted (they had denied him exactly this earlier); about sporting relations with Pakistan, he said he stuck to his stand of not playing; and he stressed he had never laid down the condition that he didn't want Azharuddin in the team. 'I have played under him and he has played under me, so there is no problem,' he pointed out. (In an interview to television commentator Harsha Bhogle twenty days after this press meet, he continually emphasized that he expected '100 per cent effort" from the players. There were repeated lines like "What's the point in playing if you can't put in 100 per cent effort?' 'When you play for India you have to be committed. There are times when lethargy sets in, and that is the time to pull up your socks,' and 'there are ups and downs, sometimes you may perform well, sometimes not, but putting the effort into it all the time, that is very important. That is what I'm looking for.' These lines at that time may have read more like exhortations to the players than anything else. In retrospect, they seem suggestive, for Tendulkar in year 2000 told India's Central Bureau of Investigation or CBI looking into the match-fixing scandal that he felt Azhar was not putting in 100 per cent effort.

I asked Ajit Wadekar about this bizarre drama over captaincy. He admitted he had forced the job on Tendulkar and said it was a mistake to do so:

> I thrust it (the leadership) on him because I felt he could be a
> great captain. His batting was like Bradman's, and Bradman was

rated as the best captain. I thought, why shouldn't Sachin be thought of as the best captain? He was reluctant but finally accepted the job after two days. Unfortunately, when he was captain, we played very strong teams. When we failed, I tried to tell him it was okay and people would not blame him for our defeat. But his mindset was different. He didn't want to be the instrument of, the cause of, defeat.

Tendulkar however put all his doubts to rest and geared up wholeheartedly for the battles ahead. Till October, when the New Zealanders were scheduled to come to India for a Test and ODI series, there were four hectic tournaments scheduled abroad. In August, India would play the triangular Aiwa Cup in Sri Lanka against the hosts and Australia. Then there was the Singapore Challenge trophy against the West Indies and Zimbabwe. After that, there would be the annual Sahara Cup in Toronto, with a different format. The Kargil conflict had ensured that India and Pakistan would not play each other in Toronto, so two separate tournaments were arranged: the West Indies were brought in, and they were to play three matches each against India and Pakistan. And finally, India had to go to Kenya to play the LG Cup.

In Sri Lanka, before he could settle down again as captain, his back trouble resurfaced. He sat out one game against Australia (Ajay Jadeja led in his place) and in another, when the team, thrashed in three consecutive matches needed a win to hope for a place in the finals, batted in spite of immense pain for a hundred that led to an Indian victory. The pain was so bad that he had to be treated on the field in the middle of his knock. India nevertheless did not reach the finals and even though it managed that in Singapore, it did not win. Here too he rested for one game after his team had secured a berth in the final.

His decision to play despite all the trouble had clearly exacerbated the injury. Finally he decided not to go to Toronto and flew to Australia instead, to get himself examined by Dr Peter Barnes, a back specialist at the Australian Institute of Sports. By now theories about Tendulkar's back were getting truly wild. Newspapers and TV channels were full of stories about it. Everyone from medical experts to quacks and sundry astrologers were being asked for their diagnoses. There were full-length features detailing how his heavy bat may actually be impacting his back, how some wrong foot movement may be at the root of the problem or how just the horribly hot conditions under which the team played may be to blame. This "national" analysis of his back was rivalled in its scope and vocabulary only by the close scrutiny of the then Indian Prime Minister Atal Bihari Vajpayee's knee that was replaced in mid-2001.

Things soon came to a point where those who met Tendulkar greeted him with a "how's your back" rather than a how-are-you, and in his own words, he got "sick" of answering this, because nobody who met him seemed to have anything else to talk about.

The real worry was whether the injury would cut short his career. Luckily Dr Barnes said that wouldn't happen. According to him, Tendulkar had spondylosis, that is, a bone defect in the spine. Though it had first severely affected him in the Chennai Test early in 1999, Dr Barnes said the condition had existed for many years. 'But it would not be a major disability. It's a very common condition in a lot of sporting people, and most of them manage to work around it and keep going. He will undoubtedly, at various stages of his future career, get a bit sore in the lower back, but by doing his rehabilitation programme regularly he should be able to make these infrequent and not prolonged periods.'

The rehab programme included working out with Swiss medicine balls (rolling over them) to easing the flexibility of the back and a set of Psitzner's exercises (Psitzner was the man who treated Shane Warne after his shoulder surgery in 1998) to strengthen the lower back, pelvis, abdomen and the trunk. The regimen meant that Tendulkar would also have to miss out on the one-day tournament in Kenya.[2] He was keen to get back into action soon. 'Till I get fit, I won't give it up. I will fight to get fit,' he said.

Those who represent the very best in international cricket do have a lot in common. In demonstrating his desire to stage a fight to recovery, Tendulkar was going down the path taken by Australia's

Dennis Lillee. On the tour to West Indies in 1973, Lillee developed a severe back problem that raised the same questions as in the case of Sachin. He went through a rigorous exercise schedule and a year's painful treatment to get back on track. After that he not only played international cricket for ten more years but went on to become one of the greatest fast bowlers of all time. Tendulkar's problem was surely not as bad, but it wasn't inconsequentially minor either.

By the time the New Zealanders arrived in India in October, Sachin was feeling fully fit. And if the workout regimen had provided relief, the birth of his second child provided much delight (his first child, daughter Sara, was born in October 1997). On 23 September, his wife Anjali gave birth to a baby boy at the Breach Candy Hospital in Mumbai. The boy was named Arjun, after the warrior from the Indian epic *Mahabharata*.

The first of the three Tests against New Zealand was at Mohali in Chandigarh. There were quite a few remarkable things to note about this Test and they seemed to mark a definite shift of sorts in Indian cricket. One was linked directly to the venue as India had a new coach, Kapil Dev who had risen to international fame from this very place in 1978-79. He had taken over as coach from Anshuman Gaekwad, and given his splendid record in world cricket, it was widely expected that he would breathe new life into Indian cricket along with a committed captain. Another vital development was the dropping of Azhar. This was the first time in twelve years that he was not in the Test team. He had undergone a shoulder surgery soon after the World Cup and was therefore ruled out of some tournaments immediately after that. He was however back on the field in September, playing the Moin-ud-Dowlah tournament in Hyderabad with the zip and agility of an eighteen or nineteen-year-old. He was still not picked. The third was that three players were making their Test debut here: Devang Gandhi as an opener, Vijay Bharadwaj as an all-rounder, and M.S.K. Prasad as wicket-keeper in place of Nayan Mongia, which in itself was the fourth remarkable feature. The infusion of young blood was a bold move on the part of the selectors.

On the first day of the Mohali Test, India were bowled out for eighty-three runs. It was an awful crashout, and Tendulkar, marking a new beginning as captain in Tests, too batted with indecisive apprehension for eighteen runs.

Some pride however was restored when the team batted for the second time. India not only wiped out the deficit of 132, but also went on to notch up 505 for three before declaring. Rahul Dravid and Tendulkar got a hundred each, though the captain's was far from an authoritative knock. Creditably, New Zealand batted out 135 overs to force a draw when the advantage clearly lay with the home team. India, however, did not get too much blame, it was rather commended for staging a fightback after the first innings ruin. In the second Test at Kanpur, it won praise after its spinners fashioned an easy victory. In the third Test at Ahmedabad, played from 29 October to 2 November, there was confusion and a controversy that found its way into the CBI probe into match-fixing.

Before the onset of the match-fixing affair, however, Sachin Tendulkar settled one conundrum concerning his Test career. Why couldn't he get a double hundred in Tests, was a question that had baffled many. The settled-for answer was that he lacked the patience and single-mindedness needed for such a knock. He had not done much to rubbish this charge, and even his first double ton in first-class cricket, against the Australians at Mumbai, had come in 1998, nine years after his Test debut. At Ahmedabad, as India batted first, he got his first double ton in Test cricket and erased doubts. For him the 217 was mentally a major push, because it was after five years that he had outdone his highest Test score of 179 and reached the elusive figure of 200, that too at a time when he needed a feel-good factor about his batting after recovering from an injury. It was an extraordinary coincidence that he had got the big score on the same ground where two towering lights of Indian cricket, Sunil Gavaskar and Kapil Dev, had got world-record-setting career landmarks. Gavaskar had played a delicate little late-cut here to get his 10,000th run in Test cricket, and Kapil Dev had bettered Sir Richard Hadlee's record for the maximum number of Test wickets.

After declaring at 583 for seven, India dismissed the Kiwis for 308. A large part of the fourth day remained when the New Zealand innings folded, so India was expected to press the follow-on. Surprisingly, the Indians batted again and declared only after they were 148 for five. New Zealand then batted ninety-five overs, lost merely two wickets and saved the Test.

Tendulkar's decision not to enforce the follow-on was strongly criticized from all quarters. It was variously called bewildering, boring and dreadfully defensive. The Indians of course felt it had robbed their team of a victory, but even former New Zealand greats said they were upset by the sheer defensiveness of the act. The Indian captain defended his move saying his four specialist bowlers had been utterly exhausted by bowling a full ten hours in the New Zealand first innings and had asked for some rest. The heat was oppressive at over forty degrees celsius, he said, the bowlers had already bowled 140 overs, and to ask them to bowl another 160 (the total number of overs that could be bowled at that stage) was to run the risk of some of them collapsing.

However, the spearhead of the Indian attack, Javagal Srinath, had gone out to bat in the second innings and had spent half-an-hour in the sweltering sun (nineteen not out) before the declaration was made.

When the match-fixing scandal hit the cricket world in its face in 2000, it was inevitable that this refusal to enforce a follow-on should come under the scanner of the authorities. By that time allegations of match-fixing against Kapil Dev had also created a sensation in India, so the actions of the Indian coach became part of the CBI investigations into Indian cricket's darkest chapter, and both he and Sachin were questioned. While Kapil, along with many other cricketers like main accuser Manoj Prabhakar (who later became one of the main accused), Azharuddin, Ajit Wadekar, Nayan Mongia and Ajay Jadeja were questioned at the CBI headquarters in Delhi, Tendulkar was questioned at his Mumbai residence. That was because the media presence at the CBI office was strong throughout the months of the many depositions. If Sachin were to turn up, things would have become unmanageable.

The CBI cleared both Kapil and Tendulkar of any wrongdoing. So did the then CBI joint director K. Madhavan, who was after CBI's submission of its own report appointed by the Indian cricket Board to investigate matters on its behalf. Madhavan questioned Tendulkar in June 2001 but clarified that he had been 'examined as a witness only'.

Kapil Dev, the then coach of the Indian team at the time, said the decision of not enforcing a follow-on in Ahmedabad was taken in consultation with the captain, vice-captain and other senior players. The CBI report recorded his statement as follows:

> One day prior to the decision, there was absolutely no doubt in his mind that the follow-on should be enforced. At the end of play on the third day, the team did not meet to work out a strategy for the next day. Somewhere during lunchtime on the fourth day the bowlers, especially Srinath, complained that they were very tired and India should bat again and score quick runs and make New Zealand bat thereafter.

On being told that the bookies in Delhi allegedly knew about the decision not to give a follow-on on the night of 31 October 1999, Kapil stated that no decision to this effect was taken on the 31st and hence it was very surprising. On being asked whether somebody could have subconsciously influenced this decision on the next day, he stated that it could not be ruled out.

The investigating agency, CBI, heard Sachin out as well:

> Sachin Tendulkar, former Indian captain when asked about the India-New Zealand Test at Ahmedabad in 1999, stated that by the end of third day's play when New Zealand had lost around six wickets, he had thought to himself that he would enforce the follow-on the next day. However, the New Zealand innings dragged on till after lunch the next day and by then he, coach Kapil Dev, Anil Kumble and Ajay Jadeja decided that the follow-

on would not be enforced since the bowlers, especially Srinath, had insisted that they were very tired. Therefore it was a collective decision not to enforce the follow-on. On being asked whether anybody could have influenced this decision since the bookies in Delhi allegedly knew one day in advance that a follow-on will not be enforced, he accepted that it was possible.

As for the one-day series against the Kiwis, India had a favourable though not a completely convincing result (3-2). Meanwhile Sachin, post his injury and the Test double hundred, secured yet another record – 186 not out, the highest score by an Indian in ODIs – in the second fixture at Hyderabad. Here, as in the World Cup game against Kenya, Rahul Dravid stood alongside him, and the two had the highest ever partnership (331) in one-day cricket. Both stepped up the gear nicely after they had crossed their hundreds, and if Dravid played some classically correct drives, Sachin was all innovation. It was as if, between them, they were exploring the full range of batsmanship. The most accurate of yorkers became useless as Tendulkar got his left leg out of trouble and kept thwacking on the leg side; some balls on the off and middle were hit behind square-leg for four, and at one point, four full tosses from pacer Chris Drum were directed to four different parts of the ground.

On the whole however, New Zealand had not proved as easily beatable on the dry and flat Indian surfaces as they had looked to be. India was scheduled to leave soon for Australia, for a three-Test and a triangular one-day series. How would Steve Waugh's Aussies be on their own fast tracks? They were on a roll in any case. After their World Cup triumph, they had crushed New Zealand and Zimbabwe and, just before the Indians arrived, they had completed a clean sweep against Pakistan (3-0).

---

1 Ajit Wadekar, Madan Lal, Shivlal Yadav, Ashok Malhotra and Anil Deshpande as well as BCCI secretary, Jaywant too attended the meeting.
2 Ajay Jadeja led in Kenya, and India lost in the finals to South Africa.

an uneasy quiet

Silence will save me from being wrong (and foolish), but it will also deprive me of the possibility of being right.

— Igor Stravinsky

Action speaks louder than words but not nearly as often.

— Mark Twain

Diplomacy and reticence became significant mantras for Sachin Tendulkar during the 1999 Australia tour. He was never much of a talker anyway, preferring to concentrate on his batting. But what was definitely missing on this tour was a voice off the field, a voice that could have been immensely strong and forceful in world cricket, in the context of disturbing developments.

However, the one instance of firm talking happened before the Indians left for Australia. At the meeting held to pick the Indian squad, Sachin successfully blocked the inclusion of Mohammed Azharuddin and Nayan Mongia and unsuccessfully asked for the capping of Mumbai left-arm spinner, Nilesh Kulkarni. It was by now an open secret that Sachin and Azhar couldn't get along, and Mongia's reckless slog at Chennai was uppermost in his mind's eye. Mongia did fly to Australia as replacement for an injured M.S.K. Prasad before the second Test, but played only one tour game and was sent back to India. During his short stay in Australia, Tendulkar gave him the cold shoulder.

An early game against New South Wales at Sydney set the tone for the whole Australian tour. Umpire Darrell Hair pulled up Sourav

Ganguly for seeing a replay on the giant screen on the ground, and went in pursuit of Ajit Agarkar all the way to cover point and ticked him off. This was no isolated incident and had to be seen in the context of the past. Hair had been for the previous four years at the centre of a broadening conflict between Asian nations and Australia over umpiring. He had no-balled Sri Lanka's Muttiah Muralitharan seven times for an "illegal action" during the traditional Boxing Day Test in Melbourne in 1995. Two other Australian umpires, Ross Emerson and Tony McQuillan, had taken their cues from him, and in the same summer, no-balled the off-spinner in a one-day game against England at Brisbane. Muralitharan was then reported to the ICC's special committee, which cleared his action. But in 1999 Emerson again no-balled him, provoking an angry Lankan captain Arjuna Ranatunga to almost abandon the match. Ranatunga led his team to the edge of the boundary, where Lankan Board officials and match referee Peter van der Merwe persuaded him, with some difficulty, to take the field again. Muralitharan was heckled all over Australia during the tour, and even the Australian media raised question marks about his action. As if all this were not enough, just before the 1999 World Cup took off, Darrell Hair released his autobiography, in which he called Murali's action "diabolical". Hair had to face a two-month suspension for this. After that, however he was back in action.

Even the Pakistanis who visited Australia three months before the Indian tour had complained bitterly of the umpiring standards. Their skipper Wasim Akram had suggested after the series that one umpire from a neutral country wasn't enough; both should be neutral. Sri Lanka and Pakistan's experiences led to allegations that Australian umpires were biased against Asian countries, and by the time India reached Australian shores, even the Australian media had begun to take serious note of the problem. As was their usual practice, the media targeted the visitors, in this case the Indians, immediately on their arrival and, again in keeping with tradition, aimed especially at the touring team's captain. But to be fair to them, they asked questions about the quality of Australian umpires as well.

After the Indians got a taste of Hair's high-handedness in dealing with Sourav and Mongia, the team management insisted he be kept out of the Test series. Yet, when he was finally made to stand in the third Test at Sydney, the Indians neither protested nor asked for another umpire. Tendulkar did not say a word on the umpiring throughout the series, and even his answers to pointed questions were politically correct (more of which later). And he was the one who suffered the most due to dreadful umpiring decisions.

The first disappointment came in the first innings of the first Test at Adelaide. Here Tendulkar was leading an Indian resistance along with Sourav Ganguly and even trying an odd sort of contest with Glenn McGrath while doing so. Normally, bowlers always tried to shut out Tendulkar's strokes by bowling a tight length and restricting field placements. The Australians, and McGrath in particular, were not known for this policy. They would rather take on a batsmen, be it a Tendulkar or a Brian Lara. So McGrath bowled to him consistently outside the off-stump, inviting him to drive. The situation too was strongly in the bowler's favour. His team had rattled up 441, had by then got four Indian wickets quickly and was now waiting to run through the rest of the Indian line-up. The man they now wanted was the captain.

Since there wasn't more than one-and-a-half hours to go before the second day's play ended, Tendulkar turned extra-defensive to try and keep his wicket. He let go everything even slightly outside the off-stump, and barely scored any runs for ninety minutes. On the third morning however, he was a transformed man. He batted defiantly and assertively along with Ganguly and tackled every bowler confidently, when umpire Daryl Harper gave him out caught at short leg off Shane Warne. It was supposed to have been a bat-and-pad catch. It was not. The bat was nowhere near the ball. India then folded up for less than 300 and, needing 396 in the second innings to win the Test, lost by a huge margin of 285 runs after Tendulkar was given a second successive dubious decision. This one turned out to be highly controversial, chiefly because of the batsman's body position when he was declared out. He ducked under a short-pitched McGrath delivery, but the ball skidded through and hit his shoulder as he was crouching down. The umpire – Daryl Harper again – had no doubt that he was plumb in front. Nobody had expected a clearly shaky Indian team to chase the target, but the manner in which they went down, and the two verdicts against their captain, created quite a stir. TV replays of his LBW dismissal were relayed frequently, with Indian commentators sardonically calling it 'shoulder before wicket' and the Australian experts saying the ball's direction suggested it might just have taken the top of the bails.

When asked about the team's performance, Tendulkar said it would definitely improve in the second Test and about his own dismissal, he merely said: 'I am disappointed that I got out.' This was seen as his acceptance of the umpire's verdict, in the classical cricket tradition, and a faithful observance of ICC rules.

Neither the performance of the Indian team nor the umpiring standards of Australians improved in the rest of the series. India was crushed in the second Test at Melbourne and also in the third Test at Sydney. It was the first time since 1974 that the team had been routed 0-3. The second Test was purely Tendulkar versus Australia. He held India's first innings together with a brilliant 116 and was the last man to get out, with the team's total at just 235. Pace bowler Brett Lee made his debut in this Test and took five wickets in the first innings. He spoke of Tendulkar with awe: 'He waves his heavy bat around like a toothpick. He's just a class batsman. It's a great experience bowling to him.' Sachin's century saved his team a follow-on, and in the second innings it looked like he could even take his team to a respectable draw when he was trapped in front, just past his fifty, by Warne. The spinner proudly called it a "match-winning" wicket, and he wasn't off the mark, because after the captain's dismissal, the remaining six Indian wickets fell for merely sixty-two runs. And the third Test – the first of the year 2000 – was over in three days, its only saving grace being a hundred by V.V.S. Laxman that truly marked his emergence in Test cricket. Laxman struck twenty-seven sublime boundaries off his bat in his knock of 167.

Tendulkar was by this time hemmed in by a host of troubles as captain, because the team's show had been distressing to say the least. He was therefore so happy with Laxman's innings, he gifted him a pair of Oakley sunglasses that evening.

On the batting front, Tendulkar got his third false LBW verdict – this time given by Zimbabwean umpire Ian Robinson – in the third Test. He had hit McGrath for fourteen runs in an over and was blazing away at forty-five when the verdict came, against the same bowler. On the leadership front too, there was more trouble. There were wet patches behind the stumps on the third day, and he requested umpire Darrell Hair that sawdust be sprayed there. The request was rejected outright, and Hair also refused to intervene when Venkatesh Prasad, fielding on the boundary, was hit with shoes by a rowdy section of the crowd. The theme of bad performance and umpiring error remained unchanged for Tendulkar in the one-day triangular series. His team lost all but one game, against Pakistan at Adelaide, and at Perth, he was wrongly given out caught behind soon after he had hit four boundaries off Wasim Akram and Waqar Younis.

The real surprise of the Test and ODI series was however the size of the crowds at various venues in Australia. The Indian team had played disastrously unchallenging cricket from day one of the Test series, yet Australians gathered in large numbers to watch. The reason for this was a terrific curiosity about Tendulkar. He had first gone to the continent as an eighteen-year-old in 1992 and had made his mark with two combative Test hundreds. He had since performed consistently well against Australia, getting his first one-day hundred against them in Sri Lanka in 1994, playing a majestic knock in a lost cause in a World Cup game in 1996 and then demolishing a very strong Australian team in 1998, first in India and then in Sharjah. What was more, cricket's all-time number one batsman, Sir Don Bradman, also an Australian, had said that Tendulkar batted just like him. Tendulkar's profile in Australia was therefore extremely high, and it was a reflection of the status he had acquired in other cricket-playing countries too.

His demeanour had further enhanced this profile, so while he was certainly being seen as representing the best in international cricket, he was also being considered as an ambassador for the game. In the context of what was happening around him, it was this second role that the cricket world dearly wanted him to take up in a much more involved manner. A number of controversies were now rocking the game. Charges of match-fixing were being flung around, and the issue of Australian umpires' bias against Asian teams had reached grave proportions. Other matters concerning the game at the global level too needed urgent addressing.

The Australian media therefore throughout the series energetically sought out Tendulkar for his opinion on all subjects. He gave none, except to suggest, when asked if he had been targeted by the umpires in Australia, that the series of bad decisions against him was 'probably a coincidence'.

Some Australian mediapersons said sarcastically that it appeared as if the phrase "no comment" seemed difficult for Sachin to "pronounce". They were obviously baffled, less by the guardedness and more by the level of guardedness, because at least on the matter of umpiring, they and many former Australian greats too had severely criticized their country's representatives. Mike Howard, an accomplished journalist, had during the Test series written in *The Australian* that 'Some of the teams, especially from the sub-continent, and even the West Indies, will in future refuse to tour Australia if our umpires continue to act in such a high-handed and biased manner.' The same Howard made a passionate plea to Tendulkar to speak up, because he saw the Indian captain's press conferences as little more than well-practiced exercises in diplomatic decency. He said there was a need for a powerful, persuasive and contemporary voice from the Asian region, and no voice could be better than Tendulkar's, for he was recognized throughout the cricket world as a thoughtful and self-effacing man of integrity and dignity. According to Howard, the people of Australia wanted to know Sachin's views 'on many matters affecting cricket in India and around the world,' and they, he underlined, would 'hang on to every word' he said.

Tendulkar's reply to this was laconic. He said he wanted to concentrate on happenings on the field rather than those off it. It could have been argued that off-the-field developments invariably impacted on-field events, and on-field happenings were in themselves so controversial that they demanded serious discourse, but sensing Tendulkar's unwillingness to take the discussion any further and constrained considerably by an enormous respect for his personal integrity and dignity, nobody took the point further for the moment.

Tendulkar by now was a frazzled man, weighed down by the pressures of captaincy. Again, as in 1996-97, the sparkle and freshness he was known to exude was gone, and a look as strained as some of the moments he had recently encountered had taken over. Frustratingly, the clashes with the selectors too had shown no signs of letting up. Azhar's name had figured prominently again in the discussion when the team for the ODI series in Australia was to be chosen. The presence of an experienced batsman like him could prevent the kind of disaster the team had had in the Tests, it had been stressed. Tendulkar along with coach Kapil Dev opposed his selection firmly, although the entire selection panel seemed to have been in favour of bringing him back. Finally, the selectors relented, and Tendulkar also had his way on the wicket-keeper's slot. M.S.K. Prasad had been far from effective in Australia, so the second contentious name – that of Nayan Mongia – was brought in by the selectors. Tendulkar pressed hard and successfully for the inclusion of Mumbai stumper (and his close friend) Sameer Dighe. The door was slammed on Mongia again.

However, the two names refused to disappear easily. Soon after the team's return from the Down Under, South Africa landed on Indian shores for a two-Test and five-ODI series. The team for the first Test was to be picked on the second day of the South Africans' tour-opener against the Board President's XI at the Brabourne Stadium in Mumbai. While journalists inside the Brabourne press box were, with one eye on the ongoing tour-opener, also eagerly awaiting the team's announcement, a serious-looking Tendulkar suddenly stepped in along with the new chairman of the selection committee, Chandu Borde, and BCCI secretary, Jaywant Lele. He went up to the microphone and said: 'I have an announcement to make.' The announcement had been well prepared. He read it out:

> I want to make a few things very clear. At the beginning of the season, when the then chairman of the selection committee Mr Wadekar met me and offered me the captaincy, I showed my reluctance to accept as I was not mentally prepared at that time. In spite of that, when my name was announced, I took up the captaincy as I was one of the most experienced players and the selectors thought I was the best man for the job. I accepted the captaincy knowing the Australia tour would be very difficult, given the Australian team's recent performance: they had just won the World Cup. I tried my best but nothing worked out for the team.
>
>   But I don't want to make any excuses for our poor performance in Australia. As captain I take moral responsibility for the failure. I feel sorry for not living up to the expectations of my countrymen who always support us. After a lot of thought I have decided to step down as captain after the two Tests against South Africa. That will give the next captain some time to be prepared. I assure you I will give my best as I always have in the past, and I am ready to play in the team *under anyone and with anyone*[1].

The journalists wore a flabbergasted look for half a minute, then gathered their wits and began a volley of questions. Tendulkar took only a few, saying essentially nothing beyond what he had read out, and left the press box. Then Chandu Borde declared the team. It had both Mohammed Azharuddin and Nayan Mongia in it.

Tendulkar insisted that the inclusion of the two had nothing to do with his quitting. The timing of his announcement – just after the team had been picked, with the two controversial names in it – was nevertheless a complete giveaway, as was the odd absence of the Indian coach Kapil Dev from the selection meeting.

There was no deviation from the pattern the Indian team had

acquired in Tendulkar's last two Tests as captain. India lost both. The first Test in Mumbai was a close one chiefly due to his defiant knock of ninety-seven in the first innings when the rest of the batting was crumbling around him, but the second was a crushing innings defeat, a reminder of the way things had gone in Australia.

He had lost five consecutive Tests, and Indian cricket was clearly facing a crisis of identity and confidence. His overall record as captain – the first and second stints taken together – had proved to be thoroughly unimpressive unlike his cricketing scores: five Tests won, fourteen drawn, and fourteen lost.

Why did such a fantastic cricketer like Tendulkar fail so miserably as captain? In a country where he has always been largely deified and therefore deprived of his position as a human being prone to foibles, this question has not been adequately addressed. But we will try and face it fair and square. First, there is nothing in the history of cricket to suggest that a good cricketer will be a good captain. Or, forget talent, that a successful cricketer will be a successful captain. If this had been true, Sir Vivian Richards, Sunil Gavaskar and Kapil Dev would have been among the best and most winning captains of all time, and Mike Brearley would never have led, and if he had, he'd at best be an average leader.

Second, Tendulkar was seriously handicapped by factors that have long been the bane of Indian cricket. The selection committee was nearly all the time bent on cutting him down to size. For a man who loved to focus entirely on cricket, he had to spend much of his time fighting a bitter conflict with the committee. And, in spite of all the resistance he put up, he hardly ever got the team he wanted.

Third, and this was revealed earlier that he made it obvious, he was not sure if all the players in his team were putting in hundred per cent effort. This lack of confidence and belief, correct or not, combined with the fact that the Indian team was anything but a cohesive unit, did negatively affect him when he was in-charge. Four, along with a fragile team, he got some of the toughest assignments an Indian captain could hope to have. The Indian team has not been known to do well abroad, and he had to lead in   West Indies,

Pakistan, Australia and South Africa. Lastly there was some truth in his statement that luck sometimes didn't favour him, and the example he held out was telling. When, in Sharjah in 1997, he had sent in Robin Singh as a pinch-hitter against Pakistan, the strategic and tactical surprise was complete. The pinch-hitter got out on the first ball and Tendulkar was squarely blamed for the move and the defeat that followed. A few months later, Azharuddin, reinstated as captain, took the same gamble, against the same team, and the man he sent in was also the same. This time, Robin Singh scored a brilliant eighty-two and paved the way for one of India's most thrilling and successful run chases against Pakistan.

Tendulkar's own shortcomings as a leader were finally as responsible for the overall record as these other factors. He often got far too caught up with the team and did not allow himself a wider outlook, which he was capable of as a shrewd cricket thinker. An obsession with his own game was an asset, but excessive involvement with the other players was not exactly helpful, for it often made him escape the reality that different individuals had different levels of ability and equally varying talents for plunging themselves into a chosen course of action. If some other fielder could not dive as energetically as he did, bowl sharply or bat as if everything depended on that one innings, he would get deeply disturbed. A wider perspective would have allowed him a fairer analysis of his team, and he would not have had much difficulty thinking up intelligent ways to make the best use of the available – and surely limited – talent. Captains in the past have harnessed limited talent to produce positive results, and they continue to do so. The point is to make players work within their own framework and ability. A Tendulkar's framework can't be applicable to all, and for many in his team it was just impossible.

What he once did in domestic cricket as captain of the Mumbai Ranji Trophy team is an example of his overinvolvement and his demand for the same exacting standards that he set for himself. The wicket on which Mumbai was playing that day had a crack almost the size of a mini-crater close to the popping crease. The team's leading pace bowler Paras Mhambrey (who also played for India) saw the problem in his path and ran in with a great deal of caution for the first few balls. When Tendulkar asked, he explained the reason. Tendulkar was incensed. He insisted that Mhambrey fire in as he usually did, because the team needed wickets. Now the crack looked so dangerous that any injury caused by it could have been career-threatening. But the captain would not listen.

The same problem occurred in international cricket as well. As one of Sachin's first gurus Ajit Wadekar and then Mark Taylor, one of the most successful captains in modern cricket, pointed out, that Tendulkar spoke to his bowlers before almost every ball. The suggestions, though well-meaning, had the opposite effect: the bowlers stopped thinking for themselves. Another game, the Ranji Trophy semi-final of the year 2000, showed how unreal certain expectations could be and therefore how wrong the general strategic direction. Sachin was not the captain in this match – he had just relinquished the Mumbai captaincy, and Sameer Dighe had taken over – but as the seniormost member of the team and someone even Dighe looked up to, his word was final. First, Tendulkar decided that five fast bowlers should play in the eleven, though it was April, and the time was anything but a fast-bowler-friendly time in Mumbai. Then, standing at mid-off, he kept insisting to the fast bowlers that they should bounce. The exact word in Marathi, repeated over and over again, was 'Aapat (Bang it in).' The wicket was flat, and the bowlers not too threatening. Their attempts to bounce meant the batsmen got the ball only a little above their waist. Robin Singh, the opposing team's (Tamil Nadu) skipper, had a particularly great time playing his favourite hoick over mid-wicket, and his team piled up a huge score that was overcome only due to one of the finest innings played by Tendulkar in his entire – domestic and international cricket – career.

Such insistence also happened in Tests and one-day internationals. The reason for it was that opposing teams always unleashed the best against his team and against him in particular: the Akrams, the Donalds, the Ambroses, the Walshs and the McGraths all came charging in and reserved their nastiest for him. He certainly, did not want his bowlers to bounce at others because he was himself most often at the receiving end of this fare – he was anything but a mean cricketer. Rather, he wanted them to replicate the same quality. And that was a mistake.

Curiously, for a man best known for sure aggressiveness and constant innovation, he was also sometimes unimaginative on the field and let the game drift. When Sri Lankans Roshan Mahanama and Sanath Jayasuriya were threatening to have a dangerously durable partnership in the 1997 Test at the R. Premadasa Stadium in Sri Lanka, he did not show the kind of ingenuity he was known for. No innovative measures were taken, and though he did not have his best bowler, Javagal Srinath, and the rest of his bowling resources were hardly formidable, he did not set attacking fields or try rotating his bowlers with a more-than-normal frequency. With the severe limitations of his attack perhaps playing on his mind, he went on the defensive, with the result that the two Lankans enjoyed a world record Test stand of 576, Jayasuriya eventually helping himself to 340 and Mahanama to 225.

Similarly, in the Ahmedabad Test against New Zealand in 1999, he did not declare when the match situation and the playing conditions were completely loaded in India's favour and the onus was on the Kiwis to try and somehow save the match.

Further, due to his personal level of participation in the game, he could never be a relaxed captain, and the burden he took partly affected his batting. But worst of all, it ruined his self-belief – which was seen by the cricket world as a sign of tremendous and still-growing cricket energy, a boon for his team and his country, a danger signal for opponents but nevertheless marvellous for the spirit of international cricket. It was replaced by a look of tiredness. Thus captaincy was the reason the word "failure" came to be associated with Sachin Tendulkar for the first time in his career. The word stuck steadfastly to him till his last day as skipper. Captaincy is also one area where Tendulkar's record does not hold up in comparison with Bradman's. The Don led Australia in five series, did not lose any and in fact earned for his team the tag of "Bradman's Invincibles", on the England tour of 1948. But it isn't as if the parallels are altogether missing. Bradman's captaincy too was broken up into two stints, not by the selectors as in Sachin's case but by the Second World War that put a six-year halt to international cricket. He too felt, like Sachin did, that captaincy had made him lose a lot of sleep, and he said he was aware from the moment he took up the job that his capacity to give results in such a demanding position was limited. In what is perhaps the most bizarre similarity with Tendulkar's reign, in only his third Test as captain, the Australian newspapers were saying that Bradman was 'not getting the loyal support of all his players'. That situation changed for him soon as the legendary Stan McCabe issued a statement that everyone was behind Bradman, and the team too transformed from being a bickering unit to a solid force. Tendulkar too had felt all along that he never got support from some players. He was implacably opposed to their inclusion in the team. The moment they were picked, he brought out the resignation letter, though he publicly refrained from saying so much as a word against them and in fact strongly denied, very unconvincingly, that they were the reason for his quitting.

Cricket's vilest undercurrent came to the fore immediately after the Indians, under a new leader Sourav Ganguly, won the one-day series against South Africa 3-2. The Delhi police were listening in on to the then and now late South African captain Hansie Cronje's secret phone conversations with bookies all through the ODI series, and they brought out clinching evidence of the murky goings-on. Cronje's immediate reaction was a stout denial, but in just a few days, he confessed he had 'not been totally clean' and later admitted to 'doing matches' for the cartel of bookies. The match-fixing scandal thus exploded in the face of international cricket and, apart from denting the image of the game, messed up the course of world cricket currents horrifically. Allegations and counter-allegations became the order of the day, garbled hearsay replaced cogent conversation, and it generally became difficult to distinguish fact from fiction.

In India, talk of match-fixing had begun in the year 1997. First, during India's tour of the West Indies that year, Pradeep Magazine, a journalist with one of India's leading newspapers, *The Hindustan Times*, had reported that a bookie had asked him to help establish contact with top Indian players, including the then captain Tendulkar. Later that year, Indian Test cricketer Manoj Prabhakar had created a minor sensation by telling a weekly newsmagazine, *The Outlook,* that he had been offered twenty-five lakh rupees by a teammate to under-perform in a game in 1994. In June 1997, the BCCI asked former Indian Supreme Court judge Y.V. Chandrachud to probe Prabhakar's allegations. Chandrachud's report, out in less than six months, cleared the players of any wrongdoing.

However, talk on the possible involvement of cricketers in betting and match-fixing continued in the sub-continent in the next few years, and after Cronje's admission sparked unprecedented doubts in all cricket-playing countries. Early in May 2000, India's Ministry of Sports asked the country's premier investigating agency, to probe the entire gamut of betting and match-fixing. Several cricketers, past and present, came under the CBI scanner, and five were ultimately implicated in the match-fixing scandal in the agency's report submitted in November 2000. The Indian cricket board imposed life bans on two of them – Mohammed Azharuddin and Ajay Sharma – and suspended the other three – muck-raker Manoj Prabhakar, Ajay Jadeja and team physiotherapist Ali Irani – for five years. The match-fixing brouhaha turned extremely dramatic when Manoj Prabhakar named Kapil Dev as the man who had offered him twenty-five lakhs to under-perform in a match. Then, in a sting operation for the website Tehelka (now a magazine), he clandestinely recorded statements of various players, thus accumulating lots of delicious gossip and little else. Kapil in return promised Prabhakar "a tight slap on the face" for manufacturing lies and then famously cried in a television interview and swore his life-long devotion to clean cricket. As a follow-up to the entire affair, India's Income Tax authorities raided the houses of some famous Indian players.

Meanwhile, Hansie Cronje's depositions and sensational revelations before the Justice King Commission in his country threw up names of various cricketers, of whom Herschelle Gibbs and Henry Williams pleaded guilty. The names of cricketers from almost every cricket-playing nation were dragged into the scandal, with Pakistani, Indian and Australian players heading the list. The International Cricket Council under Paul Condon launched its own investigations into the matter.

Yet the real reason Tendulkar's voice was sought in the affair transcended all the drama. World cricket had been well and truly shaken, and the faith of millions of its followers severely eroded. Tendulkar's stature was however still special. No doubts were raised about him; he remained invincible. As one of the most highly-regarded personalities on the international scene, his words carried a credibility and authority few others could command. Many across the world, and almost everybody in the sub-continent, saw him as an insider who would talk and throw greater light on the matter and at the same time sift fact from fiction. The pitch of expectations got louder as information got increasingly muddled. Tendulkar instead opted to be circumspect and spoke with measured caution. If at all he spoke on the subject, it was with an obvious reluctance, and even then, in effect, said nothing.

It was argued that he had to be in the know of things if some members of the Indian team were involved in corrupt practices. A few instances during his two phases of captaincy, and a few in the period in between, were cited as examples. He had lost his head when some members of his team had batted recklessly on certain occasions, and it was believed that he not only strongly suspected them of foul play, but was also certain they were hobnobbing with bookies. His staunch opposition to the inclusion of some players in the team was attributed to similar suspicions about them. When, on the West Indies tour in 1997, journalist Pradeep Magazine, after being approached by bookies, had asked him for his version on the player-bookie nexus, he had told him that he too had "heard" about it. So, the case was made out; he was not entirely ignorant.

The case was buttressed by the example of an incident in Sharjah in 1998, on the eve of the final of the Coca-Cola Cup between India and Australia. This incident was narrated to Manoj Prabhakar by one of the persons whom he secretly recorded on videotape as part of his "exposé" for Tehelka.com. Apparently, Tendulkar had already gone to sleep the night before the final when he was woken up by a senior member of the Indian team management. The worried official told Sachin: 'They (some players in the Indian team) have fixed tomorrow's game.' Tendulkar told him not to worry. They could do what they wanted, he would win the next day's game for India, he promised, and asked the official to go to sleep. The next day, after he had played one of the most swashbuckling innings of his career and won the trophy for his team, the same official went up to him during the awards ceremony and congratulated him. Sachin drew his attention to some sullen faces in the team. 'Look at them,' he said, and with a wickedly boyish delight remarked how one of them was nervously biting his nails.

This story was fascinating not so much for what it was, but for the way it was completely accepted in India as genuine. It pointed to Tendulkar's position in the public eye. The belief in the story meant that people further felt that Sachin knew who the culprits were. He however consistently took the line that he knew nothing about match-fixing.

However, he later said that those guilty should be punished in such a way that nobody again dared to indulge in betting and match-fixing. When asked if cricket could ever hope to recover from the crisis, he stressed that cricket was too great a game to be permanently affected. 'This is just a passing phase. I am a positive person. I can only look at the positive side,' he noted.

When he spoke to CBI officials, he was just as succinct but, finally, not as non-committal. The CBI report said:

> On being asked whether he suspected any Indian player of being involved in match-fixing, Sachin stated that during his tenure as captain, he had felt that Mohammed Azharuddin was not putting

in 100 per cent effort and he suspected that he was involved with some bookies.

There were three other things about which he spoke to the CBI. One, the controversial declaration during the 1999 Ahmedabad Test match versus New Zealand (his statements on the declaration have been recorded in the previous chapter). Two, the allegation that a bookie called Shobhan Mehta had attended his wedding in 1995. And three, the India-West Indies game at Kanpur in 1994 in which Manoj Prabhakar and Nayan Mongia had batted extraordinarily slothfully and did not go for the runs though the target was eminently reachable. His statement to the CBI read:

> About Shobhan Mehta, the Mumbai bookie, he stated that he had never met this person nor did he invite him to his wedding. During his wedding there was tight security and only select persons were invited and nobody without a proper invitation could have gatecrashed. All speculations about himself and Shobhan Mehta were absolutely rubbish and he had never met this person any time in his life...
>
> On being asked about the India-West Indies match at Kanpur in 1994 when Manoj Prabhakar and Nayan Mongia batted slowly, he stated that he was the vice-captain during that match and he was absolutely sure that there were no instructions from the team management for Manoj Prabhakar and Nayan Mongia to bat slowly and that he was so upset with their tactics that he did not talk to them after the match.

If all this revealed a little bit about what he thought and how he felt, a statement made by one of the accused in the match-fixing scandal, the Indian team's long-time physiotherapist Dr Ali Irani, has emerged as the highest compliment paid to Tendulkar in his entire career, even a notch above the words used by Sir Don Bradman to highlight his greatness. Dr Ali Irani told the CBI that in the world of match-fixing, 'the game would be "on" only when Tendulkar got "out" because he was one player who could single-handedly win the match and upset any calculation.'

This was exactly why many people, like Sunil Gavaskar and Sachin's good friend and former India player Sanjay Manjrekar, felt his responsibility went well beyond the cricket green. They exhorted him to speak up on crucial issues, and were disappointed when he did not say much during the match-fixing controversy.

Manjrekar told me:

> The potentially explosive tensions created by the controversy could hardly be expected to inspire confidence in the Indian team. The early effects showed in two one-day tournaments — one in Sharjah and the other in Bangladesh — played soon after Cronje was caught on tape. In both places, India was crushed. In Sharjah, they played four matches and lost three of them badly. They failed to cross 200 even once, and neither Tendulkar nor Ganguly (who had by now turned into a dependable opening partner) could get a fifty. In Dhaka, the only team they managed to defeat was Bangladesh. But more than the sorry scorecards against Pakistan and South Africa in the desert and against Pakistan and Sri Lanka in Dhaka, it was the body language of the Indian players that told the full story. They were weary and low on self-esteem and spirit. Before the team left for Dhaka, in fact, coach Kapil Dev, himself surrounded by charges of fixing, had requested the Indian cricket board not to send the team at all, but the request went unheeded and the team returned defeated and further demoralized.

*

After a gap of a few months, with little change in the atmosphere and morale except for Kapil Dev's resignation as coach in the wake of the charges against him, the team went to Nairobi for the ICC knockout mini-World Cup and, like in the manner of most mercurial outfits, gave a "why-didn't-we-play-like-this-earlier" performance. The tournament was made memorable by the firing of experienced hand Tendulkar and young guns Yuvraj Singh and Zaheer Khan against Australia in the quarter-finals. India caused a momentous upset by beating Australia and with a continued display of verve went up to the finals, where they were beaten by the unlikely winner, New Zealand. From Nairobi the Indians went back to Sharjah and to their hobbling ways. With Sri Lanka and Zimbabwe as the other two teams, they expectedly reached the final along with Lanka but were absolutely flattened there, by their island neighbours. After Sanath Jayasuriya hit a rampaging 184, they were bowled out for fifty-four, their lowest ever total. All hopes created by Nairobi seemed to have been dashed.

Zimbabwe came to India towards the end of the year, and the home team registered a predictable triumph. The three-Test series was won 1-0, and the ODIs 4-1. Tendulkar got a hundred in the first Test at New Delhi, a double hundred in the second at Kanpur and one more in the third one-dayer at Jodhpur. These triumphs and tall scores against what was perceived as a clearly weaker team coincided with the submission and subsequent revealing of the CBI report on match-fixing and the action taken by the Indian cricket authorities on the basis of the report. The on-field result was thus easily cancelled out by the sordid revelations in the report.

Indian cricket, that had touched a low ebb in April 2000 when "Cronjegate" first blew up, certainly did not rise much higher in the next eight months leading up to the Board's action on match-fixing. We have seen how Sachin was reticent during this period. But how was his approach to cricket? How did he manage in the middle, with so many tensions lurking around the corner? The answer to this question offers valuable insights into the scope and scale of Tendulkar's commitment, because dourly monosyllabic though he was on matters of match-fixing, his bat was exuberant in this critical phase. And while cricket's reputation as a gentleman's game was being stained all over, he was, for his part, laying down a shining example of purity and dedication.

His first act of dedication was when Cronje was busy chatting up the bookies in the one-day series. The semi-final of India's premier domestic tournament, the Ranji Trophy, was to be played between Mumbai and Tamil Nadu bang in the middle of the India-South Africa ODI series, so it was clear Sachin could not play for his local team. He had a look at the clashing schedule and dashed off a letter to the Indian cricket board, requesting them to push back the Ranji semis by a few days, so that he could play. This was an extraordinary thing to do. He was the best batsman in the world and now had nothing to prove on the domestic circuit. The Ranji Trophy was no doubt the gateway to international cricket, but it had in the decade since 1988 – when he made his own Ranji debut – lost much of its lustre. The international cricket schedule was so punishing that India's top players could hardly find time to play the tournament. Over the years, many of those securely established in the national side were also not too keen to participate in it, and if some of them did, they were often only half-serious on the field.

Tendulkar was however an exception. He had always shown an endearing loyalty to his home team (Here I have to push the date forward to provide an outstanding example. After Tendulkar returned from the World Cup 2003, his coach Ramakant Acharekar and then Mumbai Under-14 coach Praveen Amre went to his residence to have a chat. Sachin had done spectacularly well in the World Cup and had won the Man of the Tournament award, but if they expected him to discuss the Cup animatedly, they were in for a surprise. He kept badgering them for names of talented school cricketers from the city and was keen to know the merits of each player.) He was desperately keen that Mumbai should do well in the semis that year (1999-2000). That was because in the previous year, they had even failed to reach the Super League stage, and in the year before that, they had lost the semi-final to Uttar Pradesh.

The Board meanwhile granted his request, and barely a few days after news of the Cronje-incriminating tapes hit the cricket world, Tendulkar batted his heart out at the Wankhede Stadium, playing one of the best innings of his career. If the game was a high-pressured one, the position when he came in to bat was far from comfortable for his team. Tamil Nadu had rattled up 485, and Mumbai had lost two wickets for seventy-seven. In the Ranji Trophy, matches are often decided on the basis of the first-innings lead, so crossing the Tamil Nadu score was absolutely essential. He began with a beautiful straight drive down the ground and then was a picture of unwavering application for 565 minutes. Vinod Kambli had a good partnership with him. However, often, in the middle of his knock, the aggressive left-hander would flash outside the off-stump. Every time he did this, Tendulkar walked up to him and asked him not to do anything silly, since both of them had to stay there to see the team through. Kambli however was out for seventy-five.

Amol Muzumdar then gave him solid company, and the two of them had what Sachin later described as 'the partnership of the season.' Muzumdar was finally out to arguably the best ball of the match, and after that, Sachin lost partners at the wrong time. He fought on, shelving all his flamboyance but not forgetting to punish the loose deliveries. Many of Indian cricket's stalwarts were sitting in the stands and egging him on. There was Polly Umrigar, Ajit Wadekar, Dilip Vengsarkar, Dilip Sardesai, Eknath Solkar, Milind Rege, Sanjay Manjrekar and many others, and Sachin batted as if he had to prove himself in front of all these torch-bearers of the Mumbai cricket tradition and live up to their expectations. He had batted with as much commitment, on the same ground on his Ranji debut in 1988, in front of as illustrious a crowd that had gathered only to see him. A decade had passed now, his stature in Indian and world cricket had changed considerably, but his cricket and his approach to it had not changed – that was the secret of his success.

Mumbai was still fourteen runs away from surpassing the opponents' total when last man Santosh Saxena walked in to join Tendulkar. The final few overs of the innings were tension-filled and thrilling. Sachin hit one of the fast bowlers for a straight six out of the stadium. It was a deliberately aggressive shot in the middle of the tension, he said, because a six could psychologically crush the opposition. After that, last man Saxena courageously played out one over, and then Sachin brought out the high point of his relentless struggle: he thumped the ball in the smallest of gaps between deep cover-point and deep extra-cover to take his team ahead. Always an undemonstrative man where emotions were concerned, he could not hide his happiness this time: he repeatedly pumped his fist into the air and let out a cry of delight to savour the moment. Clearly, home was where the heart was.

Just how stiffly and single-handedly he fought towards the end can be seen by a simple fact. Mumbai was 449 for eight, and then forty-one runs were added for the last two wickets. Of those runs, the number ten and number eleven batsmen, Abey Kuruvilla and Santosh Saxena, had got zero. Sachin Tendulkar was 233 not out at the end of the Mumbai innings. He later said that memories of the Chennai Test against Pakistan came to haunt him often in the middle of this knock, and he told himself that he had to finish the job for his team. He did, and said 'it was one of the best innings I have played in any form of cricket. For me, playing for Mumbai is as important as playing international cricket.' He continued his commitment in the Ranji final against Hyderabad with a fifty in the first innings and a hundred in the second that made victory smoother for his team.

Then, in October that year at Nairobi, Tendulkar played an innings of superb defiance against Australia in the quarter-finals of the mini-World Cup. The amount of runs he got wasn't big – thirty-eight – but his blistering knock seized the initiative from the Australians and helped India register a most unexpected win over the world champions. The wicket was damp and bouncy, and Glenn McGrath had set a very aggressive field thinking that the Indian openers could immediately be driven into a corner. Tendulkar seemed to be telling that there was no point hanging around the wicket. The best ploy was to attack and try to upset the bowler's rhythm and plan. He went for a pull on the first ball he faced, and missed. Then he attempted to hit a ball that was outside the off-stump in the mid-wicket region. The result was an edge that sent the ball soaring over third-man for a six. McGrath got away by mouthing some obscenities in the first over, but when he came back for his second, even the swear words didn't help. Tendulkar came down the wicket as if he were facing a spinner and bludgeoned him for a six over long-off. In the next ball, he made exactly the same movement and struck a four in the same region. Then there was another six, and some more beautifully timed boundaries before he was dismissed.

The way the ball had gone off his bat in the brief display was amazingly authoritative, and it set the tone for youngsters like Yuvraj Singh who went on to make his mark in international cricket in that game with fluent strokeplay. In the final reckoning, though India lost the mini-World Cup finals to New Zealand, in the shock win in the quarters over Australia, his thirty-eight had the same importance as Krish Srikkanth's identical score in the 1983 World Cup final. A third notable knock he played was in Sharjah, where the Indians went from Nairobi. Here, as in the semis earlier in the year, he showed his flexibility and capacity for adjustment. The track had been newly-laid, and the ball was coming on slowly off the wicket. He kept his head down and focused on getting singles and twos by piercing gaps. As the other batsmen kept disappearing at regular intervals, he got a patient hundred. So patient, that seventy-one of his runs had come in singles, and he had hit merely three boundaries and one six. He demonstrated similar patience when Zimbabwe came to India towards the end of the year: he got a double hundred in the second Test at Nagpur.

The attitude he had displayed during a disturbing period for cricket was thus special and strengthened the belief that cricket's dedicated adherents would not easily allow the game to be crippled by scandals. In him the world of cricket saw cricket at its sincerest best. He had first saluted domestic cricket by going out of his way to participate in the Ranji Trophy semi-final. In that match, he had broken a significant barrier, he had "stayed till the end" to take his team through. Then, he had outmanoeuvred the Australians by his aggressive approach in Kenya and psychologically won the match for his team. After that, he had in his own unselfseeking way curbed his natural instincts to score an extraordinarily quiet hundred against Sri Lanka on a difficult batting wicket (this flexibility explained why he had, in the same Sharjah tournament, become the highest run-getter in one-day cricket). That hundred was his twenty-sixth in one-dayers, and though India lost that game against Lanka, his success rate, despite the debate on how "effective" his hundreds were for the team's cause, was terrific. India had won twenty-one of the twenty-six ODIs in which he had got hundreds. And he had overcome yet another barrier by getting his second Test double hundred, against Zimbabwe.

In 1999, he had got his first Test double ton against New Zealand and had voiced immense relief, because as he had commented at the time: 'I had been getting out too many times in the 170s.' But some tongues were still wagging, calling the first double-century a stroke of luck. The second double ton however, silenced his detractors. In a strange way, he had once again silenced the overriding theme of the season.

---

1 Italics are mine.

convert into a new mould

I have changed my batting in every game I have
played, depending on the match position and the
nature of the wicket.

– Sachin Tendulkar

It is generally marauding emperors who describe a geographic entity
as "the final frontier", and early in 2001, the then captain of
Australia, Steve Waugh had reason to feel like one. First, his team
had been untouched by the match-fixing scandal. Second, it had
won, in a commanding fashion, fifteen Tests in a row, against various
countries and had emerged as a much superior team than the rest in
the world. Third, its public truculence and verbal combat on and off
the field, now nicely embroidered by the captain in the term "mental
disintegration", had grown with the succession of triumphs, and it
was this that made Waugh assert that "India, the final frontier",
would also be taken smoothly.

Even staunch supporters of Indian cricket did not give Sourav
Ganguly's team much of a chance against Waugh's outfit, though it
was going to play the three Tests and five one-dayers on its own soil,
where Mark Taylor's Australian team had been handed a 2-1 defeat
just a little over three years ago. That was because of three reasons.
One, Australia was by far the best team in the world, with batsmen
such as Mark Waugh, Steve Waugh, Matthew Hayden, Ricky
Ponting, Justin Langer and Michael Slater, an attacking wicket-
keeper-batsman like Adam Gilchrist, and bowlers like Shane Warne,
Glenn McGrath, Jason Gillespie and Damien Fleming. Two, India

still needed to regroup as a team in the wake of the match-fixing row. And three, Ganguly had so far had just one Test series as captain (against Zimbabwe). Waugh, on the other hand, was a "leader-conqueror" on a roll.

The series, played between India and Australia in February-March 2001, ultimately did not prove to be one-sided at all. It was a rather fascinating contest, with India's new-found fiercely competitive instincts combating what appeared to be, especially after the first Test in Mumbai, the inexorable march of the Australian machine. The turnaround caused by India was such, and the overall quality of cricket from both teams so riveting, that the media quickly called it 'the greatest Test series ever'. Even minus the exaggeration, it does surely qualify as *one* of the best Test series of all time.

Sachin Tendulkar's role in a Test series against Australia was from the start expected to be excellent. As a cricketer he treated the Australians as special because, as a unit, they played tougher than anyone else. He was also known to single out the frontline bowlers of an opposing team, and especially against Australia, he always took this strategy more seriously than against other teams. They were a team that liked to get on top early in a series, so his policy was to try and put them down before that happened. In 1998 he had, in a way, clinched the series on the very day he smashed Shane Warne all over the Brabourne Stadium to get a double hundred in the Aussies' first tour game against Mumbai. In 2001, Warne was of course again a target, but the other bowlers, especially McGrath, were as much on his mind (McGrath had not come to India in 1998).

That focus was clear from the first day of the first Test in Mumbai. Signs of Tendulkar's positivism, especially when he is looking to dominate and not just stay at the wicket, are unmistakable. One of them is his unimpeded forward defence. If, in a matter of a few deliveries or a few overs, that defence begins to get exaggerated, it means he has decided to bat utterly freely. The other sign is when he takes balls on the rise and begins exploring the region between point and mid-off, so that he can bring out the full range of his classical drives. A third is a similar exploration of the same region, but through forcing shots off the back foot. Some of these shots are off perfectly good balls, and they thread the thinnest of gaps forcefully, thanks to the punch he's got. A fourth is the straight drive that goes just past the stumps, from the far left of mid-on, to the ropes, and a fifth sign, the killing of a rising delivery either by a sharp cut or a brutal pull. Mostly, it's the blend that one gets to see, and it was the same that day.

It was not exactly dominance; it was defiance, which made the cricket all the more interesting. Batting first, India lost two wickets for very little on the first morning, but Tendulkar was not going to let that puncture his plans. He began with a cracking drive against Damien Fleming past mid-off for four, and then pulled the same bowler to the mid-wicket fence. India lost two more wickets rapidly, but he had decided not to get bogged down. He stood firmly rooted at the crease and thumped four trademark straight drives off Fleming to the ropes. Both Warne and Fleming were cut sharply when they dug in short balls, and one of the cuts made Tony Greig exclaim on air: 'First there is Tendulkar, then there's daylight, and then there's the rest.'

McGrath however was also brilliant that day. When on seventy-six, Sachin tried to drive him through the covers and was out caught behind. Once he was gone, the Indian innings lost its spine and folded up for 176. Australia was tottering at ninety-nine for five in its response to the Indian total, when Adam Gilchrist and Matthew Hayden took charge. They pulverized the Indian attack and gave their team a solid 173-run lead.

Tendulkar came out to bat in the second innings, but in a situation that raised a lot of eyebrows. The second day was nearing its end; India had lost two wickets for a little over fifty; and wicket-keeper Nayan Mongia had been sent in at the fall of the second wicket as night-watchman. In the final over of the day, Mongia was hit on the finger by a sharply-rising ball. He suffered a cut and was seen writhing in pain. He decided to go back, and Sachin came out to face the last four balls. Mongia's decision to retire invited a lot of criticism. He was accused of putting self before country and of exposing the team's best batsman when the team, already in a crisis and desperate to stage a fightback, could not afford to lose him.

Sachin of course survived the over and began the third day in ebullient style by successfully driving McGrath through the covers for a four. The positive attitude of the first innings was again all too apparent in his strokeplay, and having gone easily past his fifty, he along with the dependable Rahul Dravid looked set to rescue India from its precarious position when a freak dismissal happened. Mark Waugh pitched a flat, harmless off-spin delivery short, and Tendulkar pulled it hard. The ball hit the back of Justin Langer, who was stationed at short-leg and had turned instinctively as the batsman played the pull, and ballooned in the air. Ricky Ponting, the man at mid-wicket, went after the ball and, sprinting all the way nearly up to square-leg, made a spectacular dive, overstretched himself and picked the ball inches above the ground. Tendulkar kept looking unbelievingly at the skies as he walked back to the pavilion. After this, the other Indian batsmen behaved as if the match was over, and on the third day, it was.

Australia won for the sixteenth consecutive time in Mumbai, and it was widely expected that the Indians would be crushed in the next two Tests just as easily, to add a couple more to that tally. But then India came up with a surprise. In the second Test at Eden Gardens, Kolkata, they pulled off a sensational win after being forced to follow on. V.V.S. Laxman played a sublime innings of 281 to pull his team out of the woods, after it appeared, on the morning of the third day, that all was over. Australia had accumulated 445, bowled India out for 171 and asked India to bat again when Laxman and Dravid (180) got together, batted throughout the fourth day and piled on the pressure in a partnership of 376. When Ganguly declared on the fifth day, Australia was set 384 to win, and India had to bowl them out if they nursed any hopes of winning. That was when off-spinner Harbhajan Singh and *golmaal* bowler Tendulkar got into the act. The Hindi word *golmaal* also, amongst other things means a puzzle, mostly with a mischievous element in it. Tendulkar's spin fits this definition, because it was a mix of many turns. He delivered and had three batsmen out LBW: the dangerous Adam Gilchrist, when the score was 165 for five, the ruthless Matthew Hayden a little while later (Gilchrist and Hayden had taken the first Test away from the Indians), and after that, Shane Warne. The last dismissal was special, because Sachin foxed the leg-spinner with a googly. Of all people, Warne should have read it. He didn't, made a mess of his footwork and was caught plumb in front.

Frankly, Sachin had done nothing remarkable with the bat in the Test. He had of course begun dramatically in the first innings when Shane Warne had bowled one to him on the middle-stump, and as it spun outside the off, he had rocked on the backfoot and pulled it to mid-wicket for a four. The shot had been a signal of intent, because only a batsman wanting to send a message to the opponents would *not* play that ball through the covers. However, he had got out soon after, trapped in front by McGrath, and in the second innings too, the dismissal was quick. He had finally more than made up with the ball and played his role, as a bowler, in India's stunning victory that levelled the series and in a truly astonishing way ended Australia's string of triumphs.

His batting theme was much the same in the third Test, but unlike earlier, he did not display any sense of hurry and that brought him rich dividends. He had, at the end of the second Test, told many of his colleagues that he was keen to record a century in the series. No better opportunity could be had than the final game, which had obtained the status of a decider, and no better ground too as far as he was concerned. The venue for the last Test was Chennai's M.A. Chidambaram Stadium, one of Sachin's most loved grounds. Three years earlier in 1998, he had got a memorable 155 not out there against the Australians; this time, he got 126 – his twenty-fifth Test hundred, mainly by waiting patiently for the loose balls. He was of course dropped by Michael Slater at mid-wicket when he tried to loft off-spinner Colin Miller, and mistimed. The ball went high up in the air and would have landed straight into Slater's hands but he ran far too forward, with the result that the ball went through his hands. But that one mistake was obliterated by the elegance of another shot.

After Tendulkar hit Warne to fine-leg for two boundaries in one over, an exasperated Warne banged in a bouncer. With his feet largely static, Sachin leaned behind and played a delicate upper cut, sending the ball to the third-man boundary. His smile after he played the cut was uncharacteristically broad, and it stayed for nearly half a minute, indicating just how pleased he was with himself.

There was thus no doubt that he was enjoying his batting by blending his positive energy with a measure of caution. However, there was a small disruption in the party when, with India needing 154 to win in the second innings, Sachin tried to get away from a rising Gillespie delivery and only succeeded in gloving it to slip. He was only on seventeen then, and his team was still quite a distance away from the target. The team lost some other batsmen too very quickly after that and made heavy weather of a small target. Finally, bowling hero Harbhajan Singh, in a tense ninth wicket partnership with Sameer Dighe, knocked off the winning runs, and the joy returned. Tendulkar, in a rare show of exuberance, was seen uncorking champagne and spraying it all over the dressing room. His mood reflected the general sentiment in India. Against all expectations, the team had come into its own and caused an upset that had made the entire cricket world sit up and take notice. Most vitally, it had, after being down and out, turned the tables on a team that had known nothing but success, a team that had come to be ranked as one of the best of all times.

Not to be put down for long, Australia came back to win the one-day series 3-2. Tendulkar's approach here too shifted progressively from unbridled to controlled aggression. In the first two one-dayers, he tried to fire from the first ball in his over-anxiety to stamp his dominance and got out without registering a big score. In the third ODI at Indore, he buried his impatience and scored a hundred almost at will, with intelligence and innovation. As the Aussies focused on the off-stump line for him, he repeatedly stepped across the line and guided the ball to fine-leg for boundaries. This frustrated the Australian bowlers, and he took the fullest advantage of it. In the process he became the first batsman to reach 10,000 runs in the history of one-day cricket, and in the fifth game at Goa, he completed a double by taking his hundredth ODI wicket. The bowler against whom he took his 10,000th run was special – Shane Warne – and so was the wicket he claimed as his hundredth – Steve Waugh.

All through the Australia series, India was witness to a strange spectacle in the stands across the country. The spectacle, *per se,* was not new. It had been seen before, but it seemed to have assumed astounding proportions now. Whenever a batsman who batted ahead of Tendulkar got out, celebrations would break out in the stands, as if it were the opposition that had lost a wicket. Nobody has ever asked those who came in before Tendulkar what they felt when the crowds first prayed for their dismissal and then actually rejoiced over it. It must have felt terrible. The crowds' consciousness however seemed to have been captured only by one man. As Sachin walked in to bat, a gigantic roar invariably went up in the stadium, whether the match was being played in northern Delhi, deep southern Chennai, the western state of Gujarat or Orissa in the east. It was clear that spectators had come only to see him, for every good stroke of his brought forth whoops of joy and thunderous clapping, a fiftieth or a hundredth run took the decibel levels still higher, and notably, at all three Test centres, Mumbai, Kolkata, and Chennai, a significant section of the crowd had left the stadium immediately after he had got out.

The fact of crowds turning up just to see him was historically significant, for it made him only the third cricketer in the last three centuries to win this kind of appeal. In the nineteenth century, crowds in England flocked to see only Dr W.G. Grace, the first serious exponent of a firmly-established batting technique. In the twentieth century, it was Sir Don Bradman who assumed this position, and now, in a new century, it was Sachin Tendulkar. Bradman had seen the Indian 'almost getting there' but wasn't around when the crowds began to be obsessive; he died a day before the first India-Australia Test in Mumbai. He would have been a happy man, because he liked Tendulkar a lot. There's reason to believe

W.G. Grace wouldn't have minded either, because with this feat, the Indian had equalled him in three ways. Grace had been the first cricketer to earn a vast amount of money from the game. Tendulkar had already earned more than what his contemporaries had managed. Grace was also known for psychologically intimidating his opponents. If an innocuous young man came out to bat, he would roar, 'I will get you out, boy, I always get young 'uns out,' and when he had got him out, would follow it up with 'Come to the nets in the morning, I'll show you how to bat.' Although Tendulkar is not known for his verbal assaults, he did resort to it for the first time during the 2000 Nairobi game against Australia, when Glenn McGrath, rattled by his aggressiveness, had abused him. In return perhaps, for the first time in the 2001 home series against Australia, Sachin resorted to sledging as a regular practice and even admitted to it after he had a heated exchange with Steve Waugh on the field. 'You know one has to do it sometimes to unsettle the batsman... just a comment so that he might play a rash shot. We get a crucial wicket and we stand a better chance of winning.'

The mass adulation for Tendulkar was of course a result of genuine love and adoration, but as in the case of Grace and Bradman – and this time on a vastly more momentous scale – there was also the element of hysteria in it. This kind of frenzy is the reason why even a hundred from him is generally not considered "enough", and if the hundred is followed up by a thirty or forty, he is said to have 'lost his form'. It was as if in the year 2001, the process of deification that had been set in motion in 1998, had reached its own "logical conclusion." Matthew Hayden was quick to observe the Indian attitude towards Tendulkar and told an Australian newspaper in an interview immediately after the engrossing series that 'He is a God in India and people believe luck shines in his hand. It is beyond chaos... it is a frantic appeal by a nation to one man.' Tendulkar was embarrassed by the statement. He told the Press Trust of India (PTI), after first politely saying that 'It is nice of him (Hayden) to have given that compliment,' that: 'All I want to say right now is that I am very happy with the way things have gone. It is all because people have always supported me, encouraged me all the time. But I do not think anyone can become God or even come close to it. I have played cricket and enjoyed it. I just feel happy I have done something for the country. I am a normal person who plays cricket. People watch me play and they get pleasure out of it. So I am nothing more than that.'

However, in retrospect, it can be said that the series against Australia, both in terms of the crowd response and his own reflections on his performance, significantly altered the mental make-up of Tendulkar. Due to the extent of popular acclaim, he began to feel much more responsible towards his team, the spectators and the country, though he denied he was feeling any greater pressure. Where the batting was concerned, his exuberance had indeed forced him to make errors, but just a little bit of control over it had brought him big scores in crucial games. The two factors however worked on his mind and marked the beginning of his new approach to batsmanship. It is today common to see Tendulkar graft for runs. He has cut out a number of strokes and consciously attempts to stay at the wicket and get a substantial score. The roots of this attitude were laid during the Australia series, and they struck deeper into the earth soon after, in the middle of India's tour of Zimbabwe.

Tendulkar along with the rest of the team did well in the one-dayers there but, in the second Test at Harare, he played a very wide delivery into the hands of the man at point to set off an Indian collapse that led to its defeat. India had won the first Test at Bulawayo, and an exhilarated Sachin there had picked up a stump as souvenir because during his career till that point in time, the only other victories his team had registered outside India were in the sub-continent (Colombo in 1993 and Dhaka in 2000). The Harare collapse saw Zimbabwe deny India an overseas series win, and Tendulkar came in for a lot of criticism from one of his mentors and idols, Sunil Gavaskar. 'Why blame V.V.S. Laxman when the best batsman in the universe gets a half-century and then gets out, when a big score from him is the crying need of the team?' he asked. To rub it in further, Gavaskar said the Australians were right in considering their captain Steve Waugh the best Test batsman in the world, for he had the ability to win and save games for his team overseas.

The fact that Tendulkar got a lot of rest after the Zimbabwe tour due to a foot injury meant that he got more time to think about this criticism, and his own responsibility towards the team. He had suffered a hairline fracture on his right toe during the last one-dayer in Zimbabwe and was ruled out of the tour to Sri Lanka, which was scheduled immediately after the Indians returned from the African nation. His back problem the previous year had forced him to opt out of some one-dayers, but this was the first time he was missing out on a full-fledged three-Test series (he had played eighty-four consecutive Tests). He hated being away from the cricketing action but there were going to be some positives too. 'If there's a break, players can spend some time with their families and go out to play with a fresh mind. And even sitting at home, one can analyse one's game and get better,' he said.

*

After the sabbatical at home, it was time for a little celebration for Sachin Tendulkar. Soon after the Australians had left, the Mumbai Cricket Association had in a glittering function attended by state dignitaries and the city's and country's top cricketers, felicitated Tendulkar and named the stand above the MCA pavilion at the Wankhede Stadium as the 'Sachin Tendulkar enclosure'. This was a big honour for him on his home turf. Coincidentally, four of the five men after whom the other stands and enclosures in the stadium were named – Sunil Gavaskar, Vijay Merchant, Polly Umrigar and Vijay Manjrekar – would be the ones into whose mould he would soon settle as a batsman, making a definitive shift from his first ten years of unbridled aggression in international cricket. In Zimbabwe, he had become India's second highest run-getter in Tests, overcoming Dilip Vengsarkar's 6,868. A celebration of that feat too was accompanied by a heightened sense of duty, for he would now be expected to be as dependable as Vengsarkar. Then Shane Warne's autobiography hit the stands in Sydney in August 2001. Warne had made a candid confession in the book – that he was "Tendul-corized" in India and Sharjah. To top it all, it was revealed in the same month that Sir Don Bradman had included Tendulkar in his "Dream Team". He was the only cricketer still playing and the only one from the sub-continent to have made it to Bradman's all-time eleven which was heavily tilted in favour of Australian players, according to the book *Bradman's Best* written by Roland Perry on the basis of extensive chats with the Don. Tendulkar was thrilled, even if that raised the bar of expectations still higher. 'It is a great honour, the greatest thing to happen,' he said. 'It is important when Sir Don speaks anything and especially when he selects me in his team, there cannot be a better thing than that. There are some great names missing and to see my name in it, I am more than thrilled. After Sir Don and before Gary Sobers (in the batting order), what else can you ask for?'

One thing he did desperately ask for: the healing of the toe injury in time for the South Africa tour starting in September 2001. To his immense relief, all was well with the toe soon, and he was declared fit to go.

After its triumph against Australia at home, India had won a Test each against Zimbabwe and Sri Lanka on foreign soil but had failed to convert these into series victories. Zimbabwe had levelled the Test series, and Lanka had beaten India 2-1. In the triangular one-day series in Zimbabwe (with West Indies as the third team), India had lost the finals to the Windies, and in Lanka too (with New Zealand as the third team), they lost the final to the home team. Therefore, a Test series and ODI tournament win overseas was still necessary to shore up Indian cricket's morale, and if it came against a strong team like South Africa, it would carry immense value. Tendulkar certainly thought it possible, despite India's far-from-impressive record in that country. His argument was that the new Indian team was very promising, its average age was twenty-four, and all it needed was 'the opportunity of playing more together and gaining more experience'.

The triangular one-day series was played before the Tests against South Africa. The third team was Kenya, so the final was expected to be India versus South Africa. But the Indians managed to create absolute uncertainty by going down to Kenya at Port Elizabeth and left themselves no option but to win the final league game if they were to qualify. Tendulkar marked his return to the international arena in the very first one-dayer against South Africa by getting 101. His opening partner Ganguly too got a hundred there, but their runs came to naught as India lost the game. In the must-win final league game, the two again got together for a fruitful partnership and, crossing their individual hundreds again, bettered two records: one, their own world record stand of 252 against Sri Lanka in 1997, and two, the number of hundred-run-plus partnerships (fifteen) between Gordon Greenidge and Desmond Haynes of West Indies. The sixteenth hundred-plus stand between Tendulkar and Ganguly was worth 258 in all, and it also yielded a result different from the first one-dayer. India won and was through to the finals.

Tendulkar's patience with the bat was already becoming evident in the one-dayers. In the first match, his hundred had been a very calm one, and even in the middle of the record partnership in the last league game, where he had himself got 146, he had hit the ball in the air only when there was a need to do so. This was unlike the Tendulkar the world knew.

The story of the finals was however something the Indians and the cricket world were getting increasingly familiar with. India went down for the ninth consecutive time in a final, with both its openers failing miserably to click. This was the first time when talk of Tendulkar's failure in the finals began to gather momentum. He had missed four of those finals due to enforced breaks, but in the five that he had played, he had accumulated a total of ninety-one runs, a bad tally at any rate.

On the first day of the first Test at Bloemfontein, it was further clear that victory on foreign soil was easy to talk about but difficult to achieve unless some of the Indian batsmen's glaring shortcomings on lively pitches were sorted out. India lost four wickets in the first one-and-a-half hours for sixty-eight. At this point, Virender Sehwag, making his Test debut, joined Tendulkar at the crease. Sehwag had created a mini-sensation on his one-day debut in Sri Lanka in August that year. He had opened the innings in the absence of Tendulkar and had got a hundred in just sixty-nine balls against New Zealand. What caught everyone's attention was that the twenty-two-year-old, hailing from the Najafgarh suburb of Delhi, had a height, build and countenance similar to that of Tendulkar, and was also in the habit of playing ferocious attacking shots on both sides of the wicket. Sachin had himself been pleased with his hundred, which he saw at home on television, and had sent him a congratulatory message. Now, as he joined Tendulkar in the middle, with S.S.Das, Rahul Dravid, V.V.S. Laxman and captain Ganguly all back in the pavilion for little, he was visibly tense. 'My first line to him,' Tendulkar later said, 'was "I know you're tense. I too was tense in my first Test. You're never going to be this tense again, so enjoy the moment."'

From then on, the two took charge. Tendulkar's batting that day could be characterized as a mix of two methods – brutality and innovative skills combined with the patience of the Gavaskars, the Merchants and the Manjrekars that he was so keen to cultivate. He played true to India's finest batting traditions, because he brought out the delicate cut that Vijay Merchant played immaculately during his days, the upper cut that Gavaskar had used to beautiful effect against the West Indies pacers in 1983-84 and the Vijay Manjrekar late cut that had often left the best of bowlers gaping in wonder at the sheer artistry of it all. The South Africans under Shaun Pollock wore similar expressions that day as Sachin repeatedly and deliberately sent the ball through, past and over the slip cordon and in the vacant third-man region for perfectly-placed fours. He repulsed the South African attack so forcefully that their bowlers, starting off in a position of strength and threatening to rip through the Indian innings, lost their spirit and character. A little before lunch, he hit eight fours in eighteen balls, and continuing his incandescent display after the break, took the initiative away from the home team. He was finally out for 155, with the team score at 288, when he pulled Makhaya Ntini, and Neil McKenzie, running in from the square-leg fence took a good catch.

Sehwag had kept relatively quiet at the other end and given him perfect company in their fifth-wicket stand of 220. With Tendulkar gone, he cut loose and got a hundred on debut. He too was out towards the end of the day, but when stumps were drawn, India had reached a score that had looked highly unlikely in the morning: 372 for seven. Sadly, the team did not capitalize on the psychological advantage that Tendulkar and Sehwag had wrested. The Test was over in four days. South Africa won it by nine wickets. If the 155 was one of Tendulkar's best Test innings – Indian coach John Wright rated it as the best ever he had seen in Test cricket – then it had suffered the same fate as the other two, equally fighting hundreds from him: one in Perth in 1992, when he was all of eighteen, and the other in Chennai in 1999, against Pakistan.

From the second Test onwards, the performance of either team became a matter of secondary importance, for the tour was fatally punctured by the ball-tampering controversy single-handedly generated by match referee Mike Denness. One of the severe casualties of the controversy was Tendulkar, and there is definitely truth to the belief that the dragging of his name into it made it a much more sensitive matter internationally than it otherwise might have been.

When India was desperately struggling to save the second Test at Johannesburg on the fourth day, match referee Denness pulled out of his bag a damning document, slapping varying sentences against six Indian players: captain Sourav Ganguly, Virender Sehwag, Harbhajan Singh, Deep Dasgupta, S.S. Das and Sachin Tendulkar. While the first five were accused of excessive and intimidatory appealing, and Sehwag also of using crude or abusive language, potentially the most damaging allegation was made against Tendulkar. He was found guilty of tampering with the ball. The elaborately spelled out official judgement read:

By acting on the match ball, Mr Tendulkar brought the game into disrepute (ICC Players and Team Officials Code No.2) and has been fined seventy-five per cent of his match fees, plus a one-Test match ban. The ban will be suspended until the last day of December 2001.

Effectively, Denness had called Tendulkar a cheat. Now, impeccable behaviour was never an underestimated feature of Tendulkar's career, and his status in India and elsewhere as a cricket icon and a symbol of sporting excellence was more than special. The charge expectedly raised a storm of protest in India. Nobody, from former Test cricketers, to administrators and officials, minced any words. The verdict was called absolutely incorrect, biased, disgraceful, and even draconian. India's cricket-crazy population was outraged, the media went ballistic, and the issue was also brought up in the Parliament for discussion, with the elected representatives there milking the flood of national sentiment to the maximum.

Despite his pronouncement, the match referee had in any case almost everything going against him. Point number one was that the on-field umpires had not complained to Denness. According to ICC regulations, the referee could initiate action in case the umpires, the manager of a team, the CEO of the Board of a country or the ICC chief executive himself reported to him that they had found the shape of the ball purposely altered. Denness had acted on the basis of television footage forwarded to him by a TV producer, and there was nothing in the ICC rules that said the media could report alleged violation of rules to the match referee. However, if that point was technical – and it no doubt was – Tendulkar's fault too was strictly a technical one. He told Denness in his explanation that he was merely cleaning grass and mud off the seam, and the video evidence showed him doing just that. Law 42 of cricket, covering fair and unfair play, said a player could take mud off the ball, but it had to be done under supervision of the umpire. So there was contravention to the extent that he had not done it before the umpire. But he had certainly not tampered with the shape of the ball, and his act of cleaning on his own, born of a lack of awareness about the concerned rule, looked bewilderingly inconsequential in view of the strong language and punishment it had invited.

A few related developments further aggravated the situation. The press meet held at Johannesburg to announce the verdict against the six Indian players turned farcical because the man who had given the verdict, Mike Denness, was present and was yet prohibited by the ICC from saying so much as a word (the verdict was announced by Gerald Majola, head of the United Cricket Board of South Africa). The Indian media in particular was impatient to ask Denness questions, because news of the punishment for the players had leaked the day before the press conference, and the correspondents were furious in anticipation and even otherwise. When it was clear he would not speak, Ravi Shastri, former India player and then TV commentator, stood up and asked what Denness was doing there in that case, since 'we all know what he looks like'. Then, the print and visual media in the sub-continent quickly and extensively brought to the fore all the recent episodes of excessive appealing and egregious on-field behaviour on the part of "white" players. The case of Michael Slater, who had claimed a catch-that-wasn't in the Mumbai Test earlier in the year and then walked up to Rahul Dravid in intimidating fashion and abused him, was the starkest example of how so many players from Australia, England and South Africa had got away without even a warning. Footage of Slater's act, along with those of many others, was shown over and over again on television, and more than just a hint was made that the action against Sachin and the five others was laden with racial overtones.

The feeling that Asians were being targeted was already strong in the region; it became stronger, and there were even unfounded suggestions that the pursuit of Tendulkar, India's top cricketer, was being treated by the South Africans as some sort of retribution against India, where Hansie Cronje had been caught and disgraced. The public outcry showed no signs of diminishing, only of further building up. This was because the central figure in the matter was a national icon with a spotless record and reputation. The papers wrote in their editorials that the then Indian cricket board chief Jagmohan

Dalmiya should 'not hesitate to convey India's strongest displeasure to the ICC', but Dalmiya went a step beyond that. He threatened to bring the team back home if Denness was not removed for the third Test (the Indians had somehow saved the second Test on the last day with gritty batting).

India's clout in international cricket was massive, and the threat could not be ignored. The South African Board was in a tight spot. It was willing to replace Denness, but the ICC stood firmly by him. Finally, with a great deal of difficulty, an odd settlement was worked out: the South African Board would indeed replace Denness with South Africa's Denis Lindsay, but the third Test would not be recognized as an official one by the ICC since it had not okayed the replacement.

India eventually went down badly in the "unofficial" Test at Centurion, losing by an innings and seventy-three runs, and the series was South Africa's, which it would have been even if the final Test had not been played. Tendulkar's form too was patchy. After the wonderful 155 that he started off with, he had got fifteen, one, twenty-two (not out), twenty-seven and forty. The aspersions cast on his character, and the indignation provoked by these, however, had put all scores on the backburner. Well before the numbers, came the name. If the fixers' deal, that a match would be "on" only after Tendulkar got out, was the supreme tribute to his attitude and commitment, the placing of name over numbers (which are so crucial in cricket) was a further testament to the kind of reputation he had acquired.

England was to come to India for three Tests and five one-dayers soon after the Indians returned from South Africa. In an attempt to placate the powerful Indian cricket board, a week before the India-England series got under way, the ICC cleared Tendulkar of the ball-tampering allegations, saying he was only guilty of cleaning the ball without the umpire's permission. But the ICC did not withdraw the sentence of 'immediate one-Test ban' against Virender Sehwag. The ICC and the Indian cricket board seemed set on a collision course on this issue, for the ICC insisted it would label the first Test against England too "unofficial" if Sehwag played. The Indian Board finally relented and did not pick Sehwag for the first Test, and the crisis blew over.

However, a crisis of serious confrontation between Tendulkar and England engulfed the entire series and, with Tendulkar really hating it this time, invited greater parallels with Sir Don Bradman. The then England captain Nasser Hussain and his largely inexperienced team – none of them had played a Test in India before – decided from the word go, that they were going to treat Tendulkar as an exceptional case. They planned to have an 8-1 field for him and bowl to him wide outside the off-stump. The policy was first implemented after he had settled well in India's first innings in the first Test at Mohali. England, batting first, had been bowled out for 238, and in response, Deep Dasgupta and Rahul Dravid had had a "slow" partnership in order to try and acquire a big lead. The 25,000-strong Mohali crowd got increasingly impatient with their defensive play and heckled them at regular intervals. They had come only to see one man bat, and they were now showing the dangerous side of an obsession. When Sachin came in at the fall of Dasgupta's wicket, the stands exploded. The Englishmen were already in some awe, because the British media had focused almost all its attention on him. The Tendulkar phenomenon and his position in modern India held a tremendous fascination for them, and they wrote untiringly about his Hindu roots and upbringing, his approach to cricket, his astounding success and the feeling of hero worship that he had stirred through the length and breadth of the country. The crowd reaction was a boisterous proclamation of his larger-than-life status, and it somehow got to the England players too, for they had seen nothing like this before.

After he had hit five boundaries for a quick thirty-one not out on the second evening, England lapsed into negativity on the third morning. They had packed off-side fields for him and for much of the time bowled at least five inches outside the off-stump. The plan was: if you can't get him out, tire and frustrate him into submission. It worked, because after a reasonably dry run at the wicket, he edged

Matthew Hoggard to the wicket-keeper. Sachin had scored eighty-eight by then, but for the new England attack, the thrill of the dismissal equalled that of getting someone out for naught.

India won the first Test by ten wickets on the fourth day itself. The fear of a 0-3 whitewash, that India had handed England during its last visit in 1993, was very real, and therefore one of Hussain's top priorities was to increasingly shut out Tendulkar. The Indian batting revolved around him, so checking him was the best way to make the entire line-up vulnerable, the England camp reasoned.

So the game of patience intensified in the second Test at Ahmedabad. Tendulkar came out to bat on the third day, not out overnight for two, and the seamers straightaway started giving him extra-width. He defensively pushed the ball around for some time. His team's situation was difficult. The visitors had got 407 in their first innings, two Indian wickets had gone down quickly, and on the third morning, the bowlers had accounted for Rahul Dravid and Sourav Ganguly without too much delay. Tendulkar had tired of the inflexible line in the first Test and gifted his wicket. The Englishmen were sure he would try and get back at them this time, to somehow prove he couldn't be bogged down all the time. As they were on top, the situation was just right to frustrate him, Mathew Hoggard, Andrew Flintoff and Craig White, with an 8-1 field to back them, did not deviate from their chosen area. Sachin was soon turning his wrists and getting himself the odd run. At lunch, he decided that his show of defiance could now be launched. He and his new batting partner V.V.S. Laxman had got their eye in, and it was anyway too much for him to allow stalling tactics for long.

Before the bowlers could reconcile themselves to his changed approach, he had got to his fifty after lunch. So the seamers tried to bowl even further outside the off-stump. The result was unforgettable, for the bowlers, their captain and spectators at the Motera Stadium who too had eyes just for him (security at the stadium was visibly stepped up after lunch as news came in of the attack on the Indian Parliament by terrorists, and not too many people were expected to walk in – the opposite happened: as news spread that Tendulkar was batting, the crowd swelled to over 30,000 post-lunch).

Hoggard ran in and bowled one six inches wide of the off-stump. Tendulkar came forward, as he had been doing for quite a while, and turned his wrists at the very moment of impact, whipping the ball through mid-wicket for four. Hoggard was stunned by the stroke but also greatly encouraged. He now had reason to bowl still wider. He did, and again, an identical stroke was produced, and the man at mid-on had to get the ball back from beyond the ropes. The crowd went crazy in its approval, the bowler couldn't hold back a grin of amazement as he walked back to his mark, and Hussain decided to play a little safe by stationing a man at mid-wicket. Hoggard bowled the next ball at the same spot. Tendulkar's wrists turned a little bit more than they had on the previous two deliveries, and the ball was sent square on the on-side, fetching him two runs. He was in complete command of the proceedings and, with a flick over mid-wicket for four, secured a place alongside Steve Waugh and Allan Border on the list of Test centurions.

His twenty-seventh Test ton (only Bradman and Gavaskar were now ahead) had pulled his team back from a perilous situation and left English shoulders drooping. Subsequently, it was a very lazy uppish shot to mid-off that cost Tendulkar his wicket. It was not the first time he had thrown his wicket immediately after crossing three figures, and he was horribly upset at what he had done.

But England, who fought spiritedly and forced a draw, acknowledged that their strategy against Tendulkar would have to change for the third Test at Bangalore. Nasser Hussain said: 'People will adapt. When they have worked it out, you have to move on to something else. We felt we had him in the morning. Then, after lunch, he came out and said, "Enough of this – I am Sachin Tendulkar." It was one of the finest innings I have seen.' By this time the Indian and the English media had already roundly criticized the overuse of the outside-the-off-stump line. The chief argument made against it, perhaps more scathingly by the English media than the local one, was that it took the fun out of the game and would alienate spectators, who were in any case not too enthused by Test cricket.

What Nasser Hussain did in the final Test at Bangalore prompted comparisons with the now legendary Bodyline case. Douglas Jardine, the prime villain of the Bodyline affair, had called the short and intimidating leg-side stuff unleashed at the best batsman of his time, Don Bradman, as "leg theory". Hussain seemed to be using his own version of "leg theory" against the best batsman of the modern era–Sachin Tendulkar. To add to it, the similarities between Jardine and Hussain were far too many. Apart from the fact that both were skippers of the English team, like Jardine, Nasser was born in India (in Chennai, to be specific), and physically the resemblance was remarkable: tall and tough, always sporting a big cap, and beneath it the same long face, the deep-set eyes, a huge angular nose, and a gruff countenance. Hussain could really get under someone's skin, and with Tendulkar, he succeeded brilliantly. Although he could reduce the runs with a much lesser degree of success than what Jardine had – Sachin averaged seventy-six in the series, while Bradman's average had come down to between fifty and sixty in the Bodyline series – he most certainly made the Indian lose nerve and cool more than once in the Bangalore Test which finally ended in a draw due to rain. But the tense on-field drama made it anything but a tame draw.

Hussain's tactic was to get his tall left-arm spinner Ashley Giles to pitch outside the right-hander's leg-stump, into the foot-marks and even beyond, so that all of Tendulkar's strokes except a very risky sweep would be automatically eliminated. Not that this was an invention. Under Mike Atherton's captaincy, England's very own Dominic Cork had tried the tactic against Brian Lara at Trent Bridge in 1995, Zimbabwe's Heath Streak had done the same against England at Bulawayo in 1996, and just one week before the India-England Test at Bangalore, South Africa's Claude Henderson had attempted it in a Test in Adelaide. However, nobody had been half as relentless as Giles. Nearly ninety per cent of his deliveries to Tendulkar landed a foot outside the leg-stump. The leg-side field was packed, even the wicket-keeper James Foster persistently stood a few yards outside the leg-stump, and the right-hander had little option but to mostly use his pads and, sometimes, his backside, to keep the balls away.

If the trick was to frustrate Tendulkar, it worked. The first sign of its effectiveness was the look on his face. He was clearly annoyed as he failed to score runs off seventy-five of the first ninety-two balls he faced. The second sign was a tense finger-wagging altercation he had with the England captain during the final drinks interval on the second day. By this time, he was thoroughly fed up, because all the classical cricket strokes had been cut out by the "leg theory". However, England had still not been entirely successful, because the whole idea was to make him chuck his wicket out of sheer exasperation. This was where the "leg theory" became, wholly unintentionally, a tribute to Tendulkar, much like the admission of his incorruptible character by the bookies. By adopting a negative strategy, Nasser Hussain and his team were conceding that conventional ways were not enough to get him out.

Sachin's impatience, though, increased, and it did look as if he just might eventually fall prey to reckless shot-making. Meanwhile, young gun Virender Sehwag came in to bat and tried some desperate hitting against Giles. Seeing Sehwag get away with slogs, the piqued Tendulkar, not out on a good seventy-plus in those trying circumstances, impulsively decided that he too would turn on the heat. That was Hussain and Giles' ultimate triumph. Sachin fleetingly and attractively cracked Giles for twelve runs in an over but, not content with that, tried another big hit in the left-armer's very next over and was out stumped for the first time in his Test career. The England team celebrated crazily, as if they had got him for zero. The fact was that he had scored ninety; that clearly wasn't far too much for an inexperienced and limited attack that thought it would otherwise not get him out at all.

England's odd strategy, and the tensions it had generated both on and off the field, sparked a hot debate in the cricket world. Strong arguments were made both for and against it. Those who saw nothing wrong with it said:

> It is the batsman's responsibility to counter what is offered to him, just as it's a bowler's job to face the consequences of his length and line.
>
> It's not that the stuff was unplayable. Sehwag got plenty of runs by attacking Giles, and so did Tendulkar himself when he took on the left-armer. So the argument that the line ruled out stroke-making was only partly true.
>
> Most importantly, the tactic worked. Giles did make the batsman lose his patience and come too far down the wicket for a clean stumping. Tendulkar had pulled his team out of a tough situation, avoided the follow-on, but he was out before he could reach his hundred. India had won the series 1-0, but in making this tactic work, Hussain had nearly neutralized the win. That was real achievement for a team that was expected to go down 0-3.

Those who thought Hussain's tactics indefensible said:

> The line cut out ninety-five per cent of a batsman's strokes, thus killing the bat-versus-ball contest and ruining the entertainment, which was the whole point of the game.
>
> It was a terrible advertisement for Test cricket, which badly needed absorbing stuff to pull in the crowds.
>
> The umpires certainly had adequate powers to deal with Hussain's tactics well before they had got out of hand. The ICC rules stated: 'For bowlers whom umpires consider to be bowling down the leg side as a negative tactic, the one-day international wide interpretation will be applied. Any off-side or leg-side delivery which in the opinion of the umpire does not give the batsman a reasonable opportunity to score shall be called a wide.' What more unambiguous laws did the umpires need to act? They ought to have stamped out the blatant negativism.
>
> Such tactics would also help ordinary and ineffective bowlers hide their lack of ability. All in all, they needed to be outlawed.

England may have got Tendulkar out eventually but their success was not unqualified. In moral terms, they had been defeated.

Historically, it is remarkable how similar these opinions were, in both letter and spirit, to those voiced in 1932 for and against Douglas Jardine and his executor-in-chief, Harold Larwood. Novelist and playwright A.A. Milne, creator of *Winnie the Pooh*, had defended the theory of Bodyline by saying:

> If modern batsmanship is really so unadventurous and inflexible that after three failures it announced itself beaten and calls for the laws to be altered, why, then, let the laws be altered; let everybody go on making runs, the artisan no easily than the master; and let us admit frankly that the game is made for the batsmen only, and that it ceases to be cricket as soon as it can no longer be called 'a batsman's paradise'.

B.J.T. Bosanquet, the inventor of the googly, who had in support of the delivery bowled outside the leg stump then said:

> Such a ball cannot hit the wicket, and therefore presents no danger to the batsman unless he plays at it. Therefore any batsman who can use his feet has merely to move inwards and let the ball pass him, unless he thinks he can make a scoring stroke off it. If the bowler tires of this game and bowls on the off or middle stump, the batsman has a large unguarded area into which to make the stroke... It is the ball which pitches on the wicket which is dangerous, not the ball which must miss it.[1]

Journalist Dr E.P. Barbour, who opposed the negative line, commented:

> If continued and extended to all grades of cricket as they should be if they are fair, the end-result of such tactics will be the disappearance from first-class cricket of every champion... Perhaps a more serious aspect still is the imminent danger to the good fellowship and friendly rivalry that has always been associated with cricket.

Finally, the target himself, Don Bradman, had hit the nail on the head:

> Undoubtedly Bodyline was a reaction against the dominance of the bat over the ball, magnified by my own fortuitous 1930 season in England. But it was the wrong remedy. Killing a patient is not the way to cure his disease.

Unlike in the aftermath of the Bodyline series, no new laws were enacted to stamp out the new leg theory in 2001. Barely had the storm over Hussain's tactics blown over when, on the eve of the fourth one-dayer against England in Kanpur, Tendulkar received news that on 27 January 2002, his agent Mark Mascarenhas had died in a road accident. Mascarenhas' car had rammed into another vehicle near Nagpur in Maharashtra, and he had succumbed to head injuries. This was a big blow to Tendulkar. The two had met recently during the third-day ODI at Chennai. 'I am shattered. Our relationship was not that of an agent and his client. He was a very, very close friend of mine, more of a family member,' he said. He had resigned with the agent's firm, WorldTel, in 2001 for the handling of his endorsements and marketing. The new deal was supposed to be worth Rs. 800 million, far in excess of the original 1996 deal that had made him the richest name in international cricket. Mascarenhas had also unveiled plans to start a global chain of restaurants carrying Sachin's name (The first of these outlets, called Tendulkar's, opened in the plush Colaba locality of Mumbai early in 2003, and the second one, called Sachin's, opened in the Mumbai suburb of Mulund in October 2004).

Over the years, Mascarenhas had set himself up as a challenger to Australia's Kerry Packer. Like Packer, he had exploited the television appeal of cricket and, after securing the TV rights for the 1996 World Cup, had succeeded in beaming cricket to countries that had not seen live cricket on the small screen earlier. However, WorldTel had come under the Indian investigative authority CBI's scanner after it was alleged that it had joined hands with India's national TV network Doordarshan and the ICC to fatten up the telecast fees for the mini-World Cup in Dhaka in 1998.

At Kanpur, Sachin insisted he would play despite "the irreparable loss" and scored eighty-seven not out off sixty-six balls to take his team beyond England's total with more than ten overs to spare. So involved was he in his batting that day, that even after he had hit a six to finish the game, he took guard, unaware that the match was over. He won the Man of the Series award in the ODI series, but at least here, there was no doubt that the moral victory was England's. They had come back from being 1-3 down to level the series.

*

Tendulkar had been suffering from a minor knee problem towards the end of the series against England. Once Hussain's team had left in February 2002 and he had notched his twenty-eighth Test hundred against Zimbabwe at home in the same month, he asked the Board for some time to recover and opted out of the one-day series against Zimbabwe. This was because he was keen to get well for India's tour to the West Indies, which was to begin in March 2002. Curiously, while for Tendulkar this was the third time in four years he was sitting out due to an injury, his chief batting rival not merely in the Caribbean but in world cricket, Brian Lara, who had similarly suffered a spate of injuries over the years, was also waiting anxiously to get back in shape for the contest against the visiting Indians. Lara had in the previous year batted brilliantly against Sri Lanka in the Tests, getting scores of 221, 178 and 130 in a losing cause. His splendid run had come to a sharp halt when he collided with Marvan Atapattu on the field and broke his elbow. He was nevertheless expected to be ready for action by the time the Indians landed; the pre-series talk focused on the duel-to-come between the two gladiators.

Ultimately, it was Tendulkar's batting that grabbed most of the attention. This was due to a peculiar mix of success and failure he enjoyed on the tour. The success was in keeping with his consistency; the failure was news; and the two were bound by a common thread called tempered batting. In the West Indies, its ascendancy was complete.

At this point in time, Tendulkar was one short of equalling Sir Don Bradman's tally of twenty-nine Test hundreds and was expected to reach the landmark in the very first of the five Test matches. He fell short by twenty-one runs in the first Test at Georgetown but got it in the second, at Port-of-Spain. As expected, the achievement won him plaudits from across the world.

His twenty-ninth ton in Test cricket also attracted attention due to one more reason: he took his own time for it and spent nearly twenty minutes in his nineties. This was very unlike the aggressive batsman the world knew. He was keen this new avatar, of a batsman willing to spend more time in the middle, albeit for fewer runs. During his knock of seventy-nine in the first Test too, when he had bailed India out of trouble from twenty-one for two in response to West Indies' 501, he had played the waiting game.

Despite his age – twenty-nine – he saw himself as an elder statesman in a young team; there were new strokeplayers in the team like Virender Sehwag, V.V.S. Laxman, and also Yuvraj Singh in the one-dayers, who could now contribute to the Indian team. In his thirteenth year in international cricket, he had a much bigger responsibility of "carrying" the team with him. Many felt he was making a big mistake by curbing his natural instincts and thought he'd be most effective playing his attacking game. They were perhaps right, but they neglected a central factor that influences human character: experience. That had altered him. He had only known an increasing weight of responsibility since he was sixteen, and in 2002 things had reached a point where his basic human vulnerability was being labelled a weakness. His position was similar and yet fundamentally different from that of Brian Lara. If Lara did not score in a few innings, he could take it easy, because the Caribbean would not experience any tumult. If on the other hand, Sachin went without a big innings in four knocks, there would be a mini-upheaval in his country. That was his, and the game's, status in the Indian sub-continent. He therefore felt he owed it to himself and his team to score nothing less than a hundred runs per innings.

Then came the three zeroes in four Test innings, for the first time in his career (eight was what he got between the zeroes). The zeroes were blown up. What's wrong with him? Why can't he get runs, worried cricket watchers asked. In four out of five innings, he had got out LBW, so that mode of dismissal triggered furious debate. Some said he was playing far too much across the line, and others pointed out that he was getting behind the ball so much that he could be easily be a candidate for LBW.

What made his failings worse was that they matched that of his team. After winning the second Test in which he had got his hundred, India had gone down terribly in the third at Trinidad and had somehow managed to save the fourth. They blew the chance to record a rare overseas series win when they lost the decider at Jamaica. The only plus the Indians could take from this Test was Tendulkar's return to form. He was fluent in the first innings with his forty-one and when his team was given 408 to chase for victory, batted with authority to try and keep his team's challenge intact. However, he was bowled for eighty-six by one from left-arm pacer Pedro Collins – the third time he had got Tendulkar in the series – that nipped back sharply and kept low, and the match was over. His final average for the Tests (41.38) was far above Lara's (28.86), but in spite of the sense of accountability with which he had batted, he had not done in the decider what Lara had done twice against the Australians three years ago. The question whether he could somehow find for his team an escape route to victory in the face of insurmountable odds was therefore still very much alive.

He was for the first time in eight years moved down the order, at number four, in the one-dayers against the West Indies. Sehwag was asked to partner Ganguly as opener. The decision was a major one and raised eyebrows, though captain Ganguly said the move was meant only to provide more stability to the middle order. Tendulkar had had phenomenal success in the opening slot, and it was generally agreed that the more balls he faced, the better it would be for his team. There was talk that he was unhappy, and a statement he made several months later revealed that he indeed was, but his dedication to the team's cause was total. He sat out the fourth one-dayer with an injured shoulder but risked further injury to play in the fifth, which was a decider. He top-scored with sixty-five in seventy balls and helped his team post a fighting score of 260 that finally won it the series. 'There were some shots I just couldn't play, because the shoulder was stiff. I had to change my game in order to try to stay in the middle,' he said after the match. But people in India were disappointed with Tendulkar and with the rest of the team, and justifiably so. The West Indies tour was India's best chance to break the sixteen-year jinx of not winning a series abroad. They had an added advantage: the West Indies' team was at its worst; it had lost fourteen of its last nineteen Tests, out of which five were consecutive defeats leading up to the India series; their main players had not been successful, and no new talent was forthcoming; and the wickets in West Indies were not radically different from those in India. With so many things going its way, India had failed to do well.

The next stop was England, where the weather and the pitches were going to be nowhere close to those in the sub-continent. So nobody thought things would go smooth for the Indians. The breaking of at least one jinx in England, in the shorter version of the game, therefore came as a tremendous boost to the spirit of Indian cricket. The team chased 325 in the finals of the NatWest Tri-Series Trophy against England and pulled off a smashing win in the last over. Its ability to chase big totals, especially in crucial games, was under doubt, had been open to serious investigation. Here the team actually overcame an early batting collapse. Among the senior batsmen who had left early was Tendulkar, once again triggering talk of how he couldn't come through in the finals. He had scored fourteen before getting out needlessly after a desperate heave against harmless spin. As he left the field, many thought the Indian challenge was over, but young Turks Yuvraj Singh and Mohammed Kaif took hold of the match on their own. The NatWest triumph has since acquired the significance of a landmark in modern Indian cricket, for it instilled a sense of self-belief that the Indians lacked earlier and proved the existence of a "real" team as against a set of individuals.

His failure in the finals apart, Tendulkar set a personal example for his team through the tournament in three respects: run-scoring, commitment, and the will to break a jinx. He got two hundreds – one against England, the other against Sri Lanka. Both were studies in how to build and pace one's innings. Nasser Hussain admitted so much when he said, 'We learned from him today how to go about a one-day innings.' The same knock was a personal jinx-breaker, for Tendulkar had in all these years not got an ODI hundred against England and was keen to set the record straight. Then there was commitment. He lost his ninety-two-year-old grandmother, Indumati Tendulkar, the day before one of the league games. He was given the option of not attending the practice session before the game but still chose to participate. And in one of the games, there was instant innovation. He got ready to play the reverse-sweep well after a slow-medium bowler had released the ball. The moment the ball landed on its length, he had a change of mind and finally played a powerful and well-timed cut. The opposition was flabbergasted.

The five-Test series that India levelled 1-1, thus further extending its wait for a series win abroad, was proof of how the more things changed, the more they remained the same. Initially there was doubt about Sachin's form; he was out for six and twelve in the first Test at Lord's. If the single digits evoked the memory of West Indies, the trap to which he fell in the second innings took the memory a little further behind, to England's tour of India early in the year. As soon as he came out to bat, Hussain posted men at his favourite spots – deep-point and deep square-leg – and minimized the runs. A frustrated Tendulkar soon tried an ambitious hit and was bowled.

With him went the Test, but what created a bigger scare was that with him also walked off the field an intruder, nicely dressed in a blue shirt and a tie. Tendulkar's security had been upgraded earlier in the year following terrorist threats of a kidnap, which were being taken seriously since the hijacking of an Indian passenger aircraft towards the end of 1999 and the attack on the Indian Parliament in September 2001. Indian officials had even spent a fortnight in England before the tour examining security arrangements. Particular care was being taken to prevent spectators from walking on to the grounds, and yet, at a place like Lord's where, once in a while, security personnel even prevented former Test greats from entering with or without proper passes, a man had not merely slipped in but walked all the way up to the boundary with Tendulkar.

Panic buttons were pressed and the Marylebone Cricket Club promised to investigate the security slip-up, but when nobody expected it, Tendulkar made a personal request that the offender not be charged. It turned out that the twenty-four-year-old intruder was a member of Australia's Melbourne Cricket Club. An admirer of Tendulkar's, he had patted him on his shoulder on his way to the pavilion and told him: 'You're my hero. Don't worry, everything is going to be all right.' According to the Indian team's spokesperson Ranga Reddy, Sachin merely felt that since the man had not said anything bad or tried any physical assault, he should be only mildly punished and did not merit as harsh a treatment as confiscation of his passport or deportation. The Indian management however took the matter seriously and the MCC decided it would go ahead with the prosecution.

The talk of loss of form was demolished in the second Test at Trent Bridge. Tendulkar hit a flurry of brilliant shots to breathe life into a fast-disappearing Indian challenge and, as he entered the nineties, suddenly put his foot on the brakes, just as he had done in the Caribbean; only the result was different here. He was out before he could reach his hundred. India somehow forced a draw and in the third Test at Headingley, came back to level the series. The highlight of that Test was Tendulkar and Ganguly's combined carnage. After Tendulkar had been positive in defence for most part of the second day, reaching his thirtieth hundred – again after half-an-hour in the nineties – and thus bettering Bradman's tally of Test hundreds, Nasser Hussain opted for the new ball in the last session to try and get him and his partner Ganguly out.

The Indians, batting first, were already in a good position, and Hussain had to prevent the situation from getting out of hand, else England would have too much to score simply to avoid a follow-on. For their part, the Indians decided to step up the gear because, one, the light seemed to be swiftly deteriorating, and it was possible that the day's play could be cut short, and two, if they could get quick runs and hike the swelling total further, they could put the home team under enormous pressure. What followed was mayhem, as both batsmen hit a series of courageous sixes and got ninety-six runs off the last 11.1 overs of play. The way he went about hitting the fast bowlers on his county ground, especially on the on-side, Tendulkar could well have been playing eight-overs-a-side tennis-ball cricket, with his own interpretation of the leg theory. There was total abandon and yet no blunders. Andrew Caddick was belted twice over mid-wicket for six. One of these sixes was slightly bizarre. It was hit while Tendulkar was coolly walking into his stroke and could have been used as justification for Yorkshire's decision to name a hospitality box after him at Headingley's new East Stand.

Soon, Caddick, as well as England's most successful bowler of the season, Matthew Hoggard, were forced out of the attack. Hoggard had had a taste of Tendulkar's fury at Trent Bridge earlier, where he was hit off successive deliveries through extra-cover point and with absolute control through the slips for four. It was as if Sachin was deliberately taking on the opposition's best bowler, and he stuck to this policy at Headingley too. Ashley Giles, Tendulkar's tormentor in India, then came on to bowl and was hit for twenty-three in a single over. On the final ball of the day, Ganguly was bowled for 128, and Tendulkar stayed unbeaten on 185. England could not recover from this pounding which *The Guardian* called 'the torture of a thousand hits' and lost their way in the Test after Tendulkar was out on the third morning for 193.

Sunil Gavaskar was delighted that Tendulkar had crossed Bradman's tally of twenty-nine Test hundreds. He had severely criticized him in the last one year for getting out when the team needed him most and had praised Steve Waugh in no uncertain terms. After Sachin's display at Headingley, the man to score most hundreds in Tests (thirty-four) told England's *Daily Telegraph* that Tendulkar was "better" than Bradman. This was a bold statement to make, because nobody had come even close to the Don's average of ninety-nine runs per Test innings. Gavaskar argued: 'For all Bradman's achievements, Tendulkar is the closest thing to batting perfection I've seen in terms of technique and temperament. If you have a look at some of the films of Bradman, you will see his bat came from third-man. Because Bradman was Bradman, he could see the ball incredibly early and score at a phenomenal rate. Tendulkar's bat comes down very straight, he is perfectly balanced off either foot, and there isn't a shot he can't play. He is probably the most complete batsman the game has seen.'

Tendulkar's opinion of himself was however not the same. 'I have statistically crossed Bradman but I can't be compared with him. He isn't a normal person. You can only dream of scoring a hundred once in every three innings.'

He had another proud moment, and another century, coming his way in the final Test at the Oval. He became the twenty-fifth man in cricket history and the first man in his twenties, to play a hundred Tests. He was understandably overjoyed, for only Gavaskar, Kapil Dev and Dilip Vengsarkar from his own country had entered the elite group. 'This is such a happy moment for me,' he said as Mumbai Cricket Association president Sharad Pawar handed him a circular plaque created in his honour by the Cricket Club of India on the morning of the Test (5 September 2002). The plaque had Tendulkar's image carved at the centre, his autograph below that, and was dotted with the mention of all the hundred Tests he had played since his debut in 1989 against Pakistan at Lahore. His family had decided against attending his hundredth Test, as they feared "it could make him extra-conscious", but some close friends had made their own arrangements. Vinod Kambli could not be physically present as he had, around the same time, to fly to Boland in South Africa to play first-class cricket, but a few days before taking the flight, he had gone to Mumbai's famous Siddhivinayak Temple to pray for Sachin.

Mumbai player Sameer Dighe, who was playing for Scholes CC in Yorkshire, had driven four hours to witness the moment. Yet another senior Ranji player Amol Muzumdar had come down from Newcastle, where he was playing for Tynemouth CC, and former India cap Nilesh Kulkarni had undertaken a three-and-a-half-hour journey from Liverpool, where he was playing for Hightown CC.

Tendulkar said he had not really set out to play a hundred Tests: 'I didn't set out to play a specific number of Tests. I wanted to enjoy every challenge put before me. In thirteen years I have learnt a lot and there is still much to learn. Each and every moment I have enjoyed and cherished. It is good to feel you have achieved something in life and contributed to the best of your abilities. It feels all the more great because only three Indians have played a hundred Tests earlier.' To cricket lovers, he said: 'Life would be boring if people didn't expect anything from you. At times the expectations have been high but they have helped me. But I try to live up to my own expectations and set attainable targets for myself, rather than those of others, which may be very, very tough. You have to be realistic.'

This was unusual for someone who always believed that silence was golden. There was another, very rare, admission that he made on the England tour in the middle of the Test series, and that was much more remarkable because it focused on the art of batting. It was a subject people wanted to pick his brains on, and on which he never spoke, at least before the public. For the first time perhaps, on Hampshire's Rosebowl Cricket Ground on 4 August 2002, Tendulkar addressed a substantial crowd of young cricketers on the essentials and finer points of batting. In the young crowd were some people who themselves knew more than a few things about cricket: Richie Benaud, Barry Richards, Michael Atherton and Ravi Shastri. They listened as keenly as the youngsters as Sachin held forth by the side of the main pitch.

He began by demonstrating how to find the ideal batting grip for oneself. From the way he went about it, it was clear he had given the matter considerable thought. He first placed the bat on the ground, exactly between his legs, then bent down, placed the right hand just centimetres above the splice, placed the left hand on top of it and lifted the bat easily and naturally. 'That is your natural and perfect grip,' he told the youngsters.

TV commentator Mark Nicholas then asked him: 'Your top and bottom hand go down the handle, unlike the conventional top-hand grip of most batsmen.' To this, he replied that his grip helped him play his shots freely and to manoeuvre at the last moment but made it clear that keeping one's hands close to the body and the elbow straight and not sideways was the correct, most suitable and advantageous stance. He then challenged certain orthodoxies. He never took stance at the same spot for every ball, he said, he just stood wherever he felt most comfortable. Contrary to what a coaching manual would say, he pointed out that great batting didn't have much to do with great foot movement. More vital was the co-ordination of the head and the hands. Keeping the head still helped to sight the moving ball and its behaviour off the wicket, and the head must not bob about otherwise too. Mental stillness was as important; that was how a batsman should be, he stressed. Even otherwise, commitment on either foot had to wait till the point that it became absolutely necessary.

Throughout the exposition that was telecast live on Channel 4, Tendulkar smiled often, but the impression that the youngsters and the seniors got was that he was extremely serious and viewed batting with a certain reverence. It had more than the quality of a craft for him; it was art, and it had to be treated as such, he seemed to feel.

*

Back in the sub-continent, the Indian team, feeling truly confident, reached the final of the ICC Champions Trophy or the mini-World Cup in Sri Lanka. The final was however a washout. Soon after, at home, they beat Carl Hooper's struggling and Lara-less[2] West Indians in the first two Tests and were in a spot in the third and final Test at Kolkata, when Tendulkar pulled the team to safety with a superb 176. India had conceded a 139-run lead in the first innings and were down at eighty-seven for four in the second when he took over and, in the company of the classy V.V.S. Laxman who himself got 154 not out, batted for seven hours to force a draw. 'Someone has stood up and delivered in a crunch situation,' captain Sourav Ganguly said, not oblivious to the criticism that Tendulkar had often invited for not doing precisely that.

During the Kolkata knock, Tendulkar strained his hamstring and missed the ODI series against the West Indians but was fit for the New Zealand tour, which proved to be a sheer disaster for the Indians. They were demolished 0-2 in the Tests and 2-5 in the one-day series, with every player struggling against the rising and moving ball. Things came to such a point on this tour that a score in excess of a hundred for the Indians began to look very decent.

Yet even the unmitigated disaster in Kiwiland did not crush the Indians' hopes for the World Cup, which was scheduled to be held in South Africa in February-March 2003. Whether their airy dismissal of the New Zealand wickets as "unfit for international cricket" was justified or not, the air of confidence was clear and palpable. This was an indicator of how the psychology of the Indian team had changed for the better in the previous two years – that is, since Australia's tour of India early in 2001 – due to sheer coming together, hard work and some deserved successes. Tendulkar reflected the hopes of the entire Indian camp when he said the team was the best India had seen since the Hero Cup-winning squad in 1993-94 and had a good chance to lift the World Cup:

> I think this is one of the best teams I've been part of. It's a very good combination. If the top order fails, the lower middle-order clicks. If the bowling doesn't do very well, the batting makes up for it. In England, when we bowled on decent tracks, the bowlers did an excellent job. Some brilliant catches have been taken, especially by Yuvraj (Singh) and Mohammed (Kaif) – they have really raised the standard.
>
> We've been improving for the last 20 months, and we've won games in every country we've gone to. All the players have been able to put things together when it mattered. It is because

everyone from number one to eleven has performed that we've produced consistent results. We should carry the confidence forward.

Two questions persisted, however, even at the moment the Indian team boarded the flight to South Africa, in the middle of the by-now usual pre-World Cup hype and hardsell. One was about the clash between the ICC and the Indian players over the issue of freezing, for a specified period, personal endorsements that conflicted with those of the Cup's official sponsors. That was a matter of secondary importance for most cricket followers in India, though. The overriding question for them was Tendulkar's position in the batting order, and it expectedly set off a raging debate nationwide, especially after captain Sourav Ganguly said before the team left Indian shores that, 'We don't have any other batsman of his class and temperament, we need Sachin to lend stability to the middle order.' Tendulkar had been sent in at number four in the West Indies, after 193 innings as an opener. It had not affected his performance, since he had got two superb hundreds in the NatWest Series and good scores even otherwise. But there were fierce arguments made against placing him at number four in the all-important World Cup. It wasn't going to be wise to hold the team's best batsman back when he could take advantage of field restrictions in the first fifteen overs, it was said. Besides, Tendulkar must be given a chance to play the maximum number of overs in order to try and gain a psychological edge over the opposition, it was argued.

Sachin wasn't happy either. 'I had a chance to dictate terms when I opened the innings. When I go in now, the terms are set for me and I have to play accordingly,' he had said, challenging the assertion that his presence in the middle order made the batting look deep and that his and Rahul Dravid's experience needed to blend with the emerging talents of Yuvraj Singh and Mohammed Kaif. The statistics supported his position: thirty of his thirty-three ODI hundreds, most of which had resulted in an Indian win, had come in the opening slot, and his average as an opening batsman exceeded by over ten runs in the number four position. Former cricket greats too stood solidly behind him. Reflecting the widening sentiment, they said that if he were kept at number four, it would be a case of the Indians shooting themselves in the foot. Finally, he was again given the opening slot at the start of the tournament, and that made a world of difference.

---

1   Mudar Patherya, Wills Book of Excellence Cricket, Orient Longman Ltd., 1987.
2   Brian Lara was hit by jaundice during the mini-World Cup.

senior statesman

In-form or out of form are phrases that do not
mean anything when Tendulkar is at the crease.

— Inzamam-ul-Haq

World Cup 2003 was going to be, for cricket-lovers worldwide, the opportunity to see for one last time – on a grand scale – the brilliance of players such as the sultans of swing, Wasim Akram and Waqar Younis, the gentle warrior Javagal Srinath, the vastly talented but greatly under-rated Aravinda De Silva, the elegant Saeed Anwar, and two champions from South Africa, the host nation – Allan Donald and Jonty Rhodes.

Tendulkar and Brian Lara had both launched their international careers at about the same time as some of these retirees. The two were yet nowhere close to retirement, but the fact was that they had recently turned into senior statesmen. They were expected to play this role for their respective teams while still being among the top entertainers in the tournament. For this, the competition was immense from players other than those mentioned above. There were pacers like Bret Lee, Shoaib Akhtar, Glenn McGrath and Jason Gillespie, spinners like Mutthiah Muralitharan, Harbhajan Singh, Saqlain Mushtaq and Daniel Vettori (an under-rated and highly effective bowler, according to Tendulkar), all-rounders like Chris Cairns and Andrew Flintoff, and in terms of sheer batting competition, a procession of attractive players like Adam Gilchrist, Ricky Ponting, Matthew Hayden, Damien Martyn, Virender Sehwag, Yuvraj Singh, Stephen Fleming, Nathan Astle, Craig McMillan, Michael Vaughan, Marcus Trescothick, Inzamam-ul-Haq, Yousuf

Youhana, Sanath Jayasuriya, Marvan Atapattu, Hashan Tillekeratne, Mahela Jayawardene, Chris Gayle, Ramnaresh Sarwan and Shivnarine Chanderpaul.

Both the Indians and Pakistanis, who along with the Sri Lankans and Bangladeshis formed the throbbing heart of international cricket, scrutinized the itinerary, the team groupings and the points system with a zeal as passionate as ever, but nothing thrilled their sense of anticipation as much as the match marked for 1 March 2003: India versus Pakistan. They promptly called it the final before the final. Tendulkar began to hear of the game from the day the schedule was declared. 'There were more than 365 days for the tournament to start. Yet wherever I went, people would invariably bring up the subject and tell me we had to win on 1 March,' he said. Some of the demands were extremist: do what you will in the World Cup, win it or don't, but make sure you win that day.

By the time 1 March arrived, India were already through all their other first-stage matches and had been a part of some super-charged drama, some of it completely unforeseen.

Their Cup campaign started against Holland. Though Holland were minnows, Tendulkar's performance against them was going to be closely watched because people in India were debating whether he could be as effective as in earlier World Cups with a mixed year behind him, a far more watchful attitude to batting and obviously altered body language since he had been asked to bat at number four. The final question was settled first. Tendulkar opened with Virender Sehwag. And signs that the other questions too could well be on their way to being solved were obtained when Tendulkar got a sound fifty-two, with seven boundaries. He had been the highest scorer for his team in the 1992 World Cup and the overall highest scorer in 1996. In this match, he overtook Javed Miandad, who had an aggregate of 1,083 runs in five World Cups, as the highest run-getter in the tournament (Miandad had played thirty-three matches, and Tendulkar ten less than that, for the same number of runs). In spite of getting an unimpressive 204, India won the match with some comfort.

The general consensus was that India's second match, against Australia at SuperSport, Centurion, would be its most significant in terms of the eventual progress it could make in the World Cup. This thinking turned out to be true, for the beating it took here impacted on its psychology in the final against the same opponents. Firstly, points gained by a win against Australia would make India's entry into the Super Six stage easier. India had been placed in Group A, which had acquired the label of Group of Death. This was because while three of the six teams in it were going to advance to the Super Sixes, it had four formidable outfits – Australia, India, Pakistan and England – and a fifth, Zimbabwe, could pull an unpleasant surprise any day. The second, more important point, was that a win against a very strong team would give the Indians the boost that was necessary for them to regroup in view of the defeats they had faced in New Zealand only recently. The Indians could then march ahead with a real chance of lifting the Cup. History too supported this theory. The Australian team was the most powerful in the world, just as Clive Lloyd's West Indians had been in 1983. India had beaten the West Indies in a league game in 1983 and had then gone on to lift the Cup.

While all this was true, the desire to see a good performance was unfortunately not dictated adequately by this logic. The exploitation of the World Cup in cricket's biggest market, India, had been enormous, and much of the cricket-loving public, in any case vulnerable more to feeling about the nation's cricket than rationale, had been swayed by manufactured sentiment. The media, the corporate world and the entertainment industry had all gotten together almost to create the impression that other cricket-playing countries were going to gather in South Africa only to present the World Cup to the Indian team.

If this made matters difficult for Sourav Ganguly's team, what didn't help at all was that the Indians put up an awful performance against the Aussies.

Tendulkar had done well against Australia all through his career, so he was expected to lead from the front. He began doing that straightaway. After watching McGrath and Lee in the first five overs, he broke loose with a ferocious shot through the covers off Lee in the sixth over. His biggest achievement, though, was that he disturbed McGrath's line and length in the seventh over. McGrath bowled one fractionally outside off-stump, and he hit it as hard as he could over point for four. Two balls later, he played a forward defensive stroke that took the ball beyond mid-off for four. He then ruined the line some more: he deliberately started walking across outside off-stump and started pushing the ball to the on-side for quick runs. But just as he had begun to establish supremacy, he was brought to a halt by a sad collapse at the other end.

Ganguly tried to hit a wide Bret Lee ball in the sixth over and nicked it to the keeper. Sehwag, at one-drop, tried to hit an even wider ball and left soon after. In came Rahul Dravid, who played twenty-three balls without a run and soon played on to the stumps. Yuvraj Singh and Mohammed Kaif followed him as if in a procession, Yuvraj caught plumb in front while trying to play McGrath across the line and Kaif, when there was a need to hang on, attempting a hook off Gillespie and spooning a catch to mid-wicket.

With the score reading fifty for five and with Dinesh Mongia, the last recognized batsman, as partner, Tendulkar decided not to play any expansive shots and began to work the ball around. However, when he was on thirty-six and the team score seventy-eight after twenty-seven overs, Jason Gillespie bowled him a slower one. He tried to play it to fine leg but committed two obvious errors in doing so: one, he did not read the pace, and two, he walked into the shot. The ball struck his pad and from the moment it did, he knew he was out. India were bowled out for 125 and, while fielding, the drooping shoulders and defeatist stance of the team members were indication enough that they were not able to put up a fight.

The capitulation generated fury across India, and the rage degenerated into violent demonstrations. Ganguly's effigies were burned in his hometown Kolkata, slogans were raised against the team by organized crowds across the country, and Mohammed Kaif's house in Allahabad was pelted with stones, paint and oil. Armed policemen were stationed outside Tendulkar's residence in Le Mer building in Bandra in Mumbai, and also outside the homes of vice-captain Rahul Dravid, Javagal Srinath and Anil Kumble in Bangalore. The fans did not relent. Before they had left for South Africa, the players had involved themselves in a spate of commercial shoots and these, seen as ventures to earn fast bucks, were held against them. They were called heroes confined to advertisements, spoiled darlings with an easy-going attitude to their profession, and worse.

The team, hurting from the defeat, was further pained by these reactions. Tendulkar was among the first to go up to Kaif and tell him not to worry. That was not enough, for all his countrymen had to be placated to prevent uglier protests. So in an unprecedented move, the man most popular in India, Sachin himself, was asked to make a statement on behalf of the team, to the nation. The statement he read out to reporters had as much self-reproof in it as a plea for support:

> This is to all the well-wishers in India. I am here on behalf of the Indian cricket team. We ourselves are very disappointed with the kind of performances we have put up and I also understand the disappointment you have gone through. I am just here to assure all of you that we will be fighting in all the games until the last ball is bowled. So please continue to support us, as you have done in the past.

From the next match onwards, it was a transformed Indian team that took over. It won all its remaining league encounters – against Zimbabwe, Namibia, England and Pakistan respectively – and walked determinedly into the Super Sixes. The team's sports psychologist Sandy Gordon, who had had a stint with Australia earlier, had coined the slogan "Now or Never" to guide it through the World Cup. There were other motivational messages too, pasted all over the dressing room at various venues. They seemed to have been taken extra-seriously now, and the most obvious sign of the team's focus was the football-style huddle all the players got into at the fall of every opposition wicket. The huddle was first seen in the inaugural match against Holland, but the body language of the Indians exuded positivism in the real sense from the third game against Zimbabwe. The huddle was more than a celebration; it was a chance for every player to say something about the team's performance and the route it had to take (Javagal Srinath spoke the most). The players also did not stint in their praise for one another, and the outcome of this was that Tendulkar was by consensus given the name *Bhagwan* (God). He was the one they were looking up to, the other players told him, he had to play friend, philosopher, and guide in this mission.

His eighty-one against Zimbabwe helped India win easily and got him the Man of the Match award. He played all the shots in his catalogue, and the momentum he obtained early in the innings never slowed down, right until the moment he was bowled beautifully by Grant Flower. Bowling gentle left-arm spin, Flower pitched one on the middle and leg. It turned just a little bit to beat the batsman and took the bail, leaving Sachin clueless about what had happened.

The match against Namibia was on a slow wicket at the Maritzburg Oval. India were lucky to bat first but even while Tendulkar tried early to play forcing shots off the back foot, the ball just would not arrive. After he was dropped in the thirteenth over, he decided to work the ball around. He played as late as possible and got his highest World Cup score of 152 runs off 151 balls. The strike rate and the pattern of the innings showed how effectual he could be while playing a quiet game. He had played seventy-four dot balls and taken forty-nine singles. What made all the difference was that he had hit eighteen boundaries.

The most memorable moment of the knock was a straight hit that nearly smashed Pakistani umpire Aleem Dar's head. The umpire, showing astoundingly quick reflexes, ducked in time and fell to the ground. The first thing he did, even before he got back on his feet, was to say a prayer. 'I could have been killed,' he said after the game. 'I was saved because of my good eyesight. I still play cricket, you know. I haven't seen a more powerful drive in my four years of umpiring at the international level. But actually I quite enjoyed the incident. Sachin was very apologetic about it and kept saying sorry for the next two overs.'

England, against whom India were to play next, tried their own version of 'mental disintegration' against Tendulkar a few days ahead of the match. Fast bowler Andrew Caddick called him 'just another batsman who could be trapped'. The media splashed his statement all over newspaper pages and asked Tendulkar for his response. He gave none.

India chose to bat first against England on a wicket that promised both pace and bounce. In the previous year, India had played two full series against England, and each time it was Sehwag who started attacking from the word go while Tendulkar looked more inclined to stay in the middle. This time there was a turnaround, and Tendulkar brought out all the strokes he had intentionally cut out recently. He looked keen to play in the air, and to pull and hook. He had decided to change his stance after the Zimbabwe game, to keep more distance between his feet so that he could be ready to play certain shots. He displayed more than a few courageous hits here; he lost balance and nearly fell while playing a hook off Caddick. He drove with an exaggerated front foot movement through the covers, stood up on his toes and flicked Caddick twice to the square-leg fence, then stood up again on his toes and pulled him to the mid-wicket boundary. But the shot of the match was the one that sent the ball soaring over mid-wicket for six. After bowling a few balls up to him, Caddick opted to bowl one outside off-stump, at shoulder-height. Tendulkar had anticipated it, and getting himself quickly into position, he pulled the ball haughtily, out of the ground. Caddick's bowling partner James Anderson, who had bowled impressively in some of the earlier games and was spoken of as a threat to India, was taken off the attack after he was carted for twenty-six runs in four overs. Tendulkar reached his fifty in as many balls and got out immediately after that. He looked to play Flintoff through point, but the pace off the wicket deceived him. The ball hit the bottom of his bat and went into the hands of point.

After India had put up 250 – a fighting score on a bouncy wicket – Srinath bowled one of the most outstanding spells of his career, keeping the line tight and beating the England batsmen over and over again, although it was Ashish Nehra who created a semi-sensation by taking six wickets for twenty-three runs and leading India to victory by eighty-two runs. However, *The Times* in London chose to put Nehra in the shade and reserved its ecstatic lines for Tendulkar. Never mind if he had knocked off England, the paper wrote: 'He batted like God. In a trance of utter brilliance, he reached fifty as if it was just a station on his way, and then, just as the journos reached wearily for the Thesaurus, bewilderingly he steered the ball straight to Paul Collingwood. That, perhaps, is the trouble with instant brilliance: it is not supposed to last forever.'

The Indian public and the media had begun by first calling him "God" in 1998. His fellow team members had taken up the chorus and labelled him *Bhagwan* at the start of World Cup 2003. Now the British media was carrying the bug of deification further.

All the excessive prose, however, wasn't enough to give Tendulkar peace about the prospect of dealing with Pakistan. He had been waiting for 1 March to arrive for a long time, and twelve days away from the day, he had lost all sleep. He had the confidence of welcoming an engagement with Pakistan, yet his restlessness was acute because he couldn't wait to go out and start the battle. In the middle of this bout of insomnia, he played three critical matches – against Zimbabwe on 19 February, against Namibia on 23 February and against England on 26 February. The fact that he had soundly struck the ball in all three games, instead of calming him, fuelled his impatience and further ruined his sleep.

Like other players, of course, he also used the technique of visualization. During practice sessions, he visualized himself batting against Pakistan in front of a packed and boisterous crowd. He accordingly tweaked his positive energies, but he knew as well as anybody else that no amount of preparation could help if the cricket between the ears was disturbed during the moment of reckoning. It was this cricket, more than that played between twenty-two yards, that so often decided India-Pakistan encounters.

When he finally walked out to bat at the Centurion, the match was beautifully poised. Pakistan had batted first and scored 273, thanks mainly to Saeed Anwar who had held the innings together with a fine hundred. The pendulum had swung both ways in the first half. Taufeeq Umar had had a good fifty-eight-run first-wicket partnership with Anwar. Zaheer Khan had bowled erratically at the start, and Nehra too had been taken for runs. Then Khan had bowled Umar, and the dangerous Inzamam-ul-Haq, after striking an effortless boundary off the first ball bowled to him by Kumble, had run himself out without adding anything more, thus placing India on top. Anwar and Yusuf Youhana had then strung a good partnership, and after Shahid Afridi got out cheaply, Younis Khan (thirty-one), Rashid Latif (twenty-nine not out in twenty-five balls) and Wasim Akram (fifteen off the final over bowled by Nehra) had got valuable runs. India felt they had given away thirty runs more than they should have, but 273 was now irreversible; the point was to chase it.

Tendulkar's thrill-a-minute response to the Pakistan bowling attack comprising Wasim Akram, Waqar Younis and Shoaib Akhtar has been well-documented, both on video and in writing, and the innings has found a place for itself in World Cup history as one of the most exciting match-winning knocks, comparable with Alvin Kallicharan's assault on Dennis Lillee in the 1975 World Cup, Clive Lloyd's hundred in the final of the same World Cup, Vivian Richards' domination of England in 1979, Kapil Dev's rescue act against Zimbabwe in 1983, Inzamam's heroics in 1992 and Jayasuriya's knockout performances in 1996. But what makes it so special? Is it the ninety-eight runs he scored in seventy-five balls? To say that would be to reduce cricket to mere statistics. The real outstanding feature of the innings was that it was a definition of positive cricket. This is how Tendulkar defined positivism in that knock:

- In all the earlier World Cup games, Tendulkar had been at the non-striker's end when the first ball was bowled. Here, he insisted he would take strike.

- He met the very first ball bowled by Akram assertively with the full face of the bat. When Akram pitched the third ball at a perfect length but fractionally off-line, he stood up on his toes and played a firm back-foot push through the covers for four. That stroke carried a message: the situation was tense and he would of course try to stay at the wicket, but whenever he got the slightest chance to play an attacking shot, he would go for it.

- He ended the between-the-ears contest in the second over. Shoaib Akhtar had become, earlier in the tournament, the man to bowl the fastest delivery in international cricket, and there had been much talk of how the Indians would be able to face up to his pace. After he had bowled three okay deliveries here, he bowled one wide outside the off-stump. Tendulkar had to stretch his arms almost full-length to reach it. He still got the ball in the middle of the bat and slapped it over third-man for a sensational six. Off the next ball, he played the peculiar flick that is his own invention in modern-day cricket. The ball was struck very late, and the wrists rolled in such a way that the bat ended in a vertical position, the bottom hand resting right above the top one as the ball rushed to the boundary. The next ball saw a purely forward defensive stroke, except that the result was something a defensive shot didn't normally produce. The ball rolled past the left of mid-on, for four.

- Akhtar was taken off the attack immediately. Zaheer Abbas, one of Pakistan's greats, said the very fact that a team that boasted of having the fastest bowler on earth, had to stop him after just one over, was a signal that it felt completely crushed. The mind-game had been won. What followed later was unavoidable, he said.

- A study done in 2004 by the *British Medical Journal* went a step further, saying that Tendulkar's hit over third-man may have marked a definitive shift in Indo-Pak cricket. The study noted that Pakistan had gained a psychological edge over India after Miandad hit the last ball in the 1986 Australasia Cup final for six. That six never really left the Indian players' consciousness, and Pakistan's advantage persisted up till World Cup 2003, because the Indians felt they could at any moment pull something special out of their bag. Tendulkar's six ended that mental supremacy and turned the tide against Pakistan, the study suggested.

- Tendulkar played the forcing shot off the back foot and the peculiar flick repeatedly in the first few overs. Akram and Waqar, in particular, were too aware that these were his favourite shots, and his poise and power that day were enough to suggest the worst to them. Even after the sixth over, when Waqar Younis dismissed Virender Sehwag and Sourav Ganguly off successive deliveries, he didn't stop the strokeplay. In fact, soon after their dismissals, he hit a forcing shot off Akram through the covers that forced TV commentator Robin Jackman, at a loss for words, to keep saying 'Oh...oh...oh...oh' till well after the ball had crossed the ropes. Tendulkar himself was so happy at the shot that even after he had completed the follow-through of the bat, he stood in the same position for a few seconds, as though savouring the moment. In his flourish, he also gave a chance. Uncharacteristically, he tried to hit Akram over the top in the "V" in the seventh over itself. Abdul Razzaq, who stood a little too ahead at mid-off, managed to get his fingers to the ball but couldn't hold on to it. More than the spilled catch, it was Akram's response to the fielder that showed how worried the Pakistanis were about Tendulkar's form. '*Tujhe maloom hai tune kiska* catch *chhoda hai?* (Do you know whose catch you have dropped?)' Akram asked the fielder angrily.

- Tendulkar's reaction on reaching his fifty was extraordinary. He pumped both fists in the air and raised his bat in the direction of the Indian dressing room. This was how he usually reacted to a hundred. The reaction to this fifty showed the value he had set on the innings.

- He began cramping in the middle of the innings, and the cramps got worse as the innings progressed, making running difficult. There came a point where he started hobbling and had to be treated by the physiotherapist between overs. Bafflingly, for a long time, he refused to take a runner. His logic was this: the batsman who has played a shot is the best judge of whether runs can be taken, and how many. A runner has no clue about this. That logic could indeed hold, but it wasn't wise to stretch it beyond a certain level of discomfort. He did, underlining unintentionally that even cramps couldn't obstruct the chase.

- Some of the front-foot strokes he played in the "V" with a hurting left leg were startling. He had to stretch the left leg considerably as he went into these shots, and he experienced stabs of pain as he completed them. The best shots were the on-drives. The on-drive is the most difficult shot to play, because cricket is a side-on game, and while playing this drive, the right-hand batsman has to open up to the extent of entirely exposing his right shoulder. That can create technical problems, but for Tendulkar, there was an additional factor to consider: the on-drive can not only sometimes make a right-hand batsman stretch his left leg more than he normally does, he may also have to move the right leg around a bit to obtain the correct balance for the shot. This didn't pose too much difficulty for Tendulkar, and all the on-drives, even those against spin, went with notable power and exquisite timing.

- Negativism on the part of others too highlighted his own positives. When he was running with some difficulty, the Pakistani fielders kept targeting his end whenever they had to throw. They were looking for a run-out, but former Pakistan Test cricketer Rameez Raja, a commentator on TV, unfortunately said with reference to the throws that 'if you can't get him out, injure him'. He also said that if Tendulkar asked for a runner, Pakistan should not give him one. This was more out of a sense of helplessness than a desire to see Tendulkar injured. However, it reflected a sentiment that only Don Bradman had generated earlier: that legal measures were not enough to get him out.

- Tendulkar guided all his batting partners – Sehwag, Kaif (who played so responsibly after the fall of two quick wickets that

Tendulkar could relax) and Rahul Dravid – through the innings, telling them they had to stay cool and stay till the end to see the team through.

When he got out for ninety-eight off a scorcher from Akhtar, there was worry again in the Indian camp. Kaif had already departed for thirty-five, and with Tendulkar the fourth man out, there were nearly a hundred runs still to get for a team that was known for sudden collapses. That did not happen this time, as Yuvraj Singh showed as cool a mind as Dravid's and together, they reached the target in the forty-sixth over. Tendulkar made no effort to hide his excitement after receiving the Man of the Match award. He said at the presentation ceremony:

> This has always been a special game for us. It's the fourth World Cup we've beaten them (Pakistan) in a row, and nothing means more than this to us. I'm very excited about the victory, and I'd like to congratulate all the team-mates. Specially I'd like to congratulate Yuvraj because he's done well so many times during pressure situations, and obviously Rahul Dravid was as solid as ever. (Pointing to spectators) I'd like to thank all the people for supporting us. Thank you very much.

Asked about his own aggressive display, he said:

> The ball was coming on quite nicely, and I was picking the line and length early, so I thought, why not go and play some aggressive cricket.

The victory led to crazy street celebrations across India, and the media reflected the massive surge of sentiment. The focus was obviously Tendulkar. 'Super Sachin sends 'em Pak-ing,' said the headline in *The Times of India*, 'Sachin! Sachin! Sachin! Sachin!' screamed *The Asian Age*, 'Pakistunned!' said *The Pioneer*, 'We did it. Now for the Cup,' exhorted *The Hindustan Times*, and *The Hindu* line was 'Celebrate Countrymen, we did Pak them off!'

In 1996, the Indian team had got carried away by its quarter-final triumph against Pakistan and had then lost its way. The 2003 team did not explode in self-congratulation, though there was no shortage of people who suggested the World Cup was over since the team had defeated the arch rivals. As it went into the Super Sixes, its focus was intact, and all the praise heaped on Tendulkar did not affect him.

. India won all its Super Six matches, against Kenya, Sri Lanka and New Zealand respectively. Against Kenya and New Zealand, Tendulkar got out for five and fifteen, respectively, as the team chased 225 and 146. Playing his favourite flick against Kenya, he failed to keep the ball down and was caught by a fielder cleverly placed to the right of the square-leg umpire. Against the Kiwis, he hit three sensational boundaries before Jacob Oram at point took a blinder off a fiercely struck square-cut. In both matches, it was feared his early dismissal could set the team back. That did not happen, and Tendulkar was glad this wasn't an outfit that crashed all too predictably. The Lankans suffered as he got a smashing ninety-seven against them, playing many of the strokes that he had played against Pakistan – including an upper-cut over third-man for six.

Seeing the nature of the wickets, Tendulkar, high on confidence, had batted with an exaggerated forward defence in all the Super Six games. However, the semi-final India played against Kenya was on a wicket where the ball came slowly on to the bat. He changed his approach here, waiting for the ball and playing mostly off the back-foot. He pulled happily, however, got eighty-three and then picked two wickets to see his team through.

India had got through to the finals after twenty years. The first time they had reached the coveted place, in 1983, they had lifted the Cup. Expectations were therefore sky-high in the sub-continent, especially because this team looked sincere, hardworking and focused on its goal. Outside India, Australia were the clear favourites. They were by far the best team in the tournament, miles ahead of India, which was obviously second best. They had also won their matches more comfortably than the Indians, and in the one match where they had played Ganguly's team, there had been no contest at all.

In the final on 23 March too, there was no contest. The Indian decision to bowl first boomeranged as Adam Gilchrist and Matthew Hayden built an opening stand of 105 off fourteen overs, with the bowlers spraying the ball over the place, and then Aussie skipper Ricky Ponting and Damien Martyn had a record 234-run partnership for the third wicket. Both Ponting and Martyn went berserk, hitting the ball all over the Wanderers at Johannesburg, but it was Ponting's one-handed six over mid-wicket that symbolized Australia's domination as they rattled up a mammoth 359 in fifty overs.

No one had chased so much in ODI history earlier, and the only way to do it on wickets that were not really flat was to try and hit even the very good balls – that too from the word go. It was going to be risky. Tendulkar had been the star batsman in the tournament so far, with 106 fifties, which were actually two nineties, two eighties and two fifties. If there was one man who was considered capable of bringing India within reach of the target, it was him. He felt that the responsibility for getting quick runs early on was his and decided to get going straightaway. The first message India needed to give the Australians was that despite the huge total, they were deadly serious about chasing it. That could be done only by hitting early boundaries, and Tendulkar, the tension palpable on his face as he came out to open the innings, made the first attempt at this off the fourth ball against Glenn McGrath. Much unlike his normal approach to McGrath, he took a slightly short ball from outside the off-stump and pulled it in the mid-wicket region for four. The next ball too was short, and he tried a similar pull. The difference this time was that the ball came on quickly, and he had neither adequate time nor place to adjust his shot. The result: the ball went high in the air, and McGrath accepted the caught-and-bowled happily. That was the end of India's World Cup campaign. Sehwag did play some attacking cricket but after Tendulkar got out, India were never really in the game. They fell 125 runs short.

Tendulkar, who had had a super tournament with 673 runs in eleven games and three Man of the Match awards, was named Man of the Tournament. He had guided the Indian team through the championship, overshadowed all other individuals from all other teams and had in the process become the highest run-maker in World Cup history. More than anything else, he had set a very high standard of cricketing excellence. The winning captain, Ricky Ponting, said he was the best batsman he had played against, and Andy Flower of Zimbabwe told all World Cup followers that they were wrong in expecting others to bat as well as he did. 'He is the best in the world. The rest of us, who are more human, make mistakes sometimes. People watch him bat and they think all of us should bat as well as he does. It doesn't quite work like that,' Flower said.

The world however saw a very tearful Sachin receiving the trophy for the best player from West Indian legend Sir Gary Sobers. He'd have loved to exchange that trophy for the Big One.

*

Soon after the World Cup, it was revealed that Tendulkar had played the entire tournament through pain. He had torn a ligament and tendon on the ring finger on his left hand during the New Zealand tour in late 2002 and early 2003. The injury had been exacerbated during the World Cup, and every time he caught the ball, he had felt tremendous pain.

After the Cup, doctors who examined the finger advised surgery. So he ruled himself out of the triangular series to be held in Bangladesh in April 2003 and flew to the US with wife Anjali, herself a doctor, for the surgery. On 29 April, he underwent an hour-long operation at the Sinai Hospital in Baltimore. He would need three months for rehabilitation, surgeon Dror Paley told him. The rehab programme would include "occupational therapy to work on a range of motion and grip strength" and exercises such as opening and closing the palm and squeezing a ball.

Luckily, the Indian team, which had played non-stop cricket for eighteen months, was scheduled to have a break of four months. So Sachin had time till September to rest. As far as international cricket was concerned, it was going to be a five-month-long break. The next international fixture was against New Zealand in October. It was the Irani Trophy between the Ranji champions and the Rest of India that would be played at the start of the new season, in September. He was clear that he wanted to be ready for the Irani Trophy game, for his team, Mumbai, had won the Ranji Trophy, and he knew that the encounter against Rest of India should be a tough one.

Before all that could happen, though, there was an unsavoury controversy. It wasn't the first one to surround Tendulkar, but it was the first in which it was hard to give him the benefit of doubt.

Formula One world champion Michael Schumacher had presented Tendulkar with a Ferrari 360 Modena in the year 2002, after he had surpassed Sir Don Bradman's tally of twenty-nine Test hundreds. The car arrived in India early in August 2003, and Sachin asked the government if he could be exempt from paying Rs thirteen million as import duty on it. The Indian government then waived the 120 per cent duty it usually levied on all imported cars, and there was, for the first time in the country, very strong criticism of Tendulkar in the public sphere. It made the first serious dent in his God-like status and poularity.

People asked why he wanted a write-off when he was the world's richest cricketer. He said he had asked for it because other cricketers had got similar concessions in the past. On this, some argued that the government had to bear the greater part of the blame. Sportspersons would ask for concessions, but it was the government's job to prove that the law was equal for all, they said. Angry letter-writers to national newspapers pointed out how India's hockey players were humiliated at airports by officials who spent hours checking their baggage. They stressed that the duty would have helped alleviate the suffering of poor farmers who sweated in the fields to make the country self-sufficient in food. Other notable things that could be done in a poor country with Rs thirteen million were explained in meticulous detail.

Yet the question was emphatically not of money alone. With his impeccable behaviour and a fine sense of decency, Tendulkar had set an example for millions in the country. Hence the criticism and on the flip side, the sycophants' argument endorsing the official line that 'he's the pride of India'. Actually, it was precisely because he was the pride of India that the Ferrari affair attracted so much notice.

Talk of the Ferrari controversy was still on when the new season began. For the Indian team, 2003-04 was going to be extremely important for retaining their image as achievers. The team had come up nicely in the last two years and had come close to achieving a major goal, but it had been swept away by the Australians in the World Cup final. It was pointless to be content with an ostensibly respectable 'number two' slot that was, in actual terms, way below that occupied by Ricky Ponting's team. The World Cup defeat had to be addressed.

The opportunity for this was to present itself soon after the start of the season. Once India had finished playing two Tests against New Zealand at home in October 2003, Australia were to arrive in India for a triangular one-day series, and after that, India would fly to Australia for four Tests and another, rather lengthy, triangular ODI series (with Zimbabwe as the third team). More than the ODI series at home, it was the battle on Australian soil that would be the clincher, the real test of will and ability. Then, if the politicians didn't act as spoilers, there would be a test of nerves. India were supposed to go to Pakistan for the first bilateral series there after a gap of fourteen years. India had never won a Test series on Pakistani soil in five decades, so this was going to be the chance.

Tendulkar's fixity of purpose was evident from the inaugural match of the season. He announced a little before Mumbai took on the Rest of India in the Irani Trophy in Chennai that his team would play to win. He led the team in such a way that Mumbai caused a near-upset against a side packed with members of the national squad. After the Rest escaped narrowly, Sourav Ganguly, their captain, made no attempt to conceal his relief. 'If we had lost, I'd have had to hear about it in the Indian dressing room for at least one year,' he said with a smile. Who he'd hear it from was an easy guess: the man who took special pride in representing his local team.

The two Tests against New Zealand, which were drawn, were hardly gripping and became lacklustre for the crowds because Tendulkar got only one fifty in four innings. If his scores weren't big, his stay at the crease also wasn't easy, thanks to spinner Daniel Vettori. He bowled brilliantly to Tendulkar, and the way he fettered him – giving him only twenty-two runs from seventy-five balls in the series – was a delight to watch for anyone who appreciated left-arm spin, sadly not a flourishing art today. Alas, cricket is not a bowler's game, and this was largely overlooked. In fact, all through the two Tests, the discussion centred not on what was happening in the middle but on what the Indian team needed to do to cope well on Australian soil and whether or why India had to agree to play in Pakistan.

However, the triangular one-day series generated great interest as Tendulkar got going at Gwalior in the first game, making a patient hundred, and then followed it up with other sizeable scores to get the Man of the Series award. The result still was the same as in the World Cup: the best individual player ended up on the losing side. In the final, Australia made 235 on a slow Kolkata wicket and then bowled India out for 198. Tendulkar scored forty-five in the final, the highest on the Indian side, which was deemed small for him and quickly added to his list of 'failures in finals'. What made the final a disaster for the Indians was that their batting line-up, which had three other in-form players in Sehwag, Dravid and V.V.S. Laxman, crumbled before an Australian attack that did not have McGrath, Gillespie, Bret Lee and Shane Warne in it. Seamers Nathen Bracken, Brad Williams and Ian Harvey and left-arm spinner Michael Clarke proved too good for the Indians.

The Indian team, till a few years ago, would have developed a siege mentality after such a defeat, especially if it had to play immediately on the soil of the country that had beaten it at home with its B-team. Ganguly's team was not such an outfit. In the last two years, it had not allowed defeats to set it back in a big way. Even after taking major blows, it had taken fresh guard; the team had hunger, and had shown steel too. Though Australia was capable of making it look like very feeble steel, and had so often poked holes in it effortlessly – Ponting in the World Cup final had done it by taking one hand off the bat handle, and Damien Martyn with a broken finger in the same game – and though the record books said India had not won in Australia for twenty-two years, the Indian team gave itself a chance as it flew Down Under, telling itself that if it gave its best, it could indeed alter the record books.

"Never Say Die" was the title of one of Steve Waugh's tour diaries, and his one constant theme throughout his nearly twenty-year-old Test career. That career was to end with the series against India. India made his principle its own and paid honour to the magnificent cricketer with an inspired performance, although the feebleness did return towards the end of the last Test, with Waugh stubbornly holding one end up under pressure in a grand summing-up of his career.

The series turned out to be special for Test cricket. India's subsequent Pakistan tour was a much-awaited one and undoubtedly, there was good cricket apart from its obvious political significance, but in pure cricketing terms, Australia was infinitely more momentous. There was hardly a boring session, the bat-and-ball contest was always fierce, and the swings in the game were enthralling. The cricket was also proof, if proof were still needed, of the fact that batting and bowling were together central to a team's effectiveness. The team that did well in one area and faltered in the other would face failure or, at best, an incomplete success.

The Australian media made predictions of a whitewash on the first day of the first Test at the Gabba. When rain interrupted the brisk run-making of Ricky Ponting and Damien Martyn that day, Australia were an enviable 262 for two. Ganguly had put them in to bat because the wicket was seamer-friendly, but the bowlers had been directionless. When nobody really expected it, the bowlers hit back on the second day. Although only sixteen overs were possible due to heavy showers, they picked up seven Australian wickets, folding the innings at 323, far short of what the home team had hoped to get. Then, at sixty-two for three on the third day, with the

rain having damaged large portions of the wicket, they looked terrible
again. Dravid and Tendulkar were gone, and although Laxman,
known for his solidity against Australia, was still around, the man
who came out to partner him was one who had question marks raised
against him. Ganguly was always considered suspect against quality
fast bowling. He had not had a single Test hundred against Australia,
Pakistan and South Africa, and here he was up on a seaming wicket.
But he surprised even his worst critics, by coming up with a gutsy ton
that helped India take a good lead. Australia still managed to set
aside some time for a potential result. They gave India 199 to chase
in the last twenty-three overs of the Test. When Sehwag and Ashish
Chopra were sent back quickly, a collapse looked possible but Dravid
and Laxman kept their heads down and blocked any further breach.

In the second Test at Adelaide, they continued from where they
had left off and played a central role in the making of history.
Responding to Australia's 556, India were a sorry eighty-five for four
when they took over, but they brought India very close to the Aussie
total. Dravid played the principal figure with a fighting double
hundred, and Laxman, the supporting and beautifully stylish hand,
with 148. Then the bowlers and fielders backed the batsmen. Ajit
Agarkar, who had at the Gabba scored his first run in eight Test
innings against Australia amid applause, bowled a full length
throughout the innings and scalped five; Tendulkar snared Damien
Martyn and Steve Waugh with gentle leg-spin; Ashish Nehra and
Anil Kumble piled on the pressure with a tight line; Ganguly set run-
denying aggressive fields; Dravid took three catches, one of them
fabulous at slip; and Sehwag plucked two. Australia were all out for
196, leaving India less than 240 to get in ample time. But against the
best in the business, even a small chase isn't complete until it is
actually over, and Australia did succeed in generating anxiety
in the visitors' camp. Dravid knew his effort in the first innings
would be meaningless if the chase for the first win in Australia in
twenty-two years wasn't a successful one. He had pride in the India
cap and commitment, and he confirmed both when, on the last day,
after hours of concentrated effort, he square-drove Simon Katich

to point, took off his cap, kissed the India crest on it and raised his bat. Sunil Gavaskar called it one of the moments a country waits for, and indeed it was. India's victory after two decades was also one of its finest ever and was the result of self-belief and real team effort.

The defeat wounded Australia's coach John Buchanan enough to dash off handwritten letters to his players. Perhaps it had something to do with Dravid's gesture, or perhaps it didn't, but Buchanan in his letter, which got leaked to the media, condemned his team's attitude as "unbaggygreen-like" and called the batting "immature".

As if in response, in the traditional Boxing Day Test at Melbourne, the doughty Australians generously gave it back to the Indians. On the first day in Brisbane, Justin Langer had scored a hundred, and Australia had crossed 250 without losing more than two wickets, yet India had fought back. Then, Dravid's double ton had placed India in a strong position in Adelaide, and Australia had collapsed at a vital juncture in both innings to give India the Test. The reverse happened in Melbourne. Indian opener Virender Sehwag got a hundred in the first innings; India looked to be on top when they crossed 250 for the loss of just one wicket on the first day; then Ponting got a solid double hundred (257) to place his team in a position from which they couldn't lose; and the Indian batting crashed out at a key point in both innings. Australia had just shown, for the nth time, why they were the top team in world cricket. This was cricket at its best.

While all this gripping action was unfolding, a terrible drama involving Sachin Tendulkar was playing itself out both as a part of the main story and as a sub-plot. Tendulkar had begun the series in blazing fashion. He had scored eighty, with fourteen boundaries, in the tour opener against Victoria at the Melbourne Cricket Ground. The knock had so much authority that all-rounder Ian Harvey had to appeal to his fielders to 'get behind the bowler rather than just enjoy watching him bat'. The Australian media too was overjoyed. *The Age* drew a comparison between Tendulkar and the construction work then going on at the MCG. 'Two sounds filled the stadium with their echoes, variously the hammering, drilling and thumping of the labourers at their toils and the sweet crack of Tendulkar's bat at play. Both promised much entertainment in the days and years ahead,' it noted. *The Australian* went a step ahead. 'He alone is enough to whet the appetite for the four Tests,' it said, and added that 'he is a must-see attraction. For a fraction of the price of a rugby World Cup ticket, it will be possible to watch one of the greats of all time bat.'

On the third ball he faced in the first Test at Brisbane, Tendulkar shouldered arms to a Gillespie delivery, thinking the ball would safely go over the stumps. Instead it cut back and struck him high on the pad. Gillespie appealed and was then about to start his walk back to his mark when umpire Steve Bucknor, as if in an afterthought, raised his finger.

The decision created an upheaval. Not only in India but in Australia too. Memories of 1999, when Tendulkar had suffered a series of bad decisions Down Under, were revived. The media showed the TV footage over and over again, with analysts drawing white lines to show how the ball would have sailed over the stumps, and there was particular emphasis on Tendulkar's stunned look at the delayed moment when Bucknor pronounced his verdict.

This was clearly an overreaction. There were three reasons why the alarm bells could have been much less noisy. First, it was only the action replays that made it clear the ball would have gone over the stumps. The umpire didn't have the benefit of slow motion. If one saw the ball in real-time, the batsman did look out. Another factor was that Sachin had not offered a shot. And the third point, to the credit of the bowler, was that Tendulkar had read the line all wrong. Shane Warne, sitting out due to a year-long ban on him, had said before the start of the tour that the Australians had over the years tried various methods to get Tendulkar out. They had tried talking to him, they had tried not talking to him. Nothing had worked. So, Warne said, the only way to deal with him was to pitch the ball at the right spot and hope. Of all bowlers, Warne said Gillespie had the best chance against Tendulkar, because he hit the seam often. Here Gillespie had forced Tendulkar into two errors of judgement in three balls. First, he had bowled one outside off and moved it away, beating him completely. A ball later, he had again pitched outside off, making Tendulkar raise his arms and place his foot forward in false anticipation. The ball had moved in and hit him in line. Gillespie unfortunately got as much acknowledgement for his skills as Daniel Vettori had earlier in the season.

Tendulkar did not get to bat in the second innings at the Gabba as Dravid and Laxman held fort. The next opportunity was in Adelaide. Australia had piled up 556, and India were eighty-one for two when he arrived at the crease. But he fell into a trap. He went for an expansive drive off a wide delivery that was cleverly bowled full by Andy Bickel and nicked to the keeper. He had improved on his zero in Brisbane with a solitary run.

By now Sachin was feeling terribly constrained. So when he was given the ball by his captain in the middle of a developing partnership between Damien Martyn and Steve Waugh, he was keen to make his contribution. The Indian bowlers had held the Australian batsmen in check by bowling a good line and length and had crippled their strokeplay. He not only kept up the good work but, bowling the sort of classical loopy leg-spin that would make Warne chuckle, he enticed both Martyn and Waugh into playing the same drive that he had been tempted into playing and induced edges to first slip in consecutive overs. These two wickets were all-important. The Waugh-Martyn stand had begun to flower; if it had blossomed fully, it could have well changed the course of the Test. After they left, the Indians choked the rest.

When India finally chased, Tendulkar came out to bat at a sensitive stage. India were seventy-nine for two, with 150 still to get. One more wicket would have meant a panic situation. He stood quietly alongside Dravid and batted with assurance. He was out when he padded up to a Stuart MacGill top-spinner. His score was then thirty-seven, and the team's score 149. After the chase was complete, Ganguly said his thirty-seven had the value of a much bigger score, because the need had been for a partnership that would ward off pressure, and Tendulkar along with Dravid had provided that. If Dravid and Laxman in the batting department and Agarkar in bowling had been the real heroes in the historic Test, Tendulkar with two prized wickets and a steady innings had played his own part.

The pressure of being Tendulkar was, however, much greater, and just how much was evident when he feather-touched the first ball he faced at Melbourne down the leg side, into the hands of the keeper. A zero, one, thirty-seven and zero was certainly an unusual sequence of scores for him. Questions now began to be asked about the drying-up of runs. What is he doing wrong? Why isn't he getting a hundred when Sehwag, Dravid, Laxman and Ganguly have all got huge scores already? He did not look out of form – his thirty-seven had been confident. It was just that he had not spent enough time at the wicket, so he hadn't been getting runs. Whether he would end the poor run finally was the question uppermost in everyone's mind as India emerged to bat again. With hardly five overs left for the end of the third day's play, India lost the second wicket. Then there was a surprise for all. Ganguly walked in ahead of Tendulkar. He wanted to protect Sachin, so that he could get him to bat the next day, and had sent a message across that Tendulkar's wicket was more vital to the team than his. Tendulkar had not seen anything like this earlier in his career. No other captain had exposed himself ahead of him; in fact, once, in the year 2001, a night-watchman who was hurt on his finger had refused to play out the last four balls of the day to protect him.

When Tendulkar did bat on the fourth day, he struck a good forty-four before falling to a trap similar to the one laid for him at Adelaide. He chased one that moved away outside off and was caught behind. At the end of five innings, his average was 16.4, and the pattern of dismissals was rather odd. He had twice got out because he had not offered a stroke, and he had twice departed playing the cover drive off widish deliveries.

So he decided to cut out the cover drive altogether in the fourth and final Test at Sydney and this had a befitting result. His score was a mammoth 301 runs in the match without once losing his wicket. Keen students of the game had felt he would surely come up with a substantial knock to correct the imbalance in scores in the series. No one knew he'd go about it this way. Several deliveries were fed to him outside off-stump, but he refused to launch into the cover drive and eschewed other risks as well. By not touching anything outside off, he forced the bowlers to pitch where he wanted and looked to playing on the on-side. During his 613-minute-long stay at the crease in the first innings for his unbeaten 241, he scored 174 on the on-side alone.

Leg-spinner Stuart MacGill bowled not too impressively, but Tendulkar, who would otherwise go after such a bowler, did nothing apart from dutifully despatching the bad ones to the fence. Not once did he get carried away, not after he had celebrated his hundred with a clenched fist and not even after he had looked at the heavens in gratitude on reaching 200. He had clearly told himself that he was going to stay not out. His innings, along with Laxman's (he fell twenty-two short of a double ton) not only shut Australia out of the decider Test, but created a very real possibility of an Indian victory. Though some bungled chances and Steve Waugh's defiance didn't allow that to happen, he got another sixty-one not out in the second innings to stamp his dominance on the Test. He had struggled for some time; now, when he had come good, he had proved impossible to get out.

Tendulkar's self-denial at Sydney led to some criticism of his style of batting; it was said that the innings was unnatural, and that the total absence of the cover drive showed he wasn't enjoying his cricket as he used to earlier. Tendulkar, actually, was responding to a trap the Australians had set for him. He had been snared twice outside the off-stump, so his refusal to play the cover drive was a matter of tactics, and it worked well for him.

Tendulkar had also honoured his and the team's situation more than his instincts. The fate of a fascinating series was at stake. He thought of three factors – the crucial nature of the Test, his own need to get a big score and his team's need for him to get a big score – before finalizing his approach.

He had also not batted only in one gear. He did step up the gears. From the first he moved to the second, and from the second to the third. It was the fourth gear that he did not turn on. And that was deliberate. He thought he must not give away his wicket, never mind if he had to miss out on the top gear, because something more than self-indulgence was needed in that vital Test. Australia is such a terrific team that to give it some time is to automatically give it a chance. Batting the team out of the game was the priority.

Given the Man of the Match award for the Sydney Test, Tendulkar said it was a special one: 'This is really memorable for me because this is the last Test match Steve Waugh is going to play, and he's been a great inspiration for me.' He defined his own innings as "relieving", as he had not had a good series. 'I knew a big innings was around the corner, so it was just a matter of hanging in there. It wasn't that I wasn't batting well. I was just missing out on one particular ball. Instead of getting beaten, I was nicking it,' he said.

He then gave India's VB Series campaign a sizzling start with a stroke-filled sixty-eight against Australia and got another good score of eighty-six against the same team en route to the best-of-three finals. Not surprisingly, it was India and Australia who made it to the ultimate clash. Suddenly talk of avenging the World Cup final defeat spread in India and among Indian spectators in Australia, who had been remarkably high in number throughout the Test and one-day series and sometimes created the impression, with their animated activity and noise in the stands, that the matches were being played in the sub-continent. The percentage of Indians scattered in various cricket-playing countries was of course significant. What swelled the numbers further was the phenomenon of Indians flying abroad to see matches. The phenomenon had begun in July-August 2002 during the NatWest Trophy and had peaked during the World Cup in South Africa. Even after that, it had shown no signs of letting up. All the noise of visiting Indian spectators in the stands, however, couldn't stop the Aussies. After winning the first final easily, they gave the Indians a repeat of the recent past in the second final. They scored 359, the exact score that they had got in the World Cup final. Tendulkar failed in both finals, again prompting talk of how he was prone to failing when it mattered the most.

There was indeed a different set of standards for him. If he got seventy, he was called "The Almighty"; if he got out cheaply, he was said to have lost his touch; if he scored a brisk ninety and got out playing an ambitious shot, he was called impetuous as ever, and if he kept his head down and stood patiently at the crease, of course, he had transformed into a "slow" batsman. It was a privilege to be Tendulkar, but it was also very hard to be the batsman who was the cynosure of cricket-lovers all over the world.

*

Whether the Pakistan tour scheduled for March-April 2004 would be played was to be known soon after the Indian team got back from Australia. Tendulkar and his family had serious security concerns, as did other Indian players. A bomb had exploded the previous year outside the hotel in Karachi where the New Zealand cricket team had been staying; some members of the terrorist group, the Al-Qaeda, were said to have slipped into Pakistan from Afghanistan and were already fomenting trouble in Pakistan; the fear of the terrorist element was real, and Tendulkar had already had security cover for two years due to kidnapping threats; and the Pakistan President, General Pervez Musharraf himself, had recently escaped two assassination attempts.

The Indian government was however determined to make the most of the recent thaw in relations between the two countries. It sent an Indian cricket board delegation to examine the security arrangements in Pakistan. The delegation gave its all-clear, and promptly, so did the government. Once that was obtained, the players' fears were greatly reduced if not wholly eliminated, and Tendulkar for one couldn't wait to get into Pakistan. He had made his Test debut there in 1989, but India had not gone back again for a full tour due to political tensions. Cricket-lovers in Pakistan too were very eager to see him play as he had come to acquire an extraordinary status in world cricket. 'It's a great feeling,' Tendulkar said soon after the tour schedule was finalized. 'At that time (1989) I was sixteen years old. Now, having been around for fourteen-and-a-half years, it's exciting that after such a long time, you are getting an opportunity to play in Pakistan.'

A fortnight before the Pakistan series, Tendulkar was hit by back trouble. He had been strictly following the individual fitness regimen prescribed for every player by the Indian team's physical trainer, Gregory Allen King, and in fact landed up well before dawn (to avoid recognition) every day at the MIG Club in Bandra in Mumbai for intensive training sessions. But the pain had surfaced suddenly. He wondered why he was afflicted with injuries every time he had to play Pakistan. In 1999, he had suffered a crippling backache in the middle of his knock at Chennai. In the World Cup game of 2003, his left foot had cramped badly. And now, there was more of it. Fortunately the pain did not exacerbate, and he was fully fit when the Prime Minister of India A.B. Vajpayee met the Indian team to wish them luck. Vajpayee told the players that they were going not just as cricketers but as ambassadors and pointed out to Sachin in Hindi: '*Khel bhi jeetiye, dil bhi jeetiye* (Win at cricket, and also win hearts).'

The five one-dayers played before the three-Test series proved why India versus Pakistan won hands down as the most engrossing contest in cricket, way ahead of an England versus Australia match. The stadia were packed to capacity. The Pakistani crowds were extremely disciplined and sporting. For the first time, a huge number of Indians were granted visas by the Pakistani government to watch the matches, and in a scene that would have looked impossible just months ago, they not only roamed Pakistan's streets carrying Indian flags and shouting slogans for their team, they also unfurled the tricolour and chanted slogans enthusiastically in the stadia.

The games were hard-fought, and India came back from 2-1 down in the series to win 3-2. Tendulkar and his opening partner Sehwag were welcomed with a deafening roar by the Karachi crowd when they walked out to bat in the first one-dayer. Sachin quickly became part of the early excitement, top-edging Shoaib Akhtar for a six, getting dropped once and then striking some good hits before getting out for a personal twenty-eight. The Indians put up a mammoth total of 349, and Pakistan chased it spiritedly. In the last few overs, Tendulkar was involved in tense action on the boundary line as the Pakistanis tried to go for the big shots. At a crucial point, when a boundary would have eased the pressure on Pakistan, he ran speedily and cut off a fiercely struck hit inches ahead of the ropes, reducing the possible runs to a couple. The match down to the wire, the last-over and last-ball specialist Javed Miandad, now coach of the Pakistan team, gesticulated wildly from the balcony of the Pakistan dressing room. That didn't really help his men who were putting up a terrific fight, but the Indian team could heave a sigh of relief, and Indian supporters in the stands, including Priyanka Gandhi, daughter of former Indian Prime Minister Rajiv Gandhi, could jump with joy only after Ashish Nehra had bowled the last ball of a disciplined final over.

The excitement levels were similar throughout the second one-dayer at Rawalpindi. Pakistan captain Inzamam-ul-Haq had made a brilliantly composed hundred in the first one-dayer and ended up on the losing side. In Rawalpindi, Tendulkar played an innings of similar quality and suffered the same result.

Pakistan batted first and put up 330. India needed someone to take charge of the chase, and Tendulkar assumed the responsibility rightaway. With the intent of batting through, he began calmly, nevertheless unfailingly hitting every loose ball for a four. Shoaib Akhtar had been wayward in Karachi. This time, he was fairly disciplined, but Tendulkar had no trouble taking him for runs. Once he had got his eye in, he was a picture of intense concentration. He kept losing partners at regular intervals but he fought on, the look of determination on his face clear and his bat answering all the queries that had been raised about his ability to deliver under pressure. He understood the bowlers' strategy of capturing him outside the off-stump and kept getting inside the line and scoring on the on-side. He crossed 13,000 ODI runs in the course of the innings and when he guided a ball to third man to become the first Indian to score a one-day hundred in Pakistan, the entire Rawalpindi crowd rose as one to give him a standing ovation. Just when he was beginning to look invincible, he hit one into the deep-mid-wicket region for the second time in an over (the earlier hit had got him a four) and was caught. He had scored 141 in 135 balls and had carried single-handedly on his shoulders the Indian innings, which ended a mere twelve runs short of its target. Shoaib Akhtar rated the innings as better than the one Tendulkar had played in South Africa in the World Cup. If not better, it was definitely as good, though a disappointed Tendulkar said the result had diminished its meaning for him.

He was out for naught in the third game, which Pakistan won to take a lead in the series, and then was out caught-behind off Akhtar for seven in the fourth ODI at Lahore's Gaddafi Stadium when India were chasing 293 under the lights; Rahul Dravid, Mohammed Kaif and Yuvraj Singh, however, made the chase look easy. Till two years ago, the team could do nothing if Tendulkar didn't fire. The situation had changed for the better. Tendulkar was now sharing the spotlight with others. They were talented, responsible, and they could be relied on to ensure that the team's challenge stayed alive all the time.

Since the levelling of the series gave the fifth ODI the status of a final, Tendulkar was determined to do well. He had been upset at the way he had lost his wicket in the last two games. He told his coach Ramakant Acharekar of his disappointment over the phone and assured him he'd do better in the decider. He was going along smoothly at thirty-seven, with the same look of determination as he had shown at Rawalpindi, when a good-length ball by Mohammed Sami took a thin edge and landed in keeper Moin Khan's hands.

However, he redeemed his pledge to the coach in his capacity as fielder. When Inzamam threatened to take the game away with a beautiful knock, Tendulkar took a match-winning catch.

India had set Pakistan a target of 293. That may have been big in another series. Not in this one. Both teams had scored, and chased, regularly in excess of 300. Besides, Inzamam, even after the early loss of wickets (he came in when his team was nine for two), looked to be in wonderful touch. He was the revelation of the series for Indian cricketers as well as Indian cricket followers. For years, his image in the neighbouring land had been unflattering. He was seen as a batsman who always threatened to be great but could never really prove his greatness, at least not against India. He had played some scintillating knocks against other teams, but he had not in any way rattled the Indian team as he should have as the successor to Javed Miandad and the backbone of the Pakistan line-up. He was perceived as a grouchy man with a boyish face who lost his head at the slightest provocation, tried to assault spectators if they heckled him, and ran himself and his partners out with ridiculous regularity. The Inzamam they were seeing in 2004 had come into his own, after a decade in international cricket. He was *khadoos*, the very picture of combat, and his best quality was his equanimity, his self-possession as he went about tackling pressure with his artistic hands. He had been compared with Tendulkar from 1992 to 1994, but comparisons had ceased soon after, because Tendulkar had taken an unassailable lead. Finally, Inzamam was making the parallels sound meaningful.

Fog usually set in on the Gaddafi Stadium late in the evening. Barely three days ago, it had created huge difficulties for Pakistani bowlers and fielders. Despite having the Indians on the mat with early wickets, they had struggled in vain under the lights to prevent them from chasing an identical score (293). Inzamam in the final looked set to do what Rahul Dravid and company had done earlier. He, along with the others, had to stay at the crease till the fog took over. He could then milk the conditions.

The Indians therefore had to latch on to the smallest chance he gave. That came when he was on thirty-eight. He danced down the track to left-arm spinner Murali Kartik and hit him straight over his head. The ball went flat and was about to sail into the stands when Tendulkar, stationed at long-on, saw a glimmer of hope. Eyes firmly fixed on the ball, he leaped to his left, placed his body in an awkward position, and plucked the ball out of the air. That was not the end of it. He landed with a precarious balance inches inside the rope and quickly pulled himself in. He had got the one man who could win the game on his own. He leaped again, this time in triumph, and sprinted towards his teammates with arms held high and in the middle of the sprint, there were whoops of delight and the odd jump. He was like a schoolboy rushing out of the school gates and running on to the streets in spontaneous celebration of an unexpected half-day leave! The catch had as much to do with his sharp antennae as his athleticism. It was this antennae, this grip over cricket psychology, that placed him above the rest. Tendulkar had seen Inzamam playing the same shot in the first game at Karachi and the fourth one at Lahore. At long-on, he was desperately hoping that Inzamam would play it again. When he did, he was ready.

Bereft of someone to guide them from one end, the remaining Pakistani batsmen lost their way. Instead of biding their time, they tried too many shots and handed the game to the opponents. Inzamam won the Man of the Series Award but he'd have liked to hold the Samsung Trophy instead.

Tendulkar was delighted at the win and dedicated it to his countrymen. 'We have been reaching the final and losing there for a while. And to do it finally in Pakistan means a lot to us. We dedicate this victory to all of India,' he said, stressing that it was teamwork that had done the trick. Where the Indians had really staked their claim to the trophy was in their bowling. Both teams had done well with the bat, but despite the mammoth totals registered at almost all the venues, the young crop of Indian bowlers – left-armer Irfan Pathan and Lakshmipathy Balaji in particular – had made a striking impression. Irfan, especially, had swung the ball in to right-handers to put them into severe trouble. One of his chief motivators, he said, was Tendulkar. He kept talking to him from his mid-off and mid-on position. Unlike the excessive talk that he gave the bowlers when he was captain, here it was mostly 'Shabash Irfan, accha dal raha hai (You're bowling well), keep it up.'

Another young cannon, Virender Sehwag, benefited immensely from Tendulkar's words. Sehwag went berserk on the first day of the first Test at Multan. The wicket was a batsman's dream, and Rahul Dravid – leading the team in place of an injured Ganguly – had been lucky to win the toss. Sehwag was past his hundred by the time Tendulkar joined him at the crease in the post-lunch session. Tendulkar told him to keep playing his natural game. But he added a warning. 'Don't try to manufacture shots, and don't play pre-meditated ones,' he told him. The team's strategy was to score massively, to try and ensure they wouldn't have to bat again. Sehwag continued to gamble, but whenever he seemed to cross the line separating attacking cricket from recklessness, Tendulkar pulled him in. He told him to be patient and guided him to his 309, the highest score ever made by an Indian in Test cricket.

When Sehwag was running riot, Tendulkar realized that all he had to do was to keep one end up. Even so, he executed two fluent cover drives – the same drives he was supposed to have dumped – early in his innings. The Pakistanis then set fielders deep on the off, and he began to place the ball in the gaps. His approach, again, was in response to the situation and the opposite team's tactics. On the second day, he began to accelerate as India moved into a strong position and contemplated giving the Pakistanis a few overs to bat towards the end of the day's play. He was six runs short of his double century in the post-tea session when Dravid announced the declaration.

The decision launched a million arguments and, in India, a nationwide trial. Those who favoured the move said it was gutsy and in the team's interest, since India were looking to pick a couple of Pakistani wickets in the remaining overs and needed adequate time to do so. Some hailed the declaration as a healthy sign that Indian cricket had finally begun to put the collective cause above individual milestones. Some media reports suggested that twelfth man Ramesh Powar had taken two messages to Tendulkar after tea, asking him to step up the run-making. However, while Yuvraj Singh had been scoring swiftly, Tendulkar, well past his hundred, had been comparatively slow. Yuvraj and he had had a partnership of 110, out of which the left-hander had got fifty-nine in sixty-six balls.

To each of these points, there was a counterpoint:

- There were eighteen overs to go before the day's play ended. True, India wanted Pakistan to bat in the last few overs. But would a couple of overs, in which he would have got the six runs needed, have made a difference?

- An individual was a part of the team, so the team's interest must include his too. It's not every day that a batsman nears 200 in Test cricket, and for an Indian cricketer, a double ton against Pakistan in Pakistan is a major career milestone.

- Tendulkar had not batted selfishly. Throughout his own innings, he had played guide to Sehwag, who'd likely have thrown his wicket earlier if Sachin weren't around to keep him calm.

- Yuvraj and Tendulkar had batted together for nineteen overs. Yuvraj had no doubt scored briskly, getting fifty-nine in sixty-six balls, but Tendulkar had not been sluggish as had been suggested. He had played eight overs and had got forty-five-plus runs in those, which meant nearly a run a ball.

- Finally, denying Sachin a milestone was akin to disappointing, even hurting, a man who gave his team everything. The way he walked back to the pavilion was very suggestive. He kept his head down till he had entered the dressing room, not looking up even once.

Tendulkar told reporters at the end of the day's play that he was "surprised" at the declaration. 'I was aware the declaration was on the cards, but I was taken by surprise at the timing. I thought maybe another two-three overs would have been enough,' he said. About the run-rate, he said: 'We were scoring at four runs an over. That is enough.' Asked if he had spoken to Dravid after he came in, he said: 'I think after the declaration there is no need to talk. You just get on with the game.' This was a stunner to the media, because Tendulkar was not known to talk about anything contentious, and "no comment", was his favourite comment. Here he had unhesitantly spoken his mind. As his comments were splashed across TV channels and newspapers, the issue blew up into a major controversy, generating the kind of public debate in India that no pressing national problem would, and spawned a host of speculative stories on what had actually happened in the dressing room. Some reports suggested the captain's final message had not reached Tendulkar at all. Powar had spoken to Yuvraj about it while handing him the gloves, and he had forgotten to tell Sachin. That sounded implausible. Other reports said Ganguly had moved about impatiently in the dressing room while Tendulkar and Yuvraj were batting, telling Dravid repeatedly, 'Usko positive khelne ko bolo (Tell him to play positive).' The same reports suggested the declaration wasn't Dravid's decision at all; it was the non-playing captain who had directed him to call the batsmen in. That was an intriguing theory but unconfirmed. Other accounts hinted at a certain resentment against Tendulkar in the Indian dressing room. One player, part of the current team, was quoted as having once told the media strictly off the record that 'All you people can only see his scores, our performance means nothing.' Parallels were then drawn with a statement that Gordon Greenidge had once apparently made after scoring a sparkling Test hundred. He had said that if only Viv Richards had got that century, the media would have gone ecstatic, but his hundred wasn't considered half as important. There was also speculation because Tendulkar had not come to field for the eighteen overs that Pakistan batted that day. And then there were two more wildly conflicting theories: one, that Dravid and he had had a ferocious argument in the dressing room, and two, that Dravid was feeling terrible about the whole thing and had gone to Tendulkar's room and apologized profusely.

Tendulkar sought to clear matters. He said he had not gone out to field because he had tweaked his ankle while batting, and since he thought it would be risky to take the field immediately, he sat out and applied ice. He clarified that he and Dravid had spoken about the declaration and sorted things out, and that was the end of it. Not only was there no bitterness between them, there had not even been an argument, he noted. Ganguly said a few days later that the declaration had been a "mistake", and so did Dravid himself. In fact, on his return from the tour, Dravid confessed he wouldn't have made the declaration if he had known India would win so easily and pointed out that the episode would stay with him forever:

I wish I had the advantage of hindsight and retrospect. If I had known that the Test would finish in four days, I would not have declared then... Both Sachin and I have a sore throat now clarifying (the issue). It has been made a bigger issue than it is. At least it is not an issue in the team. We have sorted it out. We respect each other too much to let it linger on... But I think this (issue) is going to haunt me for the rest of my life.

It was finally a non-verbal explanation offered by Tendulkar himself that ended the controversy in the real sense. By the final hour of the third day, India had five Pakistani wickets in their bag, with the score reading a little above 300, and were looking to exert further pressure in order to try and enforce the follow-on. If they could break the partnership of the last two recognized batsmen, Moin Khan and Abdul Razzaq, they could skittle out the rest, they felt. Moin Khan in particular was the danger man. Oddly, Moin looked tense when Tendulkar started the last over of the day even though the field was well spread out, and there were just two close-in fielders, both on the off, where one would expect more. The final ball of the day was a googly. It pitched on the off-side and came in. Moin didn't read it at all and got himself into an uncomfortable position while trying to defend. The ball went between his legs and hit the leg-stump. Tendulkar was ecstatic, and so were his teammates who converged on him. His happy smile, and that of the other players, stayed till they had disappeared into the dressing room. Obviously, the declaration was not an issue any more, and there was no rift in the Indian team.

India enforced the follow-on and Pakistan could never really come back into the match. Only twelve balls were needed by the visitors on the fifth day to wrap up the Test.

Tendulkar had now got over 500 runs in two Tests without getting out. However, even the Multan innings was said to be another confirmation of the fact that he had slowed down his pace, cut out some strokes and made his cricket less interesting. Those who said this failed to realize that cricket is not about hitting every ball, and it is certainly not about self-indulgence. Of course Tendulkar had been a specialist in destroying good deliveries and was now giving respect to good balls. That did not mean his cricket had become less interesting; it was just that he wasn't taking as many risks as he would have taken, say, five years ago, because he felt more responsible towards the team as a senior statesman and saw more sense in batting calmly in certain situations.

Though his "calm" was much questioned after the innings of 194, a matter that seriously called for critical thinking was not considered at all even after it came to the fore, certainly not for the first time, in the second Test at Lahore. Tendulkar got out cheaply in both innings, and Pakistan won the Test by superb bowling. One of the dismissals highlighted a bad habit he had developed of late. He crouched as the ball hit his pad, and the bowler appealed for an LBW decision, which was granted. The way Tendulkar crouched was patently wrong, and he had been, on occasions, crouching in exactly the same way for some time. When he hunkered down after the bat hit the pad, the unmistakable impression he gave was that he was desperately trying to prevent the ball from going on to the stumps. This could make both a bowler and umpire feel the ball was surely going to hit the stumps, even when that may not be the case, and could eliminate any doubt that may exist in the umpire's mind and in fact push him into lifting the finger.

In the only innings of the third Test that he batted in, it took the speed of Shoaib Akhtar to force him into a technical error. Akhtar banged in short and Tendulkar decided, on seeing the ball come off the wicket, that he'd rather get out of the way. But he had by then squared up just a little bit and exposed his right shoulder. That was a mistake, because a batsman has to be side-on. He tried to correct himself at the last moment by trying to get his shoulder and the bat out of the way, but it was too late. The ball kissed the bat and went to the keeper.

Despite these quick dismissals, Tendulkar was in a great mood on day four of the third and last Test in Rawalpindi. He had been telling his teammates since the day they lost the second Test that they need not worry. He always brought in the historical association when talking about Pakistan, whether in the matter of his injuries or the team's performances. He told them that in 1999, Pakistan had won the first Test at Chennai, then India won the second at New Delhi, and Pakistan had come back to win the third Test at Kolkata. This time, he said, India had won at Multan and Pakistan at Lahore, so in the decider Test at Rawalpindi, it was going to be India's turn.

Rahul Dravid, with a solid 270, had already helped India acquire a big lead after the Indian bowlers had first dismissed Pakistan for 224. Pakistan had lost two wickets before the end of the third day's play and appeared to be under too much pressure to clear the deficit. India needed eight wickets to secure an innings victory, but dropped six catches on the fourth morning. While having a friendly chat with umpire David Shepherd in the middle of all the catch-dropping, Tendulkar told him jocularly: 'This ball is like a hot potato. No one wants to hold it.' Tendulkar was known to be earnest on the field, and on this very tour, in the second one-dayer at Rawalpindi, he had angrily given a mouthful not once, not twice, but several times, to players who had either been sloppy in the outfield or didn't throw accurately. Now, he was relaxed and happy. He knew his team was knocking on the doors of history. In the last fifty years, India had not won a Test series in Pakistan, and here it seemed a matter of time before it broke that jinx.

He had himself been waiting for this moment for many years. For a decade and more, he had alone carried the whole team on his shoulders. His efforts had not always brought the desired results in the absence of a solid team effort. Even Brian Lara's superb double-hundred against South Africa towards the end of 2003, when Tendulkar himself was not getting runs in Australia, had not averted a defeat for the West Indies, and even his 400 not out against England in 2004, the highest ever score by a batsman in Test cricket, had not guaranteed a victory. That was because the team as a whole wasn't strong. Tendulkar had known this situation and its attendant frustrations.

He had badly wanted a strong Indian outfit that won and won regularly. He had got that in the last two years. The journey had started with the NatWest Series in England, and the 2003-04 season had shown its maturity, mental strength and ability. The team had won a Test in Australia after two decades, it had already won the ODI series in Pakistan, and it was about to clinch the Test series.

For most of his teammates, Tendulkar had been a hero, and many of its young members had grown up hero-worshipping him, so he could have been said to have provided the institutional framework for the team's new-found successes. It was therefore a noteworthy moment when, with the last Pakistani wicket remaining, Ganguly handed him the ball. Danish Kaneria was on strike. He tried a heave off the second delivery, and the ball went up in the air. In Tendulkar's own words, 'As soon as I saw two fielders getting underneath the ball, I knew we had won. I didn't even bother to see who caught the ball, I just turned around and grabbed a stump.'

*

Early in August 2004, I went to the MIG Club Ground in Bandra in Mumbai to have a chat with Sachin Tendulkar. After our chat, I waited to watch him at the nets.

I was keen to know what he was going to do at the nets. He had just returned from the Asia Cup in Sri Lanka. India had done badly there, and Tendulkar had been accused of being over-cautious against both Pakistan and Sri Lanka though he had got good scores. The defeat had invited stinging remarks from Indian cricket followers who, after the successes in Australia and Pakistan earlier that year, expected their team to bulldoze every opponent, everywhere. Also, just a week later, India was to fly to Holland for a one-day series against Australia and Pakistan, and from there to England for the NatWest Series and the Champions Trophy. I wondered if he was going to make any preparations for the Aussie and Pak attack on neutral soil, or for the English conditions. I was in for a surprise.

Tendulkar first got the ground staff to dunk almost a dozen rubber balls in a bucket of water. I had heard of, and seen, batsmen soaking tennis balls to the skin and then asking bowlers to bowl close to the rib-cage. This was a common practice, particularly when a team wanted to be ready for mean deliveries, especially against the West Indian pacers in the late 1970s and 80s. But a rubber ball seemed new to the idea of sound net practice.

Before I could think things through, Sachin went to the middle of the wicket – which was not really a wicket but a flat slab of concrete at one end of the ground – and had a bucketful of water poured on to the area where he expected the ball to land. Then he put on his batting gear, and four local fast bowlers began to unleash their nastiest best.

The point of it all became clear soon. The rubber ball was behaving more erratically than a tennis ball would. It was rearing up one moment, keeping far too low the next, sometimes stopping after pitching and sometimes, simply slipping through. It was a test for a batsman's eyesight, reflexes, footwork and timing.

Three things were noticeable. One, Tendulkar was playing the ball as late as he could. This was in preparation for the English wickets. Two, he was trying to change his shot at the last moment. This was to be his surprise package, for all three tournaments. And third, he was relentless in his pursuit of perfection. He got a faint edge to one ball and yelled 'Aaaaarrgh!' as if he had edged to McGrath, and a few times, when he lifted some balls and thought they would land into the hands of fielders, the 'Aaaaarrgh!' was repeated with much greater impatience.

He also seemed to be enjoying every moment of the practice session, laughing at the occasional joke his friends around the nets cracked to egg on the local bowlers, appreciating the good balls bowled to him and enthusiastically asking the groundsman at the end of the first half-hour session to make the contrived pitch wetter and worse. 'Aankhi paani taak (Pour some more water),' he animatedly told the gardener in his native Marathi, indicating all the danger spots where the ball could land.

A few days after this strenuous practice session, it was reported that Tendulkar was suffering from tennis elbow, a condition where the outer part of the elbow becomes tender and painful, generally because of strain, excessive wear and tear or a direct knock. The injury to the left elbow put paid to his plans: he missed the Holland series, the NatWest Trophy and the mini-World Cup.

The Indian team went down disastrously in all three tournaments. Even if it had done well, a great deal of media attention would have focused on the tennis elbow. With the team's poor show, the attention was greater. For a full three months, the Indian media every day tirelessly discussed the nature and character of the injury, the time needed for recovery and the possible impact it would have on Tendulkar's career. In what had by now become a regular pattern, lengthy articles were written, detailed graphics examining his anatomy were shown on TV channels and splashed on the pages of newspapers and magazines, and anybody and everybody from accomplished doctors to quacks and sundry astrologers was asked for expert opinions. The coverage was so extensive that when Tendulkar was finally declared fit, a national newspaper, rather aptly, published an "obituary" for the tennis elbow.

Many felt Tendulkar's absence was the main reason for the team's bad showing. Indeed, it was one of the reasons, for his name in the eleven was enough to prevent the opponents from feeling entirely at ease. It was, however, not the only reason, a fact obscured by his remarkable domination of the Indian cricket followers' collective consciousness.

The skewed analysis was carried forward to Australia's tour of India in October 2004. Tendulkar sat out the first two Tests (out of a total of four) because he was still not fit enough to play in a match. The Australians crushed India in the first Test at Bangalore, and the second, in Chennai, was drawn. The Indians needed 229 to win in the fourth innings at Chennai when the fifth day was washed out, but such was the distrust in the team's performance by now that a substantial number of its supporters believed the showers had saved India, not Australia.

During this second Test, a leading English daily in India carried a headline that reconfirmed the fact that a country desperately looking for a hero still thought it had nowhere to go but to Sachin. The newspaper's report was actually an account of the day's play and scarcely mentioned Tendulkar. The headline simply said: 'Come Back Sachin'.

When he did come back for the third Test in Nagpur, the expectations were sky-high. The Indians lost the Test without him doing much. At one stage of this match, the Indian bowlers looked ineffectual against the Australians, and this angered the spectators so much that they first booed the bowlers. Then, suddenly, they began chanting in unison: 'Tendulkar, Bowling *Kar*'. The echoes would not die down till the end of the day's play. Translated into English without the child-like rhyming, their hysterical cry was for him to take the ball into his own hands. That was half the message. The other half was implicit, as if it was logical that once he came on to bowl, the Australian batting would collapse in no time at all.

Tendulkar did not bring about any dramatic turnaround in Nagpur, but in the final Test at the Wankhede stadium in Mumbai, he did – with an innings that was outstanding and belligerent. On a wicket that could, without any exaggeration, be called near-impossible to bat on, he, along with another classy player, V.V.S. Laxman, offered cricket-lovers the definition of batsmanship.

After allowing Australia to obtain a ninety-nine-run lead in the first innings, India had begun its second innings disastrously on the third morning. The score read fourteen for two when Tendulkar walked in to bat. The Australians already led two-nil in the series; a three-nil result was now on the cards, unless Tendulkar and Laxman played the role of saviours. This was not going to be easy as a lot of dust could be seen flying off the wicket every time the ball landed. Nobody from the Indian or Australian team had been able to bat here with any comfort, and the highest partnership so far on either side had been forty-four runs.

Together, Tendulkar and Laxman got just one run in their first five overs. With the score fifteen for two, and Australia completely on top, Jason Gillespie began the eleventh over. That was the turning point. Tendulkar hit him for two boundaries with such assertion that suddenly and dramatically, the body language of the Australians changed. Tendulkar's transformation from mean to majestic rubbed off on Laxman as well, because the two then secured thirty-eight runs in four overs.

When the pacers were exhausted, Aussie captain Ricky Ponting brought on off-spinner Nathan Hauritz. Tendulkar watched him bowl his first over from the non-striker's end. In his second over, Tendulkar "welcomed" Hauritz to his home ground. He pulled the first ball hard, but it struck Simon Katich at short-leg. The next ball was cracked through the covers, for four. The third was lifted over mid-wicket, into the stands. Laxman applauded, and Tendulkar nodded to say thanks. The next ball was sent into the same region, for a boundary. In the next over, Tendulkar completed his half-century.

This was the Sachin Tendulkar the cricket world recognized, a batsman who took the battle into the opposition camp. But just when everybody spoke of how it seemed like watching a very young Sachin all over again, he got out as he had often done in the early phase of his career: impetuously. On fifty-five, he tried a sweep off Hauritz when the ball was pitched outside the off-stump, got a top edge, and was caught. But the Indians had already won the psychological battle, and Australia's panic response while chasing 107 in the fourth innings reflected that. They crashed out for ninety-three on a rapidly deteriorating wicket.

On a pitch where most batsmen had floundered, Tendulkar had stamped his authority against the best attack in the world. It was an innings only he or a Lara could have played, and it prompted a near-unanimous comment from all corners of the sub-continent: "he's back!". However, it turned out to be a flawed observation, the misjudgement proven only a few days later, when, after Tendulkar's early dismissal against South Africa, it was replaced by an equally unfounded remark: "he's finished".

Tendulkar has since been so often labelled as "finished" and then put "back in form" by the media and by cricket followers in India (and the Indian diaspora) that the matter deserves an independent examination. Before we attempt this examination in the epilogue, while also outlining the journey from 2005 to late 2007, a period which has seen the words "finished" and "back" used all too frequently, let us look at a subject that cricket-lovers will continue to discuss even years after Tendulkar's retirement: his status vis-à-vis Don Bradman.

Tendulkar and Bradman: A Comparison

Well, there's one word that moved me when a boy
that moves today... it's when the umpire, to the
general joy, pronounces 'PLAY!'

– Andrew Lang, *Play*

Sir Donald Bradman told his wife that he thought Tendulkar batted just the way he did. Sadly, he didn't elaborate, so we don't know how he compared the Indian's batting to his. In the course of this book, I have drawn comparisons with greats of the game, including the Don. However, I have deliberately left a detailed treatment of the comparison with Bradman for this, penultimate, chapter.

As Tendulkar enjoys a privileged position in international cricket and, from the standpoint of the present, looks at the future of his own, his country's and the world's cricket, it is time to look at how deeply he has fused with the Don to emerge as one of the finest flag-bearers of the global cricket tradition.

Bradman learnt his cricket on his own. His first bat was actually a stump. For hours he would hit a golf ball against the wall in the family's Bowral garden with the stump. Tendulkar's early cricket was neither untutored nor solitary, except for an hour of preferred solitude in the house every day, when he hit a ball, placed in a sock, about 2,000 times. But few know that as a child, he did play some cricket with a golf ball. For a few years of his school life, he lived at his uncle's house in Indravadhan Society at Shivaji Park, as it was a stone's throw away from the maidan where his school had its nets. After nets, he along

392 SACHIN TENDULKAR: A DEFINITIVE BIOGRAPHY

with friends Vinod Kambli, Mayur Kadrekar (one of the stars of the city's school cricket) and Santosh Jadhav would go to his uncle's place and play with a golf ball. The ball would rise nastily and give them "stickers" if it hit their body, so they tried always to get it in the middle of the bat. Many years later, when Tendulkar was in sublime form in 1998, Greg Chappell said, 'Sachin could bat okay with a stump.'

There were coaches around to knock off young Tendulkar's rough edges always, but his grip was, and is, as unusual as the Don's. Bradman's bat handle pressed against the ball of the thumb instead of resting against it. The Indian is even more odd in the eyes of the very orthodox: he holds his bottom hand centimetres above the splice instead of well above it. Both were asked to change their grips at several points in their career; both refused.

Short batsmen have usually made up for their lack of height with sure footwork, but no two players in cricket history have been surer and more nimble than the five-feet-seven-inches Bradman and the even smaller Tendulkar. This, with their hand-eye co-ordination, remarkable batspeed and the ability to judge the line and length quicker than anyone else, has given them the extra nanoseconds to play the ball that others could only hope for. Once, while facing a spinner, Bradman came down the pitch, slipped and fell, but while still on his knees, back-cut the ball for a single. Tendulkar has sometimes changed his shot *after* the ball has landed. To cite just one example, in the 2002 NatWest Series in England, he once positioned himself for a reverse-sweep after a slow-medium bowler released the ball, then had a change of heart and of body position and fiercely cut the ball through point.

The defining stroke for both has been the forcing shot off the back-foot on the off. For Tendulkar, the arc spreads a little wider than for Bradman, for his back-foot straight drive with its curtailed follow-through rolls past the stumps on the on-side. Both have also beaten everybody in terms of the sheer number of good balls they have converted into waste. The statisticians unfortunately don't count these, but since Tendulkar has in the TV age been filmed immeasurably more extensively than the Don, we can do a quick check. I will take only examples of two all-time greats who bowled to him. In Sharjah in 1994, a lovely good-length delivery from Wasim Akram was lifted over mid-wicket for six; most balls that Glenn McGrath bowled to him during his blazing innings in the 2000 mini-World Cup quarter-finals in Nairobi were spot-on, and they went off the bat with greater speed than the bowler had given them; again, in the 2001 Test series at home against Australia, McGrath had the mortification of seeing accurate balls struck nonchalantly through point, the covers and mid-off, and a back-foot stroke between cover and extra-cover off Akram in March 2003 was a challenge to a bowler's conception of precise pitching.

So what do you do when good balls don't work? Well, there's Bodyline, and there's Nasser Hussain's "leg theory". Douglas Jardine admitted his team just couldn't get Bradman out with legitimate methods when he tried the intimidatory stuff with a pack of fielders crouching on the leg, and Hussain did the same in 2001 when he set an 8-1 on-side field for Tendulkar and got his bowlers to bowl at least five inches outside leg-stump. Although cricket has produced many batting geniuses from Dr W.G. Grace to Brian Lara, the Indian and the Australian are the only two who have driven the opposition to manifestly negative methods of containment.

Swift scoring is another common quality. Bradman loved hitting boundaries. The slowest of his 117 first-class hundreds took him 253 minutes, and once, in a Test, he hit a hundred before lunch, another between lunch and tea and ended the day at 309 not out. Statistics have shown that over fifty per cent of Tendulkar's runs in an innings come in boundaries, and even in his cautious avatar, he has kept up an average of four runs an over in Tests.

Tendulkar runs his first run quicker than most contemporaries, and his conversion rate of ones into twos and twos into threes is remarkable considering that for most of his career, he has had rather unathletic partners. His running stays the same regardless of whether he's playing international cricket, a domestic tournament or a festival match. He ran swiftly in a benefit match in 2001 in Thane (near Mumbai) to get ninety runs when he had fever and had been advised against playing. The running became a source of concern to friends who knew he was ill, of surprise to spectators who appreciated the commitment in a festival game and of laughter to some who couldn't comprehend why he was taking a benefit match so seriously.

According to teammates Arthur Morris and Bill Brown, Bradman was the fastest runner between wickets in his era, and John Woodcock has written that whether he was thirty not out or 300, and whether he was batting for Bowral or in a Test at Sydney or in the Festival at Scarborough, he'd run the first run hard to put pressure on the fielder.

The desire to dominate, especially in the face of provocation, is also similar. During an innings at Blackheath, Bradman was fifty not out when an off-spinner was brought in to bowl. 'What kind of bowler is he?' Bradman asked the wicket-keeper Leo Waters. The keeper replied: 'Don't you remember? He's Bill Black. He bowled you in Lithgow a few weeks ago and has been boasting about it ever since.' Bradman then took sixty-two runs off Black in two eight-ball overs, forcing his captain to take him off.

Cut to World Cup 2003. England's Andrew Caddick boasted ahead of the India-England game that Tendulkar was "just another batsman" and could be "snared" like any other. In reply, Tendulkar began by attacking him belligerently in the game and pulled one, with a resounding crack, out of the ground. Henry Olonga got a similar response in 1998, after his dismissal of Tendulkar generated a lot of discussion. So did Shane Warne in the same year, when all eyes were on the Tendulkar-Warne contest, and Shoaib Akhtar, Wasim Akram and Waqar Younis collectively, when the world of cricket speculated on how he'd face up to their pace during India's World Cup 2003 match against Pakistan. In one evening in a Test match, he batted nearly ninety minutes without doing anything against Glenn McGrath and even letting loose deliveries pass by. Then, he perhaps told himself he was giving McGrath too much respect. The next morning, he carried out an orgy of boundary-hitting against the bowler. At Headingley in 2002, Nasser Hussain took the new ball towards the end of the second day chiefly to restrict Tendulkar, who was already past his hundred. He danced down the track to Caddick and Matthew Hoggard and hit them repeatedly into the stands. When the pacers were replaced by Ashley Giles, he took him apart in one over. That hitting, which ranks among the most audacious in Test cricket, crushed England, who then lost the Test, just as Pakistan actually lost its World Cup 2003 game in Akhtar's first over, when he was hit for a six over point and two splendid boundaries.

A shared quality of Bradman and Tendulkar was determination. When Bradman, a reserved man, did speak, he proved his words true with sheer resolve. At Leeds in 1934, Australia were thirty-nine for three at close of play on the first day. Bradman cancelled his meeting with Neville Cardus in the evening, saying he'd sleep early as he wanted to get "at least 200" the next day. Cardus pointed out that the law of averages went against him, for he had got a big score in the previous Test. 'I don't believe in the law of averages,' Bradman told him, and scored 304 the next day.

In 1998, India were under enormous pressure to win against Australia in Sharjah, and in both the games before and during the final, the Aussies rattled up big totals. Before starting the chase in the penultimate game, Tendulkar told the team management he'd ensure the team qualified for the finals, and in the final, he promised he'd take it to victory. He kept his word.

Like Bradman did in his days, Tendulkar has, in the last few years, received criticism for his occasional self-denial, clinical efficiency and lack of embellishments. Bradman's background had a role to play in what some called his machine-like approach. He had never got anything easy in life, so he would never throw away his wicket. Tendulkar has chucked his wicket far too often in his career, but has faced the same burden of greatness the Don faced after his reputation had grown: he simply can't afford to fail.

However, there are dissimilarities in their approach as well. These are chiefly due to the fact that they belong to different eras. Tendulkar loves playing in the air; Bradman hardly did that because it wasn't considered acceptable in his playing days. Bradman's range of strokes was as extensive as Tendulkar's but he did not know of at least four strokes the Indian plays. Two of them – the reverse-sweep and the inside-out hit on the off – are modern-day inventions, and two of them are Tendulkar's own inventions: a full-blooded "reverse straight drive" to fine leg, and the flick behind square-leg. While playing the flick, he rolls his wrists over to place the ball down and behind square and finishes the shot with the bottom hand above the top one, with the bat assuming a vertical position. It's a tough shot to play, because the ball must be struck very late, otherwise control would be impossible and the ball would go up in the air. Now, at least two players in international cricket have it taken up: Jacques Kallis plays it regularly and effectively, and so does Yuvraj Singh.

Above all, what makes Bradman and Tendulkar special is their ability to keep their heads (this is where the fantastic Lara loses out). Tendulkar ascended the steps that take a cricketer to the international level at a galloping rate. When he was ecstatically welcomed by the sub-continent and the rest of the cricket globe as a Test cricketer, he was at an acutely impressionable age. His spectacular early success and the praise it brought could have turned his head, and with it, exploded his reputation and future. However, he had the competitive will to ward off that danger, a willingness to learn, and a desire to achieve consistently higher levels of excellence. He did not allow his focus to waver even as his fame spread and he was, in a major disservice to him, deified by the people of his country. Public expectations were and are excessive. In the sub-continent, cricket evokes a response that is more emotional than rational, so its cricket followers are unmercifully fickle. They make someone a hero one day and bring him down the next. It is remarkable that Tendulkar has kept these cricket-lovers happy for the most part of his career. The satellite TV revolution in India began soon after he arrived on the international scene, and its full flowering took place during the course of his career. He was therefore lucky with the timing, but his focus on his work was the reason he became a greater favourite than all other personalities appearing on the small screen. A survey done by a newspaper in a remote village of Karnataka during the 2004 Indian Parliamentary polls revealed that the village locals had never heard of the Indian Prime Minister, Atal Bihari Vajpayee, but they knew who Tendulkar was and what he had done.

Indian cricket went through a difficult period in the 1990s. Tendulkar not only kept hopes alive, but was responsible for India retaining its faith in its cricketers. He has therefore been an idol for the new generation, and more than half the Indian team today derives its inspiration from him. Unlike Brian Lara, Tendulkar took the unrelenting gaze of the media well and handled wisely his status as modern cricket's international superstar. The money he earned didn't spoil him, and except for one obvious mistake of obtaining a duty waiver for his Ferrari, he has had a spotless record.

John Woodcock said of Bradman that 'his promotion from prodigy to demigod, and the adulation that went with it, he took in his stride.' He contributed to the amazing rise of Australian cricket and, like Tendulkar, created his legacy while he was still playing. He guarded his privacy as much as the Indian does, was as deeply attached to his family and its values, and went about his cricket with total professionalism. In adopting this attitude, both have emerged as ambassadors of the game and, while taking so much from it, added to its richness.

Bradman retired when he was still on top of his game, and Tendulkar must do the same. What Sunil Gavaskar has said of retirement – that one must go when others ask why rather than why not – sounds exceedingly simple but is not so for many cricketers. Like Bradman, Tendulkar, however, has made intelligent decisions all through his career, and it will be very interesting to see how he chooses his moment of departure. I would like him to go when people ask 'why' because I think the cricket world's final memories of him in action should ideally be of a batsman who dominated the bowling. Gavaskar ensured that for himself by scripting an innings of ninety-seven against Pakistan in Bangalore that is still the benchmark for batting in Test cricket; his example is a fine one to follow.

There is one more area where Tendulkar needs to do something that Bradman did. He can contribute to the game's development by speaking on the art and craft of cricket as he perceives, studies and executes it. Although he has started to get vocal about this, he must speak up. He is always in a "thinking cricket" mode and, surprisingly, not only does he not get exhausted by it, but he seems to enjoy it. Cricket for him is of the same vital importance as oxygen and for the sheer obsessional nature of his involvement in the game, he has few equals. He's therefore the best person to elucidate on the finer points of cricket. The game today has changed immeasurably since Bradman wrote his seminal work, *The Art of Cricket*. The world expects Tendulkar to spell out the art of modern cricket for the current and future generations.

Cricket today also faces many complex issues, the sort which was never encountered in Bradman's age. Tendulkar must speak on these issues (he did not say a word on the match-fixing scandal). He holds passionate views on various matters and wants several steps taken at the international level to make the game better, fairer, more structured and complete. Although reserved, he does open up before close friends. At least on some issues, he must think it safe to speak in public too. His words will have an effective resonance throughout the cricket world, which in any case has been waiting, with some frustration, to hear from him. He is a reticent man, but the interests of the game can sometimes ask for something different. For someone whose words can have a huge impact, silence is not always golden.

Finally, I must use a very personal yardstick for comparing him with Bradman. I look for an answer to one question when I'm estimating the worth of a cricketer. That question is: how did the cricketer take up challenges? The way Bradman battled Bodyline (he averaged over fifty in the series) and responded to other major challenges in his cricket career, many of them mentioned above, was exemplary. How does Tendulkar measure up?

Tendulkar's nose bled in his first Test series in Pakistan, and fielders around him did their best to hurt him psychologically. He stayed put, punched the next ball for four and eventually made his mark against Imran Khan, Wasim Akram and Waqar Younis. When the best leg-spinner of the day, Abdul Qadir, dared him to take him on, he smashed him repeatedly into the stands without losing his cool. After that, in England, he saved a Test with a superb debut hundred. From there he went to Australia and, when his team was crumbling around him, stood on the world's fastest track, Perth, against intimidatory pacers to register a fighting century. In World Cup 1992, as an eighteen-year-old, he top-scored for his team and delivered in the most high-pressure game, against Pakistan. In the Hero Cup final, when Kapil Dev was hesitant to take the ball in the last over, he literally snatched the ball from his captain and, despite his limited bowling ability, bowled an over that turned the tournament upside down. He volunteered to open the innings on the moving tracks in New Zealand in 1994 and showed how openers could combat fast bowlers early in a one-dayer. He countered Australian aggression with equal fierceness in the 1996 World Cup and moved even Bradman by his attitude. As the Australians became an all-conquering team in 1998, he attacked Shane Warne with a missionary zeal in India and unleashed a storm against the entire Aussie attack in Sharjah. Against Pakistan at Chennai in 1999, he solitarily set up a challenge and, in spite of intense physical pain, took his team to the brink of victory. In the World Cup that year, he put aside his biggest moment of grief (the death of his father), flew back to England and scored a hundred while struggling to hold back tears. When the match-fixing scandal was consuming the cricket world, he batted for his local team as if his life depended on it and, after playing one of the most focused innings of his career, exulted at his local team's triumph as if he had won the World Cup. In the historic 2001 home series against Australia, he stood alone among the ruins in the first Test, got three crucial wickets in the second to help bowl out the Aussies for a memorable win, and scored a hundred in the third. Despite provocation against Nasser Hussain's team in 2001 and during the subsequent ball-tampering controversy in South Africa, he maintained his dignity while carrying on a hard contest on the field. He went sleepless for twelve nights before the 2003 World Cup game against Pakistan and pummelled the Pakistan attack with a ninety-eight that finds a place among the finest knocks in one-day cricket. His unbeaten 241 at Sydney in 2004, the 141 in Rawalpindi in the same year that set up the match against Pakistan; the match-winning catch he took of Inzamam in the final one-dayer of a thrilling series; a fighting half-century against Australia on an impossible-to-bat-on wicket in Mumbai in 2004; his fight against and recovery from injuries in 2005 and 2006 and a remarkable string of performances in Test and one-day cricket after the World Cup disaster of 2007 that made him India's most valuable scorer (and the world's second most valuable scorer, after Matthew Hayden) in his eighteenth year in international cricket – are all signs of a cricketer who won't duck out of a difficult situation.

His entire career has been a keen and happy acceptance of challenges. That definitely makes him a wonderful cricketer.

epilogue

I'm focusing now on how I can get to the
next level as a batsman. How can I get even
more competitive? How can I get even
more consistent? How can I get better?

– Sachin Tendulkar, in an interview to *The
Guardian*, at age 37, after averaging 134.5
in a Test series against Australia in his
golden year, 2010

I write this in the last week of December 2010, just days after
Tendulkar has achieved the inconceivable in cricket: 50
hundreds in Tests. In doing so, he has redefined the boundaries
of what is possible in the game.

Nobody had thought of, or talked about, getting a double
hundred in one-dayers till he showed that it could be done.
When he reached the landmark against South Africa in February
2010, a lot of people shook their heads, wondering why the
idea had never struck them. Similarly, no one had thought
anyone could get 50 Test hundreds till he brought the target
within reach (it then became clear that it was inevitable that
he'd reach it) and then got to it, against South Africa again, on
a bouncy track in Centurion, with Dale Steyn and Co. in full
flow and India with their backs to the wall, trying to cover up a
mammoth first innings deficit.

A player who thus creates new frontiers not only leaves an
indelible mark on his sport but makes it richer, giving it a new
frame of reference that future generations would have to go by. In

this respect, Tendulkar's contribution to cricket is momentous, and as I write this, the debate on who's the better bat – he or Bradman, a subject we have dealt with in the previous chapter – has become more vigorous, and a newer frontier, of 100 centuries in international cricket, is in sight.[1]

On a deeper level, cricket's relation with Tendulkar has gone beyond the record books. He defines an era. So do Shane Warne and Brian Lara; where Tendulkar takes a step ahead is that he has been a better role model on and off the field.

Warne has admitted to taking money to provide pitch and weather reports to a man linked to bookmakers, has been suspended for a year for taking a banned diuretic, has been pulled up for excessive appealing and sledging and has text-messaged his way into deep marital trouble. Lara has fought many battles with himself and others. He almost threw his career after surpassing Gary Sobers' highest Test score, contemplated quitting the game, pulled out from tours, quarrelled with his captains, fell out with the West Indian Board and the team management on occasions and had to once even issue a public apology for hitting a chair with his bat after being given out in a Caribbean cricket championship game.

Tendulkar has neither the scandalous glamour of a Warne nor the utter unpredictability of a Lara. He represents the old-fashioned values of discipline, restraint, balance and a focus on cricket and cricket alone. He has not been accused of foul behaviour on or off the field and of ego clashes and despite so much stardom, has not lost his sense of fairness, not even during periods of serious internal conflict in Indian cricket.[2]

But bizarrely enough, while there is growing consensus worldwide on his status as a global cricket icon, and while he is seen as a player who has given youngsters across the world new dreams to dream (had they dreamt of 50 Test hundreds?), in his own country, he must still shoulder an additional responsibility – of being a symbol of hope not only on the field but on a larger, national canvas.

In 2010, public life in India was racked by a series of scams: the Commonwealth Games mess, which necessitated a probe into suspected embezzlement of funds, the Adarsh housing society scam, where politicians and bureaucrats usurped flats in Mumbai's Colaba area meant for defence personnel, and the 2G spectrum scam, which has allegedly resulted in a loss of Rs1.76 lakh crore to the Indian exchequer.

Tendulkar made the same year a veritable calendar of cricketing accomplishment: apart from getting the ODI double hundred and the highest number of runs in the IPL, he had scored seven Test hundreds till the time of writing this (one Test was left in the year as I put this down), become the highest run-maker ever, the most-capped Test player,[3] won the ICC Test player of the year award and topped the world batting rankings for the first time since 2002. And, to stick to a promise he had made his father long ago, towards the end of the year, he had turned down a Rs 20-crore-a-year offer to endorse a liquor brand.

He thus bore the responsibility of being a symbol of hope and integrity as effectively as he had done in the years preceding his 21st in international cricket. But the responsibility continues to grow.

In the wake of his golden jubilee of Test tons, I can hear loud demands being made across India: he must win the 2011 World Cup for his country.

Now, it is impossible for one player to win a World Cup for his team. He can make his personal contribution to the team cause, that's it. An example from recent years is Tendulkar's own astonishingly authoritative 175 against Australia in a one-dayer at Hyderabad in 2009.[4] He looked invincible, and ended up on the losing side. That's how the game goes.

But in India, Tendulkar is God one day, and not very god-like the next, to put it in the mildest terms. In fact, in the five years that have passed since this book was first published in March 2005, I have lost count of the number of times he has been written off and the number of times he's supposed to have come 'back' and 'silenced his critics' to show he's still the same cricketer the world has known all along.

Let us examine this peculiarly Indian approach towards Tendulkar in the sporting and social sphere. Some key developments from his troubled years 2005 and 2006 are especially instructive in this regard (the public mood has not swayed much after his consistently top-of-form performances since mid-2007, which is what makes the World Cup demand all the more vociferous and, therefore, more indicative of crowd capriciousness rather than anything else).

When Tendulkar walked back to the pavilion six short of his 35th Test hundred against Pakistan in the March-April 2005 series, many wondered if he'd get a three-figure score again: he had just recovered from a career-threatening tennis elbow injury and was just about match-fit. In November that year, when he broke Gavaskar's record of 34 Test tons, he was 'back'. Low scores against Pakistan early in 2006, and he was 'Endulkar' again, but quickly became the 'same, glorious Sachin' after a brilliant 95 in an ODI at Lahore.

At his home ground, Wankhede, in March 2006, he was booed by a section of the crowd after he got out early. Soon after, a labrum tear in the shoulder necessitated surgery and a break for some months. Even if he's back, he'll never be the same again, it was said.

A hundred against the West Indies in his return game late in 2006, and an excellent performance in South Africa meant he was 'still a long way away from retirement'.

Then came the 2007 World Cup disaster; it was apparently proof that it was all over. When, in the wake of the defeat, Tendulkar, never one to say anything contentious in public, responded to Greg Chappell's letter to the Indian Board which had raised question marks over the attitude of senior players, he was hailed as the courageous cricketer who had taken on the 'stubborn' coach who allegedly did not understand the Indian psyche.[5]

Two hundreds against Bangladesh in April-May 2007, and Sachin was the reigning king of Indian cricket again, a status reinforced several times over by his outstanding batting during the England tour from July to September 2007.[6]

India's win in the first T20 World Cup again triggered talk of how seniors like Sachin needed to call it a day; immediately thereafter, as the highest scorer in ODIs at home against Australia, Tendulkar became 'India's most precious batsman'; and at his fluent best against Pakistan in the ODI series in November 2007, he was 'vintage Sachin'. His six nineties in a single year 'shut up' everybody, and at the same time, set tongues wagging on his 'nervousness' when he approached a hundred. (For me, the nineties he scored in 2007 are a beautiful episode in the Tendulkar story; they show the humanness of a cricket genius, the vulnerability of a champion against a game's ups and downs).

In purely objective terms, Tendulkar undoubtedly suffered a slump in the two years in which he suffered serious injuries (2005 and 2006).

For the first time in his career, he felt that sometimes, runs could be difficult to get and on occasions even batted out of character and got out to some poor deliveries. The reflexes seemed to have suffered, and adjustments needed to be made. He was still among India's top scorers, though, and in 2007, he was back to batting at his best; the problem of slowed-down reflexes had disappeared. By December 2007, he was the world's second-highest run-maker of the year in one-dayers, and the fourth-highest in Tests. And from 2008 onwards, the graph has only risen.

In a welcome departure from the past, Tendulkar has also begun to speak out on certain cricketing issues. He has strongly opposed the umpires referral system, which allows teams to seek a review of an on-field umpire's decision from the third umpire. Pointing to 'an element of uncertainty in the system', he has said, 'I prefer the hotspot system to identify the contact between ball and bat. The LBW decisions are not convincing enough as the hawk eye gives a 22-yard view, which the referral system does not agree with... as to whether the ball would have hit the stumps.'

He has expressed deep displeasure over IPL rules that stipulated that only four players could be retained by a team after three years. 'That part is quite difficult to accept. We have really worked hard to build this team and have got together brilliantly. In the third year (Mumbai Indians lost in the finals), we held a couple of camps which had nothing to do with cricket. It was just to know each other well... I feel it is about building teams, not breaking them,' the Mumbai Indians captain has made clear.

He has, importantly, contributed to the debate on how we could possibly make one-dayers relevant and interesting in the era of T20 cricket. His suggestion: split a match into two innings, for each team, of 25 overs each.

How would that help? It would negate the luck factor linked to the toss, he says, and provide a level playing field for both sides in day-night games, when batting becomes difficult under lights and holding the ball gets tough because of dew. 'Today, we can tell the result of close to 75 per cent of matches after the toss. We know how conditions will affect the two teams. But it (splitting the game into two innings) is not too dependent on the toss. If it's a day-night match, both teams will have to bat under lights. In those 25 overs you can use your 10 wickets the way you want. Suppose it rains, then (also) you can plan,' he has pointed out.

So Tendulkar has filled a critical gap in his career – he is participating increasingly in cricketing discourse.

Why, then, does he still have to stand up to sterner tests on the Indian subcontinent?

There is impatient worship at work here, a worship that cannot come to terms with Tendulkar's humanness. And there is emotion, a notoriously vacillating emotion that will not tolerate any attempt at reason.

Cricket is a metaphor for life in India, and Tendulkar has been for his countrymen proof of India's ability to establish supremacy at the global level. His arrival on the scene coincided with the entry of economic reforms, and for the staggering 300-million-strong middle-class population, he represents the success and confidence that liberalization has made possible. As a surging economy gives them greater opportunities and more power in the new century, Indians are increasingly reluctant to let go of this symbol of constant reassurance, encouragement and stimulus, so they will not let Tendulkar have a bad day on the field for fear that that they might think of themselves as having feet of clay.

Thanks in part to the same commercial quotient that has made India cricket's cash capital, a lot of Tendulkar watchers have come to see cricket not as a game but as part of the entertainment industry. They think a Tendulkar innings is no different from a Hindi film or a Bollywood dance performance. If they invest time in watching him on TV or buy an expensive ticket to see him at the stadium, they think, he has to get a big score to give them value for money. Film stars can be seen dancing in a film or at a film awards function whenever a viewer pays for it; sport does not afford such certainties. If Tendulkar is likely to get a hundred, he is just as likely to get out for nothing. Yet the very nature of sport is negated and impossible demands made because Tendulkar has to conform to a peculiar Indian idea of him.

What makes Tendulkar's position in the Indian consciousness even more intriguing is that the superbly emerging cricket-crazy middle and rich classes want him to possess what they, despite all their self-righteousness, don't: a messianic zeal to do good. He must always measure up, on their behalf as it were, in terms of social and economic commitment, otherwise he be damned. And he has to be in public life what he is on the cricket field: an unselfish man always wearing himself out for a larger-than-personal cause.

He was severely criticized as self-seeking in 2003 when he asked the Indian government to waive off duty for his imported Ferrari, by the same section of the population that is constantly looking at devising new methods of tax evasion. An equally interesting case, and one not very widely known, happened late in 2004.

In November that year, Sachin along with his wife Anjali and mother Rajni attended a special screening of the national award-winning film *Shwaas* in Mumbai. The film, in Tendulkar's native language Marathi, is the sensitive story of a poignant relationship between an old man and his grandson and was sent as India's official entry to the Oscars for 2004. When Tendulkar was asked by some film enthusiasts if he would like to see the film, he promptly responded with a yes, attended the special screening and, in his own words, was thoroughly impressed.

The real story unfolded after this. The *Shwaas* team had done the film on a shoestring budget and when the decision to send it to the Oscars was made, the primary issue before it was to raise funds for the Oscar campaign. So a major and much-publicized mass funding campaign was launched in Tendulkar's home state of Maharashtra, and lots of people, including actor Amitabh Bachchan, came forward to contribute to the fund. Tendulkar was asked and he offered to auction his bat and some other cricket gear. He would also request his mates in the Indian team to give some of their own equipment for the auction, he said.

This led to a wave of disapproval. The money obtained from the auction wouldn't be Tendulkar's but someone else's, it was argued. Why couldn't he, the richest cricketer on earth, dip his hands into his own pocket when even those not really affluent were doing so, angry letter-writers to newspapers asked. The man who led the criticism was Bal Thackeray, leader of the Hindu militant political party Shiv Sena. For once, Thackeray, an avowed admirer of Adolf Hitler, found support even from confirmed liberals, many of whom, post the Ferrari controversy, had been waiting for a suitable opportunity to aim at Tendulkar.

The *Shwaas* team soon clarified that Tendulkar had indeed offered money and that they had, in an emotional response, told him: 'We want you to be with us. We need your support, not your money.' The clarification had little effect, and criticism continued for a while.

This criticism, like the one after the Ferrari affair, did not take note of a central fact: a sportsman is after all a member of his own society, and a reflection of his times. Tendulkar's gear was later put up for auction, and the response to it was said to be good, but the general view, that he had not done enough, remained. After the public indignation came a second verdict that clashed with the first. In the same month, India were playing South Africa in a Test in Kanpur, when a youngster armed with a loaded pistol sneaked into the Green Park stadium. He was spotted by a TV cameraman when he got close to Tendulkar, who was then fielding at the fine-leg boundary. The security personnel were alerted, and the armed youth was held and taken to the local police station for interrogation. The youth told the police that he was the son of the Kanpur Cricket Association president and that he had a licence for the pistol. But the very fact that he was spotted near Tendulkar sparked enormous alarm and a deep sense of concern about 'the country's favourite son'. After all, not too long ago, Tendulkar was said to have been on the hit-list of militant groups and had even been provided security cover. If the man had been caught close to any other fielder, the noises would not have been half as alarming. Sachin was and always would be special: the subject of a deep and enduring affection.

A superstitious act of Tendulkar in Pakistan 2006 was cited as 'proof' of why he deserved such affection. In the third and most crucial game of a five-match one-day series, he was dismissed for 95 after setting up the chase. Back in the dressing room, he decided to take a shower as the asking rate climbed for the new batsmen at the crease. While in the shower, he heard a roar from the crowd and asked team-mate Harbhajan Singh what the noise was about. 'Mahi (M.S. Dhoni) has just hit a four,' he was told. There was similar noise soon after, and he was told another boundary had been hit. He quickly decided that he must not change his position and kept asking for updates at regular intervals. When Dhoni and Yuvraj Singh were only a few runs away from pulling off a sensational victory, Sachin finally emerged from the shower. 'I was in for 45 minutes, my longest bath ever,' he said. He is anxious that the team does well and puts its interest above his personal disappointment at not getting a hundred, it was said.

We have earlier recounted how retirement was recommended fervently after the World Cup debacle in 2007. A few months later, when Simon Taufel wrongly gave Tendulkar out in the second Test in England, the umpire was accused of denying a genius a richly-deserved hundred, and there were passionate calls for greater use of technology so that 'God' was not thus interrupted by flawed human intervention.

To Ian Chappell, who had suggested after the 2007 World Cup that Tendulkar look into the mirror, or to Sanjay Manjrekar, who had referred to some of Sachin's low scores in Australia in 2008 as 'the elephant in the dressing room,' the Indian cricket-loving public did not say anything immediately. Soon after Tendulkar's run-making got as prolific as ever from mid-2007, and soon after he had played two brilliant match-winning knocks in Australia in the wake of Manjrekar's remarks, both Chappell and the former India team-mate were skewered.

After scoring a superb hundred in Chennai that led to a big and successful run chase on home soil against England late in 2008, Tendulkar dedicated the century to the victims of 26/11 terror attacks. The series itself had been played under a cloud of uncertainty in the wake of the attacks. 'What happened in Mumbai was extremely unfortunate. Cricket cannot lessen that. I hope this hundred will give some amount of happiness to the people. I salute the NSG commandos, Taj hotel staff, police, public and everyone,' he said. The comments came in for immediate appreciation, and Tendulkar was praised as the conscientious citizen.

This line was repeated when Tendulkar, in the midst of a native-versus-outsider controversy that raged in Mumbai in 2009, entered into the debate. In response to a question whether he felt Mumbai belonged to Maharashtra or to the whole of India, he said, 'I am a Maharashtrian and am extremely proud of being a Maharashtrian, but Mumbai is a part of India, and I play for India.'

Shiv Sena leader Bal Thackeray severely criticized Sachin for these remarks and told him to stay off the pitch of politics. But Thackeray was reproached, not only by people across the political spectrum but even by large sections of his own voter base in his state. This writer remembers hearing animated conversations on the subject across Mumbai, and especially in the Sena-dominated areas of Dadar, Mahim and Parel. There was no sympathizing with the Sena at all.

Adam Gilchrist, a favourite with many Indian cricket-lovers, had been similarly reproached across the country a little earlier when he criticized Tendulkar in his autobiography. He was forgiven, though, when he called up Tendulkar to apologize and clarified that his statements had been taken out of context.

So the verdict on Sachin Tendulkar is split. Whenever magazines do surveys to find out India's most favourite icons, he still beats presidents, prime ministers, Nobel Prize winners, business tycoons and actors to emerge as the favourite across ages, regions and economic and social sections; when the same magazines want to find out the cricketers India is most dissatisfied with, Tendulkar is somewhere on the top of that list. At one end of the measuring device there is total reliance, confidence and trust, and on the other, there is dismissive talk and suggestions that he is not doing enough. There is faith not only renewed but strengthened when he

gets a big score or makes a gesture for the team; there is
befuddlement and continual carping when he refuses to
pose as a martyr handing out his money for every worthy
cause; and there is unquestionable love, care and concern for
him. At the root of all these responses is a common belief: as
a supremely talented and driven cricketer, he can do
everything. Greatness, for Sachin Tendulkar as for anyone else,
comes at a price.

---

1   He has got 96 hundreds in international cricket at the time of writing this: 50 in
    Tests, and 46 in ODIs.
2   During the clash between Sourav Ganguly and Greg Chappell in 2005, Ten-
    dulkar, badgered for comments, reacted tellingly to Ganguly's statement after
    scoring a hundred against Zimbabwe that he had been asked to step down
    before the game. 'Matters discussed in the dressing room should not brought
    out,' Tendulkar said. Then, soon as Chappell gave Tendulkar the role of 'mentor'
    in the team set-up under Rahul Dravid, Tendulkar spoke up for Ganguly in a
    meeting with BCCI president Sharad Pawar. Ganguly deserved a better deal and
    another chance to prove himself, Tendulkar told Pawar and recommended his
    name for the Indian team that was to visit Pakistan early in 2006.
3   He overtook Steve Waugh (168 Tests) in the 3rd Test against Sri Lanka, in
    Lanka, August 2010.
4   He got to 17,000 ODI runs in this match.
5   His exact words were: 'I am shattered beyond words and I feel helpless. I've
    never felt so bad in my entire career. No matter how many tests or one-day se-
    ries you win, nothing else even comes close to a World Cup triumph. The World
    Cup was our passion, our collective goal, our dream and that has been shattered.
    We all are terribly disappointed over it. Cricket has been my life for all these
    years and will always be. I've given my heart and my soul for 17 years. No coach
    had mentioned even in passing that my attitude was not correct. Again, it's not
    that we are defending ourselves. We do realize we played badly and, as a team,
    we take full responsibility for that. But what hurt us most is if the coach has
    questioned our attitude. Tell me, the world has gone on talking about all this
    (our defeat and exit) but has anybody spared a thought for us? Did they try to
    find out what we have been going through?'
6   He fought battles with Ryan Sidebottom and James Anderson without once
    resorting to the kind of impatience he might have shown earlier. He took blows
    against Anderson and resisted the temptation of playing a shot for which the
    bowler had kept a fielder, and stayed composed in the face of Sidebottom's
    hostile stuff at Trent Bridge.

bibliography

BOOKS

A.G. Moyes, *Bradman, Angus & Robertson,* Sydney, 1948

Ajit Tendulkar, *The Making of a Cricketer: Formative Years of Sachin Tendulkar in Cricket,* published by Ajit Tendulkar for Ten Promotions, 1996

Gulu Ezekiel, *Sachin,* Penguin Books India, 2002

Harsha Bhogle, *The Joy of a Lifetime: India's Tour of England,* 1990, Marine Sports Publications, Mumbai, 1991

John Bright-Holmen (editor), *The Joy of Cricket,* Unwin Paperbacks, 1985

Michael Page, *Bradman,* Macmillan, Australia, 1983

Mihir Bose, *The History of Indian Cricket,* Andre Deutsch Ltd., 2002

Mihir Bose, *A Maidan View: The Magic of Indian Cricket,* George Allen and Unwin, 1986

Mike Marqusee, *War Minus the Shooting: A Journey Through South Asia During Cricket's World Cup,* William Heinemann, London, 1996

Mudar Patherya, *Wills Book of Excellence Cricket,* 1987

Partab Ramchand, Indian Cricket: *The Captains - From Nayudu To Tendulkar,* Marin Sports Publications, Mumbai, 1997

Pupul Jayakar, *Indira Gandhi: A Biography,* Penguin India, 2002

Ramachandra Guha, *A Corner of a Foreign Field: The Indian History of a British Sport,* Picador, 2002

Ramachandra Guha, *Spin and Other Turns: Indian Cricket's Coming of Age,* Penguin India, 1994

Ramachandra Guha, *Wickets in the East: An Anecdotal History,* Oxford University Press, New Delhi, 1992

Ramesh Tendulkar, *Prajakta* (A collection of poems), Mauj Prakashan Gruha, 2002

Richard Cashman, Dr. Players, *Patrons and the Crowd: The Phenomenon of Indian Cricket,* Orient Longman Ltd., 1980

Roland Perry, *Bradman's Best,* Bantam Press, UK, 2001

Shane Warne, *Shane Warne: My Autobiography,* Hodder and Stoughton, UK, 2001

MAGAZINES AND PERIODICALS

- Cricketer Asia
- Ekach Shatkar (Marathi)
- Sportstar
- Sportsworld
- Sportsweek
- Tehelka
- The Illustrated Weekly of India
- Wisden Cricket Monthly

index

414 SACHIN TENDULKAR: A DEFINITIVE BIOGRAPHY

Bickel, Andy, 368
Bijlani, Sangeeta, 207
Binny, Roger, 24, 52
Bishop, Ian, 96, 97, 222
Black, Bill, 394
Blackwell, Ian, 403
Bodyline case, 327-31, 393, 397
Bombay Cricket Association, 41
Boon, David, 133, 134
Borde, Chandu, 290
Border, Allan, 122, 125, 126, 128, 132, 134, 148, 171, 173, 243, 326
Borg, Bjorn, 11, 12
Bosanquet, B.J.T., 330
Bose, Gopal, 24
Bose, Subhash Chandra, 196
Botham, Ian Terence, 133, 134, 137, 140
Bowes, Bill, 139
Boycott, Geoffrey, 139-40, 141, 230, 404
Bracewell, John, 92
Bracken, Nathen, 363
Bradman, Donald, 39, 40, 82-83, 109, 142, 166, 191, 197, 207, 246, 247-50, 254, 287, 294-95, 313-14, 317, 324, 326, 327, 331, 333, 337, 338-39, 356, 391-399
Bradman, The Art of Cricket, 248, 397
Bradshaw, Ian, 187
Brandes, Eddo, 217
Brearley, Mike, 291
Brown, Bill, 393
Browne, Courtney, 187, 193
Buchanan, John, 366, 403
Bucknor, Steve, 144, 367
Burge, Peter, 155
Burke, Javed, 119
Burman, Sachin Dev, 6

C

Caddick, Andrew, 174, 338, 351, 394
Cairns, Chris, 133, 345
Captains' limitations, 210, 219
Cardus, Neville, 150, 395
CBI, 278-81, 298-99, 301
CCI, 50, 51, 219, 339
Chanderpaul, Shivnarine, 346
Chandrachud, Y.V., 294
Chandrasekhar, Bhagwat S., 6, 24, 26, 29, 83
Chapman, Percy, 82
Chappell, Greg, 123, 126, 392, 401, 405
Chappell, Ian, 28, 127, 128, 129
Charles, Prince, 189
Chauhan, Rajesh, 77, 229

Chavan, Laxman, 44, 58-59
Chidambaram, M.A., 149, 259, 311
Chopra, Ashish, 365
Churchill, Winston, 158
City, Ahmedabad, 45, 48, 214, 219, 278, 280, 294, 299, 325
City, Bangalore, 83, 171, 183, 198, 199, 226, 237, 260, 326, 327, 349, 386
City, Chennai, 44, 72, 148, 224, 226, 235, 237, 256, 258, 260, 263, 274, 276, 283, 304, 311, 313, 320, 327, 331, 336, 373, 383, 386, 397,398
City, Gwalior, 193-94, 363
City, Kanpur, 214, 237, 278, 299, 301, 331, 332, 408-09
City, Kolkata, 120, 149, 156, 157, 199, 201, 214, 215, 228, 237, 250, 261, 262, 310, 313, 341, 342, 348, 363, 383, 404
City, Mohali, 212, 277, 278, 324,
City, Mumbai, 1, 3, 5, 6, 7, 10, 13, 15, 16, 17, 18, 19, 20, 21, 22, 23, 24, 26, 28, 29, 30, 31, 32, 33, 40, 41, 42, 43, 44, 45, 46, 48, 49, 50, 51, 52, 56, 57, 65, 66, 67, 68, 69, 70, 71, 72, 74, 75, 83, 90, 91, 107, 109, 112, 114, 115, 117, 118, 120, 139, 146, 148, 153, 165, 166, 167, 169, 177, 181, 182, 187, 188, 189, 191, 194, 206, 213, 215, 219, 233, 234, 235, 249, 256, 266, 267, 268, 271, 273
City, New Delhi, 6, 122, 154, 213, 256, 261, 263, 301, 383
Clarke, Michael, 363
Clarke, Sylvester, 107-08
Close, Brian, 141
Collins, Pedro, 334
Collins, Phil, 138, 334
Compton, Dennis, 150
Condon, Paul, 297
Cooks, Jimmy, 143
Cork, Dominic, 327
Couto, Marcus, 52
Cowdrey, Chris, 96
Croft, Colin, 22
Cronje, Hansie, 213, 214, 216, 295, 297, 300, 301, 302, 322
Crowe, Martin, 132-33, 137
Cummins, Anderson, 127
Cup, Aiwa, 275
Cup, Asia, 112, 225, 226, 231, 384
Cup, Asian Test, 255, 261, 263
Cup, Coca-Cola, 238, 246, 252, 298